The
BLUE
PAGES

Second Edition

Arkape
Coll.
HF
5035
B59
2010

A Directory of Companies
Rated by Their Politics
and Practices

RELEASE

ANGIE CROUSE and the
CENTER for RESPONSIVE POLITICS

PoliPointPress

The Blue Pages: A Directory of Companies Rated by Their Politics and Practices, Second Edition

13 12 11 10   1 2 3 4 5

Production management: BookMatters
Book design: BookMatters
Cover design: BookMatters

Library of Congress Cataloging-in-Publication Data has been applied for.

ISBN-13: 978-0-9817091-4-7

Published by:
PoliPointPress, LLC
80 Liberty Ship Way, Suite 22
Sausalito, CA 94965
(415) 339-4100
www.p3books.com

Distributed by Ingram Publisher Services
Printed in the USA

Contents

About This Directory

When *The Blue Pages* first appeared in January 2006, its immediate success showed that many Americans had a shrewd understanding of our political system. By using the book to guide their purchases, thousands of conscientious consumers implicitly acknowledged that money matters in politics. But the book's remarkable sales also showed something else: if money is the problem in politics, it can also be the solution. For the first time, we could easily see and use what was always ours: namely, federally collected data on corporate campaign contributions. By putting that data in a handy directory, *The Blue Pages* let us follow the corporate money—and helped us choose how to spend ours.

Since then, the political and economic landscape has changed dramatically. Ten months after we published the first edition, Democrats gained majorities in both houses of Congress. Two years later, Barack Obama became president. His victory was historically significant, but so was an alarming economic downturn brought on by the collapse of housing values and the Wall Street recklessness that fostered it. As we go to press this time, the banks are absorbing huge sums of public money, the auto industry is on the ropes, the U.S. unemployment rate has hit a 25-year high, and the consensus among experts is that we're facing the most serious economic challenge since the Great Depression. If that weren't enough, we're also facing a global environmental crisis that the Bush administration ignored for the better part of a critical decade. Of course, some things haven't changed. Health-care costs continue to skyrocket, and the wars in Iraq and Afghanistan grind on.

Clearly it's time for a new edition of *The Blue Pages*. Like its predecessor, this one summarizes the political contributions and business practices of more than 1,000 companies. The companies are still organized alphabetically within 13 business sectors, and the index allows you to identify specific companies and brands even more quickly. But this time, we are making four major improvements:

- **Expanded and updated listings and contribution data**. The book summarizes about 10% more firms and brands, and the contribution data come from the 2008 election cycle.

- **Lobbying expenditures**. Along with direct campaign contributions, these expenditures are the main way corporate money affects politics. In 2008 alone, lobbying expenditures came to $3.3 billion.

- **More green coverage**. Author Angie Crouse specifically focused on the environmental policies and impacts of the companies she tracked.

- **New sector overviews**. We commissioned accomplished authors to write the essays that open each sector.

We didn't stop there. We also recruited Angie Crouse and the Center for Responsive Politics (CRP) for this edition. Widely acknowledged as the gold standard in research on political contributions, the nonpartisan CRP has a 26-year history of tracking the elite's influence on federal elections and policy. Those influences include campaign contributions, lobbying expenditures, lawmakers' personal finances, and Washington's revolving door.

CRP's theory is simple: if it follows the money, others can make change. For that reason, CRP makes all of its research and analysis—searchable, sortable, and now downloadable—available at its Web site, OpenSecrets.org. This year, CRP released all its archived data to the public for free, allowing everyone to use the information in new and creative (noncommercial) ways.

All of CRP's contribution data come from the Federal Election Commission (FEC). (Lobbying expenditures are pulled from the Senate Office of Public Records.) The FEC requires committees to report the names, addresses, and employers of individuals who give more than $200 to a candidate running for federal office, a political action committee (PAC), or a party committee. CRP takes that employment information and adds that company's employee contributions and PAC donations. It then tallies the overall contribution from that company and determines whether it leans Republican or Democratic. (In this book, only contributions to Democratic and Republican candidates and parties were tallied. Hence, the total figures for each company may not match what is reported on Open-Secrets.org, which includes contributions to third-party candidates and parties.) CRP then goes one step further by giving that company, union, or other special interest group one of more than 100 industry and ideological categories. This procedure allows it to do what no other organization does—track how much money any particular industry or sector is giving to lawmakers.

We were thrilled when CRP agreed to contribute the numbers to the second edition of *The Blue Pages*. (Note: CRP's participation was limited to providing data on political finance.) But how do those numbers help you? First, you'll be able to determine where your favorite businesses steer their political money. Got that new shirt from American Eagle? Well, employees there tend to give more cash to Republican candidates, PACs, and party committees. Planning a romantic getaway using Travelocity.com? Its PAC and employees favor Democrats with their cash. By consulting *The Blue Pages* before you make your purchases, you can direct your money to companies that support your values. You may not see some major companies in this edition. If they made no political contributions, they were not included.

Of course, there's more to *The Blue Pages* than numbers, however illuminating those often are. We also wanted the company listings to draw a miniature portrait of each company and its business practices. That Herculean task fell to Angie Crouse, a political researcher with a long list of credits, including her work on Joe Conason's *The Raw Deal*. Building on the research for the first edition, Angie methodically tracked each company's affiliates or parent firm, its environmental and employment policies, its legal rows, and anything else that might inform the decisions of a conscientious consumer.

The listings are meant to complement the picture provided by the numbers. Like many things in life, an enterprise may be a complex mix of virtue and vice. Some firms have stellar environmental records and lousy labor ones. Some may give generously to your favorite politicians but have legal actions against them that would shame Al Capone. Welcome to the real world. But at least now you know.

Angie used many sources in compiling the company listings, and we encourage readers to check her key sources for further information. She turned to Lexis/Nexis for information on corporate structure, such as parent and subsidiary relationships, as well as for details of pending and settled lawsuits. Addi-

tional information on legal matters came from www.
lawyersandsettlements.com. The Corporate Responsibility Newswire (www.csrwire.com) was Angie's
source for information on corporate citizenship,
sustainability, and socially responsible initiatives. For
indications of corporate performance in the areas
of human rights, social justice, and environmental
sustainability, Angie relied on reports from Green
America/Responsible Shopper (www.coopamerica.
org/programs/responsibleshopper/about.cfm). She
identified cases of human rights abuse by corporations from Human Rights Watch (www.hrw.org). She
referred to the Climate Counts (www.climatecounts.
org) scorecard, which gauges how serious companies
are about stopping climate change. She also culled,
when available, information on environmental policies
and programs from company Web sites. Finally, she
used research by the Human Rights Campaign (www.
hrc.org) to outline company benefits for domestic
partners and transgender employees.

As always, we welcome your comments and sug-
gestions about *The Blue Pages*. You can contact us
at info@p3books.com or by mail at PoliPointPress,
80 Liberty Ship Way, Suite 22, Sausalito, California
94965.

Contributors

Sasha Abramsky is a freelance journalist, a lecturer in writing at U.C. Davis, and the author of *Breadline USA: The Hidden Scandal of American Hunger and How to Fix It.*

Dean Baker is the codirector of the Center for Economic and Policy Research and the author of *Plunder and Blunder: The Rise and Fall of the Bubble Economy.*

Jane Black is a food writer at the *Washington Post.*

Michael Calabrese directs the Wireless Future Program at the New America Foundation, a nonprofit and nonpartisan think tank based in Washington DC.

Chris Colin has written for the *New York Times, Mother Jones,* and *Smithsonian* and is the author of *What Really Happened to the Class of '93.*

Malia Everette is director of Reality Tours for Global Exchange.

Carol E. Pott is a senior editor at Dolby Laboratories, Inc., and was the primary author and editor of the first edition of *The Blue Pages.*

Nomi Prins is an author, a journalist, and a senior fellow at the public policy think tank Demos.

Norman Solomon is a media critic and the author of a dozen books, including *War Made Easy: How Presidents and Pundits Keep Spinning Us to Death* and *Made Love, Got War: Close Encounters with America's Warfare State.*

Dave Zirin is the author of *A People's History of Sports in the United States* and is sports editor for the *Nation.*

Abbreviations and Acronyms

ABS	asset-backed securities
ADA	Americans with Disabilities Act
ADEA	Age Discrimination in Employment Act
BBB	Better Business Bureau
BGH	bovine growth hormone
CAFTA	Central American Free Trade Agreement
CDO	collateralized debt obligation
CERES	Coalition for Environmentally Responsible Economics
CRP	Center for Responsive Politics
CSR	corporate social responsibility
CWA	Communications Workers of America
DOE	U.S. Department of Energy
DOJ	U.S. Department of Justice
DOL	U.S. Department of Labor
EEOC	U.S. Equal Employment Opportunity Commission
EFCA	Employee Free Choice Act
EPA	U.S. Environmental Protection Agency
ERISA	Employee Retirement Income Security Act
EU	European Union
FAA	Federal Aviation Administration
FCC	Federal Communications Commission
FDA	Food and Drug Administration
FDIC	Federal Deposit Insurance Corp.
FEC	Federal Election Commission
FIRE	finance, insurance, and real estate
FLSA	Fair Labor Standards Act
FMLA	Family and Medical Leave Act
FTC	Federal Trade Commission

GLBT	gay, lesbian, bisexual, transgender
GSA	General Services Administration
HUD	Department of Housing and Urban Development
ISP	Internet service provider
LEAN	Labeling Education and Nutrition
LEED	Leadership in Energy and Environmental Design
NAACP	National Association for the Advancement of Colored People
NAFE	National Association for Female Executives
NHTSA	National Highway and Traffic Safety Administration
NIH	National Institutes of Health
NRA	National Rifle Association
NRDC	Natural Resources Defense Council
NLRB	National Relations Labor Board
OSHA	Occupational Safety and Health Administration
PAC	political action committee
PERI	Political Economy Research Institute
PETA	People for the Ethical Treatment of Animals
PVCs	polyvinyl chlorides
RICO	Racketeer Influenced and Corrupt Organizations Act
SEC	Securities and Exchange Commission
TARP	Troubled Asset Relief Program
UAW	United Auto Workers
UFCW	United Food and Commercial Workers

Frequently Appearing References

Century Council—An industry-funded nonprofit dedicated to fighting drunk driving and underage drinking.

CERES Principles—A 10-point code for environmental conduct established by a coalition of environmental groups, investment funds, and public interest groups.

Fair Labor Association—A nonprofit organization working to eliminate global apparel sweatshops.

Human Rights Campaign Corporate Equality Index—Rates large corporations on policies that affect their gay, lesbian, bisexual, and transgender employees, consumers, and investors.

Kimberley Process—Process to ensure that retail diamonds are not conflict diamonds.

Kyoto Protocol—A voluntary commitment to targets for reducing greenhouse gas emissions.

Maquilas—Factories that import materials and equipment for assembly or manufacture and that reexport the assembled product, usually to the originating country. They often demand pregnancy tests as a prerequisite to employment or insist that female workers use birth control. Pregnancy can lower a woman's chances of getting hired and can result in her termination from employment.

PERI—An independent unit of the University of Massachusetts that promotes environmental sustainability and human rights through research.

(PRODUCT)RED—A portion of profits from (PRODUCT)RED products goes to the Global Fund to invest in African AIDS programs.

SmartWay—An EPA brand designating products and services designed to minimize emissions from shipping and logistics operations.

United Nations Global Compact—A strategic policy initiative for businesses that are committed to aligning their operations and strategies with 10 universally accepted principles in the areas of human rights, labor, environment, and anticorruption.

World Diamond Council—Works to end the trade of conflict diamonds.

Acknowledgments

"Go look it up" was the response my parents gave me when I asked a question. I thank them for that—the skill has come in handy of late. This book would not have been possible without the tenacity they taught me and the hard work of several other people. Researcher Catherine "Ladybug" Miller put in long hours, and with her intelligence, dedication, and sense of humor this book was completed on a tight schedule, and I am still smiling. The staff at PoliPointPress has been indispensable. Peter Richardson gave this project direction, and it wouldn't have reached this point without his advice and leadership. He was always available, and I wouldn't blame him if he changed his phone number and didn't tell me. Melissa Edeburn's editing skills helped me keep the listings under control. John McAlester is a computer genius; his database skills made organization and work flow seamless. This second edition was also made possible by the work of the consulting editor and author of the first edition, Carol Pott. I also want to thank John Sperling for giving me the time needed to do this book.
—*Angie Crouse*

As with so many books that rely heavily on data, the true backbone of this work is in the numbers. There wouldn't be anything meaningful to say here without accurate, unvarnished research at the core. As such, the typically unsung heroes of the center's work really do need to be individually cited for their yeoman's labor, tracking the money in American politics.

Sheila Krumholz, executive director for the Center for Responsive Politics (CRP), supervised the work, and Jihan Andoni, the center's research director, managed the project from the beginning. Senior researchers Douglas Weber and Dan Auble lent their years of experience tracking political interests and their donations. Researchers Carolyn Sharpe and Erin Williams brought their expertise tracking individual donors and political action committees, respectively. Researchers Adam Crowther, Matthias Jaime, and Greg Gasiewski are the in-house experts on the often big-ticket lobbying campaigns that firms conduct in order to "grease the skids" for their legislative agendas.

CRP's IT staff, ably led by Susan Alger and including Ben Pilkerton and Hector Rivera, make it possible to profile all the millions and millions of records that our research team codes by industry and standardizes by employer and occupation on our award-winning Web site, OpenSecrets.org. Finally, our communications staff—including Dave Levinthal, Lindsay Renick Mayer, and Michael Beckel—also collaborated on this project. And they add illuminating analysis to OpenSecrets.org to show how money affects politics, policy, and—ultimately—our daily lives, and even the direction of our democracy. The CRP team strives to "count cash to make change."

The center is enormously grateful to its board of directors, individual donors, and major funders, including the Carnegie Corporation of New York, the Ford Foundation, the Joyce Foundation, the Open Society Institute, the Pew Charitable Trusts, and the Sunlight Foundation. CRP does not accept funds from corporate, trade, or labor organizations.
—*The Center for Responsive Politics*

Clothing, Shoes, and Accessories

Chris Colin

It was a minor news item that perfectly captured the strangeness of the current economic and political moment. On January 20, 2009, President Obama was at the center of the biggest, most hopeful inaugural festivities in recent memory. Three days later, Hartmarx, the century-old Chicago-based company that made his tuxedo, filed for bankruptcy.

In the story of this bankruptcy was that of the country in general. Historically, Wall Street workers had kept the company afloat. When the economy imploded and banks began to collapse, a significant chunk of New York's suit buyers started wearing sweatpants. Hartmarx had weathered the Great Depression and two world wars, but finally it was credit default swaps and collateralized debt obligations that would sink it. The irony was not lost on these Chicago clothiers. The same banks they'd supplied with suits were now receiving massive amounts of bailout money from taxpayers, but Hartmarx's campaign for a bank-sponsored bailout of its own was unsuccessful.

As with so many industries, the apparel sector has long been excoriated for its lousy labor record. Now, as the recession has decimated that sector, apparel workers are desperate to hang on to those same jobs. The situation is worst for those workers in South Asia, predictably. Tens of millions of people, mostly women, labor in the garment and textile factories of Bangladesh, Sri Lanka, India, and other South Asian countries. In early 2009, the Bangladesh Garment Manufacturers and Exporters Association estimated that Western buyers had cancelled a quarter of its orders. Given the phenomenally low wages earned in happier times—in 2006, a Chinese textile worker earned about 40 cents an hour—the economic crisis will only sink South Asia's apparel workforce into greater poverty. The effects of the slowdown on the region will likely continue to unfold for years, even if the American economy rebounds sooner.

To talk about the apparel industry, of course, is to talk about sweatshops. The topic has come to mean two things in this country: a workplace with poor safety or labor conditions and a segue to a larger

1

discussion that muddies the already opaque subject of globalization.

If Nike and the Gap brought international attention to the problems of exploited garment workers, countless other businesses have continued with equally inhumane operation, even within the United States. Nearly a century after the Triangle Shirtwaist Fire first highlighted labor issues among clothing companies, these issues persist, and the world remains addicted to cheap threads.

Ensuring responsible production is not as simple as humiliating the latest celebrity who put her name on the wrong line of pants. Even in cases where manufacturers have clamped down on labor abuses—a minority, still—environmental considerations complicate the matter further. Harmful pesticides and insecticides are often used in the growing of cotton, and toxic dyes frequently find their way into clothing.

Meanwhile, observers like Nobel Prize–winning economist Paul Krugman have argued that sweatshops offer a path to prosperity for poor countries. Not only do they provide jobs to people desperately in need, they have the potential to usher in larger reforms. Keep sending factory work to poor countries, the argument goes, and eventually those factories will have to compete for a finite pool of workers. Once labor has some leverage, these countries could see a version of what happened with Silicon Valley workplace dynamics during the tech boom. South Asian sweatshops may be a long way from offering foosball tables, but in their shifting numbers is the possibility of organizing.

Further complicating the sweatshop issue is the question of importing. Critics of quotas argue that U.S. manufacturers have long enjoyed an unfair advantage—precisely the kind of government protectionism conservatives decry when the beneficiary is a poor person rather than a wealthy corporation. But the advantage, in fact, is extended to developing countries, too. Under the quota system, nations such as Mauritius, Lesotho, and Cambodia stood a chance of competing against China; without it, some fear, jobs in the lesser-developed countries might vanish.

As for domestic clothing manufacturers, the country's largest, American Apparel, continues to confound industry critics. On the one hand, the employer of over 10,000 people has won accolades for refusing to outsource labor, for paying an average of $12 per hour to factory workers, for advocating for immigration reform, and for rejecting the use of leather, wool, fur, or other animal products in its clothes; the company also makes significant use of organic cotton. On the other hand, American Apparel has been accused of union busting, antifeminist advertising, and maintaining a culture in which sexual harassment is tolerated. Perhaps one of the chain's greatest strengths, ultimately, is its encapsulation of the contradictions inherent in the vast majority of businesses in the 21st century—contradictions that go to the heart of this very book. Finding a wholly "good" or "bad" company is nearly impossible.

To assess the clothing industry in the United States is to glimpse the power of the large corporation. Two-thirds of the 41,000 apparel manufacturers are tiny—a family operations or persons selling small lines of goods. But the vast majority of profits in the industry go to the big companies: of those 41,000, a mere 180 gobble up half the industry's revenue. A similar dynamic is found in the nation's 91,000 retail stores: the top 13% take in half the revenue.

The years ahead will undoubtedly be marked by debate over the reinstatement of quotas and by struggles over labor practices and environmental concerns. The Gap, often boycotted for its links to sweatshop labor, the violent suppression of worker protests, and even deforestation, showed signs of progress with a recent social responsibility report that admitted a variety of shortcomings. Even better, the dramatic success of small, ethically run companies such as Patagonia has focused attention on the marketability of corporate responsibility.

In the meantime, responsible consumers can take steps of their own: ask where garments are made, keep an eye out for organically grown cotton and natural or low-impact dyes, look for Fair Trade or Union Made labels, and buy secondhand or handmade clothes from independent retailers.

Top Ten Democratic Contributors

Gap, Inc.	$221,790
Next Components, Ltd.	$112,300
Limited Brands, Inc.	$107,870
J. Crew Group, Inc.	$103,190
Men's Wearhouse, Inc., The	$102,300
Mary Green Enterprises	$86,850
Macy's, Inc.	$79,034
Levi Strauss & Co.	$77,571
Gymboree Corporation, The	$72,300
Coach, Inc.	$68,170

Top Ten Republican Contributors

Limited Brands, Inc.	$367,824
Cintas Corporation	$316,200
Gap, Inc.	$182,200
J. C. Penney Company, Inc.	$105,500
Stein Mart, Inc.	$105,000
Macy's, Inc.	$93,200
Harkham Industries, Inc.	$76,600
Pendleton Woolen Mills, Inc.	$61,450
Saks, Inc.	$32,100
TJX Companies, Inc., The	$19,950

Top Ten Lobbying Spenders

Limited Brands, Inc.	$1,320,000
Hanesbrands, Inc.	$800,000
Tiffany & Co.	$560,000
Cintas Corporation	$555,000
Payless ShoeSource, Inc.	$280,000
Wolverine World Wide, Inc.	$240,000
Fruit of the Loom	$192,000
Gap, Inc.	$180,000
J. C. Penney Company, Inc.	$175,500
Dillard's, Inc.	$154,000

Abercrombie & Fitch Co.
42% | 58%
Contributions: TOTAL: *$12,600*   DEM: *$5,250*   REP: *$7,350*
LOBBY SPENDING: *$130,000*
Pending suits allege religious and racial discrimination. One of 26 retailers that agreed to a $20 million settlement in a federal class action lawsuit brought by garment workers in Saipan who alleged sweatshop practices. Paid $2.2 million to settle charges that it required employees to wear company products without compensation. Has sourced from countries with widespread, well-documented human and labor rights abuses. Cited for supplier practices that encourage sweatshop labor.

Has a written nondiscrimination policy covering sexual orientation and gender identity. Offers health insurance coverage to employees' domestic partners. Insurance for transgender employees is offered, but treatment is not covered.

Aeropostale   69%   31%
Contributions: TOTAL: *$4,800*   DEM: *$3,300*   REP: *$1,500*
LOBBY SPENDING: *$0*
Has sourced from countries with widespread, well-documented human and labor rights abuses and encourages sweatshop labor with supplier practices. Collects used jeans and donates them to homeless youth.

American Apparel, Inc.   100%   0%
Contributions: TOTAL: *$2,700*   DEM: *$2,700*   REP: *$0*
LOBBY SPENDING: *$10,000*
Several lawsuits against AAI include sexual harassment and other charges against Dov Charney, AAI's founder and co-owner. AAI is known for its no-sweat factory and the fair treatment of its workers. Operates an on-site medical clinic for employees. Offers subsidized lunches, a bike lending program, a program of paid days off, and ESL classes to employees. Promotes the fight for immigrant rights. In 2008, donated "Legalize Gay" shirts to help publicize the fight against Prop. 8, which bans gay marriage, in California.

American Eagle Outfitters, Inc.   100%   0%
Contributions: TOTAL: *$3,300*   DEM: *$3,300*   REP: *$0*
LOBBY SPENDING: *$0*
Has sourced from countries with widespread, well-documented human and labor rights abuses. Its vendor code of conduct forbids child labor, forced labor, and a workweek longer than 60 hours. Prohibits animal testing of its products. Foundation supports civic involvement, teen and college education programs, and diversification. Partners with customers to support Big Brothers Big Sisters of America, Jumpstart, and the Student Conservation Association.

Ann Taylor Stores Corporation   43%   57%
Contributions: TOTAL: *$5,260*   DEM: *$2,250*   REP: *$3,010*
LOBBY SPENDING: *$60,500*
Has sourced from countries with widespread, well-documented human and labor rights abuses. Cited for forced overtime in El Salvador, where it paid employees 60 cents per hour and had them work seven days a week. Supports women's organizations and partners with St. Jude Children's Research Hospital and Goodwill Industries. Has a written nondiscrimination policy covering sexual orientation but not gender identity.

Anthropologie, Inc.   100%   0%
Contributions: TOTAL: *$3,550*   DEM: *$3,550*   REP: *$0*
LOBBY SPENDING: *$0*
Subsidiary of Urban Outfitters, Inc.

AZ3, Inc., doing business as BCBG Max Azria
Contributions: TOTAL: *$4,500*   DEM: *$4,500*   REP: *$0*
LOBBY SPENDING: *$0*

DEM: 100%   REP: 0%

Privately held. A pending lawsuit alleges overtime violations. Has sourced from countries with widespread, well-documented human and labor rights abuses and encourages sweatshop labor with its supplier practices.

BabyUniverse, Inc.
Contributions: TOTAL: *$4,600*   DEM: *$0*   REP: *$4,600*
LOBBY SPENDING: *$0*

DEM: 0%   REP: 100%

Acquired by Toys "R" Us in 2009.

Banana Republic
Contributions: TOTAL: *$7,400*   DEM: *$2,800*   REP: *$4,600*
LOBBY SPENDING: *$0*

DEM: 38%   REP: 62%

Subsidiary of Gap, Inc.

Barneys New York, Inc.
Contributions: TOTAL: *$5,519*   DEM: *$5,519*   REP: *$0*
LOBBY SPENDING: *$0*

DEM: 100%   REP: 0%

Formerly owned by Jones Apparel Group, which sold the company in 2007 to Istithmar PJSC, an investment firm owned by the Dubai government.

Bebe Stores, Inc.
Contributions: TOTAL: *$2,300*   DEM: *$2,300*   REP: *$0*
LOBBY SPENDING: *$0*

DEM: 100%   REP: 0%

A pending lawsuit alleges FLSA violations. In 2008, settled a lawsuit alleging an FLSA violation for requiring employees to wear Bebe clothing for which they were not reimbursed. Settled multiple lawsuits in which the DOL alleged sweatshop conditions, as well as wage-and-hour overtime abuses. Has sourced from countries with widespread, well-documented human and labor rights abuses. Cited for supplier practices that encourage sweatshop labor.

Belk, Inc.
Contributions: TOTAL: *$12,300*   DEM: *$6,800*   REP: *$5,500*
LOBBY SPENDING: *$0*

DEM: 55%   REP: 45%

Donates to the United Way and the Susan G. Komen Foundation. The Belk Foundation awards grants to schools, churches, hospitals, and other charitable and community service organizations.

Bergdorf Goodman
Contributions: TOTAL: *$12,444*   DEM: *$9,194*   REP: *$3,250*
LOBBY SPENDING: *$0*

DEM: 74%   REP: 26%

Subsidiary of the Neiman Marcus Group, Inc.; parent, Leonard Green & Partners L.P. and TPG Capital L.P. Has a written nondiscrimination policy covering sexual orientation but not gender identity. Offers insurance coverage to employees' domestic partners.

Bergner's
Contributions: TOTAL: *$4,600* DEM: *$0* REP: *$4,600*
LOBBY SPENDING: *$0*
Subsidiary of Bon-Ton Stores, Inc.

0% — 100%

Bloomingdale's
Contributions: TOTAL: *$13,202* DEM: *$8,352* REP: *$4,850*
LOBBY SPENDING: *$0*
Subsidiary of Macy's, Inc.

63% — 37%

Bon-Ton Stores, Inc.
Contributions: TOTAL: *$4,954* DEM: *$2,654* REP: *$2,300*
LOBBY SPENDING: *$0*
Has donated over $3.4 million company-wide to breast cancer research facilities. Partners with Goodwill Industries. Has raised over $59 million for schools and nonprofit organizations.

54% — 46%

Brooks Brothers
Contributions: TOTAL: *$1,700* DEM: *$1,200* REP: *$500*
LOBBY SPENDING: *$140,000*
Subsidiary of Retail Brand Alliance, Inc. One of 26 retailers that agreed to a $20 million settlement in a federal class action lawsuit brought by garment workers in Saipan who alleged sweatshop practices. A pending lawsuit alleges violations of Title VII of the Civil Rights Act. Donates to the Make-a-Wish Foundation and St. Jude Children's Research Hospital. Partners with the Central Park Conservancy and nonprofit organizations working on health issues, education, and the arts.

71% — 29%

Brown Shoe Company, Inc.
Contributions: TOTAL: *$6,500* DEM: *$3,050* REP: *$3,450*
LOBBY SPENDING: *$0*
Manufactures in, and has sourced from, countries with widespread, well-documented human and labor rights abuses. Plans to open 500 stores in China. Continues to pay cleanup fees for contamination of a residential area behind a former factory. Has donated over $2.5 million to building educational, arts, and civic institutions and programs. Partners with the March of Dimes and the United Way and supports breast cancer research. Has a nondiscrimination policy covering sexual orientation but not gender identity. Offers insurance coverage to employees' domestic partners.

47% — 53%

Burlington Coat Factory Warehouse Corporation
Contributions: TOTAL: *$256* DEM: *$256* REP: *$0*
LOBBY SPENDING: *$0*
Subsidiary of Bain Capital LLC. Settled a suit with the FTC for allegedly failing to disclose the origin of textile products featured in its online catalog. Was sued by the State of California for alleged failure to disclose lead levels in costume jewelry. Supports the Leukemia & Lymphoma Society and offers child safety and wellness seminars. In 2008, partnered with One Warm Coat and Good Morning America to provide

100% — 0%

175,125 coats for those in need. Has no nondiscrimination policy covering sexual orientation or gender identity.

Calvin Klein

100%   0%

Contributions: TOTAL: *$8,900*   DEM: *$8,900*   REP: *$0*
LOBBY SPENDING: *$0*

Subsidiary of Phillips-Van Heusen Corporation. One of 26 retailers that agreed to a $20 million settlement in a federal class action lawsuit brought by garment workers in Saipan who alleged sweatshop practices. Has written a nondiscrimination policy covering sexual orientation but not gender identity.

Carolee Designs, Inc.

100%   0%

Contributions: TOTAL: *$1,500*   DEM: *$1,500*   REP: *$0*
LOBBY SPENDING: *$0*

Subsidiary of Retail Brand Alliance, Inc. Outreach focuses on breast cancer awareness and research, for which it has raised over $2 million.

Carson Pirie Scott

67%   33%

Contributions: TOTAL: *$900*   DEM: *$600*   REP: *$300*
LOBBY SPENDING: *$0*

Subsidiary of Bon-Ton Stores, Inc. Settled a discrimination case brought by the National Organization for Women by changing a policy that charged women more money for alterations than men.

Carter's, Inc.

0%   100%

Contributions: TOTAL: *$5,500*   DEM: *$0*   REP: *$5,500*
LOBBY SPENDING: *$0*

Has sourced from countries with widespread, well-documented human and labor rights abuses. Employees have raised over $800,000 for the Leukemia and Lymphoma Society since 1999.

Casual Male Retail Group, Inc.

100%   0%

Contributions: TOTAL: *$1,620*   DEM: *$1,620*   REP: *$0*
LOBBY SPENDING: *$0*

Has sourced from countries with widespread, well-documented human and labor rights abuses.

Catherine's Plus Sizes

0%   100%

Contributions: TOTAL: *$250*   DEM: *$0*   REP: *$250*
LOBBY SPENDING: *$0*

Subsidiary of Charming Shoppes.

Charming Shoppes

83%   17%

Contributions: TOTAL: *$7,400*   DEM: *$6,150*   REP: *$1,250*
LOBBY SPENDING: *$0*

A pending class action lawsuit alleges FLSA violations for forcing employees to purchase and wear its clothing on the job without reimbursement. Has sourced from countries with widespread, well-documented human and labor rights abuses. Cited for supplier practices that encourage sweatshop labor. Its Lane Bryant, Fashion Bug, and Catherine's Plus Sizes stores donated new apparel and shoes to

Hurricane Katrina victims. Focuses philanthropic efforts on women, children, and the homeless through a grant program. Donates coats to inner-city youth and professional work clothing to women exiting job-training programs.

Chico's FAS
83% | 17%

Contributions: TOTAL: *$21,095*   DEM: *$17,495*   REP: *$3,600*
LOBBY SPENDING: *$50,000*

Settled a class action suit for allegedly violating the California Labor Code for requiring employees to purchase Chico's clothing as a condition of employment. Has sourced from countries with widespread, well-documented human and labor rights abuses. Cited for supplier practices that encourage sweatshop labor. Has no nondiscrimination policy covering sexual orientation and gender identity.

Children's Place Retail Stores, Inc., The
0% | 100%

Contributions: TOTAL: *$13,600*   DEM: *$0*   REP: *$13,600*
LOBBY SPENDING: *$0*

Has sourced from countries with widespread, well-documented human and labor rights abuses. Paid a $1.5 million settlement in class action brought by shareholders alleging violations of the Securities Act for misrepresenting the financial condition of the company at its initial public offering. Two of CEO Ezra Dabah's family members landed in jail for falsifying clothing-import documents.

Cintas Corporation
3% | 97%

Contributions: TOTAL: *$326,050*   DEM: *$9,850*   REP: *$316,200*
LOBBY SPENDING: *$555,000*

Operates in and sources from countries with widespread, well-documented human and labor rights abuses. In 2008, was ordered to pay workers more than $1.1 million plus interest in back wages for violating employment law. Has a written nondiscrimination policy covering sexual orientation but not gender identity.

Citizen Watch Co. of America, Inc.
0% | 100%

Contributions: TOTAL: *$500*   DEM: *$0*   REP: *$500*
LOBBY SPENDING: *$0*

Subsidiary of Citizen Watch Co., Ltd.

Claire's Stores, Inc.
98% | 2%

Contributions: TOTAL: *$33,200*   DEM: *$32,700*   REP: *$500*
LOBBY SPENDING: *$80,000*

Acquired by Apollo Advisors in 2007. Has a written nondiscrimination policy covering sexual orientation but not gender identity.

Coach, Inc.
98% | 2%

Contributions: TOTAL: *$69,780*   DEM: *$68,170*   REP: *$1,610*
LOBBY SPENDING: *$0*

In 2008, paid $79 million to settle a class action suit alleging that information was improperly obtained from credit card transactions.

Cole Haan Holdings, Inc.
87% | 13%
Contributions: TOTAL: *$7,750*   DEM: *$6,750*   REP: *$1,000*
LOBBY SPENDING: *$0*
Subsidiary of NIKE, Inc. Has sourced from countries with widespread, well-documented human and labor rights abuses. Has a written non-discrimination policy covering sexual orientation and gender identity. Offers insurance coverage to employees' domestic partners. Insurance for transgender employees is offered, and treatment is covered.

David's Bridal
49% | 51%
Contributions: TOTAL: *$10,350*   DEM: *$5,050*   REP: *$5,300*
LOBBY SPENDING: *$0*
Subsidiary of Leonard Green & Partners L.P. Has a written nondiscrimination policy covering sexual orientation but not gender identity.

Dillard's, Inc.
74% | 26%
Contributions: TOTAL: *$32,481*   DEM: *$24,150*   REP: *$8,331*
LOBBY SPENDING: *$154,000*
Has donated over $4.5 million to Ronald McDonald House Charities. Has a written nondiscrimination policy covering sexual orientation but not gender identity.

Donna Karan International, Inc.
100% | 0%
Contributions: TOTAL: *$63,500*   DEM: *$63,500*   REP: *$0*
LOBBY SPENDING: *$0*
Subsidiary of LVMH Moët Hennessy Louis Vuitton SA. One of 26 retailers that agreed to a $20 million settlement in a federal class action lawsuit brought by garment workers in Saipan who alleged sweatshop practices. Settled a class action case alleging that it forced union workers in a New York factory to work 7 days a week, 12 hours a day, without minimum wage or overtime pay. Has written a nondiscrimination policy covering sexual orientation but not gender identity.

Dooney & Bourke, Inc.
61% | 39%
Contributions: TOTAL: *$3,800*   DEM: *$2,300*   REP: *$1,500*
LOBBY SPENDING: *$0*
Has sourced from countries with widespread, well-documented human and labor rights abuses.

Dress Barn, Inc., The
94% | 6%
Contributions: TOTAL: *$15,500*   DEM: *$14,500*   REP: *$1,000*
LOBBY SPENDING: *$0*
One of 26 retailers that agreed to a $20 million settlement in a federal class action lawsuit brought by garment workers in Saipan who alleged sweatshop practices. Has operations in and has sourced from countries with widespread, well-documented human and labor rights abuses. Cited for supplier practices that promote sweatshop labor.

DSW, Inc.
38% | 62%
Contributions: TOTAL: *$3,250*   DEM: *$1,250*   REP: *$2,000*
LOBBY SPENDING: *$0*

Was a subsidiary of Retail Ventures, Inc., until initial public offering in 2005; now it owns more than 60% of outstanding common shares and controls over 90% of the voting rights associated with these shares. Brought in federal investigators after the theft of more than 1.4 million customers' credit information. Settlement with the FTC requires it to implement an information security program and obtain security audits. Has helped to raise more than $750,000 for the March of Dimes and contributes funds to community programs aiding needy and abused children. Donated $500,000 to the New York Restoration Project.

Express, LLC
0% ▬▬▬▬ 100%
Contributions: TOTAL: *$1,740*   DEM: *$0*   REP: *$1,740*
LOBBY SPENDING: *$0*
Subsidiary of Golden Gate Capital. In 2008, agreed to a $1.7 million settlement for violations of the California Business and Professions Code. Donates to Dress for Success and Feeding America. Involved in The United Way of Central Ohio and Giving Tree Program, as well as other local charities in the Columbus, OH, and New York City areas.

Famous Footwear
100% ▬▬▬▬ 0%
Contributions: TOTAL: *$2,075*   DEM: *$2,075*   REP: *$0*
LOBBY SPENDING: *$0*
Subsidiary of Brown Shoe Company, Inc. Supports the March of Dimes.

Filene's Basement Corp.
100% ▬▬▬▬ 0%
Contributions: TOTAL: *$250*   DEM: *$250*   REP: *$0*
LOBBY SPENDING: *$0*
Subsidiary of Retail Ventures, Inc. Increasingly discounts merchandise for about one month, then gives unsold goods to charity.

Foot Locker, Inc.
72% ▬▬▬▬ 28%
Contributions: TOTAL: *$8,114*   DEM: *$5,850*   REP: *$2,264*
LOBBY SPENDING: *$0*
Subject of a class action lawsuit alleging violation of the California Labor Code. Has sourced from countries with widespread, well-documented human and labor rights abuses. Cited for supplier practices that promote sweatshop labor. Foundation supports volunteerism and disaster relief. Has donated to the Twin Towers Fund, United Way, Reading Is Fundamental, and the United Negro College Fund. Contributes to the American Cancer Society. Has a written nondiscrimination policy covering sexual orientation but not gender identity.

Forever 21, Inc.
60% ▬▬▬▬ 40%
Contributions: TOTAL: *$20,000*   DEM: *$12,000*   REP: *$8,000*
LOBBY SPENDING: *$0*
Most apparel is private label and made in Southern California. Every Forever 21 shopping bag bears the words "John 3:16."

Fossil, Inc.
33% ▬▬▬▬ 67%
Contributions: TOTAL: *$10,600*   DEM: *$3,450*   REP: *$7,150*
LOBBY SPENDING: *$0*

Has no written nondiscrimination policy covering sexual orientation or gender identity.

Fruit of the Loom
Contributions: TOTAL: *$18,600*   DEM: *$1,000*   REP: *$17,600*
LOBBY SPENDING: *$192,000*

Subsidiary of Berkshire Hathaway. Uses Latin American production to trim costs.

Gap, Inc.
Contributions: TOTAL: *$403,990*   DEM: *$221,790*   REP: *$182,200*
LOBBY SPENDING: *$180,000*

The largest specialty retailer in the United States was part of a $20 million settlement over labor abuses at a factory in Saipan. Now hires independent monitors to check factory conditions. Distinguished as one of the "100 Best Corporate Citizens." In 2009, it ranked 1st among retailers and 24th among major U.S. companies. In 2008, scored 42 out of 100 in "The Climate Counts Company Scorecard Report." In 2007 and 2008, earned the Human Rights Campaign Foundation's "Best Places to Work for GLBT Equality." Has distributed $91 million in grants worldwide. Is a partner in the (PRODUCT)RED campaign. Has a written nondiscrimination policy covering sexual orientation and gender identity. Offers insurance coverage for employees' domestic partners. Insurance for transgender employees is offered, and some treatment is covered.

Guess?, Inc.
Contributions: TOTAL: *$54,850*   DEM: *$49,850*   REP: *$5,000*
LOBBY SPENDING: *$0*

Agreed to pay a $1 million fine and subsequently moved the bulk of its operations to Mexico after the DOL charged that it operated sweatshops in Los Angeles throughout the 1990s. Supports education, environmental protection, and AIDS research and treatment. Donates to the Ronald McDonald House, Make-A-Wish Foundation, Los Angeles Children's Bureau, and Feed the Children.

Gymboree Corporation, The
Contributions: TOTAL: *$75,600*   DEM: *$72,300*   REP: *$3,300*
LOBBY SPENDING: *$0*

One of 26 retailers that agreed to a $20 million settlement in a federal class action lawsuit brought by garment workers in Saipan who alleged sweatshop practices. Has sourced from countries with widespread, well-documented human and labor rights abuses. Offers paid time off for volunteering. Has raised more than $3 million for St. Jude Children's Research Hospital. Has been involved with Junior Achievement, Grupo de la Comida, St. Anthony Foundation, and the San Francisco Food Bank.

Hanesbrands, Inc.
Contributions: TOTAL: *$16,550*   DEM: *$5,150*   REP: *$11,400*
LOBBY SPENDING: *$800,000*

Formerly Sara Lee Branded Apparel. Acquired by Hanesbrands, Inc., in 2006, after which Hanesbrands announced plans to shutter several plants. In 2008, settled a lawsuit brought by former employees for allegedly failing to pay overtime and allow for rest and meal breaks. Has sourced from countries with widespread, well-documented human and labor rights abuses. Cited for egregious labor violations at its factory in the Dominican Republic and at factories from which it sources in Bangladesh. Has no written nondiscrimination policy covering sexual orientation or gender identity.

Harkham Industries, Inc.
Contributions: TOTAL: *$76,600*   DEM: *$0*   RFP: *$76,600*
LOBBY SPENDING: *$0*

0%   100%

Parent company of Jonathan Martin Fashion Group. Manufactures and markets women's clothing under its four labels: Harkham, Hype, Jonathan Martin, and Johnny Martin.

Henri Bendel
Contributions: TOTAL: *$500*   DEM: *$500*   REP: *$0*
LOBBY SPENDING: *$0*

100%   0%

Subsidiary of Limited Brands, Inc.

Herberger's
Contributions: TOTAL: *$2,230*   DEM: *$0*   REP: *$2,230*
LOBBY SPENDING: *$0*

0%   100%

Subsidiary of Bon-Ton Stores, Inc.

Jockey International, Inc.
Contributions: TOTAL: *$12,150*   DEM: *$0*   REP: *$12,150*
LOBBY SPENDING: *$0*

0%   100%

Privately held. In 2008, sponsored an event to support cancer research. Has designated more than $1 million in direct support and sponsored fund-raising initiatives for post-adoption services. Has a written nondiscrimination policy covering sexual orientation but not gender identity.

Jones Apparel Group, Inc.
Contributions: TOTAL: *$52,988*   DEM: *$41,538*   REP: *$11,450*
LOBBY SPENDING: *$0*

78%   22%

One of 26 retailers that agreed to a $20 million settlement in a federal class action lawsuit brought by garment workers in Saipan who alleged sweatshop practices. Derives most of its garments from developing countries. Although it has a corporate code of conduct for its suppliers, abuses are common. Chairman Sidney Kimmel is a big contributor to cancer research and patient care and has committed corporate resources to raise funds for Jones New York in the Classroom, for which employees are given paid leave to donate their time. In 2008, scored 0 out of 100 in "The Climate Counts Company Scorecard Report." Has a written nondiscrimination policy covering sexual orientation but not gender identity. Offers insurance coverage to employees' domestic partners. Insurance for transgender employees is offered, but treatment is not covered.

Justin Brands
Contributions: TOTAL: *$500*   DEM: *$0*   REP: *$500*
LOBBY SPENDING: *$0*
Subsidiary of Berkshire Hathaway. Supports the Cowboy Crisis Fund and Future Farmers of America.

J. Crew Group, Inc.
Contributions: TOTAL: *$104,190*   DEM: *$103,190*   REP: *$1,000*
LOBBY SPENDING: *$0*
Subsidiary of TPG Capital L.P. One of 26 retailers that agreed to a $20 million settlement in a federal class action lawsuit brought by garment workers in Saipan who alleged sweatshop practices. Asian contractors produce about 80% of the company's merchandise. Due to the economic environment in 2009, suspended matching contributions to the company 401(k) plan through the balance of 2009 and eliminated merit-based wage increases for the entire workforce for the year.

J. C. Penney Company, Inc.
Contributions: TOTAL: *$152,600*   DEM: *$47,100*   REP: *$105,500*
LOBBY SPENDING: *$175,500*
One of 26 retailers that agreed to a $20 million settlement in a federal class action lawsuit brought by garment workers in Saipan who alleged sweatshop practices. In 2009, agreed to a $50,000 settlement in a racial discrimination lawsuit brought by the EEOC. Received a "D-" on Green America's retailer scorecard, which alleges that the company purchases clothing from known sweatshops and has sourced from countries with well-documented human and labor rights abuses. Has a minority supplier diversity program. The NAACP gave J. C. Penney a "D+" grade for its commitment to people of color. In 2009, received the ENERGY STAR Award from the EPA and DOE. Committed to building new stores with LEED certification. Supports health and welfare, education, volunteerism, and diversity. In 2008, distributed more than $9 million in grants to after-school programs. Has a written nondiscrimination policy covering sexual orientation but not gender identity. Offers insurance coverage to employees' domestic partners.

J. Jill Group, Inc., The
Contributions: TOTAL: *$200*   DEM: *$0*   REP: *$200*
LOBBY SPENDING: *$0*
Subsidiary of Talbots, Inc. Settled a lawsuit regarding a policy requiring employees to buy and wear its clothing as a condition of employment. Has donated more than $2.3 million to a compassion fund for women and children and given out more than $1.5 in grants. Has a written nondiscrimination policy that covers sexual orientation but not gender identity.

Kate Spade LLC
Contributions: TOTAL: *$250*   DEM: *$250*   REP: *$0*
LOBBY SPENDING: *$0*
Subsidiary of Liz Claiborne, Inc. Has sourced from countries with widespread, well-documented human and labor rights abuses.

Kellwood Company

0%   100%

Contributions: TOTAL: *$200*   DEM: *$0*   REP: *$200*
LOBBY SPENDING: *$0*

Subsidiary of Sun Capital Partners, Inc. Supports Boy Scouts/Girl Scouts, the University of Missouri-Columbia, Washington University, the American Cancer Society, the Missouri Botanical Garden, the St. Louis Symphony Orchestra, and Dress for Success. Has donated funds and household goods after several major natural disasters. Provides scholarships and tuition reimbursement programs for employees. Has no written nondiscrimination policy covering sexual orientation and gender identity.

Kenneth Cole Productions, Inc.

77%   23%

Contributions: TOTAL: *$13,053*   DEM: *$10,053*   REP: *$3,000*
LOBBY SPENDING: *$0*

A pending lawsuit brought by a former corporate employee alleges sexual and racial harassment. Supports Rock the Vote, Mentoring USA, and the American Foundation for AIDS Research. Established the AWEARNESS Fund, a nonprofit entity that empowers acts of service and social change. Has a written nondiscrimination policy covering sexual orientation and gender identity. Offers insurance coverage to employees' domestic partners. Insurance for transgender employees is offered, but treatment is not covered.

Kohl's Corporation

61%   39%

Contributions: TOTAL: *$4,125*   DEM: *$2,500*   REP: *$1,625*
LOBBY SPENDING: *$0*

Received a "D+" on Green America's retailer scorecard, which alleges that the company purchases clothing from known sweatshops and has sourced from countries with well-documented human and labor rights abuses. One of several major retailers that sourced from an American Samoan factory whose owner was convicted of illegal human trafficking and overseeing forced labor. Received EPA's Green Power Leadership Award and is ranked number 2 on EPA's list of top retail purchasers of renewable energy. Is installing solar power in 130 stores. Supports U.S. Youth Soccer and 156 hospitals that treat children. Will award more than $350,000 in scholarships and prizes in 2009 to recognize selfless acts by children. Matches employees' volunteer efforts with corporate grants to children's groups. Has a written nondiscrimination policy covering sexual orientation but not gender identity. Offers limited insurance coverage to employees' opposite-sex domestic partners.

Lands' End, Inc.

63%   37%

Contributions: TOTAL: *$2,050*   DEM: *$1,300*   REP: *$750*
LOBBY SPENDING: *$0*

Subsidiary of Sears Holdings Corporation. Has lost several major customers amid reports of questionable business practices and alleged labor law violations at supplier factories in El Salvador. Now has a written code of vendor conduct. Has reduced catalog paper consumption by more than 30% since 2006. Offers a ride-share program for employees. Partners with Habitat for Humanity and the American Red Cross. Has a written nondiscrimination policy covering sexual orientation and gender identity. Offers insurance coverage to employees' domestic partners.

Levi Strauss & Co.

94%   6%

Contributions: TOTAL: *$82,171*   DEM: *$77,571*   REP: *$4,600*
LOBBY SPENDING: *$125,000*

This all-American brand is now an entirely foreign-made product. Has established operating guidelines for its manufacturers and conducts audits of its factories on issues such as child labor and minimum wage. In 2008, scored 22 out of 100 in "The Climate Counts Company Scorecard Report." Has strict wastewater guidelines for its contract laundries and finishing facilities. Its foundation supports AIDS/HIV prevention, provides aid in response to natural disasters, and bolsters labor and living conditions in countries where Levi products are produced. Offers full-time employees some paid time off to volunteer. Has a written nondiscrimination policy that covers sexual orientation and gender identity. Offers insurance to employees' domestic partners. Insurance for transgender employees is offered, but treatment is not covered.

Limited Brands, Inc.

23%   77%

Contributions: TOTAL: *$475,694*   DEM: *$107,870*   REP: *$367,824*
LOBBY SPENDING: *$1,320,000*

Pending lawsuit alleges termination based on disability and sexual orientation. One of 26 retailers that agreed to a $20 million settlement in a federal class action lawsuit brought by garment workers in Saipan who alleged sweatshop practices. Has sourced from countries with widespread, well-documented human and labor rights abuses. In 2008, scored 23 out of 100 in "The Climate Counts Company Scorecard Report." Has fitted hundreds of stores with energy-efficient lighting. Keeps tons of material from going to landfills through reuse and recycling. In 2007, donated $1 million to the Whittier Peninsula Audubon Center. Supports child mentoring, education, the Komen Race for the Cure, the American Cancer Society, the Giving Tree Program, and the United Way. Has a written nondiscrimination policy covering sexual orientation but not gender identity. Offers health insurance coverage to employees' domestic partners. Insurance for transgender employees is offered, but treatment is not covered.

Liz Claiborne, Inc.

98%   2%

Contributions: TOTAL: *$49,600*   DEM: *$48,600*   REP: *$1,000*
LOBBY SPENDING: *$20,000*

One of 26 retailers that agreed to a $20 million settlement in a federal class action lawsuit brought by garment workers in Saipan who alleged sweatshop practices. Has sourced from countries with widespread, well-documented human and labor rights abuses. A founder of the Fair Labor Association. Listed by NAFE as one of the top 50 companies for female executives in 2009. In 2008, scored 15 out of 100 in "The Climate Counts Company Scorecard Report." Its foundation supports nonprofit organizations focused on family violence, women's economic self-sufficiency, and positive development programs for girls. Matches employees' charitable gifts and provides scholarships to employees' children who have demonstrated outstanding academic achievement. Has a written nondiscrimination policy covering sexual orientation and gender identity. Offers insurance coverage to employees' domestic partners. Insurance for transgender employees is offered, but treatment is not covered.

Loehmann's Holdings, Inc.

0% | 100%

Contributions: Total: *$276*   Dem: *$0*   Rep: *$276*
Lobby Spending: *$0*

Acquired by Dubai-based Istithmar PJSC in 2006. Hosts shopping nights at its New York flagship store to benefit charity. Has a written nondiscrimination policy covering gender identity but not sexual orientation.

Lord & Taylor, LLC

26% | 74%

Contributions: Total: *$950*   Dem: *$250*   Rep: *$700*
Lobby Spending: *$0*

Subsidiary of NRDC Equity Partners; parent Apollo Advisors. Supports charities in the Long Island, NY, area. Has a written nondiscrimination policy covering sexual orientation but not gender identity.

Louis Vuitton North America, Inc.

100% | 0%

Contributions: Total: *$3,300*   Dem: *$3,300*   Rep: *$0*
Lobby Spending: *$0*

Subsidiary of LVMH Moët Hennessy Louis Vuitton SA. Its cosmetic product lines were among a group of codefendants in a class action price-fixing case with a settlement involving the mass giveaway of cosmetics in 2009.

Macy's, Inc.

46% | 54%

Contributions: Total: *$172,234*   Dem: *$79,034*   Rep: *$93,200*
Lobby Spending: *$0*

Formerly Federated Department Stores. Listed by NAFE as one of the top 50 companies for female executives in 2009. Received a "C" on Green America's retailer scorecard, which alleges that the company purchases clothing from known sweatshops and has sourced from countries with well-documented human and labor rights abuses. Macys.com has a downloadable user tool for visually impaired users. Environmental goals for 2010 include reducing its energy use by 10% to 15%, increasing use of renewable power sources eight-fold, and reducing paper consumption by at least 20% from 2006 levels. Foundation supports education, women's issues, arts/culture, HIV/AIDS prevention, and education programs. Has a written nondiscrimination policy covering sexual orientation and gender identity. Offers health insurance to employees' domestic partners. Insurance for transgender employees is offered, but treatment is not covered.

Marshall Field's

100% | 0%

Contributions: Total: *$250*   Dem: *$250*   Rep: *$0*
Lobby Spending: *$0*

Subsidiary of Macy's, Inc. Settled a discrimination case by changing its policy of charging women more than men for alterations.

Marshalls
Contributions: TOTAL: *$625*   DEM: *$625*   REP: *$0*
LOBBY SPENDING: *$0*
Subsidiary of The TJX Companies, Inc.

100% / 0%

Mary Green Enterprises
Contributions: TOTAL: *$86,850*   DEM: *$86,850*   REP: *$0*
LOBBY SPENDING: *$0*
In 2008, along with the two founders of YouTube, Mary Green was accorded the Vision Award for world leadership.

100% / 0%

May Department Stores Company, The
Contributions: TOTAL: *$2,000*   DEM: *$0*   REP: *$2,000*
LOBBY SPENDING: *$0*
Subsidiary of Macy's, Inc. As of 2009, out of business.

0% / 100%

Men's Wearhouse, Inc., The
Contributions: TOTAL: *$106,090*   DEM: *$102,300*   REP: *$3,790*
LOBBY SPENDING: *$0*
Ranked 71st in *Fortune* magazine's "The 100 Best Companies to Work for in America" in 2009. CEO accepts a compensation package that is significantly lower than that for CEOs of retail competitors in order to pay higher compensation to employees. Annually, each store is allocated funds to contribute to local nonprofit organizations. Partners with organizations that help men who have conquered homelessness, addiction, and poverty. In 2008, started a drive to provide suits to clients of job-training and employment programs. Has a written nondiscrimination policy covering sexual orientation and gender identity. Offers insurance coverage to employees' domestic partners.

96% / 4%

Michael Kors, LLC
Contributions: TOTAL: *$67,970*   DEM: *$63,170*   REP: *$4,800*
LOBBY SPENDING: *$0*
Has been targeted by PETA for using fur in designs.

93% / 7%

Movado Group, Inc.
Contributions: TOTAL: *$15,000*   DEM: *$6,850*   REP: *$8,150*
LOBBY SPENDING: *$0*
Supports the arts, including the Miami City Ballet, Lincoln Center, and New York's American Ballet Theater and City Ballet. Offers insurance coverage to employees' domestic partners.

46% / 54%

Nautica Enterprises, Inc.
Contributions: TOTAL: *$9,950*   DEM: *$9,950*   REP: *$0*
LOBBY SPENDING: *$0*
Subsidiary of VF Corporation. Has sourced from countries with widespread, well-documented human and labor rights abuses. Has a written nondiscrimination policy covering sexual orientation but not gender identity.

100% / 0%

Neiman Marcus Group, Inc., The
Contributions: TOTAL: *$54,786*   DEM: *$38,271*   REP: *$16,515*
LOBBY SPENDING: *$0*

70%   30%

Subsidiary of Leonard Green & Partners LP and TPG Capital LP. One of eight firms that agreed to pay a total of $320,000 in 2008 for alleged failure to report that children's hooded sweatshirts and jackets were sold with drawstrings at the hood and neck. These products, which the firms eventually recalled, posed strangulation hazards. Has a written nondiscrimination policy covering sexual orientation but not gender identity. Offers insurance coverage to employees' domestic partners.

Next Components, Ltd.
Contributions: TOTAL: *$112,300*   DEM: *$112,300*   REP: *$0*
LOBBY SPENDING: *$0*

100%   0%

In 2008, the SEC filed a complaint against Next Components, Ltd., and its principal, Norman Hsu, alleging that they violated the Securities Act of 1933 and the Securities Exchange Act of 1934. In 2007, Hsu was indicted on federal charges of fraud and violating campaign finance laws. Public records show he has donated millions to Democratic campaigns since 2003. In 2007, the Clinton campaign returned more than $800,000 to donors whose contributions were linked to Hsu.

Nine West Group, Inc.
Contributions: TOTAL: *$2,800*   DEM: *$500*   REP: *$2,300*
LOBBY SPENDING: *$0*

18%   82%

Subsidiary of Jones Apparel Group, Inc. Has sourced from countries with widespread, well-documented human and labor rights abuses. Manufacturers are located in Brazil, China, and Italy. Has a written nondiscrimination policy covering sexual orientation but not gender identity. Offers health insurance benefits to employees' domestic partners.

Nordstrom, Inc.
Contributions: TOTAL: *$35,380*   DEM: *$21,713*   REP: *$13,667*
LOBBY SPENDING: *$0*

61%   39%

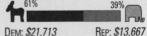

Pending lawsuit brought by the EEOC for harassment of Hispanic and African American employees. Agreed to pay a $7.5 million settlement to investors in a shareholder-filed securities fraud class action suit. One of 26 retailers that agreed to a $20 million settlement in a federal class action lawsuit brought by garment workers in Saipan who alleged sweatshop practices. Has sourced from countries with widespread, well-documented human and labor rights abuses. Is a member of the Fair Labor Association. One of several retailers ordered to give away products as settlement in a price-fixing class action suit. Ranked 72nd in *Fortune* magazine's "100 Best Companies to Work for in America" in 2009. Upgrading to energy-efficient lighting. Has a comprehensive recycling program. Supports health and human services, community development, education, scholarships, and cultural enhancement. Has a written nondiscrimination policy covering sexual orientation and gender identity. Offers insurance coverage to employees' domestic partners. Insurance for transgender employees is offered, but treatment is not covered.

Oakley, Inc.
Contributions: TOTAL: *$8,100*   DEM: *$500*   REP: *$7,600*
LOBBY SPENDING: *$0*

6% / 94%

Subsidiary of Luxottica Group, S.p.A. Has a written nondiscrimination policy covering sexual orientation but not gender identity.

Old Navy
Contributions: TOTAL: *$1,655*   DEM: *$1,405*   REP: *$250*
LOBBY SPENDING: *$0*

85% / 15%

Subsidiary of Gap, Inc.

Once Upon A Child
Contributions: TOTAL: *$500*   DEM: *$500*   REP: *$0*
LOBBY SPENDING: *$0*

100% / 0%

Subsidiary of Winmark Corporation.

Parisian
Contributions: TOTAL: *$1,000*   DEM: *$1,000*   REP: *$0*
LOBBY SPENDING: *$0*

100% / 0%

Subsidiary of Belk, Inc.

Payless ShoeSource, Inc.
Contributions: TOTAL: *$33,250*   DEM: *$18,500*   REP: *$14,750*
LOBBY SPENDING: *$280,000*

56% / 44%

Subsidiary of Collective Brands, Inc. Has sourced from countries with widespread, well-documented human and labor rights abuses. Supports local arts, education, and health and human services. Partners with Susan G. Komen for the Cure, the Fresh Air Fund, and the United Way.

Pendleton Woolen Mills, Inc.
Contributions: TOTAL: *$61,950*   DEM: *$500*   REP: *$61,450*
LOBBY SPENDING: *$0*

1% / 99%

Privately held. The EPA and the Washington Department of Ecology assert that damages to natural resources were caused by chemicals, minerals, waste, and other materials allegedly produced, generated, or disposed of by Pendleton. Its mill in Washougal, WA, was classified a Superfund site. Donates to the American Indian College Fund. Offers free educational materials to teachers.

Phillips-Van Heusen Corporation
Contributions: TOTAL: *$26,350*   DEM: *$20,750*   REP: *$5,600*
LOBBY SPENDING: *<$40,000*

79% / 21%

One of 26 retailers that agreed to a $20 million settlement in a federal class action lawsuit brought by garment workers in Saipan who alleged sweatshop practices. Has sourced from countries with widespread, well-documented human and labor rights abuses. A founder of the Fair Labor Association. Its union-made men's dress shirts bear the UNITE HERE label. Brand names: Van Heusen, Arrow, Geoffrey Beane, Calvin Klein, Stafford. Supports Ronald McDonald House, Habitat for Humanity, AIDS walks, the Special Olympics, and the United Way. Spearheading campaign for Ellis Island restoration project. Has contributed to schools, orphanages, and families in Mexico, Honduras, and the Far East. Employees organized free eye exams for poor workers in Bangladesh. Has a written nondiscrimination policy covering sexual orientation but not gender identity.

Polo Ralph Lauren Corporation

84%   16%
Contributions: TOTAL: *$38,426*   DEM: *$32,375*   REP: *$6,051*
LOBBY SPENDING: *$0*
One of 26 retailers that agreed to a $20 million settlement in a federal class action lawsuit brought by garment workers in Saipan who alleged sweatshop practices. Accused of pulling its business from factories where workers organized to demand higher wages. A pending class action lawsuit alleges labor violations, fraud, and false imprisonment. In 2007, agreed to a $1.5 million settlement in a class action suit alleging that the company requires employees to purchase company products as a condition of employment. Supports medical programs for underserved communities, cancer care, cancer prevention and research, education, and Habitat for Humanity. Proceeds of sales of an organic cotton tote go to environmental initiatives. Has a written nondiscrimination policy covering sexual orientation but not gender identity. Offers insurance coverage to employees' domestic partners.

Red Wing Shoe Company, Inc.
0%   100%
Contributions: TOTAL: *$2,900*   DEM: *$0*   REP: *$2,900*
LOBBY SPENDING: *$0*
Privately held. Company is often hit with second- and third-party suits because of workplace injuries suffered by workers wearing Red Wing boots. Red Wing boots are made in America by unionized workers.

Retail Brand Alliance, Inc.
84%   16%
Contributions: TOTAL: *$3,200*   DEM: *$2,700*   REP: *$500*
LOBBY SPENDING: *$140,000*
Holding company for Brooks Brothers.

Retail Ventures, Inc.
14%   86%
Contributions: TOTAL: *$1,750*   DEM: *$250*   REP: *$1,500*
LOBBY SPENDING: *$0*
Outreach focuses on children's health and education, women's health, and diversity staffing and training.

Ross Stores, Inc.
64%   36%
Contributions: TOTAL: *$6,350*   DEM: *$4,050*   REP: *$2,300*
LOBBY SPENDING: *$0*
In 2007, settled a suit brought by the EEOC for allegedly discriminating against an employee because of her nationality. Paid $200,000 in fines for selling highly flammable clothing in violation of federal law. Partners with a foundation that distributes retailers' donated goods. Has a written nondiscrimination policy covering sexual orientation but not gender identity.

Saks, Inc.

Contributions: TOTAL: *$89,149*   DEM: *$57,049*   REP: *$32,100*
LOBBY SPENDING: *$12,500*

64% | 36%

In 2009, settled with two former employees for age discrimination. Placed under federal order to tighten anti-money laundering practices after several alleged instances of illegal payoffs. It estimates that its voluntary partnership with the EPA to reduce emissions, eliminate energy waste, and reduce energy costs has reduced 65 million kilowatt hours of energy consumption. Supports education, breast cancer research, and preservation of natural habitats. Partners with the United Way and St. Jude Children's Research Hospital. Started "charity: water," which since 2006 has funded construction of more than 250 wells that provide clean drinking water to 150,000 people in Africa, India, and Central America. Provides disaster relief. Has a written nondiscrimination policy covering sexual orientation but not gender identity. Offers health insurance coverage to employees' domestic partners.

Shane Co.

Contributions: TOTAL: *$500*   DEM: *$0*   REP: *$500*
LOBBY SPENDING: *$0*

0% | 100%

Filed for Chapter 11 bankruptcy in 2009. Uses the Kimberley Process. Has sourced from countries with widespread, well-documented human and labor rights abuses.

Skechers U.S.A., Inc.

Contributions: TOTAL: *$10,105*   DEM: *$3,000*   REP: *$7,105*
LOBBY SPENDING: *$0*

30% | 70%

Has been fined for requiring retail workers to wear company products without compensation. Has sourced from countries with widespread, well-documented human and labor rights abuses. Its manufacturing is outsourced primarily to Chinese contractors. Donates to family-related organizations, such as the Juvenile Diabetes Research Foundation International and Habitat for Humanity.

Spiegel Brands, Inc.

Contributions: TOTAL: *$2,450*   DEM: *$2,450*   REP: *$0*
LOBBY SPENDING: *$0*

100% | 0%

Acquired by an investor group led by Granite Creek Partners in 2008; formerly owned by Golden Gate Capital. Has sourced from countries with widespread, well-documented human and labor rights abuses. Has a written nondiscrimination policy covering sexual orientation but not gender identity. Offers insurance coverage to employees' domestic partners.

Stein Mart, Inc.

Contributions: TOTAL: *$108,450*   DEM: *$3,450*   REP: *$105,000*
LOBBY SPENDING: *$0*

3% | 97%

Supports Dignity U Wear, a nonprofit organization that provides "brand new clothes for a brand new life" to help children and families in crisis.

Sterling Jewelers, Inc.

94% | 6%

Contributions: TOTAL: *$8,050*   DEM: *$7,550*   REP: *$500*
LOBBY SPENDING: *$0*

Subsidiary of Signet Jewelers, Ltd. A pending lawsuit brought in 2008 alleges sex discrimination. Has sourced from countries with widespread, well-documented human and labor rights abuses. Subsidiary Kay Jewelers supports St. Jude Children's Research Hospital, for which it has raised $14 million.

Steven Madden, Ltd.

100% | 0%

Contributions: TOTAL: *$9,441*   DEM: *$9,441*   REP: *$0*
LOBBY SPENDING: *$0*

Has sourced from countries with widespread, well-documented human and labor rights abuses. Supports the Fresh Air Fund and has helped raise funds on behalf of the Save Darfur Coalition.

Stride Rite Corporation, The

64% | 36%

Contributions: TOTAL: *$2,750*   DEM: *$1,750*   REP: *$1,000*
LOBBY SPENDING: *$0*

Subsidiary of Collective Brands, Inc. Has sourced from countries with widespread, well-documented human and labor rights abuses. Supports charities that help children, including the United Way, Netpals, and Helping Hands.

Talbots, Inc., The

63% | 37%

Contributions: TOTAL: *$12,600*   DEM: *$7,950*   REP: *$4,650*
LOBBY SPENDING: *$0*

Subsidiary of Tokyo-based retailer AEON. One of 26 retailers that agreed to a $20 million settlement in a federal class action lawsuit brought by garment workers in Saipan who alleged sweatshop practices. Has sourced from countries with widespread, well-documented human and labor rights abuses. Supports cultural, civic, health, welfare, and educational causes and scholarships for women. Has no nondiscrimination policy covering sexual orientation or gender identity.

Tiffany & Co.

97% | 3%

Contributions: TOTAL: *$36,638*   DEM: *$35,638*   REP: *$1,000*
LOBBY SPENDING: *$560,000*

Refuses to import gems from Burma, long known to use proceeds to finance human rights abuses. Supporter of the World Diamond Council. In partnership with Oxfam America's "No Dirty Gold" campaign, has made efforts to ensure that gold and diamonds are mined responsibly. Supports passage of a strong U.S. Coral Reef Conservation Act and uses no real coral. Supports reform of the General Mining Law of 1872 and legislation to assist in cleanup of abandoned hardrock mines. Its foundation supports enhancement of urban environments and culturally significant landmarks, coral reef conservation, and responsible mining. Has a written nondiscrimination policy covering sexual orientation but not gender identity. Offers insurance coverage to employees' domestic partners. Insurance for transgender employees is offered, but treatment is not covered.

Timberland Company, The
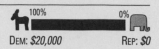
Contributions: TOTAL: *$20,000*   DEM: *$20,000*   REP: *$0*
LOBBY SPENDING: *$15,000*

In 2008, paid $7 million to settle claims that it violated federal law by sending unsolicited text advertisements to cellular phone users. Has sourced from countries with widespread, well-documented human and labor rights abuses. Uses a third party to independently monitor its manufacturing facilities, but results from the audits are for company eyes only. In 2008, launched its Earthkeeper campaign to recruit one million people to become part of an online network designed to inspire environmental behavior change. Partners with Earthwatch Institute and Conservation Alliance and is a founding member of the Organic Exchange. Supports community building, environmental stewardship, and global human rights. Offers its employees monetary incentives to purchase hybrid cars and provides sabbaticals for employees who want to pursue a dream that benefits the community. Has a written nondiscrimination policy covering sexual orientation but not gender identity. Offers insurance coverage to employees' domestic partners.

TJX Companies, Inc., The

Contributions: TOTAL: *$28,050*   DEM: *$8,100*   REP: *$19,950*
LOBBY SPENDING: *$0*

In 2008, paid more than $10 million to settle a class action lawsuit brought by consumers whose personal information was compromised by a security breach. Paid $150,000 in fines for selling highly flammable clothing. Criticized for paying low wages to its factory workers and improperly categorizing some employees as exempt from overtime pay. Shareholders and activists have pressured TJX to make sourcing of its gold and diamonds more transparent. Joined the EPA's SmartWay Transport Partnership. Supports Save the Children, Autism Speaks, and The Jimmy Fund. Has a written nondiscrimination policy covering sexual orientation and gender identity. Offers insurance coverage to employees' domestic partners. Insurance for transgender employees is offered, and some treatment is covered.

Tommy Hilfiger Corporation
Contributions: TOTAL: *$29,628*   DEM: *$25,028*   REP: *$4,600*
LOBBY SPENDING: *$0*

Acquired by Apax Partners in 2006. Privately held. One of 26 retailers that agreed to a $20 million settlement in a federal class action lawsuit brought by garment workers in Saipan who alleged sweatshop practices. A pending shareholder class action lawsuit alleges SEC violations. Agreed to pay $18.1 million to settle a federal investigation into misuse of foreign subsidiaries, allegedly to avoid taxes. Has sourced from countries with widespread, well-documented human and labor rights abuses. Supports educational opportunities.

T. J. Maxx
Contributions: TOTAL: *$2,150*   DEM: *$2,150*   REP: *$0*
LOBBY SPENDING: *$0*
Subsidiary of The TJX Companies, Inc.

VF Corporation

66% | 34%

Contributions: TOTAL: *$46,468*   DEM: *$30,858*   REP: *$15,610*
LOBBY SPENDING: <*$40,000*

In 2008, scored 4 out of 100 in "The Climate Counts Company Scorecard Report." Outreach includes support for children, teens, women who have been victims of abuse, and the fight against breast cancer. Annually recognizes the top 100 associates ranking highest in the accumulation of community service hours.

Victoria's Secret

25% | 75%

Contributions: TOTAL: *$5,050*   DEM: *$1,250*   REP: *$3,800*
LOBBY SPENDING: *$0*

Subsidiary of Limited Brands, Inc. Agreed to pay $179,300 to settle a race and religion discrimination lawsuit brought by the EEOC. Settled allegations that security vulnerabilities in its Web site had exposed its customers' personal ordering information to interception, in violation of its posted privacy policy. Has a written nondiscrimination policy covering sexual orientation but not gender identity. Offers health insurance to employees' domestic partners. Insurance for transgender employees is offered, but treatment is not covered.

Warnaco Group, Inc., The

100% | 0%

Contributions: TOTAL: *$6,850*   DEM: *$6,850*   REP: *$0*
LOBBY SPENDING: *$0*

One of 26 retailers that agreed to a $20 million settlement in a federal class action lawsuit brought by garment workers in Saipan who alleged sweatshop practices. Has sourced from countries with widespread, well-documented human and labor rights abuses. Has a written nondiscrimination policy covering sexual orientation but not gender identity.

Wet Seal, Inc., The

70% | 30%

Contributions: TOTAL: *$3,300*   DEM: *$2,300*   REP: *$1,000*
LOBBY SPENDING: *$0*

Paid $1.28 million to settle a wage hour lawsuit brought by store managers who alleged that they were denied overtime wages and wrongly classified as exempt, in violation of California law. A pending class action lawsuit alleges violation of the federal law that seeks to prevent identity theft among consumers. A pending shareholder class action suit alleges violations of the Securities Exchange Act. Supports local schools and community organizations.

Williamson-Dickie Manufacturing Company

12% | 88%

Contributions: TOTAL: *$2,100*   DEM: *$250*   REP: *$1,850*
LOBBY SPENDING: <*$40,000*

Acquired Kodiak Group Holdings in 2008. Operates sweatshops in foreign countries. Schools that purchase Dickies brand school uniforms can earn points good for computers, sporting goods, and playground equipment.

Wolverine World Wide, Inc.
Contributions: TOTAL: *$1,500*
LOBBY SPENDING: *$240,000*

33% DEM: *$500* 67% REP: *$1,000*

Supports health and human services, arts, education, research, environment, and disaster relief organizations.

Younkers
Contributions: TOTAL: *$700*
LOBBY SPENDING: *$0*

100% DEM: *$700* 0% REP: *$0*

Subsidiary of Bon-Ton Stores, Inc.

Zale Corporation
Contributions: TOTAL: *$4,550*
LOBBY SPENDING: *$0*

44% DEM: *$2,000* 56% REP: *$2,550*

Has sourced from countries with widespread, well-documented human and labor rights abuses. Founding member of the Council for Responsible Jewelry Practices, which is committed to stopping the trade in conflict diamonds. Participates in the Kimberley Process. Outreach supports children's health and well-being, medical research and treatment, and the Families of Freedom Scholarship Fund. Has a written nondiscrimination policy covering sexual orientation but not gender identity.

Computers and Electronics

Carol E. Pott

No well-informed American could have missed the historical significance of the 2008 presidential election. As the first black president, Barack Obama dominated the news both here and abroad. But for those in the computer and electronics sector, putting a Blackberry-carrying, tech-savvy Web user into the White House was even more exciting than other precedent-shattering aspects of Obama's victory.

The use of technology in Obama's campaign was another big story that quickly became politics as usual. Even the old guard had to acknowledge the power of new organizing tools and tactics, including David Plouffe's 13-million-person e-mail contact list. Not only has Obama entered office with an unmatched repository of information at his fingertips, but his type of techie-style grassroots organizing has likely revolutionized progressive politics—perhaps even politics in general. Although some still question the lasting influence of social networking sites, no one can gainsay the role of new technology on political campaigning.

Plouffe's e-mail list, fondly referred to in the media as his "13-million-mouthed dog," ushered in a president and an administration that takes tech policy (beyond cybersecurity) seriously. That approach is only fitting. After all, the federal government is the world's largest buyer of technology, and the industry has a huge impact on our culture in general. But the Obama administration has also demonstrated that it embraces the industry's advances. After it appointed the first intellectual property enforcement coordinator, a coalition of high-tech stakeholders challenged the move, arguing that overly broad intellectual property protection can quash new information technologies. The Obama administration immediately addressed that concern, but its use of Twitter, the Internet, and Obama's own Facebook page to do so signaled the beginning of a new era.

Although the past decade has brought the computer industry both boom and bust, the sector has maintained its hard-won status as a major factor in the American economy. The consumer electronics business, in particular, has held up well during the current global downturn, even with the near collapse of capital expenditures by businesses. This sector has also retained its political clout. Despite economic ups and downs, millions of dollars in contributions continue to find their way into the political coffers during each election cycle; major donations go to candidates and parties in federal elections. The sector's combined lobbying efforts from January 2005 to December 2008 exceeded $345 million—no small change.

This sector's legislative agenda is relatively straightforward. Its dependence on the Chinese and Indian labor forces means support for free trade and a liberal immigration policy. Its lobbying efforts also focus on cybersecurity, copyright law, intellectual property, patent law reform, and foreign copyright protection. Industry-wide lobbying for the Central American Free Trade Agreement (CAFTA) did not go unrewarded; the Bush administration pushed hard for approval and signed it into law in August 2005. Despite industry pressure, patent reform has stalled. Such reform has come before Congress three times over the last five years. The Senate Judiciary Committee approved the Patent Reform Act of 2009, despite mixed reactions from the industry, but industry representatives are not convinced that this legislation will be signed into law.

The industry's political contributions changed dramatically with this election cycle. Between 1990 and 2004, Democrats and Republicans split the swag almost evenly. In 2008, however, 70% of those contributions went to Democrats.

Despite being a relatively new player on the political scene, Microsoft again tops the list as the number one contributor in this sector. It increased its political contributions nearly threefold in the 2008 election cycle and shifted considerably more resources to Democrats, who received 73% of the pie, compared with 58% in the 2004 cycle. The most visible reasons for Microsoft's efforts and investment included well-publicized antitrust issues, multiple competition infringements, massive European Union (EU) fines, and the EU's continuing allegations that Microsoft shields its products from "head-to-head competition" by bundling its Internet Explorer browser with Windows.

Recently, far more attention has been focused on the computer and electronics sector's environmental impacts. News outlets report regularly on toxins used in the products and in their manufacture, and e-waste has become a common household term. Companies responded with green initiatives, sustainability solutions, and environmental programs that showered green social programs with money. Despite the economic downturn, Microsoft keeps up with its climate change policy statement; Cisco has an extensive environmental program, including energy efficiency, waste recycling, and waste reduction; and Apple's "A Greener Apple" program aggressively reduces toxic chemicals from its merchandise, recycles old products, and reduces e-waste.

With ever-expanding access to wi-fi, and Internet streaming of everything from movies to online games, Americans are increasingly wired to the teeth. No longer is it necessary to carry a boom box for portable music, when miniscule mobile phones have theater-quality surround sound and iPods do everything but walk your dog. Children learn computer skills at younger ages, increasing the gap between the computer literate and other generations. The computer and electronics industry will continue to hold sway in Washington, not only because of the nature of its products, but also because of its worldwide cultural and environmental impacts.

Top Ten Democratic Contributors

Microsoft Corporation	$2,577,710
Cisco Systems, Inc.	$974,084
International Business Machines Corporation (IBM)	$856,358
Sony Corporation	$771,941
Hewlett-Packard Company	$771,096
Oracle Corporation	$719,538
Intel Corporation	$477,698
Motorola, Inc.	$398,281
Apple Computer, Inc.	$315,323
Certain Software, Inc.	$266,818

Top Ten Republican Contributors

Microsoft Corporation	$1,005,981
Cisco Systems, Inc.	$547,056
Hewlett-Packard Company	$475,708
Intel Corporation	$370,712
Oracle Corporation	$317,385
Motorola, Inc.	$305,135
International Business Machines Corporation (IBM)	$287,762
Sony Corporation	$266,720
Electronic Arts, Inc.	$259,451
EMC Corporation	$245,350

Top Ten Lobbying Spenders

Microsoft Corporation	$17,900,000
International Business Machines Corp. (IBM)	$14,600,000
Motorola, Inc.	$12,150,000
Hewlett-Packard Company	$11,148,648
Oracle Corporation	$10,270,000
Siemens AG	$9,716,898
EDS Corporation	$6,208,648
Texas Instruments, Inc.	$4,900,000
Sony Corporation	$4,783,000
Toshiba Corporation	$4,110,000

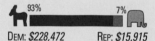

Adobe Systems, Inc.
Contributions: TOTAL: *$244,387*   DEM: *$228,472*   REP: *$15,915*
LOBBY SPENDING: *$784,930*
Ranked 11th on *Fortune* magazine's "Top 100 Companies to Work For" in 2009. Donates funds, software and training, and employee volunteers to groups and schools. Partners with a nonprofit that places individuals with disabilities in regular employment. Has a written nondiscrimination policy covering sexual orientation and gender identity. Offers insurance coverage to employees' domestic partners.

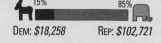

Advanced Micro Devices, Inc.
Contributions: TOTAL: *$120,979*   DEM: *$18,258*   REP: *$102,721*
LOBBY SPENDING: *$1,530,000*
Settled a class action suit alleging violations of federal securities laws, fraudulent misrepresentation, and inflation of common stock. Has sourced from countries with widespread, well-documented human and labor rights abuses. Named to 2009 Global 100 Most Sustainable Corporations in the World list. Reduced greenhouse gas emissions, normalized for production, by more than 50% between 2002 and 2006; plans an additional 33% reduction in the level of its 2006 emissions by 2010. Has a written nondiscrimination policy covering sexual orientation and gender identity. Offers insurance coverage to employees' domestic partners. Insurance for transgender employees is offered, and treatment is covered.

Agfa-Gevaert N.V.

68% DEM | 32% REP

Contributions: TOTAL: *$2,200*   DEM: *$1,500*   REP: *$700*
LOBBY SPENDING: *$0*

Foreign owned. Voluntarily supports chemical industry's "Responsible Care" initiative. Offers health insurance coverage for employees' domestic partners at its Teterboro, NJ, manufacturing facility and at its Greenville, SC, location.

Akamai Technologies, Inc.

59% DEM | 41% REP

Contributions: TOTAL: *$345,916*   DEM: *$204,066*   REP: *$141,850*
LOBBY SPENDING: *$0*

Delivers between 15% and 20% of all Web traffic. Promotes mathematics education and awards scholarships. Offers insurance coverage to employees' domestic partners.

Apple Computer, Inc.

89% DEM | 11% REP

Contributions: TOTAL: *$354,026*   DEM: *$315,323*   REP: *$38,703*
LOBBY SPENDING: *$3,010,000*

Has operations in and sources from countries with widespread, well-documented human and labor rights abuses. In 2008, scored 11 out of 100 in "The Climate Counts Company Scorecard Report." Has a free recycling program from its stores, but the program is available only to customers who buy from Apple directly. Every new Mac is Energy Star 4.0 compliant. Supports genomic research and environmental causes and research. A partner in the (PRODUCT) RED campaign. Has a written nondiscrimination policy that covers sexual orientation and gender identity. Offers health insurance coverage to employees' domestic partners. Insurance for transgender employees is offered, but treatment is not covered.

Atari, Inc.

100% DEM | 0% REP

Contributions: TOTAL: *$2,000*   DEM: *$2,000*   REP: *$0*
LOBBY SPENDING: *$0*

Subsidiary of Infogrames Entertainment, S.A. Foreign owned. Operates in and sources from countries with widespread, well-documented human and labor rights abuses.

Best Buy Company, Inc.

27% DEM | 73% REP

Contributions: TOTAL: *$230,225*   DEM: *$61,050*   REP: *$169,175*
LOBBY SPENDING: *$1,375,000*

Named in several age discrimination suits. Offers free in-store recycling for cell phones, rechargeable batteries, ink-jet cartridges, CDs, DVDs, and PDAs. Its foundation donates to schools, awards scholarships to high school seniors, and puts millions into local communities. Has a written nondiscrimination policy covering sexual orientation and gender identity. Offers insurance coverage to employees' domestic partners. Insurance for transgender employees is offered, and treatment is covered. Requires sexual orientation and gender identity diversity training for management.

Brookstone, Inc.

100% DEM | 0% REP

Contributions: TOTAL: *$4,400*   DEM: *$4,400*   REP: *$0*
LOBBY SPENDING: *$0*

Subsidiary of J.W. Childs Associates, L.P.

Canon U.S.A., Inc.

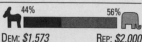

Contributions: Total: *$3,573*   Dem: *$1,573*   Rep: *$2,000*
Lobby Spending: *$0*

Subsidiary of Canon, Inc. A pending class action lawsuit alleges it knowingly sold defective PowerShot S400 digital cameras. Has partnerships with the EPA and provides funding for the Yellowstone Park Foundation, the American Cancer Society, and the American Red Cross. Supports the Canon Envirothon, which offers scholarships and prizes. Has a written nondiscrimination policy covering sexual orientation, not gender identity. Does not offer insurance coverage to employees' domestic partners.

Canon, Inc.

Contributions: Total: *$500*   Dem: *$500*   Rep: *$0*
Lobby Spending: *$0*

Foreign owned. Has operated in and sourced from countries with widespread, well-documented human and labor rights abuses. In 2008, scored 74 out of 100 in "The Climate Counts Company Scorecard Report." Its green procurement program establishes material declaration guidelines and includes inspection of suppliers' manufacturing facilities. Is shifting from truck to rail and ship transport of products to reduce carbon dioxide emissions. Supports the World Wildlife Fund. Donates digital cameras and printers to the National Center for Missing & Exploited Children.

Certain Software, Inc.

Contributions: Total: *$266,818*   Dem: *$266,818*   Rep: *$0*
Lobby Spending: *$0*

Privately held.

Cisco Systems, Inc.

Contributions: Total: *$1,521,140*   Dem: *$974,084*   Rep: *$547,056*
Lobby Spending: *$2,820,000*

In 2006, paid $91 million to settle a class action suit alleging securities violations. Has operated in and sourced from countries with widespread, well-documented human and labor rights abuses. Ranked 6th on *Fortune* magazine's "Top 100 Best Companies to Work For" in 2009. Listed by NAFE as one of the top 50 companies for female executives in 2009. Aims to reduce its greenhouse gas emissions by 25% by 2012. Part of the EPA's Green Power Partnership; ranked 8th on EPA's list of the top 25 national purchasers of green power. Foundation supports community capacity building and sustainable practices. Has a written nondiscrimination policy covering sexual orientation and gender identity. Offers insurance coverage to employees' domestic partners. Insurance for transgender employees is offered, and treatment is covered.

Cisco-Linksys, LLC

Contributions: Total: *$250*   Dem: *$250*   Rep: *$0*
Lobby Spending: *$0*

Subsidiary of Cisco Systems, Inc.

CompUSA, Inc.

Contributions: Total: *$1,810*   Dem: *$0*   Rep: *$1,810*
Lobby Spending: *$0*

Acquired by Systemax, Inc., in 2008. Has a written nondiscrimination policy covering sexual orientation but not gender identity.

Compuware Corporation

31% | 69%

Contributions: TOTAL: *$300,915*   DEM: *$91,915*   REP: *$209,000*
LOBBY SPENDING: *$36,000*

Supports the American Cancer Society, American Heart Association, Big Brothers/Big Sisters, Forgotten Harvest, and United Way. Supports Habitat for Humanity, Gleaners Community Foodbank, and the Susan G. Komen Race for the Cure through its employee volunteer program. Has a written nondiscrimination policy covering sexual orientation and gender identity. Offers insurance coverage to employees' domestic partners. Insurance for transgender employees is offered, but treatment is not covered.

Dell Computer Corporation

84% | 16%

Contributions: TOTAL: *$3,050*   DEM: *$2,550*   REP: *$500*
LOBBY SPENDING: *$160,000*

Agreed to pay $800,000 to settle allegations of security violations brought by the FTC. In 2008, scored 49 out of 100 in "The Climate Counts Company Scorecard Report." Offers free recycling of all its products. Reduces its climate impacts by purchasing a portion of electricity needs from renewable energy sources. Is a member of the EPA's SmartWay program. In partnership with The Conservation Fund and Carbonfund.org, launched Plant a Tree for Me. Foundation supports nonprofit education, health, and literacy programs. A partner in the (PRODUCT) RED campaign. Has a written nondiscrimination policy that covers sexual orientation and gender identity. Offers insurance coverage to employees' domestic partners. Insurance for transgender employees is offered, but treatment is not covered.

Eastman Kodak Company

59% | 41%

Contributions: TOTAL: *$289,386*   DEM: *$170,410*   REP: *$118,976*
LOBBY SPENDING: *$2,235,000*

A pending 2004 class action lawsuit alleges Kodak offered payments to avoid discrimination lawsuits brought by African Americans. A pending $90 million lawsuit was brought by families whose children grew up near the company's Rochester facility and developed rare cancers. In 2009, named for the fifth consecutive year to the "Global 100 Most Sustainable Corporations" list. Has sponsored Habitat for Humanity houses, donated millions to scholarships, and sponsored the NAACP, the National Gay and Lesbian Chamber of Commerce, and the United Way. Has a written nondiscrimination policy covering sexual orientation and gender identity. Offers insurance coverage to employees' domestic partners. Insurance for transgender employees is offered, and treatment is covered.

EDS Corporation

56% | 44%

Contributions: TOTAL: *$434,451*   DEM: *$241,750*   REP: *$192,701*
LOBBY SPENDING: *$6,208,648*

Subsidiary of Hewlett-Packard Company.

Electronic Arts, Inc.
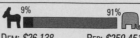
Contributions: TOTAL: *$285,589* DEM: *$26,138* REP: *$259,451*
LOBBY SPENDING: *$20,000*
A pending class action lawsuit alleges consumer fraud and privacy rights violations. Provides grants to local nonprofit organizations and schools. Matches employees' donations. Has a written nondiscrimination policy covering sexual orientation and gender identity. Offers insurance coverage to employees' domestic partners. Insurance for transgender employees is offered, but treatment is not covered.

EMC Corporation

Contributions: TOTAL: *$507,546* DEM: *$262,196* REP: *$245,350*
LOBBY SPENDING: *$2,790,000*
A pending lawsuit alleges discrimination against women in its sales force. Participates in the EPA's Climate Leaders program. Operates a water-treatment facility that recycles 100% of EMC campus water. Sponsors of the Boston Symphony Orchestra, the Leary Firefighters Foundation, and the Michael Carter Lisnow Respite Center. Has a written nondiscrimination policy covering sexual orientation and gender identity. Offers insurance coverage to employees' domestic partners.

Emerson Electric Co.

Contributions: TOTAL: *$250* DEM: *$250* REP: *$0*
LOBBY SPENDING: *$574,200*
A pending lawsuit brought by residents of a New York community alleges trichloroethylene from its local plant has contaminated their homes. Contributes millions to charities and nonprofit organizations. Has a written nondiscrimination policy covering sexual orientation but not gender identity. Insurance for transgender employees is offered, but treatment is not covered.

Energizer Holdings, Inc.

Contributions: TOTAL: *$13,900* DEM: *$5,400* REP: *$8,500*
LOBBY SPENDING: *$305,000*
Energizer is one of the largest supporters of the Rechargeable Battery Recycling Corporation. Has a written nondiscrimination policy covering sexual orientation but not gender identity.

Epson America, Inc.
Contributions: TOTAL: *$1,402* DEM: *$1,402* REP: *$0*
LOBBY SPENDING: *$10,000*
Subsidiary of Seiko Epson Corporation. Foreign owned.

Fry's Electronics, Inc.

Contributions: TOTAL: *$1,700* DEM: *$300* REP: *$1,400*
LOBBY SPENDING: *$0*

Fujifilm Co., Ltd.
Contributions: TOTAL: *$5,927* DEM: *$1,901* REP: *$4,026*
LOBBY SPENDING: *$195,000*
Foreign owned.

Fujifilm U.S.A., Inc.
21% | 79%
Contributions: TOTAL: *$950*   DEM: *$200*   REP: *$750*
LOBBY SPENDING: *$0*
Subsidiary of Fuji Photo Film Co., Ltd. Recycles single-use camera components. By fiscal 2010, some of its manufacturing facilities will reduce their unit energy consumption by 10% and carbon emissions by 20% from fiscal 1990 levels. Provides environmental education for its employees. Outreach includes an annual volunteer day, scholarships, and product donations.

Fujitsu Computer Products of America, Inc.
100% | 0%
Contributions: TOTAL: *$1,750*   DEM: *$1,750*   REP: *$0*
LOBBY SPENDING: *$0*
Subsidiary of Fujitsu Limited. Foreign owned. Has a written nondiscrimination policy covering sexual orientation but not gender identity. Offers insurance coverage to employees' domestic partners.

Fujitsu Limited
70% | 30%
Contributions: TOTAL: *$5,875*   DEM: *$4,125*   REP: *$1,750*
LOBBY SPENDING: *$0*
Foreign owned. Has operated in and sourced from countries with widespread, well-documented human and labor rights abuses. Pending lawsuits brought in 2002 by the Khulumani Support Group allege that Fujitsu and other multinational corporations knowingly aided and abetted South Africa's apartheid regime. Has a reforestation project aimed at reviving endemic species and promoting economic self-sufficiency through ecotourism in Southeast Asia. Policies target "green" suppliers, reducing chemical emissions, and achieving zero-waste emissions for Japanese plants.

GameStop Corp.
66% | 34%
Contributions: TOTAL: *$13,475*   DEM: *$8,900*   REP: *$4,575*
LOBBY SPENDING: *$0*
Partners with the Make-A-Wish Foundation. Has a written nondiscrimination policy covering sexual orientation and gender identity. Offers insurance coverage to employees' domestic partners. Insurance for transgender employees is offered, and treatment is covered.

Gateway, Inc.
29% | 71%
Contributions: TOTAL: *$7,680*   DEM: *$2,250*   REP: *$5,430*
LOBBY SPENDING: *$0*
Foreign owned. Acquired by Taiwan-based Acer, Inc. in 2007. A pending lawsuit alleges violations of the California Labor Code and breach of contract. Has faced lawsuits and been investigated by the federal government for insider trading, overstated earnings, and misleading financial statements. Has sourced from countries with widespread, well-documented human and labor rights abuses. Offers a recycling program for computers and peripherals. Foundation provides equipment and support to schools. Has a written nondiscrimination policy covering sexual orientation but not gender identity. Offers insurance coverage to employees' domestic partners.

Hewlett-Packard Company

62% | 38%

Contributions: TOTAL: *$1,246,804*   DEM: *$771,096*   REP: *$475,708*
LOBBY SPENDING: *$11,148,648*

Sources from Foxconn, a firm in China accused of engaging in sweatshop practices. Listed by NAFE as one of the top 50 companies for female executives in 2009. In 2008, scored 68 out of 100 in "The Climate Counts Company Scorecard Report." Has reduced its global warming impact through energy conservation and transportation reduction programs. Installed a solar electric power system near its San Diego facility. By 2010, says it will reduce carbon emissions from its facilities to 15 percent below 2006 levels. Designs many products to be comparatively easy to recycle and often uses recycled parts in construction. Redesigned print cartridge packaging for North America to reduce greenhouse gas emissions. Allocated cash and equipment to the World Wildlife Fund to establish three projects aimed at addressing climate change. Offers a minority scholarship program. Has a written nondiscrimination policy that covers sexual orientation and gender identity. Offers insurance coverage to employees' domestic partners. Insurance for transgender employees is offered, and treatment is covered.

Intel Corporation

56% | 44%

Contributions: TOTAL: *$848,410*   DEM: *$477,698*   REP: *$370,712*
LOBBY SPENDING: *$3,965,789*

Has sourced from countries with widespread, well-documented human and labor rights abuses. Listed by NAFE as one of the top 50 companies for female executives in 2009. In 2008, made a multi-year commitment to purchase more than 1.3 billion kilowatt hours of renewable energy certificates per year, for which the EPA named Intel a Green Power Partner of the Year and gave it the Green Power Leadership Award. Has a written nondiscrimination policy covering sexual orientation and gender identity. Offers insurance coverage to employees' domestic partners. Insurance for transgender employees is offered, but treatment is not covered.

International Business Machines Corporation (IBM)

75% | 25%

Contributions: TOTAL: *$1,144,120*   DEM: *$856,358*   REP: *$287,762*
LOBBY SPENDING: *$14,600,000*

Pending lawsuits brought in 2002 by the Khulumani Support Group allege that IBM and other multinational corporations knowingly aided and abetted South Africa's apartheid regime. Agreed to a partial settlement of $320 million for improperly converting pension plans for pre-1999 employees. More than 250 employees have filed suits claiming exposure to toxic chemicals. IBM's Endicott, NY, manufacturing facility is a Superfund site. Listed by NAFE as one of the top 50 companies for female executives in 2009. In 2008, scored 77 out of 100 in "The Climate Counts Company Scorecard Report." Has reduced its carbon emissions by 65% from 1990 levels. Purchases renewable energy. Recycles the majority of its waste. Offers free technology for use by retirees who volunteer at schools and nonprofits. Has a written nondiscrimination policy covering sexual orientation and gender identity. Offers insurance coverage to employees' domestic partners. Insurance for transgender employees is offered, and treatment is covered.

Intuit, Inc.
Contributions: Total: *$393,475*   Dem: *$263,598*   Rep: *$129,877*
Lobby Spending: *$3,440,000*

67%   33%

Eligible disadvantaged individuals have free access to tax prepara-
tion software. Environmental policies include hiring "green" vendors,
reducing its carbon footprint, and disposing of its technology-based
waste according to strict EPA guidelines. Its San Diego office is LEED-
certified. Works with the National Coalition Against Domestic Violence
and the National Endowment for Financial Education to expand the
Financial Literacy Project for Battered Women. Matches employee
charitable gifts and offers employees paid time off to volunteer. Foundation funds financial literacy programs and donates software. Has a
written nondiscrimination policy covering sexual orientation and gender identity. Offers insurance coverage to employees' domestic partners. Insurance for transgender employees is offered, but treatment is
not covered.

Lexmark International, Inc.
Contributions: Total: *$15,200*   Dem: *$3,550*   Rep: *$11,650*
Lobby Spending: *$160,000*

23%   77%

A pending class action suit alleges it maintained a "use it or lose it" policy for vacation and personal days in violation of California law. Its "pre-
bate" cartridge return program (touted as environmentally beneficial)
was called a ploy to reclaim empty cartridges, which competitors could
refill more cheaply. Will recycle for free end-of-life Lexmark-branded
products. Allows paid time off for charity work and makes matching
gifts up to $5,000 per employee. Has donated materials for Habitat
for Humanity homes. Has a written nondiscrimination policy covering
sexual orientation and gender identity. Offers insurance coverage to
employees' domestic partners. Insurance for transgender employees
is offered, and some treatment is covered.

Medis Technologies Ltd.
Contributions: Total: *$14,000*   Dem: *$14,000*   Rep: *$0*
Lobby Spending: *$0*

100%   0%

Its Direct Liquid Fuel Cell technology is green. Its Medis Power Pack
contains and uses no environmentally damaging materials or chemicals, comes only in recyclable PET packaging, and has no harmful emissions. The depleted power pack is recyclable at authorized recycling
facilities.

Microsoft Corporation
Contributions: Total: *$3,583,691*   Dem: *$2,577,710*   Rep: *$1,005,981*
Lobby Spending: *$17,900,000*

72%   28%

Its firewall software helps China keep a lid on online political dissent.
Has given more than $2.5 billion in cash, services, and software to
nonprofit organizations. Provides paid time off for volunteer work and
matches employees' donations. Ranked 38th on *Fortune* magazine's
"100 Best Companies to Work For" in 2009. In 2008, scored 38 out of
100 in "The Climate Counts Company Scorecard Report." In 2009,
introduced the Environmental Sustainability Dashboard for Microsoft
Dynamics AX, which will enable mid-size businesses to capture energy
consumption data. Partnering with The Clinton Foundation to develop

technology tools that will enable cities to monitor, compare, and reduce their greenhouse gas emissions. Has a written nondiscrimination policy covering sexual orientation and gender identity. Offers insurance coverage to employees' domestic partners. Insurance for transgender employees is offered, and treatment is covered.

Motorola, Inc.

57%   43%

Contributions: TOTAL: *$703,416* DEM: *$398,281* REP: *$305,135*
LOBBY SPENDING: *$12,150,000*

A pending suit alleges Motorola violated the Securities Exchange Act by artificially inflating the value of its stock. Other suits allege ERISA violations. In 2008, scored 66 out of 100 in "The Climate Counts Company Scorecard Report." Has reduced the carbon footprint of its operations by 25% since 2002 and offers or participates in mobile device recycling programs in 69 countries. Has reduced its hazardous waste and its water and energy use by 10% per year since 1998. Provides used cell phones to abuse victims. Has a written nondiscrimination policy covering sexual orientation and gender identity. Offers insurance coverage to employees' domestic partners. Insurance for transgender employees is offered, but treatment is not covered.

NETGEAR, Inc.

100%   0%

Contributions: TOTAL: *$4,700* DEM: *$4,700* REP: *$0*
LOBBY SPENDING: *$0*

Nikon Corporation

67%   33%

Contributions: TOTAL: *$750* DEM: *$500* REP: *$250*
LOBBY SPENDING: *$90,000*

Foreign owned. Has achieved a resource-recycling rate of 97%. Environmental goals include 30% or more improvement in overall energy efficiency of new products, compared with similar existing products, released between 2009 and 2011 and 19% or more reduction in carbon emissions per net sales over 2007.

Nintendo of America, Inc.

100%   0%

Contributions: TOTAL: *$6,050* DEM: *$6,050* REP: *$0*
LOBBY SPENDING: <*$40,000*

Subsidiary of Nintendo Co., Ltd. Donated 500 GameCube DVD-equipped entertainment centers to an organization that supports seriously ill, hospitalized children. Also supports Habitat for Humanity.

Olympus America, Inc.

74%   26%

Contributions: TOTAL: *$950* DEM: *$700* REP: *$250*
LOBBY SPENDING: *$190,000*

Subsidiary of Olympus Corporation. Manufactures self-designated "ecoproducts" aiming to promote recycling and to reduce energy consumption and the use of harmful chemicals. Its headquarters incorporates many LEED features. Sponsors a car pool program. Supports a battery recycling initiative. Sponsors a Web site to bring awareness to colorectal cancer. Has a written nondiscrimination policy covering sexual orientation but not gender identity. Offers insurance coverage to employees' domestic partners.

Olympus Corporation
Contributions: TOTAL: *$2,750*   DEM: *$1,550*   REP: *$1,200*
LOBBY SPENDING: *$190,000*

56% | 44%

Donates endoscopes to hospitals in developing nations. Has a comprehensive environmental policy aimed at reducing carbon dioxide emissions, creating recyclable packaging, and exercising "green" procurement.

Oracle Corporation
Contributions: TOTAL: *$1,036,923*   DEM: *$719,538*   REP: *$317,385*
LOBBY SPENDING: *$10,270,000*

69% | 31%

Privately held. In 2008, paid $8.95 million to settle an FLSA lawsuit alleging failure to pay overtime. Promotes "green" practices. Is adopting LEED practices for U.S. tenant improvement projects of 10,000 or more square feet. Has awarded $1 million in grants to The Nature Conservancy, the Cooperative for Assistance and Relief Everywhere, Inc. (CARE), the Dana-Farber Cancer Institute, and the American Cancer Society. Outreach also includes support for education (particularly in India) and the environment. Has a written nondiscrimination policy covering sexual orientation and gender identity. Offers insurance coverage to employees' domestic partners. Insurance for transgender employees is offered, and some treatment is covered.

Panasonic Corporation
Contributions: TOTAL: *$9,506*   DEM: *$6,250*   REP: *$3,256*
LOBBY SPENDING: *$0*

66% | 34%

Foreign owned. A pending consumer class action suit alleges that Panasonic marketed flat-screen plasma television models as high-definition televisions, which resulted in consumers paying thousands of dollars more than they would have otherwise paid. In 2006, settled a class action suit for breach of implied warranty of merchantability and unfair or deceptive business practices. By 2011, aims to reduce carbon emissions to fiscal year 2001 levels. Switches its public signs from neon to LED lighting at 8pm each evening. Has a recycling program for rechargeable batteries. Is a seven-time Energy Star winner.

PC Connection, Inc.
Contributions: TOTAL: *$250*   DEM: *$0*   REP: *$250*
LOBBY SPENDING: *$0*

0% | 100%

Written nondiscrimination policy includes neither sexual orientation nor gender identity.

Petters Group Worldwide, LLC
Contributions: TOTAL: *$47,805*   DEM: *$19,000*   REP: *$28,805*
LOBBY SPENDING: *$0*

40% | 60%

Privately held. In October 2008, filed for Chapter 11 bankruptcy protection. The John T. Petters Foundation promotes diversity in higher education and provides scholarships to students studying international business.

Polaroid Corporation
Contributions: TOTAL: *$3,105*   DEM: *$250*   REP: *$2,855*
LOBBY SPENDING: *$0*

8% | 92%

Subsidiary of Petters Group Worldwide, LLC. Filed for Chapter 11 bankruptcy protection in December 2008. A class action suit is pending for alleged ERISA violations. A pending suit for loss of pay and benefits was brought by 180 employees who were on disability when Bank One purchased Polaroid out of bankruptcy in 2002. As a member of the World Wildlife Fund Climate Savers program, Polaroid agreed to reduce its carbon dioxide levels 25% by 2010, a goal it has already exceeded. Has donated $150,000 to the Breast Cancer Research Foundation. Has a written nondiscrimination policy covering sexual orientation but not gender identity. Offers insurance coverage to employees' domestic partners.

Radio Shack Corporation

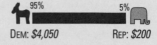
0%   100%

Contributions: TOTAL: *$3,500*   DEM: *$0*   REP: *$3,500*
LOBBY SPENDING: *$0*
Class action status was granted to a lawsuit filed by employees alleging violation of federal law and intentional avoidance to pay overtime wages. Donates $1 to the National Center for Missing & Exploited Children for every cell phone collected, refurbished, and resold. Posts information in its retail stores on missing children. Provides free child identification kits and supports programs that give children tools to avoid abduction, violence, and abuse. Has a recycling program for rechargeable batteries and cell phones. Has a written nondiscrimination policy covering sexual orientation but not gender identity.

Samsung Electronics America, Inc.

95%   5%

Contributions: TOTAL: *$4,250*   DEM: *$4,050*   REP: *$200*
LOBBY SPENDING: *$50,000*
Subsidiary of Samsung Group. Foreign owned. Pending suit claims that its laser printers defraud consumers by requiring users to change the toner cartridge before it is empty. A class action lawsuit over the health risks caused by cell phone use is pending. Has a large selection of Energy Star–rated TVs. Offers free recycling for cell phones and toner cartridges. Offers free recycling of working displays and printers at drop-off locations on purchase of a new Samsung product. Samsung's philanthropic program provides students with new digital technologies and software.

Samsung Group

63%   37%

Contributions: TOTAL: *$14,200*   DEM: *$8,900*   REP: *$5,300*
LOBBY SPENDING: *$690,000*
Operates in a country with widespread, well-documented human and labor rights abuses. Agreed to pay $90 million to settle allegations by 38 states that it participated in a conspiracy to fix prices of DRAM chips in 2007. Human Rights Watch reports that Samsung's Tijuana, Mexico, plant will not hire women thought to be pregnant, a violation of Mexican labor law. Operates a plant constructed for employees who use wheelchairs. In 2008, scored 51 out of 100 in "The Climate Counts Company Scorecard Report." By 2010, pledges to have reduced greenhouse gas emissions from its operations by 45% from 2001 levels. Has mobile phone recycling programs in 32 countries. Develops environmentally

friendly products and sponsors "Adopt-a-River" and "Adopt-a-Mountain" cleanup programs. Supports literacy, economic self-sufficiency, and child care programs for low-income families. Donates computers to elementary schools. Operates an animal companionship, assistance, and welfare program.

Seagate Technology

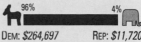

96%   4%

Contributions: TOTAL: *$276,417*   DEM: *$264,697*   REP: *$11,720*
LOBBY SPENDING: *$180,000*

A pending class action lawsuit alleges violation of the ADEA. Minimizes energy use through equipment design, facility retrofitting, and process improvements. Other programs focus on energy-use reduction, recycling, tree planting, and commuting solutions. Supports science, education, environment, health and human services, and the arts. Has a written nondiscrimination policy covering sexual orientation but not gender identity. Offers insurance coverage to employees' domestic partners.

SEGA Sammy Holdings, Inc.

100%   0%

Contributions: TOTAL: *$250*   DEM: *$250*   REP: *$0*
LOBBY SPENDING: *$0*

SEGA Corporation is a subsidiary. Foreign owned.

Sharper Image Corporation

47%   53%

Contributions: TOTAL: *$5,800*   DEM: *$2,750*   REP: *$3,050*
LOBBY SPENDING: *$0*

Filed for Chapter 11 bankruptcy protection in 2008. Has been acquired by a joint venture led by units of private investment firms Hilco Consumer Capital Corporation and Gordon Brothers Group. Named in lawsuits alleging gift-certificate violations. Has a written nondiscrimination policy including sexual orientation but not gender identity.

Siemens AG

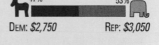

59%   41%

Contributions: TOTAL: *$437,967*   DEM: *$258,671*   REP: *$179,296*
LOBBY SPENDING: *$9,716,898*

Foreign owned. In 2009, a lawsuit accused it of giving corporate customers a bigger discount on medical imaging equipment than it gave the federal government. In 2009, federal agents from the Defense Criminal Investigations Service raided its offices, seeking documents related to military contracts. In 2008, agreed to settle a lawsuit brought against it by the German and U.S. governments; the company, which was rocked by bribery scandals, was ordered to pay over $1.3 billion in fines. In 2007, a class action lawsuit alleged it cheated workers out of overtime and break pay. Foundation provides more than $7 million annually in support of educational initiatives. Has a written nondiscrimination policy covering sexual orientation but not gender identity. Offers insurance coverage to employees' domestic partners.

Sony Corporation

74%   26%

Contributions: TOTAL: *$1,038,661*   DEM: *$771,941*   REP: *$266,720*
LOBBY SPENDING: *$4,783,000*

This Tokyo-based company owns one of the largest media groups in the United States and is often cited as an example of worrisome media consolidation. Has been boycotted for doing business with Burma, where human rights violations are common. In 2008, scored 68 out of 100 in "The Climate Counts Company Scorecard Report." Has been praised for its in-house recycling and conservation efforts. Has several music and arts education foundations.

Sony Corporation of America, Inc.

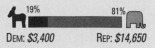
97% 3%

Contributions: TOTAL: *$160,665*   DEM: *$155,573*   REP: *$5,092*
LOBBY SPENDING: *$660,000*

Subsidiary of Sony Corporation. In 2008, on the same day it was sued for violations of the Children's Online Privacy Protection Act of 1998, Sony BMG Music Entertainment agreed to pay $1 million to settle claims that it improperly collected personal information from at least 30,000 children and disclosed some of it to other registered users. In 2008, it also settled a class action lawsuit in which it was accused of secretly installing piracy protection technology on compact discs that can make computers susceptible to damage. A pending class action suit over royalties seeks compensatory damages of $25 million. Offers free drop-off of its products for recycling at 150 collection centers. Aims to recycle one pound of old consumer electronics equipment for every pound of new products sold. Supports Teach for America, a substance abuse program, literacy, and humanitarian and disaster aid. Has a written nondiscrimination policy covering sexual orientation but not gender identity. Offers insurance coverage to employees' domestic partners.

Spectrum Brands, Inc., formerly Rayovac Corporation

19% 81%

Contributions: TOTAL: *$18,050*   DEM: *$3,400*   REP: *$14,650*
LOBBY SPENDING: *$210,000*

Filed for Chapter 11 bankruptcy in 2009. A pending civil action filed by the SEC arose out of a former holding company's fraudulent scheme to manipulate stock price. Spectrum Brands' principals—two of whom have previous convictions for money laundering and racketeering—are also under criminal indictment in the Eastern District of New York. Wal-Mart accounts for 19% of Spectrum's sales. Donated DEET-based mosquito repellents to California residents who are particularly susceptible to the mosquito-borne West Nile virus. Has a written nondiscrimination policy covering sexual orientation but not gender identity.

Sun Microsystems, Inc.

72% 28%

Contributions: TOTAL: *$337,340*   DEM: *$241,547*   REP: *$95,793*
LOBBY SPENDING: *$897,000*

Subsidiary of Oracle Corporation. Has reduced carbon emissions from its U.S. operations. Its foundation gave nearly $1.7 million to match employee donations in 2008. Has a written nondiscrimination policy covering sexual orientation and gender identity. Offers insurance coverage to employees' domestic partners. Insurance for transgender employees is offered, and treatment is covered.

Texas Instruments, Inc.

53% 47%

Contributions: TOTAL: *$178,960*   DEM: *$94,616*   REP: *$84,344*
LOBBY SPENDING: *$4,900,000*

A pending class action lawsuit filed in 2006 accuses it of contaminating a neighborhood with chlorinated solvents. Was assessed a fine for what OSHA termed "serious" violations following the death of a subcontractor at a manufacturing facility. Recognized for environmentally beneficial process changes in semiconductor manufacturing. Ranked 65th on *Fortune* magazine's "100 Best Companies to Work For" in 2009. Listed by NAFE as one of the top 50 companies for female executives in 2009. Operates a recycling program at its 11 major production sites. Supports education, arts, culture, and health and human services in the Dallas metro area. Contributed $1.8 million to the American Red Cross and Salvation Army in the wake of hurricanes Katrina and Rita. Has a written nondiscrimination policy covering sexual orientation and gender identity. Offers insurance coverage to employees' domestic partners. Insurance for transgender employees is offered, but treatment is not covered.

Toshiba America, Inc.

66% 34%

Contributions: TOTAL: *$1,930*   DEM: *$1,280*   REP: *$650*
LOBBY SPENDING: *$30,000*

Subsidiary of Toshiba Corporation. Foreign owned. In 2009, ordered to pay over $1 million in a class action lawsuit alleging that the lamps of certain Toshiba DLP televisions were susceptible to premature failure. Supplier companies have been cited for discrimination, forced overtime, and failure to pay a living wage, and the company lacks a comprehensive policy on workers' rights. In 2008, scored 70 out of 100 in "The Climate Counts Company Scorecard Report." Offers free recycling of its notebook computers; recycles non-Toshiba notebook computers for a shipping fee. Participates in the "Call 2 Recycle" program for used rechargeable batteries. Supports science and mathematics education programs, projects, and activities for schoolchildren in the United States. In 2008, donated money to the Arbor Day Foundation to plant 80,000 trees in Southern California national forests damaged by wildfires. In 2006, donated more than $80,000 in advanced technology equipment to the Partners for Healing clinic in Tullahoma, TN. Partners with Keep Houston Beautiful and the City of Houston Parks and Recreation.

Toshiba Corporation

25% 75%

Contributions: TOTAL: *$83,620*   DEM: *$21,280*   REP: *$62,340*
LOBBY SPENDING: *$4,110,000*

Foreign owned. Involved in several suits in Japan involving alleged racketeering, infringement, and extortion. Supplier companies have been cited for discrimination, forced overtime, and failure to pay a living wage, and the company lacks a comprehensive policy on workers' rights.

Xerox Corporation

70% 30%

Contributions: TOTAL: *$128,197*   DEM: *$89,592*   REP: *$38,605*
LOBBY SPENDING: *$1,725,000*

Holds a stake in a joint venture with Fuji Photo Film called Fuji Xerox. Listed by NAFE as one of the top 50 companies for female executives in 2009. In 2009, ranked 35th on DiversityInc's "Top 50 Companies for Diversity." Was the first high-tech company to join the United States Climate Action Partnership. In 2008, was the first technology company, and one of only five companies, to be named a Performance Track Corporate Leader by the EPA. Also awarded the EPA's Climate Protection Award for significantly reducing energy use and greenhouse gas emissions. Offers a recycling program for ink and toner cartridges. Supports environmental protection, education, diversity, and community activities. Offers employees a one-year paid leave to work for a community organization of their own choosing. Partners with The Nature Conservancy. Has a written nondiscrimination policy covering sexual orientation and gender identity. Offers insurance coverage to employees' domestic partners. Insurance for transgender employees is offered, and some treatment is covered.

Finance, Insurance, and Real Estate

Nomi Prins

Following a record profit year in 2006 (mostly due to intensified mortgage lending and the leveraging and repackaging of those ill-fated loans), the finance, insurance, and real estate (FIRE) sector's good times stalled in 2007. Firms like global supermarket banking giant Citigroup and brokerage goliath Merrill Lynch posted their first losses in years. By the end of 2008, the industry had entered its worst period since the Great Depression. But that didn't stop campaign contributions. Nearly $55 million of bipartisan campaign contributions flowed in to both parties ($30.8 million for Democrats, $24 million for the GOP). The money would later become a down payment on the biggest bank bailout in American history; its key component, the $700 billion Troubled Asset Relief Program (TARP), was the cornerstone of the Emergency Economic Stabilization Act, which President Bush signed into law on October 3, 2008.

How did we arrive at this state of affairs? After the spate of corporate scandals led by Enron and WorldCom in 2001 and 2002, the finance sector was in shock. Not over what had occurred, but over what the next route to making real money would be. The FIRE sector didn't exit the period unscathed, but its bruises were relatively minor—a few billion to settle class action lawsuits, and a $1.4 billion settlement initiated by New York attorney general Eliot Spitzer in 2003, which amounted to a wrist slap.

The next hot thing for the finance industry turned out to be real estate, and not just any old type: the extending, packaging, and leveraging of subprime and other risky loans. From 2001 through 2003, Federal Reserve chairman Alan Greenspan chopped interest rates from 6.5% to 1.75% to thwart the mini-recession that followed the scandals. With money rendered so cheap, banks had to find new ways to make it work for them. Lenders sought borrowers who had lower credit ratings and pushed subprime mortgage loans on these people. Wall Street investment banks and megacommercial banks knew they could use these subprime loans to stuff into all sorts of exotic concoctions, or "securitized bonds," backed by these loans.

What made this practice so inherently risky was that the rating agencies that had once been so good to Enron and WorldCom gave these asset-backed securities (ABS) ratings far better than they deserved. That green light gave Wall Street the go-ahead to repackage ABS in even more esoteric ways.

Between 2003 and 2006, the subprime market heyday, Wall Street couldn't create enough ABS. Lenders pushed more loans, because Wall Street and its client investors demanded them. The cycle spun out of control. The gods of Wall Street converted a $1.4 trillion subprime market into a $14 trillion ABS and collateralized debt obligation (CDO) market. To make matters worse, banks used these assets to borrow more money. Big supermarket banks like Citigroup, Bank of America, and JPM Chase leveraged or borrowed against them in multiples of 10 to 1. Investment banks like Goldman Sachs and Lehman Brothers went even crazier. The Securities and Exchange Commission (SEC), under the influence of these investment banks, overturned a capital rule that would have limited these firms to 12 to 1 leverage, instead allowing them 30 to 1 leverage.

After three years of rapid growth, the U.S. housing market began to run out of steam in 2005. But Wall Street banks didn't stop securitizing home loans; instead, they cranked up production and profits. That greed would spark a financial crash. By 2007, the housing market was in dire straits, and banks couldn't give away what had become known as "toxic assets." They also couldn't hold them as collateral for their borrowing anymore, because without any buyers, they were essentially valueless.

By 2008, the first major Wall Street failure occurred. Bear Stearns, the sixth largest U.S. investment bank and a big holder of toxic assets, couldn't pay its creditors. Rather than having it declare bankruptcy, Treasury secretary Henry Paulson, New York Federal Reserve president Tim Geithner, and Federal Reserve chairman Ben Bernanke pledged $30 billion of public money to back Bear's assets, paving the way for JPM Chase to take the firm over, risk-free. Six months later, Lehman Brothers blew Enron and WorldCom away as the biggest bankruptcy in U.S. history.

Lehman received no government backing, but the TARP, conceived by Paulson and approved by Congress in October 2008, sustained an imperiled industry with capital injections from an unwilling American public. The initial $700 billion fund was just the tip of the bank bailout iceberg. From the fall of 2008 through the middle of 2009, more than $10 trillion would be dumped into "saving" the financial industry in the form of direct capital, ultracheap Federal Reserve loans— for which banks could post some of their inferior assets as collateral—and FDIC backing.

Washington promised that capitalizing the banks would get strained credit to flow again to the American public. But this proved not to be the case. Goldman Sachs, which topped the campaign contribution charts for both parties, giving $4.3 million to the Democrats and $1.4 million to the GOP, also received $10 billion in TARP money, though it was never involved in consumer lending. Moreover, the government backed Goldman Sachs's trades with insurance giant AIG to the tune of $12.9 billion. JPM Chase, number two on donation charts for 2008, received federal backing for its takeover of Bear Stearns and Washington Mutual (the second largest bankruptcy in U.S. history, next to Lehman Brothers), plus $25 billion in TARP money. Citigroup, the fifth largest donor in 2008, pulled in a total of $346 billion in TARP money and other federal aid. Bank of America bagged a combination worth $163 billion.

In 2009, despite all the deregulatory recklessness that had ignited the financial crisis, Congress enacted no meaningful regulation to stabilize the industry or, more importantly, protect taxpayers. President Obama, Treasury secretary Tim Geithner, and Federal Reserve chairman Ben Bernanke talked about regulatory reform. So did Congress. But the might of the FIRE money and its lobby power prevailed. The industry was not dissected into manageable parts, which the Glass-Steagal Act of 1933 had mandated to protect the public. Instead, banks became bigger and more concentrated, and Congress and the new Obama administration largely maintained the regulatory status quo.

Top Ten Democratic Contributors

Goldman Sachs Group, Inc.	$4,522,938
JPMorgan Chase & Co.	$3,186,717
Citigroup, Inc.	$3,110,801
General Electric (GE) Company	$2,501,827
Morgan Stanley	$2,177,732
Bank of America Corporation	$1,862,545
UBS AG	$1,802,317
Blue Cross and Blue Shield	$1,543,570
Deloitte Touche Tohmatsu	$1,499,910
New York Life Insurance Co.	$1,489,408

Top Ten Republican Contributors

JPMorgan Chase & Co.	$2,023,670
Citigroup, Inc.	$1,912,313
Blue Cross and Blue Shield	$1,666,331
PricewaterhouseCoopers LLC	$1,652,607
Morgan Stanley	$1,647,918
Bank of America Corporation	$1,632,186
Deloitte Touche Tohmatsu	$1,620,175
Merrill Lynch & Co., Inc.	$1,555,439
Goldman Sachs Group, Inc.	$1,539,798
UBS AG	$1,489,397

Top Ten Lobbying Spenders

General Electric (GE) Company	$39,019,000
Blue Cross and Blue Shield	$25,586,969
American International Group, Inc. (AIG)	$21,069,000
Citigroup, Inc.	$17,280,000
United Services Automobile Association (USAA)	$13,473,636
Cerberus Capital Management LP	$10,927,782
JPMorgan Chase & Co.	$10,830,000
Blackstone Group LP, The	$10,701,933
Prudential Financial, Inc.	$10,338,063
MetLife, Inc.	$10,270,000

Accenture Ltd.

55%   45%

Contributions: Total: *$1,124,803* Dem: *$614,759* Rep: *$510,044*
Lobby Spending: *$7,575,603*

Foreign owned. Signed the United Nations Global Compact. Ranked 97th on *Fortune* magazine's "100 Best Companies to Work For" in 2009. Ranked 23rd on DiversityInc's list of the "Top 50 Companies for Diversity" in 2009. Accenture Brazil has reduced paper use by 45%. Accenture Japan has worked to conserve blue coral reefs. Promoting sustainable use of renewable forest resources. Has committed over $14 million to charitable giving programs. Has a written nondiscrimination policy covering sexual orientation and gender identity. Offers insurance coverage to employees' domestic partners. Insurance for transgender employees is offered, but treatment is not covered.

AEA Investors

97% — 3%

Contributions: TOTAL: *$238,200*   DEM: *$230,300*   REP: *$7,900*
LOBBY SPENDING: *$0*

Was sued for issuing merger proxy statements that were materially misleading and for failing to disclose full financial liability of transactions to shareholders.

Aetna, Inc.

54% — 46%

Contributions: TOTAL: *$727,757*   DEM: *$390,962*   REP: *$336,795*
LOBBY SPENDING: *$4,125,280*

A pending multistate lawsuit alleges that it and Cigna Corp. used a database rigged to underpay physicians, in violation of the RICO Act. Ranked 48th on DiversityInc's list of the "Top 50 Companies for Diversity" in 2009. Listed by NAFE as one of the top 50 companies for female executives in 2009. Its foundation supports health, education, diversity, and arts and culture. Has a written nondiscrimination policy covering sexual orientation and gender identity. Offers insurance coverage to employees' domestic partners. Insurance for transgender employees is offered, but treatment is not covered.

Aflac, Inc.

45% — 55%

Contributions: TOTAL: *$2,211,030*   DEM: *$1,004,100*   REP: *$1,206,930*
LOBBY SPENDING: *$7,310,000*

Ranked 26th on *Fortune* magazine's "100 Best Companies to Work For" in 2009. Supports health, education, youth, the arts, and the American Cancer Society. Donated $1 million for the building of the National Museum of African American History and Culture. Has a written nondiscrimination policy covering sexual orientation and gender identity.

Allstate Corporation, The

51% — 49%

Contributions: TOTAL: *$427,750*   DEM: *$217,844*   REP: *$209,906*
LOBBY SPENDING: *$8,540,000*

In 2009, settled a lawsuit accusing it of overcharging minorities. In 2008, was ordered to pay over $70 million to policyholders who state regulators allege were charged excessive home insurance rates. Settled a class action lawsuit brought for unpaid overtime for up to $120 million. Denied hundreds of policyholders payment for water damage after Hurricane Katrina. Eliminated retirement benefits for its agents and was sued for alleged nonfiduciary duty claims and ERISA violations. Listed by NAFE as one of the top 50 companies for female executives in 2009. Has invested in renewable energy projects. Recycles paper and plastics, and partners with organizations to responsibly dispose of e-waste. Foundation supports diversity, community safety, and economic empowerment programs. Has a written nondiscrimination policy covering sexual orientation and gender identity. Offers health insurance coverage to employees' domestic partners. Insurance for transgender employees is offered, but treatment is not covered.

American Automobile Association (AAA)

100%   0%

Contributions: TOTAL: *$250*   DEM: *$250*   REP: *$0*
LOBBY SPENDING: *$1,200,000*

Supports photo radar and red-light cameras. In 2006, Southern California AAA opposed California's Proposition 87 to levy a tax on producers of oil extracted in California that would go to a fund aimed at reducing petroleum consumption. Has criticized open-space measures and opposed EPA restrictions on emissions. Battled stricter vehicle-emissions standards in Maryland. Is a member of the auto industry-dominated American Highway Users Alliance, a powerful pro-pavement lobby.

American Express Company

60%   40%

Contributions: TOTAL: *$1,058,208*   DEM: *$632,107*   REP: *$426,101*
LOBBY SPENDING: *$7,110,000*

A pending class action lawsuit alleges that the terms outlined in a marketing campaign were misleading. In 2009, a class action lawsuit alleged that it misrepresented its reliance on risky credit card holders and programs in violation of federal securities laws. In 2009, a lawsuit on behalf of participants in its retirement savings plan alleged ERISA violations. Criticized for doing business with Burma. Listed by NAFE as one of the top 50 companies for female executives in 2009. Ranked 13th on DiversityInc's list of the "Top 50 Companies for Diversity" in 2009. Supports preservation of cultural and architectural heritage, leadership development, and disaster relief. Is a partner in the (PRODUCT) RED campaign. Has a written nondiscrimination policy covering sexual orientation and gender identity. Offers health insurance coverage to employees' domestic partners. Insurance for transgender employees is offered, and treatment is covered.

American International Group, Inc. (AIG)

65%   35%

Contributions: TOTAL: *$1,233,728*   DEM: *$808,054*   REP: *$425,674*
LOBBY SPENDING: *$21,069,000*

A lawsuit filed in 2009 on behalf of shareholders demands that company executives return some of the bonuses they received after AIG got $182.5 billion in government aid. Is fighting the federal government for the return of $306 million in tax payments, some related to deals conducted through offshore tax havens. A lawsuit filed in 2009 alleges fraud and breach of contract and depicts AIG as an absentee landlord to its real estate holdings. Paid $1.64 billion to settle charges of fraud, bid rigging, and improper accounting practices. The *Multinational Monitor* named AIG one of the "10 Worst Corporations" of 2008. Developing new insurance products that support the carbon credit market and address client needs related to alternative energy. Supports youth charities. Its diversity program serves people with disabilities.

Apollo Advisors LP

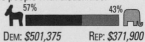

57%   43%

Contributions: TOTAL: *$873,275*   DEM: *$501,375*   REP: *$371,900*
LOBBY SPENDING: *$1,120,000*

Also known as Apollo Management. Joined forces with TPG Capital to purchase gaming company Harrah's Entertainment in 2008.

Assurant Health

49%   51%

Contributions: TOTAL: *$372,597*   DEM: *$180,900*   REP: *$191,697*
LOBBY SPENDING: *$3,556,000*

Subsidiary of Assurant, Inc. Formerly Fortis Health. The office of the Connecticut attorney general has investigated dozens of the more than 500 complaints nationwide against Assurant. According to the office, Assurant has a pattern of "bad faith" when it comes to its customers; it "creates the illusion of coverage, when in reality, it would challenge almost any expensive procedure as a pre-existing condition." Offers insurance coverage to employees' domestic partners.

Bain Capital LLC

70%   30%

Contributions: TOTAL: *$1,156,420*   DEM: *$807,720*   REP: *$348,700*
LOBBY SPENDING: *$1,510,000*

A pending lawsuit alleges gender discrimination, retaliation, and a violation of the FMLA. Has been accused of buying out companies, which then have faced layoffs, closures, and bankruptcy while Bain came out ahead. It also closed U.S. factories, causing hundreds of layoffs, and pocketed huge fees shortly before companies collapsed.

Bank of America Corporation

53%   47%

Contributions: TOTAL: *$3,494,731*   DEM: *$1,862,545*   REP: *$1,632,186*
LOBBY SPENDING: *$9,614,000*

In 2009, paid $50 billion in stock for Merrill Lynch. A pending lawsuit contends that it facilitated a fraudulent trading scheme. A pending lawsuit alleges FLSA violations. Five African American employees brought a lawsuit that alleges the bank limited them to certain clients. In 2009, ordered to pay up to $35 million to customers who incurred fees because it authorizes debit card transactions that will result in overdraft charges and provides inaccurate account balance Information. Ranked 14th on DiversityInc's list of the "Top 50 Companies for Diversity" in 2009. Listed by NAFE as one of the top 50 companies for female executives in 2009. In 2008, scored 60 out of 100 in "The Climate Counts Company Scorecard Report." Is one of the largest investors in coal and coal-fired power and has provided financing to build coal-fired power plants. Established an initiative that encourages environmentally sustainable business practices. Gives its associates $3,000 to buy a hybrid car. Supports the American Cancer Society, American Diabetes Association, and American Heart Association. Has a written non-discrimination policy covering sexual orientation and gender identity. Offers insurance coverage to employees' domestic partners. Insurance for transgender employees is offered, and some treatment is covered.

Berkshire Hathaway

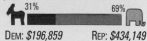

31%   69%

Contributions: TOTAL: *$631,008*   DEM: *$196,859*   REP: *$434,149*
LOBBY SPENDING: *$2,477,000*

Holds large stakes in Bank of America, M&T Bank, Sun Trust, US Bancorp, and Wells Fargo & Co. A pending lawsuit was brought by Indian tribes and fishermen against subsidiary MidAmerican Energy's PacifiCorp, whose dams on the Klamath River are alleged to be related to toxic algae. Chairman Warren Buffett has pledged to bequeath 85% of his fortune amassed from stock in Berkshire Hathaway to five foundations. Has a written nondiscrimination policy covering sexual orientation but not gender identity.

Blackstone Group LP, The   47%   53%
Contributions: TOTAL: *$1,932,301*   DEM: *$899,001*   REP: *$1,033,300*
LOBBY SPENDING: *$10,701,933*

This private equity firm owns stakes in more than 40 companies, manages hedge funds and other funds, and provides mergers and acquisitions and restructuring advice to corporate clients. In 2008, a class action lawsuit filed on behalf of purchasers of Blackstone's common stock alleged violation of federal securities laws. Has a written nondiscrimination policy covering sexual orientation but not gender identity.

Blue Cross and Blue Shield   48%   52%
Contributions: TOTAL: *$3,209,901*   DEM: *$1,543,570*   REP: *$1,666,331*
LOBBY SPENDING: *$25,586,969*

An umbrella association that licenses chapters in every state, the District of Columbia, and Puerto Rico. Following its merger with WellPoint, Blue Cross/Blue Shield (BCBS) faced lawsuits brought by doctors over late payment and low reimbursement rates. In 2008, settled a class action lawsuit filed under the RICO Act for more than $128 million. Settled a similar lawsuit in 2007 in Florida and was ordered to create a $128 million fund for physicians to recover damages. In 2007, it abruptly canceled the group insurance plan for the California Association of Realtors, which has filed suit against BCBS. Member organizations have been sued by insureds who charge that BCBS made coverage decisions without regard for medical standards or doctors' recommendations. Supports initiatives to improve health care quality and affordability.

Capital One Financial   58%   42%
Corporation
Contributions: TOTAL: *$806,820*   DEM: *$468,153*   REP: *$338,667*
LOBBY SPENDING: *$2,379,037*

In 2008, a former employee filed a pending whistle-blower lawsuit alleging approval of loans containing fraudulent information. In 2007, BBB said it had processed 6,183 complaints about Capital One in 36 months. The SEC filed charges of insider trading against its former CFO, who was ordered to pay $1.8 million. Ranked 25th on DiversityInc's list of the "Top 50 Companies for Diversity" in 2009. In 2008, scored 8 out of 100 in "The Climate Counts Company Scorecard Report." Later joined the EPA's Climate Leader Program. Four of the company's office buildings have received the EPA Energy Star certification. Supports education, community services, and violence prevention. Provides grants, loans, and equity investments for neighborhood redevelopment and affordable housing. Donated $150,000 in 2008 to a green residential project in New Orleans. Has a written nondiscrimination policy covering sexual orientation and gender identity. Offers insurance coverage to employees' domestic partners. Insurance for transgender employees is offered, and some treatment is covered.

Century 21 Real Estate LLC

7% 93%

Contributions: TOTAL: *$4,550*   DEM: *$300*   REP: *$4,250*
LOBBY SPENDING: *$0*

Subsidiary of Realogy Corporation; parent, Apollo Advisors. A pending lawsuit alleges that Town & County-Sterling Heights, a franchise of Century 21 in Michigan, steers prospective white buyers to mostly white neighborhoods and African American buyers to African American neighborhoods. A pending class action brought by former franchisees alleges consumer fraud and breach of contract. Paid $450,000 to settle allegations of federal housing discrimination and racial bias. Has raised more than $90 million for Easter Seals. Has a written nondiscrimination policy covering sexual orientation but not gender identity. Offers insurance coverage to employees' domestic partners. Insurance for transgender employees is offered, but treatment is not covered.

Cerberus Capital Management LP

43% 57%

Contributions: TOTAL: *$1,248,937*   DEM: *$535,344*   REP: *$713,593*
LOBBY SPENDING: *$10,927,782*

Cerberus purchased 80% of Chrysler from Daimler in 2007 but plans to drop its investment to 45%. Cerberus was the lead investor of a group that acquired 51% of GMAC, the financing arm of General Motors. It is a holding company for Albertsons LLC. J. Ezra Merkin, a partner in Cerberus, invested his funds in Cerberus and its portfolio companies. His Gabriel Fund was a feeder fund for Bernard L. Madoff Investment Securities LLC. Merkin served as the nonexecutive chairman of GMAC until his resignation at the insistence of the U.S. government. Aozora, a Cerberus company, lost $137 million to the Madoff LLC. Aozora was part of the investment group that acquired 51% of GMAC.

CIGNA Corporation

36% 64%

Contributions: TOTAL: *$458,095*   DEM: *$164,635*   REP: *$293,460*
LOBBY SPENDING: *$2,481,436*

The AMA filed a lawsuit charging that CIGNA used a flawed database to pay physicians artificially low rates for out-of-network care. In 2008, pharmacy benefits manager Express Scripts, Inc. and CIGNA Life Insurance Co. agreed to pay a combined $27 million to settle a New York state lawsuit over alleged drug switching. Express Scripts settled with 28 states over similar allegations for $9.3 million. Shreds/recycles 4 million pounds of paper annually. Maintains a telecommuting program. Supports health education, youth education, disaster relief, the March of Dimes, the United Way, and Susan G. Komen Race for the Cure. Partnered with Water for People, providing clean drinking water for school children in India. Has a written nondiscrimination policy covering sexual orientation. Offers health insurance coverage to employees' domestic partners. Insurance for transgender employees is offered, but treatment is not covered.

Citigroup, Inc.

62% 38%

Contributions: TOTAL: *$5,023,114*   DEM: *$3,110,801*   REP: *$1,912,313*
LOBBY SPENDING: *$17,280,000*

Received a government bailout in 2008. A pending lawsuit charges that it misled investors about its housing-market wagers. A gender discrimination lawsuit has been filed with the EEOC. Pending lawsuits brought in 2002 by the Khulumani Support Group allege that it knowingly aided South Africa's apartheid regime. Has spearheaded industry efforts to fight legislation that would restrict bank consolidation. According to a study released in 2007 by Fair Finance Watch, Citigroup extended higher-cost subprime loans to African Americans and Latinos far more frequently than to whites. Is one of the top financiers of coal mining and coal-fired power plants. In 2008, scored 60 out of 100 in "The Climate Counts Company Scorecard Report." Is directing $50 billion to support the commercialization and use of alternative energy and clean technology. Aims to reduce its emissions by 10% from 2005 levels by 2011. Purchases carbon offsets. Its foundation supports financial education, microenterprises, and the environment. Has a written nondiscrimination policy covering sexual orientation and gender identity. Offers insurance coverage to employees' domestic partners. Insurance for transgender employees is offered, but treatment is not covered.

Coldwell Banker Real Estate Corporation

58%   42%

Contributions: Total: *$667,732*   Dem: *$390,079*   Rep: *$277,653*
Lobby Spending: *$0*

Subsidiary of Realogy Corporation; parent, Apollo Advisors. Agreed to pay part of a $35 million settlement in a lawsuit brought by HUD. Paid $296,000 to settle claims of violations of federal real estate law brought by the State of Minnesota and HUD. The corporate owners of Coldwell brokerage offices in four states face fines of up to $1.1 million for violating lead paint disclosure rules. Supports Habitat for Humanity. Has a written nondiscrimination policy covering sexual orientation but not gender identity. Offers insurance coverage to employees' domestic partners. Insurance for transgender employees is offered, but treatment is not covered.

Countrywide Financial Corporation

43%   57%

Contributions: Total: *$331,443*   Dem: *$141,193*   Rep: *$190,250*
Lobby Spending: *$2,119,000*

Subsidiary of Bank of America Corporation. In 2009, SEC staff recommended civil fraud charges against former CEO Angelo Mozilo for illegal insider trading. A pending securities class action lawsuit alleges that it made false statements and material omissions regarding its business and operations. Another pending lawsuit alleges that it violated federal housing discrimination laws. In a lawsuit filed in 2009, it is accused of teaming up with KB Home to inflate prices on new homes in Arizona and Nevada. In 2008, the Florida attorney general filed a lawsuit alleging deceptive and unfair trade practices. Attorneys general in Illinois and California have also filed suit. A class action lawsuit filed in 2007 on behalf of participants in the company's 401(k) plan alleges that the defendants knew or should have known that a sharp decline in the stock's price was inevitable and that they should have taken action to protect plan participants. Has a written nondiscrimination policy covering sexual orientation and gender identity. Offers insurance coverage to employees' domestic partners. Insurance for transgender employees is offered, and some treatment is covered.

Coventry Health Care, Inc.
50%   50%
Contributions: TOTAL: *$98,850*   DEM: *$49,000*   REP: *$49,850*
LOBBY SPENDING: *$1,300,000*
Settled a lawsuit filed alleging it withheld information related to the purchase of First Health. Has a written nondiscrimination policy covering sexual orientation but not gender identity.

Deloitte Touche Tohmatsu
48%   52%
Contributions: TOTAL: *$3,120,085*   DEM: *$1,499,910*   REP: *$1,620,175*
LOBBY SPENDING: *$2,230,000*
Foreign owned. In 2008, was ordered to pay $26 million to settle a lawsuit brought by General Motors shareholders who alleged that it and GM had issued false statements regarding GM's financial status. In 2007, agreed to pay $50 million as part of a settlement of a class action lawsuit by shareholders over misleading financial statements at defunct Canadian Philip Services Corp. In 2006, Deloitte & Touche and 39 banks agreed to pay a total of $455 million to settle a lawsuit by investors in Adelphia Communications Corp., which filed for bankruptcy protection after an accounting fraud. Paid $50 million to settle SEC charges relating to the Adelphia lawsuit. Founding member of the United Nations Global Compact. Ranked 61st on *Fortune* magazine's "100 Best Companies to Work For" in 2009. Ranked 33rd on DiversityInc's list of the "Top 50 Companies for Diversity" in 2009. Has partnered with the University of Reading's Walker Institute for Climate System Research to provide scientific research on the business impacts of climate change. Supports educational programs, access to clean drinking water, sustainable economic growth, and disaster relief. Has a written nondiscrimination policy covering sexual orientation and gender identity. Offers insurance coverage to employees' domestic partners. Insurance for transgender employees is offered, and treatment is covered.

Discover Financial Services LLC
58%   42%
Contributions: TOTAL: *$65,950*   DEM: *$37,950*   REP: *$28,000*
LOBBY SPENDING: *$1,020,000*
Received about $1.2 billion from the federal government under TARP after it converted to a bank holding company. At the center of a security lapse that left the credit card data of more than 200,000 people vulnerable to fraud. Supports the Juvenile Diabetes Research Foundation, as well as employee volunteerism. Has a written nondiscrimination policy covering sexual orientation and gender identity. Offers insurance coverage to employees' domestic partners. Insurance for transgender employees is offered, but treatment is not covered.

Ditech.com
0%   100%
Contributions: TOTAL: *$1,600*   DEM: *$0*   REP: *$1,600*
LOBBY SPENDING: *$0*
Subsidiary of GMAC Financial Services LLC. A pending lawsuit brought by Georgia homeowners alleges that GMAC Mortgage Corp. and its Ditech.com brand violated the Truth in Lending Act and the Home Ownership and Equity Protection Act.

Ernst & Young LLP

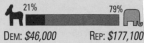

44%   56%

Contributions: TOTAL: *$2,540,377*   DEM: *$1,122,296*   REP: *$1,418,0 1*

LOBBY SPENDING: *$4,953,536*

Foreign owned. Subsidiary of Ernst & Young Global Ltd. A pending la suit was filed in 2009 against Ernst and Swiss bank UBS by investors a now-defunct fund that directed 95% of assets to Bernard Madof firm. In 2008, an investment fund filed a pending lawsuit alleging frau that led to the loss of more than $150 million of the public's money. 2009, paid $109 million to settle a class action suit alleging that it pro vided materially false financial statements for HealthSouth. In 200 settled a class action shareholder lawsuit over the fiscal health American Italian Pasta Co. Paid $3.5 million to settle its part of anothe class action lawsuit alleging that it issued false statements about th pasta company's financial status. In 2007, settled an investor clas action lawsuit filed for allegedly fraudulent accounting practices an agreed to a $1.59 million penalty imposed by the SEC. Ranked 51st o *Fortune* magazine's "100 Best Companies to Work For" in 2009. Ranke 3rd on DiversityInc's list of the "Top 50 Companies for Diversity" i 2009. Is incorporating LEED criteria into new construction. Support entrepreneurship, disaster relief, and access to higher education. Ha a written nondiscrimination policy covering sexual orientation and gender identity. Offers insurance coverage to employees' domestic partners. Insurance for transgender employees is offered, and treat-ment is covered.

Farmers Group, Inc.

21%   79%

Contributions: TOTAL: *$223,100*   DEM: *$46,000*   REP: *$177,100*

LOBBY SPENDING: *$460,000*

Subsidiary of Zurich Financial Services. In 2007, a pending class action lawsuit was filed on behalf of consumers who, since 1998, purchased a Farmers policy and who later were subject to a rate increase due to Farmers' alleged use of credit reports without the consumers' consent. Required to pay millions in lawsuits for failing to defend a negligence claim, refusing to defend its policyholders in a legal action, and han-dling a claim with bad faith. During the 2007 California wildfires, set up facilities to aid its customers. Supports education, high school athletic programs, safety programs, and the March of Dimes.

Fidelity Investments

44%   56%

Contributions: TOTAL: *$1,244,867*   DEM: *$543,721*   REP: *$701,146*

LOBBY SPENDING: *$1,115,000*

Subsidiary of FMR Corporation. In 2007, it cut by 91% its holding of PetroChina, which has alleged ties to genocide in Sudan. Is being sued over losses linked to investments in subprime mortgage-backed securi-ties. In 2007, a lawsuit alleged that Fidelity executives instructed the plaintiff to sidestep the Patriot Act. Fidelity filed its own suit to prevent the plaintiff from divulging "confidential information." In 2008, agreed to pay an $8 million penalty to the SEC to settle charges that employees improperly accepted gifts from brokers courting its business. In 2007, brokerage industry regulator NASD fined two Fidelity broker-dealer units a total of $400,000 for allegedly misleading U.S. military personnel in promoting two mutual funds. Supports civic, charitable, literacy, arts, and cultural programs and organizations. Has a written nondiscrimination policy covering sexual orientation but not gender identity. Does not offer insurance coverage to employees' same-sex domestic partners.

GE Consumer Finance, Inc. (GE Money) — 90% | 10%
Contributions: TOTAL: *$20,350*   DEM: *$18,350*   REP: *$2,000*
LOBBY SPENDING: *$0*
Subsidiary of General Electric Company. Supports health, education, disaster relief, and economic development.

GEICO Corporation — 54% | 46%
Contributions: TOTAL: *$66,499*   DEM: *$35,849*   REP: *$30,650*
LOBBY SPENDING: *$0*
Subsidiary of Berkshire Hathaway. A pending discrimination lawsuit accuses it of making education and employment status a factor in determining insurance rates. Is introducing recycling programs and energy and water-saving efforts in its offices. Partners with the Association of Zoos and Aquariums. Allows domestic partners to have joint car insurance policies. Has a written nondiscrimination policy that includes sexual orientation but not gender identity.

General Electric (GE) Company — 64% | 36%
Contributions: TOTAL: *$3,932,297*   DEM: *$2,501,827*   REP: *$1,430,470*
LOBBY SPENDING: *$39,019,000*
Multinational Monitor named GE one of the "10 Worst Corporations" of 2008. Has many convictions for environmental pollution and fraud and has been accused of human rights and labor abuses. Also accused of exposing people to nuclear radiation from its power plants and of releasing PCDs into the environment. Has spent millions on campaigns to avoid cleaning up its PCB dump sites, including 116 current or former Superfund sites. In 2008, scored 71 out of 100 in "The Climate Counts Company Scorecard Report." Its wind turbines prevent emission of as much as 18.3 million tons of greenhouse gases annually. In 2008, the GE Foundation awarded the New York City Department of Education a grant of $17.9 million. Supports math and science education, disaster relief, and micro-lending. Has a written nondiscrimination policy covering sexual orientation but not gender identity. Offers insurance coverage to employees' domestic partners. Insurance for transgender employees is offered, but treatment is not covered.

Golden Gate Capital — 58% | 42%
Contributions: TOTAL: *$61,400*   DEM: *$35,700*   REP: *$25,700*
LOBBY SPENDING: *$0*
Private equity firm with investments ranging from financial services, to semiconductors, to consumer products.

Golden Rule Insurance Company — 0% | 100%
Contributions: TOTAL: *$256*   DEM: *$0*   REP: *$256*
LOBBY SPENDING: *$0*
Subsidiary of UnitedHealth Group, Inc. Has a written nondiscrimination policy covering sexual orientation and gender identity. Offers insurance

coverage to employees' domestic partners. Insurance for transgender employees is offered, but treatment is not covered.

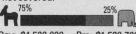

Goldman Sachs Group, Inc.
Contributions: Total: *$6,062,736* Dem: *$4,522,938* Rep: *$1,539,798*
Lobby Spending: *$6,110,000*

In 2008, received a government bailout, converted to a bank holding company, and formed subsidiary Goldman Sachs Bank USA. A pending class action securities lawsuit alleges that it misled the public by saying its research was unbiased. In 2008, paid $11.5 million to settle a class action suit filed by the University of California over the purchase of Enron Corp. securities. A $1.4 billion penalty was imposed on it and nine other investment banks in an SEC move to reform Wall Street practices. Ranked 9th on *Fortune* magazine's "100 Best Companies to Work For" in 2009. Received the 2008 Rainforest Alliance Corporate Green Globe Award. Portfolio includes investments in energy-efficiency technologies and sustainable real estate development. Is consolidating its operations into LEED-certified facilities. In 2007, donated $2 million to Morehouse College. Supports educational programs, arts and cultural institutions, and social service agencies. Has a written nondiscrimination policy covering sexual orientation and gender identity. Offers insurance coverage to employees' domestic partners. Insurance for transgender employees is offered, and treatment is covered.

Guardian Life Insurance Company of America, The
Contributions: Total: *$116,421* Dem: *$66,721* Rep: *$49,700*
Lobby Spending: *$300,000*

Privately held. A pending class action lawsuit was filed to recover overtime and other pay. Supports affordable housing, health and human services, education, and the arts and cultural institutions. Has no written nondiscrimination policy covering sexual orientation or gender identity.

Hartford Financial Services Group, Inc., The
Contributions: Total: *$721,932* Dem: *$433,705* Rep: *$288,227*
Lobby Spending: *$6,260,000*

In May 2009, won preliminary approval to receive $3.4 billion from the TARP. A class action lawsuit filed in 2009 accuses it of keeping settlement money that should have gone to accident victims. A pending class action lawsuit alleges that it concealed price manipulation and kickbacks, which inflated the stock price. In 2007, agreed to pay $115 million to settle allegations by Connecticut, Illinois, and New York that it faked bids and allowed illegal trading in some mutual funds. Participates in the EPA Energy Star program and is an EPA Climate Leader. In 2007, gave $1 million to Teach For America. Gives employees paid time off to volunteer. Has a written nondiscrimination policy covering sexual orientation and gender identity. Offers insurance coverage to employees' domestic partners.

Health Net, Inc.
Contributions: Total: *$312,468* Dem: *$187,745* Rep: *$124,723*
Lobby Spending: *$4,055,200*

An arbitration hearing revealed that it scrutinizes a claimant's original health insurance application for even minor flaws in order to justify policy cancellation once a major medical claim is made. A lawsuit revealed that it paid bonuses on the basis of number of policies canceled and resulting savings, a practice for which it was fined $1 million. Accused in a lawsuit of unfairly terminating coverage for 800 people; paid $6.3 million in damages and a $2 million penalty. In 2008, a New Jersey federal judge approved a $255 million settlement in three class action lawsuits that alleged it used a database that sometimes under-reimbursed members' insurance claims. Paid $167 million to settle a class action suit filed in federal court alleging price rigging. Supports the American Heart Association. Has a written nondiscrimination policy covering sexual orientation and gender identity. Offers insurance coverage to employees' domestic partners. Insurance for transgender employees is offered, but treatment is not covered.

HealthPartners, Inc.

83% | 17%

Contributions: TOTAL: *$57,754*   DEM: *$47,744*   REP: *$10,010*
LOBBY SPENDING: *$104,962*

Paid a $15,000 fine and agreed to modify its policies to allow for treatment of children with behavioral problems. Its Regions Hospital Foundation supports Regions Hospital in Minneapolis-St. Paul. Supports health programs in Uganda. Has a written nondiscrimination policy covering sexual orientation but not gender identity. Offers insurance coverage to employees' domestic partners.

Highmark, Inc.

49% | 51%

Contributions: TOTAL: *$19,150*   DEM: *$9,300*   REP: *$9,850*
LOBBY SPENDING: *$574,137*

In 2007, agreed to a lawsuit settlement which could cost it about $14 million for engaging in a conspiracy to improperly deny, delay, or reduce payment to physicians, physician groups, and physician organizations. Foundation supports programs for youth health, senior citizens, and the underserved and uninsured. Also supports the United Way and Go-Red for Women events and gives employees paid time off to volunteer.

HSBC Bank USA, NA

47% | 53%

Contributions: TOTAL: *$32,405*   DEM: *$15,320*   REP: *$17,085*
LOBBY SPENDING: *$280,000*

Subsidiary of foreign-owned HSBC Holdings PLC. In 2009, the NAACP filed a lawsuit accusing it of forcing African Americans into subprime mortgages while whites with identical qualifications got lower rates. Fair Finance Watch found that it extended higher-cost subprime loans to African Americans and Latinos far more frequently than to whites. A lawsuit alleges it violated federal and state labor laws in compensation matters. In 2007, agreed to pay nearly $1 million in fines and reimbursement to settle a California state lawsuit over a toxic chemical cleanup. Ranked 34th on DiversityInc's list of the "Top 50 Companies for Diversity" in 2009. In 2008, scored 65 out of 100 in "The Climate Counts Company Scorecard Report." Makes loans for and equity investments in organizations engaged in affordable housing development and economic development. Has a written nondiscrimination policy covering sexual orientation and gender identity. Offers insurance coverage to employees' domestic partners. Insurance for transgender employees is offered, and some treatment is covered.

HSBC Holdings, PLC
Contributions: TOTAL: *$925,284*   DEM: *$466,048*   REP: *$459,236*
LOBBY SPENDING: *$6,470,000*

Foreign owned. In 2009, investors in Hong Kong said they plan a multi-million-dollar lawsuit against London-based bank HSBC over the collapse of Lehman Brothers. In 2007, a U.S. real estate fund sued, alleging that HSBC's U.S. mortgage-trading operations took advantage of the crisis to profit at the expense of the fund. Engaged in a $100 million campaign to fight climate change. Was the first major bank to become carbon neutral.

Humana, Inc.
Contributions: TOTAL: *$603,850*   DEM: *$227,950*   REP: *$375,900*
LOBBY SPENDING: *$2,628,945*

A pending securities lawsuit alleges it made false statements in earnings reports related to its Medicare prescription drug plans. In 2008, agreed to pay $2.8 million to settle a class action lawsuit against it and other insurers for alleged conspiracy to suppress payments to physicians. Agreed to pay more than $1 million in back wages for FLSA violations. Scored 40 out of 100 in the 2008 Human Rights Campaign Corporate Equality Index. Partners with Energy Star. Foundation supports health and education. Has a written nondiscrimination policy covering sexual orientation but not gender identity. Offers insurance coverage to employees' domestic partners. Insurance for transgender employees is offered, but treatment is not covered.

JPMorgan Chase & Co.
Contributions: TOTAL: *$5,210,387*   DEM: *$3,186,717*   REP: *$2,023,670*
LOBBY SPENDING: *$10,830,000*

Pending lawsuits brought in 2002 by the Khulumani Support Group allege that it aided South Africa's apartheid regime. Is an investor in PetroChina, which is linked financially to the genocide in Darfur. A pending lawsuit filed in 2009 claims it knew that Bernard Madoff's investment operation was a fraud. In 2008, it and Morgan Stanley were collectively ordered to return over $7 billion to investors for misrepresentations about auction rate securities. Fair Finance Watch found that it extended higher-cost subprime loans to African Americans and Latinos far more frequently than to whites. Criticized for financing projects that put the environment at risk. Ranked 15th on DiversityInc's list of the "Top 50 Companies for Diversity" in 2009. Listed by NAFE as one of the top 50 companies for female executives in 2009. In 2008, scored 59 out of 100 in "The Climate Counts Company Scorecard Report." In 2007, helped found New York Mercantile Exchange's Green Exchange. Built several LEED-certified branches. Aims to lower its greenhouse gas emissions by 20% from 2005 levels by 2012. Supports educational and cultural initiatives and disaster relief. Has a written nondiscrimination policy covering sexual orientation and gender identity. Offers insurance coverage to employees' domestic partners. Insurance for transgender employees is offered, and treatment is covered.

J. W. Childs Associates LP

1%   99%

Contributions: TOTAL: *$175,550*   DEM: *$2,500*   REP: *$173,050*
LOBBY SPENDING: *$0*

Private equity firm that invests in consumer products, health care, and specialty retail companies.

Kaiser Permanente

86%   14%

Contributions: TOTAL: *$578,402*   DEM: *$499,700*   REP: *$78,702*
LOBBY SPENDING: *$595,000*

Has illegally canceled individual insurance policies. A pending lawsuit alleges nonpayment of emergency room treatment of HMO patients. A pending lawsuit accuses it of discriminating against children with autism. In 2007, agreed to a settlement of civil and criminal charges for patient dumping. Ranked 7th on DiversityInc's list of the "Top 50 Companies for Diversity" in 2009. Its environmental initiatives involve green buildings, environmentally responsible purchasing, and environmentally sustainable operations. Supports the uninsured and underserved. Has a written nondiscrimination policy covering sexual orientation and gender identity. Offers insurance coverage to employees' domestic partners. Insurance for transgender employees is offered, and some treatment is covered.

KPMG LLP

45%   55%

Contributions: TOTAL: *$2,209,302*   DEM: *$1,000,746*   REP: *$1,208,556*
LOBBY SPENDING: *$2,625,000*

Foreign owned. Subsidiary of KPMG International. Pending lawsuits claim that its reckless audits accelerated the collapse of New Century Financial Corp. in 2007. In 2009, the town of Fairfield, CT, named KPMG, its investment advisor, in a lawsuit after it lost money in a pension fund invested with Bernard Madoff. In 2009, two former executives were convicted of helping clients evade taxes. KPMG was fined $456 million. In 2008, it and Xerox settled a shareholder lawsuit alleging that Xerox manipulated its accounting to inflate its earnings. KPMG, Xerox's former outside auditor, had to pay $80 million. Ranked 56th on *Fortune* magazine's "100 Best Companies to Work For" in 2009. Ranked 21st on DiversityInc's list of the "Top 50 Companies for Diversity" in 2009. Is aiming for a 25% reduction in carbon emissions and a 10% reduction in waste from 2005 levels by 2010. Its Nashville office is LEED certified. Supports military troops stationed overseas. In 2008, partnered with First Book, which serves needy children. Has a written nondiscrimination policy covering sexual orientation and gender identity. Offers insurance coverage to employees' domestic partners. Insurance for transgender employees is offered, and treatment is covered.

Lehman Brothers Holding, Inc.

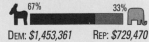

67%   33%

Contributions: TOTAL: *$2,182,831*   DEM: *$1,453,361*   REP: *$729,470*
LOBBY SPENDING: *$1,320,000*

Foreign owned. Purchased by Barclays PLC after declaring bankruptcy in 2008. Faces several ERISA lawsuits. In 2009, the Washington State

Investment Board filed a lawsuit to recover $100 million in lost investments. In 2008, a class action lawsuit filed on behalf of investors alleged it made false and misleading statements about its financial strength. In 2008, a San Mateo County, CA, investment fund accused it of fraud that led to the loss of $150 million of the public's money. Has committed $10 million to establish the Lehman Brothers Center for Global Finance and Economic Development at Spelman College.

Leonard Green & Partners LP

93%   7%

Contributions: TOTAL: *$159,700*   DEM: *$149,100*   REP: *$10,600*
LOBBY SPENDING: *$0*

This private equity firm has investments ranging from clothing retailers to restaurants.

Loews Corporation

58%   42%

Contributions: TOTAL: *$762,394*   DEM: *$441,845*   REP: *$320,549*
LOBBY SPENDING: *$9,618,368*

Diversified holding company with subsidiaries ranging from off-shore drilling to hotels. In 2008, it removed its tobacco unit from its holdings. Agreed to pay a $7.5 billion settlement for class action punitive damage claims alleging that it misled investors and smokers over the health risks associated with cigarettes. Targeted, with 11 other companies, in a slave reparation class action suit for pre-1865 gains. Has a written nondiscrimination policy covering sexual orientation but not gender identity. Offers insurance coverage to employees' domestic partners.

Lone Star Funds

31%   69%

Contributions: TOTAL: *$5,650*   DEM: *$1,750*   REP: *$3,900*
LOBBY SPENDING: *$110,000*

In 2008, found guilty of stock-price manipulation in South Korea. Paul Yoo, head of its Seoul office, was sentenced to a five-year prison term, and he was indicted for breach of trust, tax evasion, stock manipulation, and refusal to testify at the National Assembly.

MacAndrews & Forbes Holdings, Inc.

71%   29%

Contributions: TOTAL: *$656,847*   DEM: *$469,297*   REP: *$187,550*
LOBBY SPENDING: *$1,930,000*

Private equity firm has investments across a wide range of industries, from cosmetics and entertainment to biotechnology and military equipment. President and CEO Ronald Perelman agreed to pay $80 million in 2008 to settle a lawsuit accusing him of helping divert $553.5 million in notes when he controlled comic book publisher Marvel Entertainment Group. Perelman and other Marvel directors were accused of moving proceeds to some of Perelman's other companies before Marvel's 1996 bankruptcy. Supports women's health issues, education, and the arts.

MasterCard, Inc.

49%   51%

Contributions: TOTAL: *$354,878*   DEM: *$175,503*   REP: *$179,375*
LOBBY SPENDING: *$4,930,000*

In 2007, it and Visa agreed to pay the U.S. government $3.5 million for violating federal antitrust laws. Ranked 41st on DiversityInc's list of the "Top 50 Companies for Diversity" in 2009. Received the highest score possible from the Human Rights Campaign Corporate Equality Index. Supports organizations serving youth. Has an employee matching gift program. Offers campaigns to educate college students about good credit habits. Has a written nondiscrimination policy covering sexual orientation and gender identity. Offers insurance coverage to employees' domestic partners. Insurance for transgender employees is offered, and some treatment is covered.

MBNA Corporation

33% — 67%

Contributions: TOTAL: *$3,000*   DEM: *$1,000*   REP: *$2,000*
LOBBY SPENDING: *$0*

Subsidiary of FIA Card Services; parent, Bank of America Corporation. A class action lawsuit claims that it violated federal securities laws by issuing material misrepresentations to the market. A pending class action lawsuit alleges that it sold private information belonging to its credit card customers. A proposed class action lawsuit was filed in 2008 against it and Bank of America for allegedly false and misleading statements in "live check" loan solicitations. In 2009, it and parent FIA Card Services were ordered to pay a total of $6.325 million to a settlement fund to resolve a class action lawsuit for allegedly misleading advertising for certain Access Check offers. In 2007, agreed to pay $147,000 to settle a discrimination lawsuit. Has a written nondiscrimination policy covering sexual orientation and gender identity. Offers health insurance coverage to employees' domestic partners. Insurance for transgender employees is offered, and some treatment is covered.

Medica, Inc.

79% — 21%

Contributions: TOTAL: *$8,930*   DEM: *$7,080*   REP: *$1,850*
LOBBY SPENDING: *$0*

Its foundation funding focuses on health care literacy, reduction of socioeconomic disparities in health care, and efforts to address the health care needs of Minnesota communities. Has a written nondiscrimination policy covering sexual orientation but not gender identity. Offers insurance coverage to employees' domestic partners.

Mercury General Corporation

0% — 100%

Contributions: TOTAL: *$51,500*   DEM: *$250*   REP: *$51,250*
LOBBY SPENDING: *$0*

Has been involved in several investigations involving political contributions to get legislation passed. Has a written nondiscrimination policy covering sexual orientation but not gender identity.

Merrill Lynch & Co., Inc.

47% — 53%

Contributions: TOTAL: *$2,936,116*   DEM: *$1,380,677*   REP: *$1,555,439*
LOBBY SPENDING: *$9,120,000*

Acquired by Bank of America Corporation in 2008 after it lost $51.8 billion in mortgage-backed securities. A pending lawsuit alleges that its effort to market credit default swaps to MBIA was part of a strategy to off-load deteriorating U.S. subprime residential mortgages. In 2008, the State of Massachusetts filed a lawsuit alleging fraud in the sale of esoteric debt securities to the City of Springfield. In 2009, settled with the Ohio State Teachers' Retirement System for $475 million after allegations related to subprime-related securities. In 2009, paid $75 million to settle an ERISA lawsuit. In 2009, paid $1.55 million to settle a lawsuit brought by the EEOC alleging discrimination against an employee because of his nationality and religion. In 2007, an arbitration panel ordered it to pay $1.6 million to an employee fired because of his ethnicity. Has a written nondiscrimination policy covering sexual orientation and gender identity. Offers insurance coverage to employees' domestic partners. Insurance for transgender employees is offered, and some treatment is covered.

58%   42%

MetLife, Inc.
Contributions: Total: *$1,259,416*   Dem: *$726,907*   Rep: *$532,509*
Lobby Spending: *$10,270,000*

A pending lawsuit contends that it paid the Indiana Teachers' Association Administrative Services to promote it over other insurance options. A pending lawsuit brought by the SEC claims a former MetLife broker stole $6 million from MetLife customer accounts. In 2009, a jury ordered it to pay $55 million in punitive damages and $155,000 in compensatory damages for failure to process a valid claim. In 2008, a client won $285,000 in a civil case against MetLife for misappropriation of money. A pending lawsuit filed in 2001 alleges that it pays women less than men in similar positions. Listed by NAFE as one of the top 50 companies for female executives in 2009. Ranked 43rd on DiversityInc's list of the "Top 50 Companies for Diversity" in 2009. Received Energy Star ratings for nine of its sites. Has invested $1.1 billion in renewable energy projects. Foundation supports educational, health and welfare, civic, and cultural organizations. Has a written nondiscrimination policy covering sexual orientation and gender identity. Offers insurance coverage to employees' domestic partners. Insurance for transgender employees is offered, but treatment is not covered.

57%   43%

Morgan Stanley
Contributions: Total: *$3,825,650*   Dem: *$2,177,732*   Rep: *$1,647,918*
Lobby Spending: *$5,880,000*

Changed its status from investment bank to bank holding company in 2008. The SEC has filed a lawsuit against two ex-Morgan Stanley advisers for allegedly circumventing market timing restrictions. In 2008, it and JPMorgan were ordered to return over $7 billion to investors to settle allegations that they made misrepresentations about auction rate securities. In 2007, agreed to pay $4.4 million to settle a class action lawsuit with brokerage clients. Paid a $15 million civil penalty for failing to produce records during an SEC investigation in a timely manner. In 2007, agreed to pay $46 million to settle gender discrimination allegations. Outraged U.S. unions by telling clients to pull their money out of heavily unionized industries. Has committed to reducing its 2006 level of greenhouse gas emissions by up to 10% by 2012. Supports HRH The Prince of Wales' Rainforests Project.

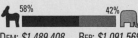

58%   42%

New York Life Insurance Co.
Contributions: Total: *$2,580,977*   Dem: *$1,489,408*   Rep: *$1,091,569*
Lobby Spending: *$10,090,000*

In 2009, a jury awarded $6 million in an age discrimination lawsuit. In 2008, paid $14 million to settle a lawsuit alleging that it improperly directed pension funds into its own mutual funds, costing its pension participants millions. Foundation focuses on the needs of children. Has a matching gift program for donations to educational institutions. Has a written nondiscrimination policy covering sexual orientation and gender identity. Offers insurance coverage to employees' domestic partners. Insurance for transgender employees is offered, and some treatment is covered.

PacifiCare Health Systems LLC

33% / 67%

Contributions: TOTAL: *$7,600*   DEM: *$2,500*   REP: *$5,100*
LOBBY SPENDING: *$0*

Subsidiary of UnitedHealth Group, Inc. A pending lawsuit alleges that some HMO members were prescribed medication subsequently pulled from the market because of serious side effects. Named with other insurance companies in a pending class action lawsuit, filed by doctors and states in federal court, alleging violation of the federal RICO Act. It and its parent are alleged to have delayed processing of new contracts and terminations, and to have given patients misinformation about their doctors' participation status in their plans. In 2009, UnitedHealth/PacifiCare made $5.7 million in grants to promote health information technology and medical education in California, as required by state regulators when they approved the merger of the two companies in 2005. Has a written nondiscrimination policy covering sexual orientation and gender identity. Offers health insurance coverage to employees' domestic partners. Insurance for transgender employees is offered, but treatment is not covered.

PricewaterhouseCoopers LLC

46% / 54%

Contributions: TOTAL: *$3,047,071*   DEM: *$1,394,464*   REP: *$1,652,607*
LOBBY SPENDING: *$4,990,584*

Privately held. A class-certified wage and hour lawsuit is pending. A class action lawsuit charges that it has "recklessly or intentionally" certified inaccurate financial statements for AIG since 1999. In a pending lawsuit against it and other investment companies, two clients allege they lost millions after their money was steered into an illegal tax haven. In 2009, PwC and its Bermuda affiliate paid the State of New Jersey $5.85 million to resolve allegations of fraud and accounting improprieties at Tyco International Ltd. that resulted in significant losses for New Jersey's pension fund portfolio. In 2007, agreed to pay $225 million to settle a class action lawsuit brought by Tyco shareholders. In 2007, it and IBM Corp. agreed to pay a total of nearly $5.3 million to settle allegations that they made improper payments on government technology contracts. Ranked 58th on *Fortune* magazine's "100 Best Companies to Work For" in 2009. Ranked 5th on DiversityInc's list of the "Top 50 Companies for Diversity" in 2009. Subsidizes its employees' mass transit costs. Supports inner-city youth education, disaster relief, assistance efforts in Darfur, and the United Way. Has a written nondiscrimination policy covering sexual orientation and gender identity. Offers insurance coverage to employees' domestic partners. Insurance for transgender employees is offered, but treatment is not covered.

Progressive Corporation, The

80% — **20%**

Contributions: TOTAL: *$23,116*   DEM: *$18,466*   REP: *$4,650*
LOBBY SPENDING: *$0*

A lawsuit alleges rampant steering in violation of New York statutes. Four pending class action suits allege breach of contract and fraud for the purchase of after-market replacement parts for vehicle repairs. Four class actions allege violation of the federal Equal Credit Opportunity and Fair Credit Reporting acts. Matches funds to eligible charitable organizations to which its employees contribute. Attempts to conserve the natural setting of its campuses by working with builders to save old-growth trees and protect wetlands. Has a written nondiscrimination policy covering sexual orientation and gender identity. Offers health insurance coverage to employees' domestic partners. Insurance for transgender employees is offered, but treatment is not covered.

Prudential Financial, Inc.

59% — **41%**

Contributions: TOTAL: *$1,140,332*   DEM: *$675,028*   REP: *$465,304*
LOBBY SPENDING: *$10,338,063*

In 2009, a shareholder filed a class action lawsuit alleging concealment of the company's business and financial condition in documents related to an initial public offering of common stock. In 2008, the SEC sued Prudential for alleged violations of the Securities Exchange Act. Fined $2 million and censured by the National Association of Securities Dealers; ordered to pay another $9.5 million to customers for questionable sales practices. Implicated in California's insurance scheme scandal involving bid rigging and kickbacks. Listed by NAFE as one of the top 50 companies for female executives in 2009. Ranked 45th on DiversityInc's list of the "Top 50 Companies for Diversity" in 2009. Foundation supports public education and economic development. Supports neighborhood revitalization. Has a written nondiscrimination policy that covers sexual orientation and gender identity. Offers insurance coverage to employees' domestic partners. Insurance for transgender employees is offered, but treatment is not covered.

Safeco Insurance Company of America

62% — **38%**

Contributions: TOTAL: *$42,822*   DEM: *$26,722*   REP: *$16,100*
LOBBY SPENDING: *$0*

Subsidiary of Liberty Mutual Group. A pending lawsuit in California alleges that it illegally surcharged customers due to their lack of prior continuous automobile insurance coverage. A pending lawsuit alleges it implemented an auditing program to reduce payouts under the medical payments coverage of property and casualty insurance. Implicated in California's insurance scheme scandal involving bid rigging and kickbacks. Supports education, health and human services, access to health care for low-income individuals, and home rehabilitation services. Provides agent-directed grants and sponsorships to nonprofit organizations. Offers employees paid time off to volunteer. Has no written nondiscrimination policy covering sexual orientation or gender identity. Offers insurance coverage to employees' domestic partners.

State Farm Insurance Companies
36% | 64%

Contributions: TOTAL: *$579,469*   DEM: *$208,767*   REP: *$370,702*
LOBBY SPENDING: *$5,805,504*

More than 15 affiliated privately held companies. A pending lawsuit brought by a New York physician alleges that it and other codefendents created fraudulent documents for the purpose of denying claims and that it paid kickbacks to independent medical examiners. A class action lawsuit over its handling of thousands of claims for hail damage is pending. Ordered to reevaluate claims filed after Hurricane Katrina on which it refused to pay a dime. An agreement with the State of Mississippi resulted in payouts of $74 million to the victims. Listed by NAFE as one of the top 50 companies for female executives in 2009. Has reduced its greenhouse gas emissions by more than 38% since 2002. Its composite Energy Star rating is 82, indicating that State Farm buildings, on average, are more energy efficient than 82% of comparable buildings. Outreach focuses on education, auto and home safety, and home ownership. In 2008, the State Farm Youth Advisory Board, in partnership with State Farm, awarded over $4 million for youth-led, service-learning-based projects. Has a nondiscrimination policy covering sexual orientation and gender identity. Offers no insurance coverage to employees' domestic partners. Insurance for transgender employees is offered, and treatment is covered.

Sun Capital Partners, Inc.
35% | 65%

Contributions: TOTAL: *$246,575*   DEM: *$87,050*   REP: *$159,525*
LOBBY SPENDING: *$0*

This private equity firm has investments ranging from clothing to faucets to home furnishings to restaurants. Has no written nondiscrimination policy covering sexual orientation or gender identity.

TPG Capital LP
79% | 21%

Contributions: TOTAL: *$773,785*   DEM: *$610,300*   REP: *$163,485*
LOBBY SPENDING: *$1,480,000*

Also known as Texas Pacific Group. Private equity firm has investments ranging from telecommunications to apparel to energy to casinos. In 2008, it led a $7 billion investment in Washington Mutual. On September 25, 2008, Washington Mutual was taken over by the government, costing TPG a $1.35 billion investment. TPG was a leading investor during the 2006-2008 buyout boom.

Tracinda Corporation
54% | 46%

Contributions: TOTAL: *$90,250*   DEM: *$49,150*   REP: *$41,100*
LOBBY SPENDING: *$0*

This private equity firm has investments in hotels and casinos.

TRT Holdings, Inc.
1% | 99%

Contributions: TOTAL: *$227,801*   DEM: *$3,250*   REP: *$224,551*
LOBBY SPENDING: *$0*

Diversified holding company for Texas billionaire Robert Rowling. TRT owns the Omni Hotel chain and Gold's Gym International. In addition, it is involved in oil and gas exploration through Tana Exploration Company. Other business interests include real estate.

UBS AG

55%   45%

Contributions: Total: *$3,291,714*   Dem: *$1,802,317*   Rep: *$1,489,397*
Lobby Spending: *$1,270,000*

Foreign owned. In 2009, federal authorities filed a lawsuit to force it to turn over information on U.S. customers who hid their accounts in violation of tax laws. UBS agreed to pay the U.S. government $780 million and later made a deal expected to result in identification of Americans who controlled 4,450 accounts. In 2009, an investor filed a class action lawsuit alleging violations of U.S. federal securities laws. As a result of its alleged malfeasance, UBS faces a fine of $1.2 billion and possibly a felony indictment. In 2008, the New York attorney general filed a securities fraud lawsuit against UBS Securities LLC and UBS Financial Services, Inc. (collectively "UBS"). UBS customers hold more than $25 billion in illiquid, long-term paper as a result of UBS's fraudulent misrepresentations and illegal conduct. In 2007, a shareholder sued UBS, contending it misled investors about write-downs related to securities linked to U.S. subprime mortgages. Endorses the United Nations Global Compact. Supports education and community building. Matches employee donations, and offers employees paid time off to volunteer. Has a written nondiscrimination policy covering sexual orientation and gender identity. Offers insurance coverage to employees' domestic partners. Insurance for transgender employees is offered, but treatment is not covered.

**United Services Automobile
Association (USAA)**

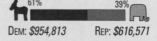

0%   100%

Contributions: Total: *$500*   Dem: *$0*   Rep: *$500*
Lobby Spending: *$13,473,636*

Privately held. In 2008, a jury awarded $3.6 million to a Marine captain serving in Iraq after concluding that USAA tried to cheat him out of coverage. Involved in several notable discrimination suits involving alleged civil rights and federal tort law violations, as well as libel and slander. Recognized as a family-friendly employer. Its foundation supports education in financial management. Has no written nondiscrimination policy covering sexual orientation or gender identity.

UnitedHealth Group, Inc.

61%   39%

Contributions: Total: *$1,571,384*   Dem: *$954,813*   Rep: *$616,571*
Lobby Spending: *$9,774,000*

In 2009, agreed to pay $350 million to settle class action lawsuits over reimbursements for out-of-network medical services. In 2008, agreed to pay $895 million to settle a lawsuit brought by the California Public Employees' Retirement System that alleged improper backdating of stock options. Also paid $17 million to settle a second suit for ERISA violations. In 2007, agreed to pay at least $12 million to end state investigations into the processing and payment of claims. Two of its buildings meet LEED standards. In 2009, UnitedHealth/PacifiCare made $5.7 million in grants to promote health information technology and medical education in California, as required by state regulators when they approved the merger of the two managed-care giants in 2005. Foundation focuses on improving the quality and cost-effectiveness of medical care and expanding access to health care services. Matches employee donations. Has a written nondiscrimination policy covering sexual orientation and gender identity. Offers insurance coverage to employees' domestic partners. Insurance for transgender employees is offered, but treatment is not covered.

U.S. Bancorp

44% | 56%

Contributions: TOTAL: *$548,861*   DEM: *$239,920*   REP: *$308,941*
LOBBY SPENDING: *$910,000*

Being investigated over possible breaches of fiduciary duty related to compensation for certain senior officers. In 2007, was ordered to pay $17.6 million in a civil lawsuit brought by the trustee overseeing the bankruptcy of a company that defrauded investors out of $45 million. Paid $2.5 million to settle allegations of negligence when a former broker bilked 38 clients out of $1.4 million. In 2008, scored 17 out of 100 in "The Climate Counts Company Scorecard Report." Has implemented practices to guide its lending to businesses that have high conservation values. Has committed $1 billion to environmentally beneficial businesses. Its foundation and community development loan program support affordable housing, economic revitalization, education, and the United Way. Has an employee volunteer program and offers matching donations. Has a written nondiscrimination policy covering sexual orientation and gender identity. Offers insurance coverage to employees' domestic partners. Insurance for transgender employees is offered, but treatment is not covered.

Vanguard Health Systems

54% | 46%

Contributions: TOTAL: *$134,950*   DEM: *$73,350*   REP: *$61,600*
LOBBY SPENDING: *$140,000*

Subsidiary of The Blackstone Group LP. Nurses in four cities filed lawsuits alleging that more than 17 hospitals conspired to maintain artificially low wages. Provides funding to local charitable foundations and activities. Maintains several school-based clinics and outreach for educational programs. Has no written nondiscrimination policy covering sexual orientation or gender identity.

Vestar Capital Partners LP

84% | 16%

Contributions: TOTAL: *$234,250*   DEM: *$196,500*   REP: *$37,750*
LOBBY SPENDING: *$50,000*

This private equity firm has investments ranging from frozen food to medical equipment.

Visa, Inc.

57% | 43%

Contributions: TOTAL: *$307,158*   DEM: *$176,076*   REP: *$131,082*
LOBBY SPENDING: *$10,150,000*

Supports small enterprise development through micro-finance programs, village banking initiatives, economic self-sufficiency programs, entrepreneurship, and humanitarian aid. Developed a "virtuous circle" system to help world economies grow, support themselves, and prosper.

Visa U.S.A., Inc.

52% ▬▬▬▬▬ 48%

Contributions: TOTAL: *$235,156*   DEM: *$122,599*   REP: *$112,557*
LOBBY SPENDING: *$9,670,000*

Subsidiary of Visa, Inc. In 2007, it and Visa agreed to pay the U.S. government $3.5 million for violating federal antitrust laws. Named as a defendant in an antitrust class action filed on behalf of a group of small businesses alleging that several banks illegally fix the price of credit card transaction fees. Has a written nondiscrimination policy covering sexual orientation and gender identity. Offers insurance coverage to employees' domestic partners. Insurance for transgender employees is offered, but treatment is not covered.

Wachovia Corporation

40% ▬▬▬▬▬ 60%

Contributions: TOTAL: *$2,441,620*   DEM: *$985,156*   REP: *$1,456,464*
LOBBY SPENDING: *$3,141,000*

Subsidiary of Wells Fargo & Co. In 2009, a judge blocked it from foreclosing on a shopping center until a lawsuit involving a derivative interest rate swap and alleged extortion, fraud, and deceptive trade practices goes to trial. A pending class action lawsuit accuses it of ERISA violations. In 2008, it was fined $10 million and ordered to distribute up to $125 million to customers who were financially harmed when it allowed fraudulent telemarketers to use its accounts. In 2008, scored 30 out of 100 in "The Climate Counts Company Scorecard Report." Is a signatory to the Equator Principles. Does not finance logging in ecologically valuable and vulnerable areas. Plans to reduce its absolute carbon emissions by 10% from 2005 levels by 2010. Purchases renewable energy where available and recycles paper. Supports educational improvement and neighborhood strengthening. Its employee volunteer program provides grants and matching donations. Has a written nondiscrimination policy covering sexual orientation and gender identity. Offers insurance coverage to employees' domestic partners. Insurance for transgender employees is offered, and treatment is covered.

Washington Mutual, Inc. (WaMu)

58% ▬▬▬▬▬ 42%

Contributions: TOTAL: *$643,816*   DEM: *$371,896*   REP: *$271,920*
LOBBY SPENDING: *$1,899,000*

Subsidiary of JPMorgan Chase & Co. A pending lawsuit brought by its investors is notable for its citations from 89 "confidential witnesses," who allege that WaMu's officers and directors misrepresented the company's financial results, secretly undermined its risk-management policies, corrupted its appraisal process, and abandoned appropriate underwriting standards for home loans. Was one of the country's leading subprime lenders and has been criticized for targeting African Americans with subprime loans. Supports neighborhoods through affordable housing loans, financial education, and community-building efforts. Matches employee donations dollar for dollar up to $10,000 per employee each year. Has a written nondiscrimination policy covering sexual orientation and gender identity. Offers insurance coverage to employees' domestic partners. Insurance for transgender employees is offered, and treatment is covered.

WellPoint, Inc.
33% | 67%

Contributions: TOTAL: *$983,496* DEM: *$319,970* REP: *$663,526*
LOBBY SPENDING: *$5,350,000*

The nation's largest health insurer, it provides health insurance under the Blue Cross and Blue Shield names and under the entities Anthem, HealthLink, and UniCare. In 2009, a class action complaint accused it of colluding in a price-fixing scheme to set artificially low reimbursement rates for out-of-network care. A former executive filed a pending whistle-blower lawsuit. In 2008, was ordered to pay $11.8 million to settle claims from 480 California hospitals that allege it did not cover the bills of patients who were dropped after treatment. Listed by NAFE as one of the top 50 companies for female executives in 2009. Ranked 44th on DiversityInc's list of the "Top 50 Companies for Diversity" in 2009. Foundation focuses on initiatives related to health-care accessibility, affordability, and quality. Supports the March of Dimes, the United Way, and efforts to reduce childhood obesity. Provides assistance to community health clinics. Matches employee donations 50 cents on the dollar. Has a written nondiscrimination policy covering sexual orientation and gender identity. Offers insurance coverage to employees' domestic partners. Insurance for transgender employees is offered, but treatment is not covered.

Wells Fargo & Company
49% | 51%

Contributions: TOTAL: *$1,846,723* DEM: *$898,231* REP: *$948,492*
LOBBY SPENDING: *$4,184,740*

Received $25 billion under the TARP. Is one of the largest single stockholders in the GEO Group, a private prison outfit with prisons and detention centers, several of which have been accused of human rights abuses. In 2009, the NAACP filed a lawsuit accusing it of forcing African Americans into subprime mortgages while giving lower rates to whites with identical qualifications. In 2008, the City of Baltimore filed a lawsuit contending that its lending practices discriminated against African American borrowers. In 2007, agreed to pay up to $6.8 million to settle a class action lawsuit alleging improper nonprime mortgage lending practices in California. Ranked 31st on DiversityInc's list of the "Top 50 Companies for Diversity" in 2009. Earns praise as a family-friendly employer. In 2008, scored 31 out of 100 in "The Climate Counts Company Scorecard Report." Has provided $4 billion in environmental financing since 2006. In 2008, gave $1.5 million to three national home-owner-counseling organizations. Supports education, human services, community development, disaster relief, arts and culture, and civic and environmental programs. Has a written nondiscrimination policy that covers sexual orientation and gender identity. Offers insurance coverage to employees' domestic partners. Insurance for transgender employees is offered, and treatment is covered.

Zurich Financial Services
24% | 76%

Contributions: TOTAL: *$814,704* DEM: *$198,986* REP: *$615,718*
LOBBY SPENDING: *$6,920,329*

Foreign owned. In 2008, agreed to pay a $25 million penalty to settle civil securities-fraud charges from the SEC. In 2007, subsidiary Zurich Capital Markets paid $16.8 million to settle with the SEC for helping four hedge funds avoid detection when making frequent trades in mutual fund shares. In 2006, subsidiary Zurich American Insurance Company was ordered to pay $153 million in an agreement with Connecticut, Illinois, and New York to settle allegations that it rigged bids and secretly paid insurance brokers to steer business to Zurich. Also in 2006, nine states reached a $171 million settlement with Zurich American, again relating to bid rigging and price-fixing. Its Climate Office works with its business units to shape and implement its climate change strategy. Supports organizations that enhance the lives of children, improve safety, expand educational opportunities, improve health and human services, and encourage civic participation. Supports arts and culture and the environment. Matches employees' donations.

Food and Beverage

Sasha Abramsky

A little over a century after the publication of *The Jungle*, Upton Sinclair's exposé of the meatpacking business, a rash of books and documentaries are once more sounding the alarm about what we eat and how we eat it. Books like Michael Pollan's *Omnivore's Dilemma* and Eric Schlosser's *Fast Food Nation*, as well as Morgan Spurlock's *Supersize Me* documentary, have put the spotlight on the world of food production and consumption. After years of willful ignorance, the public finally is waking up to the dangers of obesity, junk food, and unregulated industrial agriculture.

Scares over salmonella in peanut and pistachio products, huge recalls of beef—including some that ended up in school cafeterias—and a global panic over tainted Chinese milk have shifted public sentiments about how food is produced. So, too, did the video footage—virally distributed over the Internet—of sick cows at a California abattoir being driven to the slaughter, and thus into the human food chain.

The new Obama administration has indicated that after years of lax enforcement and underfunded inspection agencies, it will take an aggressive stance to ensure that the nation's food supplies are safe. It has also made clear that it will enforce labor laws more assertively, giving activists some reason to hope that the more scandalous conditions faced by farm laborers and slaughterhouse workers might be ameliorated. That gels well with recent consumer campaigns and workers' protests to push Taco Bell, Burger King, and other companies to ensure better pay for produce pickers.

Seeing the writing on the wall, many of the nation's largest food and beverage companies began channeling huge sums of money to the Democrats during the last election cycle. If they couldn't prevent politicians who favored more regulations from coming to power, they could at least try to influence those politicians. In fact, in a stunning indication of larger changes in political fortune, the five food and beverage organizations that donated the most to political campaigns in 2008—the National Beer Wholesalers' Association, American Crystal Sugar, Anheuser-Busch, Dairy

Farmers of America, and the Wine and Spirits Whole-salers of America—all contributed more heavily to the Democrats than to the Republicans. As like as not, this shift had more to do with pragmatism than idealism. Quite sensibly, these big players were determined to keep their places at the DC table.

All of these expenditures may well bear fruit. Agriculture secretary Tom Vilsack has long been viewed as something of a friend to agribusiness, lobbying for expanded use of ethanol in the nation's vehicle fleet and defending genetically engineered crops. As new regulations are crafted and old ones properly enforced, his will likely be a voice of "moderation" that food industry groups can turn to if the going gets too rough and the proposed reforms become too sweeping for them to stomach.

As the economic crisis has worsened, the spotlight has also turned to food affordability and access issues. In 2008, Raj Patel's book *Stuffed and Starved* focused attention on global food security issues and looked at how millions of people are currently priced out of the food supply system despite a global food glut. Belatedly, the feds have pumped more money into feeding the country's poor again. This effort was, in part, an emergency response to the fact that during George Bush's presidency, the plight of America's poor worsened, commodities prices soared, and increasing numbers of working families found it impossible to make ends meet. The Farm Bill, passed in 2008, once again extended huge subsidies to agribusiness; yet it also set aside billions of dollars for government food programs, including USDA contributions to food banks around the country, which keep millions of working poor Americans afloat nutritionally.

In the post-bubble economy, record numbers of people (approximately 30 million) now rely on food stamps, and millions more on food charity. Many of them work at near minimum-wage jobs in the food and service sector—McDonalds or Wal-Mart, for example. Ironically, they eat food bank donations supplied, in many cases, by these very same employers. Wal-Mart now trucks food to charity distribution centers in all 50 states. It's cheaper, apparently, to make charitable donations than to pay workers a true living wage.

In the years ahead, the food and beverage industries will likely be scrutinized more closely than they have been in decades. More generally, the country's food production and distribution systems will remain a focal point for journalists' and consumers' attention. Stay tuned: this part of the economy is likely to change significantly during this book's lifetime.

Top Ten Democratic Contributors

American Crystal Sugar	$1,255,900
Anheuser-Busch Companies, Inc.	$1,172,888
Altria Group, Inc.	$680,084
Dairy Farmers of America, Inc.	$523,950
Safeway, Inc.	$373,733
Brown-Forman Corporation	$306,195
E. & J. Gallo Winery	$302,084
PepsiCo, Inc.	$297,856
Dean Foods Company	$245,725
Kraft Foods, Inc.	$238,151

Top Ten Republican Contributors

Anheuser-Busch Companies, Inc.	$903,800
Altria Group, Inc.	$818,757
American Crystal Sugar	$698,250
Dairy Farmers of America, Inc.	$485,000
Pilgrim's Pride Corporation	$473,451
Publix Super Markets, Inc.	$428,702
Dean Foods Company	$397,350
Safeway, Inc.	$392,069
PepsiCo, Inc.	$371,200
United Dairy Farmers, Inc.	$314,300

Top Ten Lobbying Spenders

Altria Group, Inc.	$28,485,000
Anheuser-Busch Companies, Inc.	$6,900,000
Kraft Foods, Inc.	$6,010,000
Nestlé S.A.	$4,265,487
Mars, Inc.	$4,140,000
Tyson Foods, Inc.	$3,791,433
Diageo PLC	$3,500,000
Diageo North America	$3,420,000
Sara Lee Corporation	$2,850,000
Pernod Ricard S.A.	$2,695,000

7-Eleven, Inc.
29% / 71%
Contributions: Total: *$13,750* Dem: *$3,950* Rep: *$9,800*
Lobby Spending: *$210,466*
Parent company, Seven & I Holdings, Co., Ltd., is foreign owned. Pending class action lawsuit brought by former employees alleges California Labor Code violations regarding minimum and overtime wages. Agreed to stop advertising cigarettes near products that appeal to minors and paid a $375,000 settlement. The blind community has commended 7-Eleven for installing tactile point-of-sale devices. Has been subject to several environmental lawsuits, including one alleging leaking of petroleum. Has contributed more than $100 million in cash and in-kind products to support police, school and youth sports programs, and community events. Has a written nondiscrimination policy covering sexual orientation but not gender identity. Offers insurance coverage to employees' domestic partners.

Ahold USA, Inc.
100% / 0%
Contributions: Total: *$6,282* Dem: *$6,282* Rep: *$0*
Lobby Spending: *$0*
Subsidiary of Royal Ahold N.V. In 2008, it discontinued the sale of shark, Chilean sea bass, and orange roughy until issues regarding the sustainability of these species have been addressed. Purchases locally grown and produced products in many locations. Installed solar panels at one store. Supports hunger relief. Has a written nondiscrimination policy covering sexual orientation and gender identity. Offers insurance coverage to employees' domestic partners. Limited insurance for transgender employees is offered, and limited treatment is covered.

Albertsons LLC
7% / 93%
Contributions: Total: *$27,050* Dem: *$1,850* Rep: *$25,200*
Lobby Spending: *$0*
Subsidiary of SUPERVALU, Inc. A pending lawsuit against it and pharmacy subsidiaries alleges a violation of California's Confidential Medical Information Act. In 2007, a class action lawsuit awarded $53.3 million to former employees for unpaid overtime. Two pending lawsuits were brought by the EEOC on behalf of former employees who claim they were punished because of their opposition to Albertsons' discriminatory employment practices. Two pending lawsuits allege Albertsons violated California antitrust law and hurt consumers by discouraging competitive pricing when it formed an alliance with Safeway, Inc./Vons and the Kroger Co./Ralphs Grocery Company. Workers affiliated with the UFCW Union claim to have been intimidated by Albertsons when it violated federal labor rules by forcing employees to watch and discuss anti-union videos. Allows its pharmacists to refuse to fill prescriptions for the morning-after pill. Does not distribute irradiated food or sell milk from cows treated with BGH. Has contributed $3.1 million to muscular dystrophy research. Has a written nondiscrimination policy covering sexual orientation and gender identity. Offers health insurance coverage to employees' domestic partners. Insurance for transgender employees is offered, but treatment is not covered.

Altria Group, Inc.
Contributions: TOTAL: *$1,498,841*   DEM: *$680,084*   REP: *$818,757*
LOBBY SPENDING: *$28,485,000*

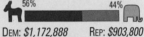

Controls about half of the U.S. tobacco market. Supports FDA regulation of tobacco products. *Multinational Monitor* named it one of the "10 Worst Corporations" of 2008. Believes immigration reform should provide for a reliable source of legal foreign workers to fill important agricultural and scientific positions that cannot be filled by the domestic workforce. Invests in environmental programs for responsible water, solid waste, and land management. Provided funds for a cigarette litter prevention program. Contributes to arts, hunger, AIDS, education, and domestic violence prevention programs. Has a written nondiscrimination policy covering sexual orientation but not gender identity. Offers insurance coverage to employees' domestic partners.

American Crystal Sugar
Contributions: TOTAL: *$1,954,150*   DEM: *$1,255,900*   REP: *$698,250*
LOBBY SPENDING: *$1,315,955*

In 2008, a chemical spill at its Hillsboro, ND, factory allowed sulfur dioxide to escape into the atmosphere. Investments have been made in water treatment, odor elimination, and air pollution reduction.

Anheuser-Busch Companies, Inc.
Contributions: TOTAL: *$2,076,688*   DEM: *$1,172,888*   REP: *$903,800*
LOBBY SPENDING: *$6,900,000*

Foreign owned. In 2008, acquired by Belgian brewer InBev, now Anheuser-Busch InBev. Named as a defendant with several other beer companies in class actions alleging that its marketing of alcoholic beverages to underage consumers causes human suffering and economic injuries. In 2008, scored 50 out of 100 on "The Climate Counts Company Scorecard Report." Its 12 U.S. breweries recycle or reuse more than 99% of their solid waste. Says it will brew one in seven beers using alternative fuels by 2010. Founding member of the Wildlife Habitat Council, which has certified 10 of its facilities as "Wildlife at Work" for projects that help create a healthy natural world. Supports education, health care, human services, minority leadership and economic development, cultural enrichment, and environmental conservation. Has invested more than $750 million to promote responsible drinking. Has a written nondiscrimination policy covering sexual orientation and gender identity. Offers insurance coverage to employees' domestic partners. Insurance for transgender employees is offered, and some treatment is covered.

Bacardi Limited
Contributions: TOTAL: *$124,701*   DEM: *$13,250*   REP: *$111,451*
LOBBY SPENDING: *$1,270,000*

In 2008, paid $550,000 and agreed to donate and preserve land valued at $1 million after violating the federal Clean Water Act. Indicted on charges of allegedly making an illegal $20,000 campaign contribution to the PAC founded by Republican Tom DeLay. The DeLay-Bacardi connection seems to be strengthened by the "Bacardi bill," which would give Bacardi the rights to the Havana Club label in the United States. Bacardi has been named, with other alcohol producers, in several suits for encouraging alcohol consumption by minors. Outreach includes the Century Council.

Bacardi U.S.A., Inc.

11%   89%

Contributions: TOTAL: *$113,000*   DEM: *$12,250*   REP: *$100,750*
LOBBY SPENDING: *$1,270,000*

Privately held. Subsidiary of Bacardi Limited. Member of the Distilled Spirits Council, a trade group that lobbies against restrictions on alcohol sales and contributes primarily to Republican campaigns. Named in various lawsuits filed by watchdog groups and consumer attorneys claiming alcohol producers market to minors.

Beam Global Spirits & Wine, Inc.

73%   27%

Contributions: TOTAL: *$8,250*   DEM: *$6,000*   REP: *$2,250*
LOBBY SPENDING: *$605,000*

Subsidiary of Fortune Brands, Inc. Named with other alcohol producers in several suits for encouraging alcohol consumption by minors. Member of the Distilled Spirits Council, a trade group that lobbies against restrictions on alcohol sales and contributes primarily to Republican campaigns. Outreach includes the Century Council. Supports local service agencies, medical research, hunger cessation, and environmental preservation.

Ben & Jerry's Homemade, Inc.

100%   0%

Contributions: TOTAL: *$23,450*   DEM: *$23,450*   REP: *$0*
LOBBY SPENDING: *$0*

Subsidiary of Unilever N.V. Offers Fair Trade Certified™ vanilla, chocolate, and coffee flavors. Works with Certified Humane Cage-Free egg suppliers. Invests in renewable energy, carbon offsets, and efficiency projects in its manufacturing plants. For the sixth year in a row, offset all 5,140 tons of carbon emissions created in its Vermont manufacturing operations through renewable energy credits. Offers employees paid time off for community service projects and a $1,000 hybrid automobile purchase incentive. Supports projects and groups that promote positive social and environmental change. In 2007, sponsored a resolution calling for the use of economic sanctions and diplomatic pressure to protect the people of Darfur. Offers insurance coverage to employees' domestic partners.

Best Brands Corporation

83%   17%

Contributions: TOTAL: *$4,200*   DEM: *$3,500*   REP: *$700*
LOBBY SPENDING: *$0*

Subsidiary of Value Creation Partners, Inc.

Birds Eye Foods, Inc.

0%   100%

Contributions: TOTAL: *$1,251*   DEM: *$0*   REP: *$1,251*
LOBBY SPENDING: *$0*

Subsidiary of Vestar Capital Partners LP. The Birds Eye brand is represented in the United Kingdom by the private equity firm Permira.

BI-LO, LLC
Contributions: TOTAL: *$200*   DEM: *$200*   REP: *$0*
LOBBY SPENDING: *$0*

100%   0%

Subsidiary of Lone Star Funds. Supports education, hunger relief, and children's services.

Boston Beer Company, Inc., The
Contributions: TOTAL: *$10,150*   DEM: *$7,900*   REP: *$2,250*
LOBBY SPENDING: *$10,000*

78%   22%

The company's most notable brand is its Samuel Adams line of beers. Named as a defendant with several other beer companies in class actions alleging that marketing of alcoholic beverages to underage consumers causes human suffering and economic injuries.

Brown-Forman Corporation
Contributions: TOTAL: *$528,295*   DEM: *$306,195*   REP: *$222,100*
LOBBY SPENDING: *$690,000*

58%   42%

Member of the Distilled Spirits Council, a trade group that lobbies against restrictions on alcohol sales and contributes primarily to Republican campaigns. Its Fetzer Vineyards subsidiary is certified organic. Company distilleries claim to follow strict environmental procedures, though they continue to be cited for excessive emissions. Has a third-party verified greenhouse gas inventory showing a 10% reduction in emissions for its U.S. and Canadian operations between 2005 and 2007. Has implemented several water preservation and conservation projects. Outreach includes the Century Council, of which it is a founding member. Supports agricultural scholarships, child protective services, and school gardening and composting projects in Sonoma County. Supports the educational system, social service agencies, and the arts in Louisville, KY.

Bumble Bee Foods, LLC
Contributions: TOTAL: *$11,500*   DEM: *$6,250*   REP: *$5,250*
LOBBY SPENDING: *$165,000*

54%   46%

Privately held. Subsidiary of Centre Partners Management, LLC. Fended off California's appeal to have mercury warnings placed on tuna can labels. Outreach includes breast cancer awareness and hunger relief efforts.

Cadbury PLC
Contributions: TOTAL: *$6,008*   DEM: *$1,458*   REP: *$4,550*
LOBBY SPENDING: *$100,000*

24%   76%

Foreign owned. Implemented a strict code of conduct for operations, including human and labor rights initiatives, after several lawsuits. Fined for violations of sanctions for exports to Sudan. Engaged in a pilot program to provide advice to help farmers reduce carbon emissions from milk production. Foundation supports education, health and welfare, and environmental sustainability projects. Founded Africa Aid to support education, capacity building, and sustainable environmental practices and to assist children orphaned by HIV/AIDS. Has a written nondiscrimination policy covering sexual orientation but not gender identity. Does not offer insurance coverage to employees' domestic partners.

Campbell Soup Company

41%   59%

Contributions: Total: *$82,101*   Dem: *$33,907*   Rep: *$48,194*
Lobby Spending: *$104,484*

In 2009, signed the United Nations Global Compact. In 2008, ranked second (behind Google) on the Corporate Social Responsibility Index 50, a list of the most socially responsible companies in the United States as judged by consumers. In 2008, subsidiary Pepperidge Farm joined with FuelCell Energy, Inc., and Connecticut Clean Energy Fund to open the country's largest fuel cell power plant at its Bloomfield, CT, bakery. Foundation supports educational, cultural, and residential projects that promote sustainable development. Supports breast cancer research, education, screening, and treatment. Has a written nondiscrimination policy covering sexual orientation and gender identity. Offers insurance coverage to employees' domestic partners. Insurance for transgender employees is offered, and treatment is covered.

Cargill, Inc.

29%   71%

Contributions: Total: *$342,392*   Dem: *$98,517*   Rep: *$243,875*
Lobby Spending: *$2,060,219*

Largest privately held firm in the United States. *Multinational Monitor* named Cargill, Inc., one of the "10 Worst Corporations" of 2008. Operates 13 silos in the Amazon rainforest and is the leading soy producer and exporter in the region. In 2006, Greenpeace activists shut down its main European soybeans export facility in the Amazon, which was operating illegally. Sued with other large poultry producers for alleged CERCLA violations. Paid $24 million in a class action settlement for allegedly fixing the price of corn-based sweeteners. Paid $7.7 million in one suit and over $400,000 in another suit for allegedly misrepresenting animal feed. Poses a threat to farmers by pushing its genetically modified products onto the market, aggressively seeking patents for its seeds, and suing farmers that unknowingly cultivate Cargill-patented products. Has tried to "green" its image with NatureWorks PLA, a biodegradable synthetic material that uses a corn base instead of petroleum, but does not publicize the fact that the corn base is genetically modified. Supports higher education, housing, food, and environmental stewardship. Has a written nondiscrimination policy covering sexual orientation and gender identity. Offers health insurance coverage to employees' domestic partners. Insurance for transgender employees is offered, and some treatment is covered.

Cargill Meat Solutions Corporation

44%   56%

Contributions: Total: *$2,250*   Dem: *$1,000*   Rep: *$1,250*
Lobby Spending: *$0*

Subsidiary of Cargill, Inc. Subsidiary Excel Corp. is a major supplier of irradiated meat products. Stated that Congress must provide employers better tools to enforce immigration and that its intent is to hire only those people who have the legal right to be in the United States. In 2008, donated $1 million to the office of diversity and dual career development at Kansas State University to establish the Cargill Project Impact Diversity Partnership. Encourages supplier diversity. Has a written nondiscrimination policy covering sexual orientation and gender identity. Offers health insurance coverage to employees' domestic partners. Insurance for transgender employees is offered, and some treatment is covered.

Caribou Coffee Company, Inc.
Contributions: Total: *$14,600*   Dem: *$13,600*   Rep: *$1,000*
Lobby Spending: *$0*

93% | 7%

Bahrain-based investment group Arcapita owns 60% of Caribou Coffee. The goal of this Fair Trade–certified company is to have 50% (three times the industry rate) of its coffees Rainforest Alliance Certified™. Offers organic blends. Supports environmental stewardship, medical, and educational programs in coffee-producing communities. Focuses charitable efforts on breast cancer, children's literacy programs, and the environment.

Chiquita Brands International, Inc.
Contributions: Total: *$4,000*   Dem: *$0*   Rep: *$4,000*
Lobby Spending: *$290,000*

0% | 100%

In 2007, Chiquita Brands pleaded guilty to doing business with a terrorist organization and agreed to pay a $25 million fine. Cited for operating in Colombia in a way that threatens unionized workers, restricts organized labor, and violates basic rights. Accused of using pesticides banned in the United States, exposing thousands of banana pickers in Central America to known toxins. Several lawsuits were filed after over 200 people became ill with an E. coli infection from eating Chiquita's bagged fresh spinach. Three of the lawsuits were settled in April 2007, more than 90 are pending. In 2007, in response to the spinach recall, subsidiary Fresh Express voluntarily provided $2 million to fund research to help the fresh-cut produce industry prevent E. coli contamination. Recycles 100% of the plastic bags and twine used on its farms. Has cut pesticide use by 26% and provides better protective gear for workers. Promotes nature conservation awareness and creates new sources of income for people in Costa Rica. Outreach focuses on programs and organizations that support the health and well-being of the communities where its employees live and work. Provides assistance following major disasters. Has a written nondiscrimination policy covering sexual orientation but not gender identity.

Chocoladefabriken Lindt & Sprüngli AG
Contributions: Total: *$4,950*   Dem: *$2,650*   Rep: *$2,300*
Lobby Spending: *$0*

54% | 46%

Foreign owned. Supports autism advocacy organization, Autism Speaks.

Clif Bar, Inc.
Contributions: Total: *$3,800*   Dem: *$3,800*   Rep: *$0*
Lobby Spending: *$0*

100% | 0%

Company uses fair-trade and organic ingredients as well as environmentally sound production processes. Plants trees with American Forests, and several of its farmers use wind turbines. Helps organizations and individuals earn money for charity by collecting used wrappers and shipping them for free to TerraCycle, which weaves the wrappers into a material from which eco-chic products are made. Donates 2 cents for each wrapper to a nonprofit of the collector's choice. Provides mind-body enrichment opportunities to employees and encourages volunteerism. Has eco-friendly commuting program for employees. Supports environmental stewardship and breast cancer prevention.

Coca-Cola Enterprises, Inc.

40% ▬▬▬▬▬ 60%

Contributions: TOTAL: *$286,074*   DEM: *$114,624*   REP: *$171,450*
LOBBY SPENDING: *$419,000*

It's many alleged abuses include use of paramilitary groups to kill union activists in South America, major environmental offenses at its plants in India, and promotion of child labor in El Salvador. Two international water rights campaigns have targeted it for high-volume pumping in areas facing extreme shortages of potable water. Ranked 9th on DiversityInc's list of the "Top 50 Companies for Diversity" in 2009. In 2008, scored 61 out of 100 in "The Climate Counts Company Scorecard Report." In 2009, introduced a bottle made from a recyclable plant-based plastic. Working toward recycling the equivalent of 100% of its packaging. Has the largest fleet of hybrid electric delivery trucks in North America. In 2009, committed $30 million to provide access to safe drinking water to communities throughout Africa. Has made efforts to expand AIDS treatment to workers at its African bottling plants. Supports youth development and education, environmental conservation, and community and economic development. Has a written nondiscrimination policy covering sexual orientation and gender identity. Offers health insurance coverage to employees' domestic partners. Insurance for transgender employees is offered, and treatment is covered.

ConAgra Foods, Inc.

20% ▬▬▬▬▬ 80%

Contributions: TOTAL: *$182,610*   DEM: *$37,210*   REP: *$145,400*
LOBBY SPENDING: *$335,000*

Voluntarily recalled all its peanut butter products in 2007 after an outbreak of salmonella. Found guilty of health code violations and bacterial contaminations at its food processing facilities, which in some cases have been linked to deaths. Has had significant problems with regard to factory farming, consumer health and safety, and genetic engineering. Sued for negligence by former workers with a severe obstructive lung disease due to chronic exposure to diacetyl. Pleaded guilty and paid a criminal fine for violating the Clean Water Act. In 2008, scored 21 out of 100 in "The Climate Counts Company Scorecard Report." Supports hunger cessation, disaster relief, and food safety programs. Has a written nondiscrimination policy covering sexual orientation and gender identity. Offers insurance coverage to employees' domestic partners.

Constellation Brands, Inc.

60% ▬▬▬▬▬ 40%

Contributions: TOTAL: *$227,060*   DEM: *$135,260*   REP: *$91,800*
LOBBY SPENDING: *$0*

Member of the Century Council. Installed a solar-powered energy plant at a winery in California in 2009. Studying ways of reducing air emissions and treating wastewater in various parts of the world. Exploring new uses for wine-making byproducts, such as nutraceuticals made from grape seeds and skins. Supports breast cancer research, zoos, African wildlife, preservation of American beaches, and reforestation.

Also supports the arts, education, health, and specific needs of communities where it conducts business.

Cott Corporation
Contributions: TOTAL: *$1,301*   DEM: *$0*   REP: *$1,301*
LOBBY SPENDING: *$0*

0% — 100%

In 2009, Wal-Mart Stores ended the soft-drink maker's exclusive supply agreement in the United States.

Cumberland Packing Corp.
Contributions: TOTAL: *$28,500*   DEM: *$28,500*   REP: *$0*
LOBBY SPENDING: *$0*

100% — 0%

Its artificial butter flavorings are suspected of being the cause of popcorn worker's lung.

Dairy Farmers of America, Inc.
Contributions: TOTAL: *$1,008,950*   DEM: *$523,950*   REP: *$485,000*
LOBBY SPENDING: *$2,384,000*

52% — 48%

Privately held. In 2009, a number of dairy farmers filed a class action lawsuit alleging millions have been stolen through the filing of false nonfat dry milk prices with the USDA. In 2008, ordered to pay $12 million in fines and amend its trading practices to settle a federal investigation into a possible price manipulation scheme. Awards scholarships.

Dannon Company, Inc., The
Contributions: TOTAL: *$1,000*   DEM: *$500*   REP: *$500*
LOBBY SPENDING: *$0*

50% — 50%

Subsidiary of foreign-owned Groupe Danone. Subject of a federal lawsuit filed in 2008; the proposed class action accuses the company of lying in advertisements about the "clinically proven" ability of Activia, Activia Lite, and DanActive to regulate digestion or improve the body's immune system. The FTC fined it $15,000 for falsely implying that some flavors in its Pure Indulgence frozen yogurt line were low in fat and calories. Named as a defendant in a lawsuit alleging that the dairy industry and several food companies are falsely marketing dairy consumption as a way to lose weight. No longer uses milk from cows injected with BGH. Meets or exceeds the regulatory standards of all federal, state, and local environmental agencies. Annually awards a $30,000 grant to each of four programs nurturing healthy eating habits among children.

Davide Campari-Milano S.p.A.
Contributions: TOTAL: *$4,600*   DEM: *$0*   REP: *$4,600*
LOBBY SPENDING: *$0*

0% — 100%

Foreign owned. Italian distributor for Brown-Forman Corporation's spirit portfolio. Member of various organizations that promote responsible drinking programs and education.

Dean Foods Company
Contributions: TOTAL: *$643,075*   DEM: *$245,725*   REP: *$397,350*
LOBBY SPENDING: *$1,414,000*

38% — 62%

Exposed for country-of-origin labeling violations on its Birds Eye Foods, Inc., brand. Subject of concerns regarding discrimination, transparency, price-fixing, and monopoly of the dairy market. Although Dean

Foods owns Horizon Organic, it does not guarantee hormone-free and antibiotic-free products under its other brand names. Supports health/nutrition, education, and environmental stewardship and conservation. Has a written nondiscrimination policy covering sexual orientation but not gender identity. Offers insurance coverage to employees' domestic partners. Insurance for transgender employees is offered, and treatment is covered.

Dean's Beans Organic Coffee Company

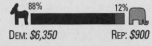

Contributions: TOTAL: *$2,000*   DEM: *$2,000*   REP: *$0*
LOBBY SPENDING: *$0*

All its whole bean coffees are certified organic, Fair Trade, and kosher. Uses recyclable bags for most orders and reusable buckets for all deliveries. Has installed solar panels on its beanery's roof. A partner in CHICA, a Guatemalan indigenous girls' empowerment organization. Supports micro-credit, health care, and reforestation projects and projects to keep indigenous communities intact.

Del Monte Foods Company

Contributions: TOTAL: *$7,250*   DEM: *$6,350*   REP: *$900*
LOBBY SPENDING: *$238,000*

Its record is marred by many charges of human rights violations. One of several defendants in a pending lawsuit alleging false and misleading marketing statements regarding the contents of pet food. A member of Coalition to Advance Healthcare Reform, a lobby aimed at mandating health insurance. Played a major role in revitalizing the historical waterfront area of San Francisco. Supports the American Heart Association, Animal Friends, and several food banks and hunger relief organizations. Has a written nondiscrimination policy covering sexual orientation but not gender identity. Offers insurance coverage to employees' domestic partners.

Delhaize America, Inc.

Contributions: TOTAL: *$0*   DEM: *$0*   REP: *$0*
LOBBY SPENDING: *$180,000*

Subsidiary of Delhaize Group. Pending class action lawsuit seeking more than $5 million for the alleged theft of customers' personal information from subsidiary Hannaford Bros. Co.

Delhaize Group

Contributions: TOTAL: *$60,800*   DEM: *$19,450*   REP: *$41,350*
LOBBY SPENDING: *$180,000*

Delhaize Belgium achieved its target of keeping its energy use at 2003 levels, in spite of square footage growth. Supports hunger cessation, health care, and education.

Diageo Chateau & Estate Wines Company, The

Contributions: TOTAL: *$500*   DEM: *$500*   REP: *$0*
LOBBY SPENDING: *$0*

Subsidiary of Diageo PLC.

Diageo North America

67%   33%

Contributions: TOTAL: *$197,112*   DEM: *$132,128*   REP: *$64,984*
LOBBY SPENDING: *$3,420,000*

Subsidiary of Diageo PLC. In 2008, the Alcohol and Tobacco Tax and Trade Bureau accepted $100,000 to resolve alleged violations of the Internal Revenue Code. Diageo North America and other alcohol producers and distributors were sued by the Colombian government and several regional authorities for alleged unfair competition, racketeering, kickbacks, and money laundering. Member of the Distilled Spirits Council, a trade group that lobbies against restrictions on alcohol sales and that contributes primarily to Republican campaigns. Turns charcoal from vodka production and berries and seeds from gin production into fertilizer for one facility's 30-acre farm. Has a written nondiscrimination policy covering sexual orientation and gender identity. Offers insurance coverage to employees' domestic partners. Insurance for transgender employees is offered, and treatment is covered.

Diageo PLC

67%   33%

Contributions: TOTAL: *$197,612*   DEM: *$132,628*   REP: *$64,984*
LOBBY SPENDING: *$3,500,000*

Foreign owned. Settled a class action suit alleging its advertising campaigns were targeting juvenile consumers. Named in various lawsuits filed by watchdog groups and consumer attorneys claiming alcohol producers market to minors. Member of the Century Council. Part of a joint venture in a bioenergy facility in Scotland. Two bottling facilities convert municipal solid waste into power and steam instead of sending it to a landfill. Participant in the EPA's SmartWay program. Foundation supports (with more than $34 million annually) responsible drinking programs, microenterprise development, environmental conservation, disaster relief, and access to clean drinking water.

Dole Food Company, Inc.

12%   88%

Contributions: TOTAL: *$42,845*   DEM: *$5,100*   REP: *$37,745*
LOBBY SPENDING: *$375,000*

Multinational Monitor named Dole one of the "10 Worst Corporations" of 2008, the same year that it was named one of the "World's Most Ethical Companies" by *Ethisphere Magazine,* a national publication of the think tank Ethisphere. In 2008, fined $58.4 million by the European Commission for its role in a price-fixing cartel. In 2007, ordered to pay $2.5 million in punitive damages to five Nicaraguan workers exposed to the pesticide DBCP in the 1970s. Paid $1 million to settle a class action suit brought by employees who were not given proper notification of a plant closing in California. Uses organic farming methods for banana production in Peru. Banana waste from its facility in Stockholm is used to produce biogas, which is mainly used for vehicle fuel. Recycles plastic in Colombia at Recicla, a microfinance company partially funded by Dole and owned and operated by 60 mothers and their dependents. Supports environmental stewardship and social, educational, and cultural programs in the countries in which it operates. Has a written nondiscrimination policy covering sexual orientation but not gender identity. Offers insurance coverage to employees' domestic partners.

Dreyer's Grand Ice Cream Holdings, Inc.

4% 96%

Contributions: TOTAL: *$134,400*   DEM: *$6,000*   REP: *$128,400*
LOBBY SPENDING: *$0*

Supports educational and family causes in communities where it has a presence. Provides a bus free of charge to nonprofit groups and schools within a 60-mile radius of Pleasanton, CA. Employees who volunteer at least eight hours per month may request a $200 donation for the organization from the Dreyer's Foundation. Offers insurance coverage to employees' domestic partners.

Dr Pepper Snapple Group, Inc.

80% 20%

Contributions: TOTAL: *$3,800*   DEM: *$3,050*   REP: *$750*
LOBBY SPENDING: *<$40,000*

Formerly Cadbury Schweppes Americas Beverages. In a 2006 report by the Container Recycling Institute and As You Sow, Cadbury Schweppes earned an F in every area surveyed: use of recycled content, increases in recovery and recycling, and reduction of material used in beverage containers. Is replacing its coolers and vending machines with Energy Star–rated equipment. In many plants, is replacing empty package water rinsers with air rinsers, saving approximately 10,000 gallons per line per day at each site. In 2008, it introduced a reduced-weight two-liter bottle, eliminating more than 1 million pounds of plastic each year. Gives employees one paid day off per year to volunteer. Has donated to the Muscular Dystrophy Association, the Hispanic Heritage Foundation, the American Diabetes Association, and the Juvenile Diabetes Research Foundation. Has a written nondiscrimination policy covering sexual orientation but not gender identity. Does not offer insurance coverage to employees' domestic partners.

Dunkin' Brands, Inc.

32% 68%

Contributions: TOTAL: *$85,250*   DEM: *$27,650*   REP: *$57,600*
LOBBY SPENDING: *$390,000*

Owned by a group of private investment firms, including Bain Capital, the Carlyle Group, and Thomas H. Lee Partners. In 2008, began to assess the impact of its business on the environment in order to set measurable goals for improvement. Foundation supports emergency response organizations. Foundation has donated more than $1.9 million to organizations that support U.S. soldiers, hunger relief, and police and firefighters. Has a written nondiscrimination policy covering sexual orientation but not gender identity. Offers insurance coverage to employees' domestic partners.

E. & J. Gallo Winery

92% 8%

Contributions: TOTAL: *$327,587*   DEM: *$302,084*   REP: *$25,503*
LOBBY SPENDING: *$100,000*

For every acre of land planted in vineyard, one acre of property is set aside for wildlife habitat. Supports education, arts, and causes in its local community. Has a written nondiscrimination policy covering sexual orientation but not gender identity.

Energy Brands, Inc.

100% 0%

Contributions: TOTAL: *$1,000*   DEM: *$1,000*   REP: *$0*
LOBBY SPENDING: *$0*

Also known as Glacéau. Subsidiary of Coca-Cola. In a class action lawsuit filed in 2009, accused of making deceptive health claims about its Vitamin Water line of beverages.

FIJI Water Company LLC
100% | 0%
Contributions: TOTAL: *$500*   DEM: *$500*   REP: *$0*
LOBBY SPENDING: *$0*
Subsidiary of Roll Corporation. Partnered with Conservation International to become the first "carbon negative" company in its industry and to save the largest rainforest in Fiji. Is reducing its packaging and expanding recycling programs and incentives. Has taken direct responsibility for providing water access to the villages that surround the water source it uses. Built schools in local villages and provides teacher training and educational materials. Outreach includes disaster relief, environmental conservation, medical research, hunger cessation, and the arts. Foundation supports education access and development, infrastructure development, and health and sanitation development.

Florida's Natural Growers
10% | 90%
Contributions: TOTAL: *$2,550*   DEM: *$250*   REP: *$2,300*
LOBBY SPENDING: *$0*
Subsidiary of Citrus World, Inc. Privately held. Solar panels atop the Grove House Visitors Center collect solar energy to provide 30% of the center's power. In the plant, on-site co-generators burn natural gas.

Food 4 Less of Southern California, Inc.
3% | 97%
Contributions: TOTAL: *$36,000*   DEM: *$1,000*   REP: *$35,000*
LOBBY SPENDING: *$0*
Subsidiary of The Kroger Co. Donated food, water, and other supplies to firefighters and evacuees during wildfires in Southern California in 2007. Also donated to the American Red Cross Wildfire Relief Fund.

Food Lion, LLC
34% | 66%
Contributions: TOTAL: *$49,950*   DEM: *$17,200*   REP: *$32,750*
LOBBY SPENDING: *$180,000*
Subsidiary of Delhaize America, Inc.; parent, Delhaize Group. Has 400 stores labeled Energy Star stores, half of the total number of Energy Star stores in the United States. Has a cardboard recycling program. Has raised over $19 million for Easter Seals. Raised over $3.7 million for Children's Miracle Network hospitals. Outreach also includes support for hunger cessation, education, and other nonprofits. Has a written nondiscrimination policy covering sexual orientation and gender identity. Offers insurance coverage to employees' domestic partners. Limited insurance for transgender employees is offered, but treatment is not covered.

Fortune Brands, Inc.
58% | 42%
Contributions: TOTAL: *$124,429*   DEM: *$72,580*   REP: *$51,849*
LOBBY SPENDING: *$725,000*
Accused, with other alcohol producers, in several class action suits of encouraging and profiting from underage alcohol use. Has environmental stewardship and conservation programs throughout its production

facilities. Supports education and social causes in communities where it has a presence. Has a written nondiscrimination policy covering sexual orientation but not gender identity.

Fred Meyer Stores, Inc.
Contributions: Total: *$7,327*   Dem: *$770*   Rep: *$6,557*
Lobby Spending: *$0*
Subsidiary of The Kroger Co.

11% | 89%

Frito-Lay, Inc.
Contributions: Total: *$5,201*   Dem: *$3,850*   Rep: *$1,351*
Lobby Spending: *$80,000*

74% | 26%

Subsidiary of PepsiCo, Inc. Paid $1.5 million in fines and legal costs in 2008 to settle a lawsuit for not posting warnings of cancer-causing chemicals in its products. In addition, it agreed to reduce the amount of acrylamide in its chips by about 20% over three years. Paid OSHA $57,000 in fines following the drowning death of an employee. Uses renewable energy and recycles heat and steam from its plants. Is working to reduce its level of energy use per bag of chips to 45% less than its 1999 level by 2017. In 2007, used 1 billion gallons less water to make potato chips than it did in 1999. Participates in the EPA's SmartWay program. In 2008, SunChips brand committed $1 million dollars to support the economic infrastructure of Greensburg, KS. Has a written nondiscrimination policy covering sexual orientation and gender identity. Offers insurance coverage to employees' domestic partners. Insurance for transgender employees is offered, and some treatment is covered.

Fry's Food & Drug Stores
Contributions: Total: *$1,000*   Dem: *$750*   Rep: *$250*
Lobby Spending: *$0*

75% | 25%

Subsidiary of The Kroger Co. Settled a RICO violations lawsuit for $5.1 million. Has a written nondiscrimination policy covering sexual orientation but not gender identity. Offers insurance coverage to employees' domestic partners.

General Mills, Inc.
Contributions: Total: *$411,827*   Dem: *$212,112*   Rep: *$199,715*
Lobby Spending: *$1,534,300*

52% | 48%

Many of its products contain genetically modified ingredients. Has fought efforts to require that such foods be labeled. As a member of the Grocery Manufacturers of America, a powerful lobbying group, General Mills spends millions to influence governmental diet recommendations and other food issues. Pending lawsuit brought by workers exposed to artificial butter flavorings, which are suspected of causing a lung disease. Committed to the use of whole grains in all of its cereals. Is investing $2 million to create 150 jobs at Siyeza, Inc., a company offering ownership stake opportunities to employees. Ranked 99th on *Fortune* magazine's "100 Best Companies to Work For" in 2009. Ranked 47th on DiversityInc's list of the "Top 50 Companies for Diversity" in 2009. Listed by NAFE as one of the top 50 companies for female executives in 2009. In 2008, scored 39 out of 100 on "The Climate Counts Company Scorecard Report." Has partnered with the NIH to raise awareness of heart disease in women. Has provided more than 5 million free books inside cereal boxes. Donates to breast cancer research, hunger cessation, rural businesses, and education. Donated $5 million for sustainable agricultural development in Malawi and Tanzania. Has a written nondiscrimination policy that covers sexual orientation and gender identity. Offers insurance coverage to employees' domestic partners. Insurance for transgender employees is offered, but treatment is not covered.

Ghirardelli Chocolate Company

54%   48%

Contributions: TOTAL: *$4,950* DEM: *$2,650* REP: *$2,300*
LOBBY SPENDING: *$0*
Subsidiary of Chocoladefabriken Lindt & Sprüngli AG.

Giant Food Stores LLC

28%   72%

Contributions: TOTAL: *$1,816* DEM: *$500* REP: *$1,316*
LOBBY SPENDING: *$0*
Subsidiary of Ahold USA, Inc.; parent, Royal Ahold N.V. Offers natural, organic, and locally grown products. Collects customers' plastic bags to be recycled into park benches and recycles its cardboard boxes. Delivery trucks are programmed with anti-idling mechanisms. Supports health and wellness, hunger cessation, and multicultural educational events. Has a written nondiscrimination policy covering sexual orientation and gender identity. Offers insurance coverage to employees' domestic partners.

Godiva Chocolatier, Inc.

100%   0%

Contributions: TOTAL: *$6,900* DEM: *$6,900* REP: *$0*
LOBBY SPENDING: *$0*
Foreign-owned subsidiary of Yildiz Holding AS in Turkey.

Gorton's

100%   0%

Contributions: TOTAL: *$200* DEM: *$200* REP: *$0*
LOBBY SPENDING: *$0*
Subsidiary of Nippon Suisan (USA); parent, Japan's Nippon Suisan Kaisha Ltd. Purchases from environmentally responsible suppliers and has eliminated unsustainable products. Installed energy-efficient lighting, reducing electricity use. Reduced water use by 8 million gallons a year. Increased use of rail freight, reducing greenhouse gas emissions. Has a written nondiscrimination policy covering sexual orientation but not gender identity.

Goya Foods, Inc.

68%   32%

Contributions: TOTAL: *$9,500* DEM: *$6,500* REP: *$3,000*
LOBBY SPENDING: *$0*
Was issued a warning by the FDA for false and misleading labeling. Found guilty of 40 unfair labor practices. Said it would never recognize or bargain with a union. The employees voted to unionize and are represented by UNITE HERE. After 10 years of decisions by the circuit courts in favor of the employees, the NLRB still can't bring Goya to the bargaining table. Supports Hispanic culture, community building, leadership, and families and children in need.

Great Atlantic & Pacific Tea Company, Inc., The (A&P)

Contributions: TOTAL: *$17,667*　DEM: *$16,867*　REP: *$800*
LOBBY SPENDING: *$30,000*

Subsidiary of Tengelmann Warenhandelsgesellschaft KG (Germany). Named with other New York grocers in several class action lawsuits for FLSA violations. Settled one of the lawsuits for $3.1 million. One of four supermarket chains in New York City sued by the Legal Action Center for allegedly discriminating against homeless people by refusing to redeem their bottles and cans. Pending lawsuit alleges ADEA violations. Installing energy-efficient lighting in its stores. Recycles 100,000 tons of cardboard a year and gives customers a cash credit for using reusable bags. Supports education, community building, and children's health and welfare.

Green Mountain Coffee Roasters, Inc.

Contributions: TOTAL: *$61,000*　DEM: *$57,750*　REP: *$3,250*
LOBBY SPENDING: *$0*

Sells some Fair Trade Certified™ coffees. Grants 100 stock options to all full-time employees after their first year of employment. Offers training in financial literacy. Is awarding $800,000 in grants to nonprofits to find solutions to climate change. Was commended for the design and efficiency of its "green" roasting facility in Vermont. Cut its normalized solid waste stream by 11% by composting. Has installed a biodiesel fueling station for its Waterbury, VT, fleet. Total outreach to local and coffee-growing communities is over $1.1 million through grant making, volunteerism, and product donations. Each year, donates at least 5% of its pre-tax profits to social and environmental projects. Has a written nondiscrimination policy covering sexual orientation but not gender identity. Offers insurance coverage to employees' domestic partners.

Hain Celestial Group

Contributions: TOTAL: *$39,950*　DEM: *$39,950*　REP: *$0*
LOBBY SPENDING: *$0*

Makes products with ingredients that are grown without artificial pesticides, fertilizers, or chemicals. Has an extremely strict supplier verification program. Offers insurance coverage to employees' domestic partners. Limited insurance for transgender employees is offered, and some treatment is covered.

Hannaford Bros. Co.

Contributions: TOTAL: *$10,100*　DEM: *$2,000*　REP: *$8,100*
LOBBY SPENDING: *$0*

Subsidiary of Delhaize America, Inc.; parent, Delhaize Group. A pending lawsuit alleges failure to maintain the security of customers' confidential financial and personal data. Recycles more than 60% of all its waste. More than 40% of its stores recycle organic material. Through a business partnership, used plastic pails and pill bottles are recycled to produce decking boards. Implemented energy reduction measures and became an Energy Star partner with the EPA. Four Hannaford supermarkets use renewable energy from rooftop solar panels. Hannaford Trucking is a partner in the EPA's SmartWay program. Outreach includes environmental stewardship, health care, hunger cessation, and educational programs. Has a written nondiscrimination policy covering sexual orientation and gender identity. Offers insurance coverage to employees' domestic partners. Insurance for transgender employees is offered, but treatment is not covered.

H. E. Butt Grocery Company (H-E-B)

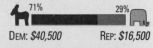
45%   55%

Contributions: TOTAL: *$21,400*   DEM: *$9,650*   REP: *$11,750*
LOBBY SPENDING: *$0*

In 2009, its regional vice president was elected chair of the United Negro College Fund's Leadership Advisory Council. Recycles aluminum, steel, plastic, oil, cardboard, and computers. Saves 6.2 million gallons of water each year by reusing condensation from manufacturing steam equipment. Charter partner in the EPA's SmartWay program. Supports education and hunger cessation. Has a written nondiscrimination policy covering sexual orientation but not gender identity. Offers insurance coverage to employees' domestic partners. Limited insurance for transgender employees is offered, but treatment is not covered.

Heineken N.V.

100%   0%

Contributions: TOTAL: *$1,450*   DEM: *$1,450*   REP: *$0*
LOBBY SPENDING: *$0*

Subsidiary of L'Arche Holding SA. Named with other alcohol producers in several suits for encouraging alcohol consumption by minors. Operates clinics with its own doctors and nurses to provide medical aid for its employees in sub-Saharan Africa. Also offers preventive items such as bednets and condoms. Environmental goals include a 15% reduction in energy use by 2010 and installation of 16 wastewater treatment plants in Africa and the Middle East by 2012. Supports HIV/AIDS education.

Heineken USA, Inc.

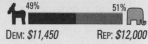
71%   29%

Contributions: TOTAL: *$57,000*   DEM: *$40,500*   REP: *$16,500*
LOBBY SPENDING: *$280,000*

Subsidiary of Heineken N.V. Supports the National Multiple Sclerosis Society, the American Diabetes Association, the Muscular Dystrophy Association, the New Orleans Musicians Clinic, and HIV/AIDS education. Offers disaster relief funding. Donates money to organizations for which employees volunteer. Has a written nondiscrimination policy covering sexual orientation but not gender identity. Offers insurance coverage to employees' domestic partners.

Hershey Foods Corporation

49%   51%

Contributions: TOTAL: *$23,450*   DEM: *$11,450*   REP: *$12,000*
LOBBY SPENDING: *$880,000*

A pending lawsuit alleges price-fixing. Sources cocoa from plantations that employ slave labor and trafficked child labor. Has agreed to work toward ending illegal child labor on cocoa farms vis-à-vis the voluntary Harkin-Engel Protocol. However, the protocol expired in 2005, and the chocolate industry failed to develop a system to certify that its products are sourced without the use of forced child labor. Paid an $85,000 settlement to the FTC for violations of the Children's Online Privacy Protection Act. Provides subsidized in-house child care, flextime, telecommuting, job-share options, and extensive family leave. Environmental outreach includes resource conservation, emissions reduction, recycling, and waste reduction. Supports the Chesapeake Bay Foundation, the Pennsylvania Resource Council Lens on Litter Program, and the Pennsylvania Envirothon. Outreach includes child welfare, health and human services, education, and diversity efforts. Has a written nondiscrimination policy covering sexual orientation and gender identity. Offers insurance coverage only to employees' opposite-sex domestic partners. Insurance for transgender employees is offered, but treatment is not covered.

H. J. Heinz Company

44% | 56%

Contributions: TOTAL: *$196,478*   DEM: *$86,228*   REP: *$110,250*
LOBBY SPENDING: *$200,000*

Pending lawsuit brought for its failure to post warnings of cancer-causing chemicals in its cooked potato products. Fined $200,000 following an OSHA violation that resulted in the death of an employee. Faces controversies over its marketing of breast milk substitutes, baby food, snack foods aimed at children, and infant formula. Ending the use of GMOs in its U.S. baby food products. Seeking to reduce its greenhouse gas emissions by 20% by 2015. In project development stages to convert potato peels into bio-fuel. Supports research into treatment of childhood anemia. Distributes packets of micronutrients to needy children. Has a written nondiscrimination policy covering sexual orientation and gender identity. Offers insurance coverage to employees' domestic partners. Insurance for transgender employees is offered, but treatment is not covered.

Hormel Foods Corporation

35% | 65%

Contributions: TOTAL: *$16,950*   DEM: *$5,950*   REP: *$11,000*
LOBBY SPENDING: *$366,855*

Subsidiary Mountain Prairie Farms was fined $116,000 for safety and environmental violations on its Colorado hog farm. Environmental goals include reducing water and energy use by 10% and increasing recycling by 50%. Supports hunger cessation. Has a written nondiscrimination policy covering sexual orientation but not gender identity.

Hy-Vee, Inc.

22% | 78%

Contributions: TOTAL: *$14,951*   DEM: *$3,350*   REP: *$11,601*
LOBBY SPENDING: *$0*

Privately held. Working toward Energy Star certification of a number of its stores. Working to improve the fuel efficiency of its trucking fleet. Recycles cardboard, plastic, tin cans, and paper. Provides containers for plastic bag recycling at most store locations. Awards scholarships. Has a written nondiscrimination policy covering sexual orientation and gender identity.

IGA, Inc.

7% | 93%

Contributions: TOTAL: *$3,350*   DEM: *$250*   REP: *$3,100*
LOBBY SPENDING: *$0*

Privately held. IGA, Inc., does not control pricing, procedures, or policies in any individual IGA store because the stores are part of its voluntary supermarket network.

Interstate Bakeries Corporation
3% | 97%
Contributions: TOTAL: *$9,700*   DEM: *$300*   REP: *$9,400*
LOBBY SPENDING: *$0*

Has a written nondiscrimination policy covering sexual orientation but not gender identity.

Jamba Juice Company
100% | 0%
Contributions: TOTAL: *$4,000*   DEM: *$4,000*   REP: *$0*
LOBBY SPENDING: *$0*

Outreach supports environmental stewardship, physical fitness, youth activities, and nutrition education efforts.

Jewel-Osco
100% | 0%
Contributions: TOTAL: *$250*   DEM: *$250*   REP: *$0*
LOBBY SPENDING: *$0*

Subsidiary of Albertsons LLC; parent, SUPERVALU. Has a written nondiscrimination policy covering sexual orientation and gender identity. Offers insurance coverage to employees' domestic partners. Insurance for transgender employees is offered, but treatment is not covered.

J. M. Smucker Company, The
5% | 95%
Contributions: TOTAL: *$73,050*   DEM: *$3,800*   REP: *$69,250*
LOBBY SPENDING: *$0*

Offers organic fruit spreads. Has a written nondiscrimination policy covering sexual orientation but not gender identity.

Kellogg Company
70% | 30%
Contributions: TOTAL: *$141,775*   DEM: *$99,875*   REP: *$41,900*
LOBBY SPENDING: *$857,231*

The Center for Science in the Public Interest threatened to sue Kellogg over its advertising and marketing of unhealthy foods to children. Agreed to increase the nutritional value of children's cereals and snacks. With three other food companies, it created the Alliance for American Advertising, a lobbying group that disputes any link between advertising and childhood obesity. Cited for enclosing toys containing mercury batteries in cereal boxes. Has worked to block U.S. legislation requiring producers to label items containing GMOs. Listed by NAFE as one of the top 50 companies for female executives in 2009. In 2008, scored 35 out of 100 in "The Climate Counts Company Scorecard Report." Fined by the EPA in two cases for hazardous chemical releases. Environmental targets for 2015 include 15% to 20% reductions from 2005 baselines in energy use, greenhouse gas emissions, water use, and waste per metric ton of food produced. Supports the Alliance for Youth. Outreach includes donating products to the hungry, educating young people about proper nutrition, and working to reduce global malnutrition. Supports United Way campaigns. Has a written nondiscrimination policy covering sexual orientation but not gender identity. Offers insurance coverage to employees' domestic partners only in some subsidiaries.

Kendall-Jackson Wine Estates, Ltd.

100% 🐴 ▬▬▬▬▬▬▬ 0% 🐘

Contributions: TOTAL: *$27,078*   DEM: *$27,078*   REP: *$0*
LOBBY SPENDING: *$20,000*

Privately held. Cleared 600 acres of old-growth oak trees in California, prompting local officials to put a land stewardship proposition on the ballot. Partners with the nonprofit Hungry Owl Project and the Owl Box Adoption Program. Offers insurance coverage to employees' domestic partners.

Kraft Foods, Inc.

56% 🐴 ▬▬▬▬▬▬▬ 44% 🐘

Contributions: TOTAL: *$423,172*   DEM: *$238,151*   REP: *$185,021*
LOBBY SPENDING: *$6,010,000*

Helped create the Alliance for American Advertising, which disputes any link between childhood obesity and advertising targeted to youth. Pending class action lawsuit brought by employees who allegedly were not paid for time spent donning and doffing personal protective equipment and walking to and from their work stations. Its coffees are not Fair Trade. Its foods contain unlabeled GMOs, and it has fought to prevent the passage of labeling requirements. Has been recognized for progress in supporting diversity in the workplace and for agreeing to improve environmental and labor standards in the coffee industry. Listed by NAFE as one of the top 50 companies for female executives in 2009. Listed as one of the "100 Best Companies for Working Mothers" by *Working Mother* magazine for the seventh year in 2008. Scored 39 out of 100 in "The Climate Counts Company Scorecard Report" in 2008. Two of its plants use bio-methane from on-site waste treatment systems to replace 30% to 35% of their annual natural gas purchases. Partnered with the Rainforest Alliance. Supports projects focused on world hunger, healthy lifestyles, and disaster relief. Has a written non-discrimination policy covering sexual orientation and gender identity. Offers insurance coverage to employees' domestic partners. Insurance for transgender employees is offered, but treatment is not covered.

Kroger Co., The

40% 🐴 ▬▬▬▬▬▬▬ 60% 🐘

Contributions: TOTAL: *$120,164*   DEM: *$48,215*   REP: *$71,949*
LOBBY SPENDING: *$195,310*

Two pending lawsuits allege violation of California antitrust law when Kroger formed an alliance with Albertsons, LLC and Safeway, Inc./Vons that required all three companies to lock out union employees if a strike were called. Has made no discernible commitment to selling Fair Trade products. Continues to use unlabeled GMOs in its store brand products. Scored 75 out of 100 on the 2008 Human Rights Campaign Corporate Equality Index. Operates a landfill gas plant adjacent to its Turkey Hill Dairy, reducing diesel fuel use by an estimated 150,000 gallons per year. Since 2000, has reduced overall energy consumption by more than 22%. Recycles corrugated cardboard. Donates to Feeding America. Has a written nondiscrimination policy covering sexual orientation but not gender identity. Offers insurance coverage to employees' domestic partners.

Land O'Lakes, Inc.

54% 🐴 ▬▬▬▬▬▬▬ 46% 🐘

Contributions: TOTAL: *$337,155*   DEM: *$181,855*   REP: *$155,300*
LOBBY SPENDING: *$830,000*

In 2008, ordered to pay $1.6 million in a negligence lawsuit for distributing alpaca feed contaminated with salinomycin, resulting in the death of 69 alpacas. Foundation helps rural communities in the areas of human services, education and youth, civic activities, and the arts. Has a written nondiscrimination policy covering sexual orientation but not gender identity. Offers insurance coverage to employees' domestic partners. Limited insurance for transgender employees is offered, and some treatment is covered.

LVMH Moët Hennessy Louis Vuitton SA
Contributions: Total: $20,225 Dem: $20,025 Rep: $200
Lobby Spending: $0

99% / 1%

Has sourced products from countries with widespread, well-documented human and labor rights abuses. Has a global charter that defines environmental protection criteria and goals. Supports the arts, youth programs, public health, medical research, and the Twin Towers Fund.

Manischewitz Company, The
Contributions: Total: $5,500 Dem: $0 Rep: $5,500
Lobby Spending: $0

0% / 100%

Subsidiary of R.A.B. Holdings, Inc. Sued by 10 deaf employees who alleged discrimination and civil rights violations. Agreed to a $1 million fine after pleading no contest to antitrust violations in its matzo marketing.

Mars, Inc.
Contributions: Total: $57,476 Dem: $32,551 Rep: $24,925
Lobby Spending: $4,140,000

57% / 43%

A pending lawsuit alleges Mars and 11 other chocolate makers engaged in price-fixing. Products of a subsidiary in Thailand (manufacturers of Pedigree and Whiskas cat and dog foods) were found to contain molds and were alleged to be responsible for renal and kidney failure in pets. Is a founding member of the World Cocoa Foundation. Supports the Sustainable Tree Crops Program in West Africa. Uses GMOs in its products. Operates a week-long employee volunteer program. Outreach includes education and research, hunger cessation, sustainable development projects and medical clinics in Africa, and education in the Middle East. Has a written nondiscrimination policy covering sexual orientation and gender identity. Offers insurance coverage only to employees' opposite-sex domestic partners. Insurance for transgender employees is offered, but treatment is not covered.

Meijer, Inc.
Contributions: Total: $81,000 Dem: $14,750 Rep: $66,250
Lobby Spending: $0

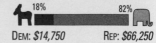
18% / 82%

Privately held. In 2009, OSHA fined it $35,000 for safety violations. Escaped paying a fine imposed by the Indiana Election Commission for admitting it had given too much cash to three legislative candidates, who later returned the money. Forced to allow employees to wear union insignia after it violated the NLRA. Has launched numerous green initiatives, including construction of LEED-certified stores, recycling of plastic bags, and sale of green products. Installing wind turbines at headquarters and local stores. Supports hunger cessation, health and wellness, and nature conservancy. Has a written nondiscrimination policy covering sexual orientation but not gender identity. Refuses insurance coverage to employees' domestic partners.

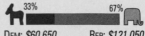

Miller Brewing Company
Contributions: TOTAL: *$316,230*   DEM: *$187,850*   REP: *$128,380*
LOBBY SPENDING: *$1,882,048*

Subsidiary of Molson Coors Brewing Company. Named with other alcohol producers in several suits for encouraging alcohol consumption by minors. Several informal boycotts were called by interest groups due to racially discriminatory advertising or language on its products. Has many union disputes with distributors and laborers. Recycles 99.9% of all packaging waste. At its Irwindale brewery, recycles brewery wastewater to generate biogas. Supports HIV/AIDS education, hunger cessation, at-risk youth, domestic violence issues, and alcohol education. Has a written nondiscrimination policy covering sexual orientation and gender identity. Offers insurance coverage to employees' domestic partners.

Molson Coors Brewing Company
Contributions: TOTAL: *$181,700*   DEM: *$60,650*   REP: *$121,050*
LOBBY SPENDING: *$1,652,000*

Before its merger with Molson, Coors Brewing Company had numerous civil rights violations and citations for unfair labor practices. Funds voter advertising, recently giving at least $100,000 to influence a California vote allowing for personal data collection and to support a referendum in Michigan banning affirmative action. Has donated money to conservative watchdog groups that target universities over the use of race in admissions policies. Named as a defendant in class actions alleging that marketing of alcoholic beverages to underage consumers causes human suffering and economic injuries. Agreed to a $71,000 fine for violations stemming from an explosion at a Virginia plant that killed two workers. In 2008, endorsed the United Nations' CEO Water Mandate. Joined the EPA's Climate Leaders initiative. Recycles spent yeast and waste beer into ethanol. Participates in several recycling, water conservation, and forest preservation programs. In 2008, scored 34 out of 100 on "The Climate Counts Company Scorecard Report." Has a written nondiscrimination policy covering sexual orientation and gender identity. Offers insurance coverage to employees' domestic partners. Insurance for transgender employees is offered, and some treatment is covered.

Mrs. Fields' Original Cookies, Inc.
Contributions: TOTAL: *$250*   DEM: *$0*   REP: *$250*
LOBBY SPENDING: *$0*

Subsidiary of Capricorn Holdings, Inc. Paid a $100,000 settlement to the FTC for violations of the Children's Online Privacy Protection Act.

Murphy-Brown LLC
Contributions: TOTAL: *$6,600*   DEM: *$1,250*   REP: *$5,350*
LOBBY SPENDING: *$0*

Subsidiary of Smithfield Foods, Inc. Is the world's largest hog producer. Is phasing out individual gestation stalls on all sow farms. Cited for releasing nitrogen-rich wastewater into local rivers. Has established field borders on over 40,000 acres of its North Carolina property, where naturally occurring vegetation is allowed to grow. Devotes research money to documenting and reducing antibiotic use in pork, as well as eliminating use of human-grade antibiotics. Supports the communities surrounding its operations.

Nabisco
40% ◀ ▶ 60%
Contributions: TOTAL: *$2,500*   DEM: *$1,000*   REP: *$1,500*
LOBBY SPENDING: *$0*
Subsidiary of Kraft Foods, Inc. Continues to market unlabeled GMOs, including some in products targeted to children. Has a written non-discrimination policy covering sexual orientation and gender identity. Offers insurance coverage to employees' domestic partners. Insurance for transgender employees is offered, but treatment is not covered.

Naked Juice Company
0% ◀ ▶ 100%
Contributions: TOTAL: *$1,000*   DEM: *$0*   REP: *$1,000*
LOBBY SPENDING: *$0*
Subsidiary of PepsiCo, Inc. Sells only non-GMO products. Its bottles are 100% PVC free and recyclable, and they contain 20% to 30% postindustrial recycled content. Voluntarily purchases carbon credits to completely offset its electricity use. Byproducts are used by local farmers for animal feed. Transitioning to hybrid vehicles for juice delivery.

National Grape Cooperative Association, Inc.
59% ◀ ▶ 41%
Contributions: TOTAL: *$11,000*   DEM: *$6,500*   REP: *$4,500*
LOBBY SPENDING: *$35,000*
Terminated the memberships of grape suppliers in an alleged price-fixing scheme to reduce supply and fraudulently increase prices. In 2008, signed a new contract with Teamsters Union 397.

Nestlé S.A.
26% ◀ ▶ 74%
Contributions: TOTAL: *$356,673*   DEM: *$92,334*   REP: *$264,339*
LOBBY SPENDING: *$4,265,487*
Foreign owned. Has business dealings in Burma, which is known for its human rights abuses. Sued for its complicity in the murder of Luciano Enrique Romero Molina, a Colombian trade unionist and former Nestlé employee who helped expose Nestlé's use of expired milk in its Milo brand drink. Pending lawsuit alleges it and 11 other chocolate makers engaged in illegal price-fixing. Its aggressive marketing of infant formula in developing countries inspired an ongoing international boycott. Its U.S. division produces and sells infant formulas and other foods with unlabeled GMOs. Repeatedly sued for the impacts of its bottled water operations on communities and for false advertising of its products. In 2008, it scored 61 out of 100 in "The Climate Counts Company Scorecard Report." Supports nutrition education, hunger cessation, HIV/AIDS education, and agricultural assistance.

Newman's Own, Inc.
100%   0%
Contributions: Total: *$2,000*   Dem: *$2,000*   Rep: *$0*
Lobby Spending: *$0*
Privately held. All after-tax profits and royalties go to charity, supporting causes such as camps for ill children, UNICEF, and Habitat for Humanity.

Nippon Suisan Kaisha, Ltd.
30%   70%
Contributions: Total: *$11,210*   Dem: *$3,310*   Rep: *$7,900*
Lobby Spending: *$0*
Foreign owned. Its plants are switching from petroleum to city gas, which has lower carbon emissions. Supports environmental education and youth sports. Provides in-house fisheries training for young Maori.

Ocean Spray Cranberries, Inc.
72%   28%
Contributions: Total: *$22,250*   Dem: *$16,000*   Rep: *$6,250*
Lobby Spending: *$760,000*
Uses methane gas from a nearby landfill to power its manufacturing operation in Wisconsin.

Odwalla, Inc.
56%   44%
Contributions: Total: *$900*   Dem: *$500*   Rep: *$400*
Lobby Spending: *$0*
Subsidiary of Coca-Cola. Uses organic fruit when possible. Converts wastewater to methane gas. Supports the Organic Farming Research Foundation, Conservation International, and community projects. Coordinated a consumer-driven project that donated 60,000 trees to state parks across the United States in 2008.

Pathmark Stores, Inc.
92%   8%
Contributions: Total: *$10,250*   Dem: *$9,450*   Rep: *$800*
Lobby Spending: *$0*
Subsidiary of The Great Atlantic & Pacific Tea Co.; parent, Tengelmann Warenhandelsgesellschaft KG (Germany). Has been the subject of several injury-related lawsuits. Supports children's causes, coat drives, hunger relief, diabetes issues, and heart health. Has sponsored Black History Month events. Has a written nondiscrimination policy covering sexual orientation but not gender identity. Offers insurance coverage to employees' opposite-sex domestic partners. Insurance for transgender employees is offered, but treatment is not covered.

Pepperidge Farm, Inc.
36%   64%
Contributions: Total: *$6,750*   Dem: *$2,450*   Rep: *$4,300*
Lobby Spending: *$0*
Subsidiary of the Campbell Soup Company. Installed two fuel cells at its bakery in Bloomfield, CT. Has a written nondiscrimination policy covering sexual orientation and gender identity. Offers insurance coverage to employees' domestic partners. Insurance for transgender employees is offered, and treatment is covered.

PepsiCo, Inc.
45%   55%
Contributions: Total: *$669,056*   Dem: *$297,856*   Rep: *$371,200*
Lobby Spending: *$2,176,636*

Under fire for major environmental problems caused by its bottling plants in India, where some states have banned its products in government and educational institutions. Accused of pumping aquifers dry in areas where people are poor and water is difficult to find. Opposed deposit legislation endorsed by environmental groups. Asked its suppliers to discontinue the use of genetically modified seed, but gave $127,000 to defeat an Oregon measure that would require the labeling of genetically modified foods. Has been sued by the State of California and the ACLU over toxic contents in its snack foods. Ranked 24th on DiversityInc's list of the "Top 50 Companies for Diversity" in 2009. In 2008, scored 37 out of 100 in "The Climate Counts Company Scorecard Report." Awarded a 2009 Energy Star Award by the EPA in recognition of its purchase of green energy, the largest in history and enough to power 100% of its energy needs. Environmental goals include reducing water consumption by 20%, electricity consumption by 20%, and fuel consumption by 25% per unit of production by 2015 compared with 2006. Made a $5 million grant to Save the Children. Foundation supports water management programs. Has a written nondiscrimination policy that covers sexual orientation and gender identity. Offers insurance coverage to employees' domestic partners. Insurance for transgender employees is offered, and some treatment is covered.

Perdue Farms, Inc.

41% 59%

Contributions: TOTAL: *$28,250*   DEM: *$11,550*   REP: *$16,700*
LOBBY SPENDING: *$175,000*

Two pending class action lawsuits allege that it disposes of excess giblets by stuffing them into whole chickens. Agreed to $10 million in back pay to settle a class action lawsuit. Has a long history of environmental violations, labor union clashes, anti-union practices, wage and hour disputes, and worker safety/injuries. Accused of animal cruelty in governmental investigations. Has a partnership with the Poultry Welfare Program and an on-site program to help ensure humane treatment. Operates the first-of-its kind facility to convert poultry litter into an organic fertilizer. A pilot recycling project at its Dillon, SC, processing plant recycled 2 million pounds of solid waste in one year. Its Shore Water Conservation initiative reduced water use by an average of 2 million gallons per week per plant. Partners with the Center for Inland Bays to improve water quality. Exploring alternative energy sources, including poultry fat, to replace fuel oil in its processing plants. Is an EPA SmartWay Transport Partner. Outreach includes partnership with Feeding America.

Pernod Ricard S.A.

82% 18%

Contributions: TOTAL: *$2,725*   DEM: *$2,225*   REP: *$500*
LOBBY SPENDING: *$2,695,000*

Foreign owned. Complies with several ethical codes concerning advertising for alcoholic beverages. Its goal is to reduce its energy consumption by 10% per product unit by 2011. Has reduced its carbon dioxide emissions. Recycles about 90% of plant waste at its bottling facilities. Several of its plants are engaged in water conservation efforts. Promotes sustainable agriculture.

Pilgrim's Pride Corporation
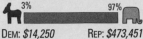
Contributions: TOTAL: *$487,701*   DEM: *$14,250*   REP: *$473,451*
LOBBY SPENDING: *$80,000*
Filed for Chapter 11 bankruptcy in 2008. Feeds its poultry natural grains and pure water; adds no hormones or preservatives. Encourages its contract farmers to store poultry litter in litter sheds until it is needed for crop fertilization. Its boilers are fueled by environmentally friendly fuels. Supports hunger relief, cancer research, adult education, and local nonprofit organizations. Has no written nondiscrimination policy covering sexual orientation or gender identity.

Pillsbury Company, The
83%   17%
Contributions: TOTAL: *$13,180*   DEM: *$10,880*   REP: *$2,300*
LOBBY SPENDING: *$0*
Subsidiary of General Mills. Has a written nondiscrimination policy covering sexual orientation but not gender identity.

Pinnacle Foods Group, Inc.
4%   96%
Contributions: TOTAL: *$20,750*   DEM: *$750*   REP: *$20,000*
LOBBY SPENDING: *$0*
Subsidiary of The Blackstone Group LP. Settled with the Center for Science in the Public Interest over false labeling on its Aunt Jemima products.

POM Wonderful LLC
100%   0%
Contributions: TOTAL: *$1,500*   DEM: *$1,500*   REP: *$0*
LOBBY SPENDING: *$180,000*
Subsidiary of Roll Corporation.

Publix Super Markets, Inc.
17%   83%
Contributions: TOTAL: *$514,812*   DEM: *$86,110*   REP: *$428,702*
LOBBY SPENDING: *$0*
In 2008, settled a consumer class action alleging that two of the company's soft drinks tended to contain benzene at levels exceeding the maximum safe level for drinking water. Ranked 88th on *Fortune* magazine's "100 Best Companies to Work For" in 2009. Has reduced carbon dioxide emissions through conservation projects. Has installed solar panels at two of its stores. Offers reusable and 100% recyclable bags. Member of the EPA's Climate Leaders program. Supports seafood sustainability programs, Special Olympics, children's issues, and hunger relief. Has a written nondiscrimination policy covering sexual orientation but not gender identity.

Quality Food Centers, Inc.
0%   100%
Contributions: TOTAL: *$300*   DEM: *$0*   REP: *$300*
LOBBY SPENDING: *$0*
Subsidiary of Fred Meyer Stores, Inc.; parent, the Kroger Co.

Raley's, Inc.
5%   95%
Contributions: TOTAL: *$10,800*   DEM: *$500*   REP: *$10,300*
LOBBY SPENDING: *$0*

Sued for violating contract terms in a lawsuit brought by the United Wholesaler & Retailers union. Has installed solar panels at one store. Uses an exhaust filtration system that makes its trucks the cleanest Class 8 diesel trucks in day-to-day operation. Offers produce from local growers. Makes reusable canvass bags available to customers. Supports hunger relief efforts. Has a written nondiscrimination policy covering sexual orientation but not gender identity.

Randalls Food Markets, Inc.
100% / 0%
Contributions: TOTAL: *$250*   DEM: *$250*   REP: *$0*
LOBBY SPENDING: *$0*

Subsidiary of Safeway, Inc. A Dallas store was found to have sold adulterated "beef" (beef containing 25% other meat products) in violation of state law. Received a good corporate citizen award by the Sanitation District of Los Angeles County for consistent compliance with its wastewater discharge requirements. Has a written nondiscrimination policy covering sexual orientation but not gender identity. Offers insurance coverage to employees' domestic partners. Insurance for transgender employees is offered, but treatment is not covered.

Red Bull GmbH
100% / 0%
Contributions: TOTAL: *$500*   DEM: *$500*   REP: *$0*
LOBBY SPENDING: *$0*

The Swedish government opened an investigation into the safety of Red Bull energy drink after three people died, allegedly due to the consumption of Red Bull in combination with alcohol or in excess after exercise. Supports a yearly music academy and several stunt competitions.

Robert Mondavi Corporation, The
91% / 9%
Contributions: TOTAL: *$5,300*   DEM: *$4,800*   REP: *$500*
LOBBY SPENDING: *$0*

Subsidiary of Constellation Brands, Inc. Facing a $10.8 million lawsuit brought by shareholders for breach of fiduciary duties and breach of contract. Paid $120,000 in fines and agreed to spend $30,000 to educate the wine industry on illegal gratuities following an independent counsel investigation of its relationship with former agriculture secretary Mike Espy. Has sustainable farming, biodiversity, and environmental conservation programs. Is the only winery to date to receive an "Innovator" award from California's EPA. Sponsors events to benefit local cultural organizations and research into wine cultivation and refinement. Supports local youth, health care, and housing services in Napa Valley.

ROCKSTAR, Inc.
0% / 100%
Contributions: TOTAL: *$5,000*   DEM: *$0*   REP: *$5,000*
LOBBY SPENDING: *$0*

Many LGBT and ally groups are calling for consumers to boycott Rockstar Energy Drinks. Michael Weiner (aka Michael Savage, radio host of Savage Nation), cofounder of Rockstar Energy Drink, and his son, Russell Weiner, currently the CEO of Rockstar Energy Drink, are outspoken supporters of marriage being defined as between a man and a woman. The Weiners are co-founders of the ultra-right-wing Paul Revere Society.

Roll International Corporation
Contributions: TOTAL: *$179,050*   DEM: *$166,200*   REP: *$12,850*
LOBBY SPENDING: *$50,000*

Holdings include FIJI Water Company, POM Wonderful, Paramount Farms (the world's largest grower, processor, and supplier of almonds and pistachios), and Paramount Citrus (a leading producer of fresh citrus fruits).

Royal Ahold N.V.
Contributions: TOTAL: *$20,914*   DEM: *$11,682*   REP: *$9,232*
LOBBY SPENDING: *$0*

Paid $1.1 billion to settle shareholder lawsuits after executives at former subsidiary U.S. Foodservice were found to have committed serious accounting fraud. Czech Republic officials uncovered evidence that subsidiary Hypernova had been falsifying employee time sheets, failing to pay overtime wages, and paying female employees less than their male counterparts. Criticized for a lack of action regarding the plight of agricultural workers who earn poverty wages. Uses energy-saving devices in stores and has recycling programs. Makes donations to offset its carbon footprint. Environmental goal is to reduce its 2008 baseline carbon emissions per square meter of sales area by 20% by 2015. Supports environmental stewardship, hunger cessation, and social issues in areas where it has a presence.

Russell Stover Candies, Inc.
Contributions: TOTAL: *$83,900*   DEM: *$0*   REP: *$83,900*
LOBBY SPENDING: *$0*

Privately held. No information on outreach, benefit structure, environmental impact, or legal or labor issues.

SABMiller PLC
Contributions: TOTAL: *$327,821*   DEM: *$193,900*   REP: *$133,921*
LOBBY SPENDING: *$1,882,048*

Foreign owned. Miller's purchase by South African Breweries in 2002 produced SABMiller PLC. In the United States, the company owns 58% of MillerCoors, a joint venture with Molson Coors. See Miller Brewing Company and Molson Coors for its U.S. contribution record. In 2008, scored 48 out of 100 in "The Climate Counts Company Scorecard Report." Reuses its treated wastewater. Supports HIV/AIDS, public health initiatives, education, and environmental stewardship. Promotes enterprise development through cash grants, training, and mentoring within the communities in which it operates.

Safeway, Inc.
Contributions: TOTAL: *$765,802*   DEM: *$373,733*   REP: *$392,069*
LOBBY SPENDING: *$2,210,000*

Named in a lawsuit alleging violation of California antitrust law for forging an alliance with Albertsons, Inc., and the Kroger Co./Ralphs Grocery Company that required all three companies to lock out union employees if a strike were called. Is responsible for part of a $22.4 million settlement in a class action suit for failure to pay overtime. Scored 75 out of 100 on the 2008 Human Rights Campaign Corporate Equality Index. Has committed to reducing its greenhouse gas emissions by 6% from 2000 levels. Is powering 23 California stores with solar energy. Offers training programs in source reduction, recycling, and environmental compliance. Member of the EPA's SmartWay Transport Partnership. Its foundation has raised over $1 billion for hunger relief, as well as millions for local schools and youth groups, Easter Seals, breast cancer and prostate cancer causes, the Muscular Dystrophy Association, and emergency relief in areas struck by natural disasters. Has a written non-discrimination policy covering sexual orientation and gender identity. Offers insurance coverage to employees' domestic partners. Insurance for transgender employees is offered, but treatment is not covered.

Sara Lee Bakery Group
Contributions: TOTAL: *$250*   DEM: *$0*   REP: *$250*
LOBBY SPENDING: *$0*
Subsidiary of Sara Lee Corporation. The EPA fined its Earthgrains division $5.25 million for "the largest-ever corporate-wide violations" of ozone protection regulations. Has reduced its water use and the amount of solid waste going to landfills. Has a written nondiscrimination policy covering sexual orientation but not gender identity. Offers insurance coverage to employees' domestic partners. Insurance for transgender employees is offered, but treatment is not covered.

Sara Lee Corporation
Contributions: TOTAL: *$59,754*   DEM: *$51,704*   REP: *$8,050*
LOBBY SPENDING: *$2,850,000*
Was one of the several food companies implicated in a cover-up of a massive accounting scandal at U.S. Foodservice (formerly owned by Royal Ahold). Workers at Sara Lee garment supplier Monclova International in Mexico have alleged labor violations. Paid $310,000 in fines and agreed to upgrade a wastewater treatment system that allegedly exceeded effluent release levels more than 1,500 times in a one-year period. In 2008, scored 13 out of 100 on "The Climate Counts Company Scorecard Report." Focuses its environmental sustainability efforts on water, energy, packaging, and solid waste. Its foundation supports women's issues, housing, and hunger relief. Has a written nondiscrimination policy covering sexual orientation but not gender identity. Offers insurance coverage to employees' domestic partners. Insurance for transgender employees is offered, but treatment is not covered.

Sara Lee Foods
Contributions: TOTAL: *$250*   DEM: *$0*   REP: *$250*
LOBBY SPENDING: *$0*
Subsidiary of Sara Lee Corporation. Paid $3.5 million to settle 139 racial discrimination suits filed by employees of one of its plants. Sells little Fair Trade coffee and earned the lowest rating of all U.S. coffee roasters for its treatment of farmers. Has a written nondiscrimination policy covering sexual orientation but not gender identity. Offers insurance coverage to employees' domestic partners. Insurance for transgender employees is offered, but treatment is not covered.

Schwan Food Company, The
Contributions: TOTAL: *$70,000*   DEM: *$12,000*   REP: *$58,000*
LOBBY SPENDING: *$50,000*
Privately held. Supports youth issues, arts, education, and charity.

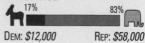

Skyy Spirits, LLC
Contributions: TOTAL: *$4,600* DEM: *$0* REP: *$4,600*
LOBBY SPENDING: *$0*
Subsidiary of Davide Campari-Milano, S.p.A. Named with other alcohol producers in several suits for encouraging alcohol consumption by minors. Supports San Francisco, CA, HIV-awareness organizations, as well as the local LGBT community.

Smith's Food & Drug Centers, Inc.
Contributions: TOTAL: *$1,410* DEM: *$250* REP: *$1,160*
LOBBY SPENDING: *$0*
Subsidiary of Fred Meyer Stores, Inc.; parent, The Kroger Co.

Smithfield Foods, Inc.
Contributions: TOTAL: *$208,665* DEM: *$66,950* REP: *$141,715*
LOBBY SPENDING: *$2,507,000*
Has filed a racketeering lawsuit against the UFCW International union on the theory that speaking out about labor, environmental, and safety issues in order to pressure the company to unionize amounts to extortion like that used by organized crime. In testimony before a Senate committee, was exposed for union-busting tactics. Meat packers at Smithfield endure poor working conditions, which at its Tar Heel, NC, plant have not improved even after a 2002 lawsuit found the company guilty of violating human rights there. That plant is the only meatpacking plant in the United States to have its own private police force. Settled with the State of North Carolina for $65 million and agreed to upgrade its wastewater treatment facility. Has implemented over 150 recycling and conservation projects. Devoted $15 million for research into better and safer methods of hog waste disposal. Supports education, nutrition, and hunger cessation. Has a written nondiscrimination policy covering sexual orientation but not gender identity.

Smoothie King Franchises, Inc.
Contributions: TOTAL: *$2,000* DEM: *$0* REP: *$2,000*
LOBBY SPENDING: *$0*
Franchise owner shipped smoothies to troops stationed in Iraq.

Spectrum Organic Products
Contributions: TOTAL: *$2,300* DEM: *$2,300* REP: *$0*
LOBBY SPENDING: *$0*
Subsidiary of Hain Celestial Group. Joined in the boycott of the Canadian Fishing/Seafood Industry against the killing of baby seals. Uses only small-scale organic farms with sustainable practices and active biodiversity of crops. Its palm oil supplier, DAABON, allocates a percentage of its export revenues to fund social projects in Colombia. Products are free of GMOs. Participates in a biofuel research cooperative. Supports Children's Heartlink, an international nonprofit organization addressing heart disease among needy children in developing countries.

Starbucks Corporation
Contributions: TOTAL: *$150,286* DEM: *$139,894* REP: *$10,392*
LOBBY SPENDING: *$1,028,000*

Paid more than $100 million to employees in California to settle a suit alleging that it violated a state law that prohibits managers and supervisors from sharing in employee tips. Refuses to guarantee that its products contain no GMOs. Fair Trade Certified™ coffee comprises only a fraction of the company's sales. Ranked 24th on *Fortune* magazine's "100 Best Companies to Work For" in 2009. In 2008, scored 49 out of 100 on "The Climate Counts Company Scorecard Report." Purchases wind renewable energy certificates to offset its carbon footprint. Striving to buy, sell, and use environmentally friendly products. Its foundation has provided more than $22 million in grants to benefit communities around the world. Is a partner in the (PRODUCT) RED campaign. Supports Conservation International, the Earthwatch Institute, the African Wildlife Foundation, Save the Children, and Mercy Corps. Has a written nondiscrimination policy covering sexual orientation and gender identity. Offers insurance coverage to employees' domestic partners. Insurance for transgender employees is offered, and some treatment is covered.

Stater Bros. Holdings, Inc.
94% | 6%

Contributions: TOTAL: *$4,150* DEM: *$3,900* REP: *$250*
LOBBY SPENDING: *$0*

In 2008, contributed more than $15 million to nonprofit organizations focusing on hunger relief, children's health, youth and adult education, elderly care and services, and help for veterans. Has no written nondiscrimination policy covering sexual orientation or gender identity. No information on insurance coverage to employees' domestic partners.

Stop & Shop Supermarket Company, The
38% | 62%

Contributions: TOTAL: *$12,816* DEM: *$4,900* REP: *$7,916*
LOBBY SPENDING: *$0*

Subsidiary of Ahold USA, Inc.; parent, Royal Ahold N.V. Paid a $25,000 fine to the DOL for violation of child labor laws. In 2008, was awarded LEED certification for 51 of its buildings. In Massachusetts, has helped state officials create an infrastructure and set standards for organic recycling. Has a recycling program for plastic bags, sells reusable shopping bags, and gives a $.05 credit for each bag brought from home. Participates in the EPA SmartWay Transport Partnership. Partnered with the New England Aquarium, engaging in environmentally friendly seafood practices. Supports hunger cessation, cancer care and research, children's services, and education. Has a written nondiscrimination policy covering sexual orientation and gender identity. Offers insurance coverage to employees' domestic partners.

Sunny Delight Beverages Co.
0% | 100%

Contributions: TOTAL: *$5,350* DEM: *$0* REP: *$5,350*
LOBBY SPENDING: *$0*

Privately held portfolio company of J.W. Childs Associates, L.P.

SUPERVALU, Inc.
46% | 54%

Contributions: TOTAL: *$184,804* DEM: *$84,753* REP: *$100,051*
LOBBY SPENDING: *$960,000*

Pending class action lawsuit alleges that it routinely mislabeled "Choice beef" as "genuine Black Angus." Is a member of the lobbying special interest group Coalition to Advance Healthcare Reform. Recently entered the EPA's GreenChill Partnership. Has invested $100 million on energy projects. Sells reusable grocery bags. Outreach includes hunger cessation, health and nutrition, environmental stewardship, and the United Way. Has a written nondiscrimination policy covering sexual orientation and gender identity. Offers insurance coverage to employees' domestic partners. Insurance for transgender employees is offered, but treatment is not covered.

Sweetbay LLC (formerly Kash n' Karry Food Stores, Inc.)

100% | 0%

Contributions: TOTAL: *$250*   DEM: *$250*   REP: *$0*
LOBBY SPENDING: *$0*

Subsidiary of Delhaize America, Inc.; parent, Delhaize Group. Accused of violating child labor laws by the U.S. DOL, fined $46,000 in civil penalties. Also cited for 19 violations involving the sale of adulterated beef and the mislabeling of foreign-grown produce as local. Offers a line of natural and organic products. Outreach includes nutrition and wellness, hunger cessation, cultural diversity, and early education. No information on benefit structure.

Swift & Company

28% | 72%

Contributions: TOTAL: *$99,200*   DEM: *$27,750*   REP: *$71,450*
LOBBY SPENDING: *$380,000*

Subsidiary of JBS S.A. In 2006, the U.S. Department of Homeland Security's Immigration and Customs Enforcement division questioned employees at all of Swift's six plants in an identity theft investigation. Swift is constructing a biogas facility at one of its meat processing facilities. Supports disaster relief efforts. Supports the United Way.

Tate & Lyle PLC

37% | 63%

Contributions: TOTAL: *$55,144*   DEM: *$20,394*   REP: *$34,750*
LOBBY SPENDING: *$0*

Foreign owned. Is the world's supplier of sucralose, the low-calorie sweetener sold under the name SPLENDA. Reducing its carbon footprint with a new biomass boiler at one of its refineries. Supports education, the environment, health, and the arts.

Thai Union Frozen Products PLC

Contributions: TOTAL: *$0*   DEM: *$0*   REP: *$0*
LOBBY SPENDING: *$260,000*

Participates in a mangrove forestation project. Supports educational institutions, needy children, and the underprivileged.

Tops Markets, LLC

50% | 50%

Contributions: TOTAL: *$900*   DEM: *$450*   REP: *$450*
LOBBY SPENDING: *$0*

Subsidiary of the private equity unit of Morgan Stanley. Outreach includes hunger cessation, education, juvenile diabetes, and health care.

Trader Joe's Company, Inc.

90% | 10%

Contributions: TOTAL: *$9,678*   DEM: *$8,728*   REP: *$950*
LOBBY SPENDING: *$0*

Subsidiary of TACT Holding; parent ALDI Group in Germany. A recent investigation by the AFL-CIO–affiliated Solidarity Center found that Trader Joe's is sourcing shrimp from plants in Thailand and Bangladesh where workers as young as eight years old are subject to sweatshop conditions. Carries some Fair Trade products. All products with Trader Joe's private label are sourced from non-genetically modified ingredients. Carries only cage-free hen eggs and does not support testing on animals. Does not purchase seafood items from areas where seals are being killed. Supports hunger cessation. Offers insurance coverage to employees' domestic partners.

Trinchero Family Estates
Contributions: TOTAL: *$28,100*   DEM: *$28,100*   REP: *$0*
LOBBY SPENDING: *$0*
Formerly Sutter Home Winery.

100% | 0%

Tyson Foods, Inc.
Contributions: TOTAL: *$275,929*   DEM: *$167,819*   REP: *$108,110*
LOBBY SPENDING: *$3,791,433*

61% | 39%

A pending lawsuit maintains that it continues to market its chicken as antibiotic-free despite a government directive to cease that practice. Facing a federal class action suit for allegedly smuggling illegal workers into the United States. Paid $1.5 million to settle discrimination allegations by the DOL. Involved in several lawsuits over allegations that it doesn't pay its workers for the time it takes to don and doff gear. Paid $6 million in fines following an investigation of influence brokering and illegal gratuities in connection with former agriculture secretary Mike Espy. Like others in the poultry industry, lobbies Congress to exempt manure from being labeled a hazardous substance under the federal Superfund law. Has a joint venture to produce synthetic fuels made from renewable feedstocks. Some of its farmers use chicken-litter fertilizer on crops. Operates wastewater treatment plants. Is a SmartWay Transportation Partner with the EPA. Supports hunger relief, education, environmental protections, and family and community initiatives. Has a written nondiscrimination policy covering sexual orientation but not gender identity. Refuses insurance coverage to employees' domestic partners.

Tyson Fresh Meats, Inc.
Contributions: TOTAL: *$1,150*   DEM: *$0*   REP: *$1,150*
LOBBY SPENDING: *$0*

0% | 100%

Subsidiary of Tyson Foods, Inc. A pending class action lawsuit alleges that it doesn't pay its workers for the time it takes to don and doff gear. Supports hunger relief, education, and environmental stewardship. Has a written nondiscrimination policy covering sexual orientation but not gender identity. Refuses insurance coverage to employees' domestic partners.

United Dairy Farmers, Inc.
Contributions: TOTAL: *$315,800*   DEM: *$1,500*   REP: *$314,300*
LOBBY SPENDING: *$0*

0% | 100%

Pending lawsuit brought by a former employee alleges race discrimination and violation of the FMLA. Only bottles milk from farms that pledge not to use artificial growth hormones.

White Wave Foods

Contributions: TOTAL: *$7,700*   DEM: *$6,700*   REP: *$1,000*
LOBBY SPENDING: *$380,000*

Subsidiary of Dean Foods Company. Fought against the merger of parent Dean Foods Company and Suiza Foods Corp., the nation's two largest dairy producers. Whenever possible, purchases ingredients from American farms; supports organic standards; prohibits the use of pesticides, herbicides, and synthetic fertilizers; and ensures that no GMOs are in its products. Participates in the EPA's Climate Leaders Program. Purchases renewable energy credits to offset its carbon footprint. Offers a free public transportation pass to employees. Supports an employee volunteer program.

Whole Foods Market, Inc.

Contributions: TOTAL: *$66,775*   DEM: *$41,425*   REP: *$25,350*
LOBBY SPENDING: *$142,295*

Subsidiary of Leonard Green & Partners L.P. None of its employees are union members. It opposes union organizing and reportedly has terminated employees who solicit union participation. Carries only a limited variety of Fair Trade Certified™ products. Is not fully transparent about the use of GMOs in store-brand products and has ignored shareholder requests for information on the use of toxic chemicals in products it sells. In 2009, it ranked 22nd on *Fortune* magazine's "100 Best Companies to Work For," a list it has made for 11 consecutive years. Scored 90 out of 100 on the 2008 Human Rights Campaign Corporate Equality Index. Offsets 100% of its energy use with wind energy credits. Is transitioning to all-natural fiber packaging for its food containers and utensils. Supports hunger cessation in Rwanda and the United States and combating poverty in developing countries. Also supports projects that relate directly to organics and environmentally friendly production methods, animal welfare, sustainable seafood, and healthy families and nutrition. Has a written nondiscrimination policy covering sexual orientation and gender identity. Offers insurance coverage to employees' domestic partners. Insurance for transgender employees is offered, but treatment is not covered.

Wine Group, Inc., The

Contributions: TOTAL: *$40,800*   DEM: *$300*   REP: *$40,500*
LOBBY SPENDING: *$0*

Privately held. Is the third largest wine company in the United States in terms of sales volume.

Winn-Dixie Stores, Inc.

Contributions: TOTAL: *$2,275*   DEM: *$1,750*   REP: *$525*
LOBBY SPENDING: *$0*

Supports women and children, breast health, education, disaster relief, hunger cessation, and Special Olympics. Has partnered with the American Cancer Society to create three lodges for cancer patients and their families traveling away from home during outpatient treatments. Has a written nondiscrimination policy covering sexual orientation but not gender identity. Refuses insurance coverage to employees' domestic partners.

Health and Beauty

Dean Baker

The health and beauty sector, which is dominated by the pharmaceutical and medical supply industries, has good reason for making large contributions to political campaigns. Government-granted patent monopolies are the basis for most of the profit in these industries. Without these monopolies, the vast majority of drugs would be selling for $4 per prescription at Wal-Mart. Medical supplies and tests would also have very limited markups.

Campaign contributions from the pharmaceutical and medical supply industries are first and foremost about increasing the value of these monopolies. The industries seek protection against competition in all forms—for example, limiting the ability of patients to import drugs from Canada and other countries. They also seek to extend their monopolies overseas, pushing increased patent protection as a central component of trade deals, such as the recent pacts negotiated with Colombia, Panama, and South Korea.

The pharmaceutical and medical supply industries also rely on government support for the development of new drugs and other products, primarily through the $30 billion annual budget for the National Institutes of Health (NIH). These industries have been consistent supporters of increasing the budget for NIH, with the expectation that they would gain ready access to any potentially profitable findings.

The pharmaceutical and medical supply industries also count on friendly relations with the Food and Drug Administration (FDA) so they can receive quick approvals for their drugs and devices. The medical device industry is likely to be especially concerned, in the current session of Congress, over efforts to reverse a recent Supreme Court ruling that protects manufacturers from liability for FDA-approved devices. In fact, if the tide flows the right way, the pharmaceutical industry may seek the same sort of protection that the court granted device makers.

The pharmaceutical industry also is very concerned about the government's role as a purchaser of drugs. The Medicare drug benefit makes the federal government the country's largest single payer for prescription drugs. However, the bill was deliberately written to prevent the government from using the market power that its size implies.

With health-care costs imposing the major source of pressure on the budget in the years ahead, there will be efforts to allow Medicare to negotiate drug prices directly with the pharmaceutical industry, a position endorsed by President Obama during his campaign. In fact, President Obama's budget already calls for reducing the payments made for prescription drugs through the Medicaid program. Every dollar saved by the government is a dollar out of the profits of the pharmaceutical industry, and therefore grounds for serious concern.

The pharmaceutical and medical supply industries will play a central role in the debate over health-care reform, trying to ensure that any reform does not impinge on their profits. They will be especially concerned about any efforts to change the fundamental structure of the industry—for example, by advocating publicly financed clinical drugs trials, as suggested by Nobel Prize–winning economist Joseph Stiglitz.

With so much money at stake, it is not surprising that the pharmaceutical industry, along with other companies in the health and beauty sector, was a big contributor in the last election cycle. The larger category accounted for $14.8 million in contributions in the last election sector. This investment was almost evenly divided between parties; the Republicans received 50.4% of the industry's contributions, and the Democrats, 49.6%. The top contributors in the sector were Pfizer at $1.7 million, Amgen at $1.4 million, and GlaxoSmithKline, which contributed $1.2 million. Johnson & Johnson finished in fourth place, also crossing $1 million.

The political influence purchased with these campaign contributions will undoubtedly be an important factor in the health-care reform debate. Few politicians are anxious to cross such a politically powerful industry. Its clout will make meaningful health-care reform considerably more difficult.

Top Ten Democratic Contributors

Pfizer, Inc.	$1,115,048
Johnson & Johnson	$855,276
Amgen, Inc.	$837,814
GlaxoSmithKline Plc	$627,904
Merck & Co., Inc.	$607,820
Eli Lilly & Co.	$573,732
Abbott Laboratories	$548,193
CVS Caremark Corporation	$381,952
Wyeth	$365,628
McKesson Corp.	$321,341

Top Ten Republican Contributors

Pfizer, Inc.	$1,048,363
GlaxoSmithKline PLC	$970,046
Amgen, Inc.	$886,400
Abbott Laboratories	$676,613
Eli Lilly & Co.	$652,871
Merck & Co., Inc.	$650,671
Johnson & Johnson	$568,091
McKesson Corp.	$408,790
Novartis AG	$382,251
Schering-Plough Corporation	$374,495

Top Ten Lobbying Spenders

Amgen, Inc.	$26,410,000
Pfizer, Inc.	$25,980,000
Eli Lilly & Co.	$16,762,220
GlaxoSmithKline PLC	$15,230,000
Johnson & Johnson	$14,620,000
Novartis AG	$12,499,420
Hoffman-La Roche, Inc.	$12,161,339
Bayer AG	$11,730,980
Bayer Corporation	$10,030,980
Abbott Laboratories	$9,590,000

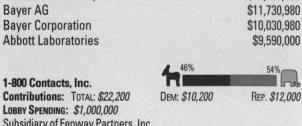

1-800 Contacts, Inc.
Contributions: TOTAL: *$22,200*   DEM: *$10,200*   REP. *$12,000*
LOBBY SPENDING: *$1,000,000*
Subsidiary of Fenway Partners, Inc.

24 Hour Fitness Worldwide, Inc.
Contributions: TOTAL: *$3,500*   DEM: *$2,750*   REP: *$750*
LOBBY SPENDING: *$0*
Subsidiary of Forstmann Little & Co. Accused in a pending class action lawsuit of not honoring a contract renewal offer to members. A pending

lawsuit for unpaid overtime was brought under the FLSA. Two pending lawsuits allege sexual harassment and retaliation. Sponsors the Lance Armstrong Foundation, the Magic Johnson Foundation, and the Safe Surfin' Foundation.

Abbott Laboratories

 45% | 55%

Contributions: Total: *$1,224,806* Dem: *$548,193* Rep: *$676,613*
Lobby Spending: *$9,590,000*

Pending lawsuits allege it unlawfully monopolized the market for boosted protease inhibitors used to treat medical disorders caused by HIV. Pending class action lawsuit brought by employees alleges it created a new firm in order to slash retirement benefits. In 2008, agreed to pay $28 million to settle Medicaid fraud allegations brought by the State of Texas. In 2008, agreed to pay $184 million to settle antitrust claims relating to its drug TriClor. Agreed to pay $37.5 million to settle nationwide claims by consumers that they were overcharged for HIV/AIDS drug Norvir in 2008. Has no policy against animal testing for its products. Has reduced its carbon dioxide emissions and water use. In 2008, its Michigan nutrition plant was named Outstanding Business Recycler of the Year by the Michigan Recycling Coalition. The nonprofit Abbott Fund was instrumental in constructing Tanzania's first pediatric HIV/AIDS clinic in 2008. Has a written nondiscrimination policy covering sexual orientation but not gender identity. Offers insurance coverage to employees' domestic partners. Insurance for transgender employees is offered, but treatment is not covered.

Alberto-Culver

22% | 78%

Contributions: Total: *$14,350* Dem: *$3,150* Rep: *$11,200*
Lobby Spending: *$0*

Named as a defendant in a suit that alleged wrongful death for decedent beautician exposed to vinyl chloride on the job. Does not conduct animal testing for its products. Expects to achieve zero landfill by 2010 at two of its plants. Plans to reduce its global operations waste by 95% of 2007 levels by 2014. Is reducing its greenhouse gas emissions as measured against its 2008 emissions. Grant program funds health care, education, and women-in-the-workplace projects. Gives 325 scholarships annually to children of employees. Has a written nondiscrimination policy covering sexual orientation but not gender identity.

AmerisourceBergen Corp.

34% | 66%

Contributions: Total: *$397,500* Dem: *$135,600* Rep: *$261,900*
Lobby Spending: *$2,740,250*

In 2007, the DEA temporarily suspended operations at one of the company's distribution centers in Florida due to its alleged failure to adequately control its supply of Hydocodone. In 2006, settled a complaint alleging that it distributed a counterfeit drug. Has a written nondiscrimination policy covering sexual orientation but not gender identity.

Amgen, Inc.

49% | 51%

Contributions: Total: *$1,724,214* Dem: *$837,814* Rep: *$886,400*
Lobby Spending: *$26,410,000*

Pending lawsuit alleges that it illegally marketed Enbrel and Aranesp. In 2008, agreed to pay $200 million to settle an antitrust lawsuit relating to sales of its oncology products Aranesp, Neupogen, and Neulasta. Foundation focuses on advancing science education and improving quality of care and access for patients. Has a written nondiscrimination policy covering sexual orientation but not gender identity. Offers insurance coverage to employees' domestic partners. Insurance for transgender employees is offered, and some treatment is covered.

Aveda

100%   0%

Contributions: TOTAL: *$98,200*   DEM: *$98,200*   REP: *$0*
LOBBY SPENDING: *$0*

Subsidiary of Estée Lauder Companies, Inc. One of the most progressive companies in the United States, with stellar environmental policies and labor practices. Does not conduct animal testing for its products. Has not signed the Compact for Safe Cosmetics. Has pledged to avoid the use of products made from clear-cut old-growth temperate rainforests and to source responsibly produced wood products. Most of its plastic bottles use a minimum of 80% postconsumer recycled material. Is the 32nd largest buyer of green energy in the United States. Funds environmental, sustainability, and indigenous peoples projects. Has a written nondiscrimination policy covering sexual orientation and gender identity. Offers insurance coverage to employees' domestic partners. Insurance for transgender employees is offered, and treatment is covered.

Avon Products, Inc.

100%   0%

Contributions: TOTAL: *$62,688*   DEM: *$62,488*   REP: *$200*
LOBBY SPENDING: *$260,000*

Was the first major cosmetic company to announce a permanent end to animal testing. Has not signed the Compact for Safe Cosmetics. Scored 60 out of 100 on the 2008 Human Rights Campaign Corporate Equality Index. Listed by NAFE as one of the top 50 companies for female executives in 2009. In 2008, scored 29 out of 100 in "The Climate Counts Company Scorecard Report." Has reduced overall energy consumption per unit produced by 35%, water consumption per unit by 10%, and greenhouse gas emissions per unit by 30%. Every new Avon facility in the United States is designed according to LEED standards. The Avon Foundation supports breast cancer research, domestic violence prevention, and emergency relief. Has a written nondiscrimination policy covering sexual orientation and gender identity. Offers insurance coverage to employees' domestic partners. Insurance for transgender employees is offered, and treatment is covered.

Bally Total Fitness Holding Corporation

67%   33%

Contributions: TOTAL: *$6,000*   DEM: *$4,000*   REP: *$2,000*
LOBBY SPENDING: *$0*

In December 2008, filed for Chapter 11 bankruptcy protection for the second time in 17 months. Paid $24,000 in a race discrimination suit brought by the EEOC in 2007. Class action lawsuit brought over "unreasonable initiation fees" in 2007. Has a company-wide recycling program and uses eco-friendly flooring. Bally never dumps used fitness equipment in landfills but always donates or recycles it.

Bare Escentuals, Inc

Contributions: TOTAL: *$2,500* DEM: *$2,000* REP: *$500*
LOBBY SPENDING: *$0*

Partners with organizations that advocate education, detection, and treatment of various skin conditions. 100% of the profits from certain products provide funding to Lupus Foundation of America, National Rosacea Society, and the Skin Cancer Foundation. Also contributes to the Sunshine Lady Foundation, which invests in organizations dedicated to helping women and children.

Bath & Body Works

Contributions: TOTAL: *$1,050* DEM: *$750* REP: *$300*
LOBBY SPENDING: *$0*

Subsidiary of Limited Brands, Inc. Does not conduct animal testing for its products. Has a written nondiscrimination policy covering sexual orientation but not gender identity. Offers insurance coverage to employees' domestic partners. Insurance for transgender employees is offered, but treatment is not covered.

Bausch & Lomb, Inc.

Contributions: TOTAL: *$16,050* DEM: *$9,850* REP: *$6,200*
LOBBY SPENDING: *$40,000*

Subsidiary of Warburg Pincus LLC. Makes charitable contributions and offers grants targeting eye health. Has a written nondiscrimination policy covering sexual orientation and gender identity. Offers insurance coverage to employees' domestic partners. Insurance for transgender employees is offered, but treatment is not covered.

Bayer AG

Contributions: TOTAL: *$340,525* DEM: *$140,678* REP: *$199,847*
LOBBY SPENDING: *$11,730,980*

Foreign owned. In 2009, named one of DiversityInc's Top 10 Companies for Global Diversity. Has come under fire for the use of child labor on cottonseed farms in India. Germany banned a line of pesticides manufactured by Bayer's agrochemical subsidiary after millions of honeybees died after the chemicals' application in 2008. Offers adoption assistance to employees. Has a written nondiscrimination policy covering sexual orientation and gender identity. Offers insurance coverage to employees' domestic partners. Insurance for transgender employees is offered, but treatment is not covered.

Bayer Corporation

Contributions: TOTAL: *$304,226* DEM: *$121,450* REP: *$182,776*
LOBBY SPENDING: *$10,030,980*

Subsidiary of Bayer AG. In 2009, required by the FDA and the attorneys general of 27 states to air new advertisements for the birth control pill Yaz to correct overstatements of the pill's benefits. Fined and issued citations by OSHA after one of its manufacturing facilities exploded, killing two people, in 2008. In 2007, it paid $8 million to settle a lawsuit over the cholesterol drug Baycol, which was found to have serious muscle-weakening side effects. Recognized in 2009 by *Working Mother* magazine as one of the 100 best companies in the United States for working mothers. Funds community partnership programs in the United

States. Offers adoption assistance to employees. Has a written nondiscrimination policy covering sexual orientation but not gender identity. Offers insurance coverage to employees' domestic partners. Insurance for transgender employees is offered, but treatment is not covered.

Bobbi Brown Professional Cosmetics, Inc.

100% 0%

Contributions: TOTAL: *$50,576*   DEM: *$50,576*   REP: *$0*
LOBBY SPENDING: *$0*

Subsidiary of Estée Lauder Companies, Inc. Does not conduct animal testing for its products.

Bristol-Myers Squibb Company

36% 64%

Contributions: TOTAL: *$452,882*   DEM: *$161,854*   REP: *$291,028*
LOBBY SPENDING: *$9,545,520*

A pending lawsuit claims that it failed to alert the public to the serious risk of heart attack, stroke, blood disorders, and death caused by its drug Plavix. Pending lawsuits involve the antibiotic Tequin, which is allegedly tied to a high incidence of diabetes. In 2007, agreed to pay more than $515 million to settle civil suits over fraudulent drug marketing and pricing schemes. Paid $13 million to settle a class action lawsuit alleging that it artificially inflated the price of certain medicines. Is a 2008 Best Company for Working Mothers according to *Working Mother* magazine. Listed by NAFE as one of the top 50 companies for female executives in 2009. One of its biopharmaceutical manufacturing facilities conforms to LEED certification. Is targeting a 10% increase in fuel economy for its U.S. fleet. Has cut its carbon emissions by 10%. Has decreased its hazardous waste disposal. Provides its medicines free of charge to some people. Sponsors endangered species and habitats. Has a written nondiscrimination policy covering sexual orientation and gender identity. Offers insurance coverage to employees' domestic partners. Insurance for transgender employees is offered, and treatment is covered.

Bumble & Bumble

100% 0%

Contributions: TOTAL: *$2,300*   DEM: *$2,300*   REP: *$0*
LOBBY SPENDING: *$0*

Subsidiary of Estée Lauder Companies, Inc.

Burt's Bees

100% 0%

Contributions: TOTAL: *$47,300*   DEM: *$47,300*   REP: *$0*
LOBBY SPENDING: *$0*

Subsidiary of the Clorox Company. Its products are certified by the Natural Products Association, which requires products to be made with at least 95% all-natural ingredients. Has cut its electricity use by 14% per sales dollar and reduced manufacturing-related water use by more than 20%. Has cut its waste to landfill by over 50%. Aims to reduce its U.S. greenhouse gas emissions by 35% per dollar sales by 2011. Its 2020 sustainability goals include sustainable products and packaging, zero landfill waste, 100% renewable energy, and LEED-certified facilities. Employees who purchase or lease a vehicle that runs entirely on fuel other than petroleum are eligible for a one-time match of $1,500 from the company. Partners with the Nature Conservancy, the Conservation Alliance, and the National Arbor Day Foundation.

Cerner Corporation
36% | 64%
Contributions: TOTAL: *$120,822* DEM: *$43,808* REP: *$77,014*
LOBBY SPENDING: *$670,000*
Community outreach includes the First Hand Foundation, which helps needy children receive health care. Has a written nondiscrimination policy covering sexual orientation and gender identity. Offers insurance coverage to domestic partners. Insurance for transgender employees is offered, but treatment is not covered.

Chanel, Inc.
48% | 52%
Contributions: TOTAL: *$10,760* DEM: *$5,160* REP: *$5,600*
LOBBY SPENDING: *$0*
Subsidiary of Chanel SA. Was among a group of codefendants in a class action price-fixing case with a settlement involving the mass giveaway of cosmetics in 2009. Uses phthalates in its products.

CIBA Vision Corporation
35% | 65%
Contributions: TOTAL: *$1,435* DEM: *$500* REP: *$935*
LOBBY SPENDING: *$0*
Subsidiary of Novartis AG. Has a written nondiscrimination policy covering sexual orientation and gender identity. Offers insurance coverage to employees' domestic partners. Insurance for transgender employees is offered, but treatment is not covered.

Colgate-Palmolive Co.
91% | 9%
Contributions: TOTAL: *$108,023* DEM: *$97,923* REP: *$10,100*
LOBBY SPENDING: *$40,000*
Named as a codefendant in a pending lawsuit brought by the American Lung Association and several environmental watchdogs seeking disclosure of ingredients in its detergents. A pending lawsuit alleges a hostile work environment due to pornography in the workplace. Does not conduct animal testing for its products. Listed by NAFE as one of the top 50 companies for female executives in 2009. Considered a family-friendly employer. In 2008, scored 44 out of 100 in "The Climate Counts Company Scorecard Report." Foundation supports dental health education for children. Has a written nondiscrimination policy covering sexual orientation and gender identity. Offers insurance coverage to employees' domestic partners. Insurance for transgender employees is offered, but treatment is not covered.

Conair Corporation
36% | 64%
Contributions: TOTAL: *$13,350* DEM: *$4,850* REP: *$8,500*
LOBBY SPENDING: *$0*
Privately held.

Coty, Inc.
93% | 7%
Contributions: TOTAL: *$4,500* DEM: *$4,200* REP: *$300*
LOBBY SPENDING: *$0*
Privately held. Has not signed the Compact for Safe Cosmetics. Some of its products have been tested and contain phthalates. Sponsors the "Linked Against Leukemia" initiative.

Cover Girl
Contributions: TOTAL: *$500*   DEM: *$500*   REP: *$0*
LOBBY SPENDING: *$0*

Subsidiary of Proctor & Gamble. It has removed phthalates from its nail polishes.

Curves International, Inc.
Contributions: TOTAL: *$114,967*   DEM: *$4,667*   REP: *$110,300*
LOBBY SPENDING: *$0*

This faith-based, private company claims to be the largest fitness franchise business in the world. The founders have been major contributors to conservative causes, including antigay and prolife causes.

CVS Caremark Corporation
Contributions: TOTAL: *$712,841*   DEM: *$381,952*   REP: *$330,889*
LOBBY SPENDING: *$5,845,510*

A pending lawsuit alleges some pharmacies illegally filled prescriptions for brand-name drugs with generic drugs without the prescribing doctors' permission. In 2008, agreed to pay $36.7 million to settle a lawsuit alleging drug substitution and insurance fraud. Agreed to a $38.5 million settlement in a multistate civil deceptive practices lawsuit in 2008. Was fined more than $226,000 in 2007 after a DOL investigation found dozens of stores changed employee time cards and violated child labor laws. CVS Caremark Charitable Trust awarded $6.4 million in 2008. Has a written nondiscrimination policy covering sexual orientation and gender identity. Offers insurance coverage to employees' domestic partners. Insurance for transgender employees is offered, but treatment is not covered.

Dial Corporation
Contributions: TOTAL: *$24,700*   DEM: *$14,200*   REP: *$10,500*
LOBBY SPENDING: *$40,000*

Privately held. In 2006, the EEOC sued for alleged gender bias.

Drugstore.com, Inc.
Contributions: TOTAL: *$950*   DEM: *$950*   REP: *$0*
LOBBY SPENDING: *$150,000*

Its distribution centers use recycled cardboard and all-vegetable inks. Foundation focuses on improving the health and well-being of individuals in transition in the communities where the company operates.

Dr. Bronner's Magic Soaps
Contributions: TOTAL: *$220*   DEM: *$220*   REP: *$0*
LOBBY SPENDING: *$0*

Privately held. Seeks to market only fair-trade and fully organic products. Recent charitable giving to social and environmental causes has roughly matched total after-tax income.

Eli Lilly & Co.
Contributions: TOTAL: *$1,226,603*   DEM: *$573,732*   REP: *$652,871*
LOBBY SPENDING: *$16,762,220*

Pending racial discrimination lawsuit. In 2009, pleaded guilty to a charge that it illegally marketed the antipsychotic drug Zyprexa for an unapproved use. In 2008, agreed to pay at least $1.2 billion to settle lawsuits from people who claimed they had developed diabetes or other diseases after taking Zyprexa. The same year, the company agreed to pay $15 million to settle a lawsuit filed by the State of Alaska over allegations that it concealed data about the side effects of Zyprexa and cost the state Medicaid program millions of dollars because of an increased incidence of diabetes. Outreach focuses on children's diabetes and assistance to tuberculosis patients. Has a written non-discrimination policy covering sexual orientation and gender identity. Offers insurance coverage to employees' domestic partners. Insurance for transgender employees is offered, and some treatment is covered.

68%   32%

Equinox Fitness Clubs
Contributions: TOTAL: *$7,101*   DEM: *$4,801*   REP: *$2,300*
LOBBY SPENDING: *$0*
Privately held.

90%   10%

Estée Lauder Companies, Inc.
Contributions: TOTAL: *$261,950*   DEM: *$234,500*   REP: *$27,450*
LOBBY SPENDING: *$320,000*
Among a group of codefendants in a class action price-fixing case with a settlement involving the mass giveaway of cosmetics in 2009. Does not conduct animal testing for its products. It has not signed the Compact for Safe Cosmetics. Has pledged to avoid the use of products made from clear-cut old-growth temperate rainforests and to source responsibly produced wood products. Its Breast Cancer Awareness Campaign provides the bulk of funding for the Breast Cancer Research Foundation. Has a written nondiscrimination policy covering sexual orientation and gender identity. Offers insurance coverage to employees' domestic partners. Insurance for transgender employees is offered, and treatment is covered.

100%   0%

Estée Lauder Cosmetics
Contributions: TOTAL: *$40,735*   DEM: *$40,735*   REP: *$0*
LOBBY SPENDING: *$0*
Subsidiary of Estée Lauder Companies, Inc.

64%   36%

Gillette Co., The
Contributions: TOTAL: *$7,000*   DEM: *$4,500*   REP: *$2,500*
LOBBY SPENDING: <*$40,000*
Subsidiary of Procter & Gamble. Does not conduct animal testing for its products.

39%   61%

GlaxoSmithKline PLC
Contributions: TOTAL: *$1,597,950* DEM: *$627,904*   REP: *$970,046*
LOBBY SPENDING: *$15,230,000*
Foreign owned. Questions have arisen about its outsourcing of drug trials overseas, such as in Argentina, where 13,000 children were test subjects and where some parents allegedly had not been informed of the testing. Has committed to reduce its energy and climate change impact per unit of sales by 45% of 2006 levels by 2015. Says it will reduce all its drug prices to 25% of Western prices in the 50 least developed countries (LDCs), release intellectual property rights for substances and processes relevant to neglected diseases into a patent pool to

encourage new drug development, and invest 20% of profits from the LDCs in medical infrastructure for those countries. The Access to Medicine Foundation ranked it number 1 of 20 of the largest global drug companies of 2008. Partners with WHO in seeking to eliminate the disease lymphatic filariasis. Supports nonprofit organizations to help improve health and education in underserved communities.

GNC Corp. (formerly General Nutrition Centers)
8%   93%
Contributions: Total: *$10,000* Dem: *$750* Rep: *$9,250*
Lobby Spending: *$0*
Subsidiary of Ares Management LLC. A pending class action lawsuit claims it damaged franchisees through unfair business practices. Has several pending class action lawsuits related to its purported muscle-building and athletic performance-enhancing products such as Creatine. Raises money for the Children's Hospital of Pittsburgh.

Gold's Gym
14%   86%
Contributions: Total: *$18,051* Dem: *$2,550* Rep: *$15,501*
Lobby Spending: *$0*
Subsidiary of TRT Holdings, Inc. A jury awarded $11 million in 2008 for a personal injury due to an equipment failure resulting in quadraplegia. In 2007, settled a lawsuit with the EEOC relating to creation of a hostile work environment.

Hoffman-La Roche, Inc.
60%   40%
Contributions: Total: *$458,104* Dem: *$276,241* Rep: *$181,863*
Lobby Spending: *$12,161,339*
Subsidiary of Roche Holding AG. A number of pending lawsuits allege Its drug Accutane Is linked to side effects such as psychiatric issues. In 2008, paid $12.8 million in a case that linked the use of Accutane to the onset of inflamatory bowel disease. In 2008, a former employee filed a claim for sexual harassment and dismissal for refusing to engage in illegal marketing practices. Has incorporated hybrid vehicles into its U.S. fleet. Has a written nondiscrimination policy covering sexual orientation and gender identity.

Jewel-Osco
100%   0%
Contributions: Total: *$250* Dem: *$250* Rep: *$0*
Lobby Spending: *$0*
Subsidiary of SUPERVALU, Inc. In 2008, received the Illinois EPA's "Partners for Clean Air" award. Outreach focuses on hunger relief, nutritional education, and environmental stewardship.

John Paul Mitchell Systems
100%   0%
Contributions: Total: *$250* Dem: *$250* Rep: *$0*
Lobby Spending: *$0*
Privately held. First hair care company to publicly oppose animal testing. Uses solar panels to generate electricity in Hawaii. Supports efforts to battle the problem of land mines. Funds the planting of enough trees to offset all carbon emissions from its manufacturing and distribution. A portion of the sales of all Tea Tree products funds American Forests' Global ReLeaf and Wildfire ReLeaf programs.

Johnson & Johnson

Contributions: Total: *$1,423,367*   Dem: *$855,276*   Rep: *$568,091*
Lobby Spending: *$14,620,000*

A pending lawsuit alleges subsidiary Janssen Pharmaceutica defrauded Texas to get on the state's Medicaid list. Is a codefendant in a pending class action lawsuit alleging misrepresentation of the health risks associated with exposure to bisphenol A (BPA) from its polycarbonate plastic baby bottles and training cups. Pending lawsuits allege tendon ruptures resulting from use of its drug Levaquin. Is a codefendant in a pending class action lawsuit alleging negligence or wrongdoing after a study revealed that many of its products for children contain probable cancer-causing chemicals. In 2009, spent at least $68.7 million to resolve U.S. lawsuits filed by women who suffered blood clots, heart attacks, or strokes after using the Ortho Evra birth control patch. Has paid tens of millions in wrongful death suits involving its pain treatment patch Duragesic; another 60 Duragesic lawsuits are pending in the United States. Paid a final settlement of $15 million in 2006 toward any remaining death and injury cases related to its drug Propulsid. Ranked number 1 by *DiversityInc* magazine on its "2009 DiversityInc Top 50 Companies for Diversity." *Working Mother* magazine has named it one of the "Top 100 Companies for Working Mothers" every year. The EPA has designated it a National Environmental Performance Track Corporate Leader. Sponsors programs to make children safer, provides resources for caregivers, and encourages the recruitment and retention of nursing professionals in the United States. Has a written nondiscrimination policy covering sexual orientation and gender identity. Offers insurance coverage to employees' domestic partners. Insurance for transgender employees is offered, and treatment is covered.

Kiehl's Since 1851 LLC

Contributions: Total: *$500*   Dem: *$500*   Rep: *$0*
Lobby Spending: *$0*
Privately held.

Kimberly-Clark Corporation

Contributions: Total: *$20,721*   Dem: *$7,471*   Rep: *$13,250*
Lobby Spending: *$280,000*

Named as a codefendant in a pending class action lawsuit alleging negligence or wrongdoing after a study revealed that many of its products for children contain probable cancer-causing chemicals. Is a codefendant in a pending class action lawsuit alleging misrepresentation of the health risks associated with exposure to BPA from its polycarbonate plastic baby bottles and training cups. Paid $165,000 in fines and damages in 2008 for air pollution from a fire it allowed to smolder. Criticized for contributing heavily to the cutting of ancient forests. Has yet to establish benchmarks for using recycled or sustainable materials. Named a 2009 Energy Star Partner of the Year by the EPA. Ranks 9th on EPA's Fortune 500 Green Power list. In 2009, awarded $1.5 million in college scholarships through its charitable foundation. Has a written nondiscrimination policy covering sexual orientation and gender identity. Offers insurance coverage to employees' domestic partners.

Lancôme US
100% / 0%
Contributions: TOTAL: *$3,200*   DEM: *$3,200*   REP: *$0*
LOBBY SPENDING: *$0*
Subsidiary of L'Oréal SA.

Longs Drug Stores Corporation
33% / 67%
Contributions: TOTAL: *$25,650*   DEM: *$8,450*   REP: *$17,200*
LOBBY SPENDING: *$49,500*
Subsidiary of CVS Caremark Corporation.

Luxottica Group S.p.A.
74% / 26%
Contributions: TOTAL: *$3,800*   DEM: *$2,800*   REP: *$1,000*
LOBBY SPENDING: *$0*
Foreign owned. A pending class action lawsuit concerns allegations of over-prescribing and breach of optometrist/patient privilege.

L'Oréal SA
68% / 32%
Contributions: TOTAL: *$33,900*   DEM: *$23,000*   REP: *$10,900*
LOBBY SPENDING: *$0*
Foreign owned. A pending lawsuit brought by a former employee claims that the company used chemicals banned in foreign countries and attempted to hide that fact. Has no policy against animal testing for its products. Community outreach includes a UNESCO project to encourage women to take up science professions.

L'Oréal USA
57% / 43%
Contributions: TOTAL: *$25,450*   DEM: *$14,550*   REP: *$10,900*
LOBBY SPENDING: *$0*
Subsidiary of L'Oréal SA. Pending class action lawsuits allege it made false claims for its products. A codefendant in a class action price-fixing case with a settlement involving the mass giveaway of cosmetics in 2009. Has not signed the Compact for Safe Cosmetics. In 2008, scored 58 out of 100 in "The Climate Counts Company Scorecard Report." Funds fellowships for its "Women in Science" program. Participates in a college scholarship program to assist young African Americans who attend selected Historically Black Colleges and Universities. Gave the "NY Coalition of 100 Black Women" a grant to expand. Has a written nondiscrimination policy covering sexual orientation but not gender identity.

Mary Kay Cosmetics
35% / 65%
Contributions: TOTAL: *$6,500*   DEM: *$2,300*   REP: *$4,200*
LOBBY SPENDING: *<$40,000*
Privately held. Does not conduct animal testing for its products. Has not signed the Compact for Safe Cosmetics. Partnered with the Arbor Day Foundation to plant 100,000 trees in the Bitterroot National Forest. Its charitable foundation has the mission to eliminate cancer and to end the epidemic of violence against women.

Max Factor
100% / 0%
Contributions: TOTAL: *$2,300*   DEM: *$2,300*   REP: *$0*
LOBBY SPENDING: *$0*
Subsidiary of Procter & Gamble. Has not signed the Compact for Safe Cosmetics.

McKesson Corp.

44% 56%

Contributions: TOTAL: *$730,131*   DEM: *$321,341*   REP: *$408,790*
LOBBY SPENDING: *$1,785,000*

In 2009, agreed to a $493 million settlement stemming from allegations of deliberately reporting false and inflated average wholesale prices for some drugs. In 2008, a $15 billion lawsuit alleged racketeering related to price-fixing. Is building its newest distribution center to LEED certification standards. Foundation awards 160 scholarships to employees' children and gives over $250,000 in cash grants to employees' favorite schools through its matching gifts program. Has a written nondiscrimination policy covering sexual orientation but not gender identity. Offers insurance coverage to employees' domestic partners. Insurance for transgender employees is offered, but treatment is not covered.

McNeil Consumer Health Care

87% 13%

Contributions: TOTAL: *$1,950*   DEM: *$1,700*   REP: *$250*
LOBBY SPENDING: *$160,000*

Subsidiary of Johnson & Johnson. In 2007, a jury awarded $5 million in a Tylenol-related wrongful death lawsuit. Settled a lawsuit over false claims relating to its product Splenda in 2007.

Merck & Co., Inc.

48% 52%

Contributions: TOTAL: *$1,258,491*   DEM: *$607,820*   REP: *$650,671*
LOBBY SPENDING: *$9,470,000*

In 2008, paid $650 million to settle two lawsuits that alleged it violated federal law by not offering the government the same deep price discounts it gave hospitals that showed preference to its products. In 2008, paid $58 million as part of a multistate settlement of allegations that its ads for the painkiller Vioxx played down the drug's associated health risks. In the same year, claims were filed for alleged misrepresentations and information withholding in approval submissions and filings with the FDA for its drug Vytorin. In 2007, paid $2.3 billion in back taxes, interest, and penalties. In 2009, signed on to the United Nations Global Compact. Ranked 8th on DiversityInc's list of the "Top 50 Companies for Diversity" in 2009. In 2007, it agreed to resolve violations of federal and state water pollution control regulations by paying $10 million to deploy systems that will prevent such discharges. Received the 2009 Energy Star Sustained Excellence Award from the EPA. Is increasing the number of people eligible for the Merck Patient Assistance Program, which provides medicines for chronic conditions. In 2008, awarded more than $8 million in grants to combat HIV and AIDS. Has donated over 2 billion MECTIZAN tablets to fight the spread of river blindness. Has a written nondiscrimination policy covering sexual orientation and gender identity. Offers insurance coverage to employees' domestic partners. Insurance for transgender employees is offered, and some treatment is covered.

M.A.C. Cosmetics, Inc.

100% 0%

Contributions: TOTAL: *$5,600*   DEM: *$5,600*   REP: *$0*
LOBBY SPENDING: *$0*

Subsidiary of Estée Lauder Companies, Inc. Its AIDS Fund (MAF) works to fight the stigma and shame associated with HIV and AIDS in the United Kingdom.

Neutrogena
Contributions: Total: *$2,100*   Dem: *$0*   Rep: *$2,100*
Lobby Spending: *$0*

Subsidiary of Johnson & Johnson. Pending lawsuits allege skin injuries related to use of the company's products. In 2006, was one of the defendants in a class action lawsuit alleging misleading claims for sunscreen products. Has not signed the Compact for Safe Cosmetics.

Novartis AG
Contributions: Total: *$684,023*   Dem: *$301,772*   Rep: *$382,251*
Lobby Spending: *$12,499,420*

Foreign owned. A pending $200 million class action lawsuit alleges gender discrimination. A pending lawsuit claims that the company inflated prices paid by the Alabama Medicaid program. A pending lawsuit brought by a former employee alleges that she was wrongfully discharged as a direct result of her refusal to participate in activities she believed were illegal. Pending lawsuits regard use of Triaminic children's cold remedy and complications arising from use of Elidel. Ranked 20th in 2009 DiversityInc's "Top 50 Companies for Diversity." *Working Mother* magazine listed it as one of the 100 Best Companies for Women in 2008. In 2009, generic subsidiary Sandoz withdrew from the International Federation of Pharmaceutical Manufacturers and Associations (IFPMA) after it was criticized for violating IFPMA's code of ethics in the labeling of its products. Named a leader in sustainability in the health products industry by the 2008 Dow Jones Sustainability Index. Its foundation seeks to bring an end to leprosy and malaria. Has a written nondiscrimination policy covering sexual orientation and gender identity. Offers insurance coverage to employees' domestic partners.

Pearle Vision
Contributions: Total: *$5,600*   Dem: *$5,600*   Rep: *$0*
Lobby Spending: *$0*

Subsidiary of Luxottica Retail (U.S.). A 2006 lawsuit alleged unlicensed practice of optometry, deceptive marketing, and unfair business practices. Its foundation funds vision preservation grants and scholarships to students pursuing degrees in optometry.

Pfizer, Inc.
Contributions: Total: *$2,163,411*   Dem: *$1,115,048*   Rep: *$1,048,363*
Lobby Spending: *$25,980,000*

In 2009, settled a lawsuit brought in Nigeria regarding the testing of a drug on children, allegedly without parental permission. In 2008, settled the majority of cases arising from consumer fraud and from use of its drugs Celebrex and Bextra. The FDA has received hundreds of reports of serious and sometimes fatal injuries linked to the company's anti-smoking drug Chantix. Listed by NAFE as one of the top 50 companies for female executives in 2009. Supports efforts against malaria, HIV/AIDS, and blindness due to trachoma infection. Has a written nondiscrimination policy covering sexual orientation and gender identity. Offers insurance coverage to employees' domestic partners. Insurance for transgender employees is offered, and some treatment is covered.

Playtex Products, Inc.
27% | 73%
Contributions: TOTAL: *$9,450*   DEM: *$2,550*   REP: *$6,900*
LOBBY SPENDING: *$0*
Subsidiary of Energizer Holdings, Inc. In 2008, named as a codefendant in several class action lawsuits alleging misrepresentation of the health risks associated with BPA exposure through use of polycarbonate plastic baby bottles and training cups. In 2006, named as a defendant in a class action lawsuit alleging misleading claims for sunscreen products. Supports the National Breast Cancer Foundation.

Procter & Gamble
43% | 57%
Contributions: TOTAL: *$580,816*   DEM: *$252,309*   REP: *$328,507*
LOBBY SPENDING: *$6,030,171*
Named as a codefendant in a pending lawsuit brought by the American Lung Association and several environmental watchdogs seeking disclosure of ingredients in its detergents. Named as a codefendant in a pending class action lawsuit alleging negligence or wrongdoing after a study revealed that many of the company's products for children contain probable cancer-causing chemicals. Is a codefendant in a pending class action lawsuit alleging misrepresentation of the health risks associated with exposure to BPA from its polycarbonate plastic baby bottles and training cups. Ranked 11th on DiversityInc's list of the "Top 50 Companies for Diversity" in 2009. Listed by NAFE as one of the top 50 companies for female executives in 2009. In 2008, scored 69 out of 100 in "The Climate Counts Company Scorecard Report." Has not signed the Compact for Safe Cosmetics. Has collaborated with the CDC to develop safe drinking water systems that people can easily use in their homes. Has a written nondiscrimination policy covering sexual orientation and gender identity. Offers insurance coverage to employees' domestic partners.

Reckitt Benckiser, Inc.
60% | 40%
Contributions: TOTAL: *$4,950*   DEM: *$2,950*   REP: *$2,000*
LOBBY SPENDING: *$0*
Subsidiary of foreign-owned Reckitt Benckiser PLC. Named as a codefendant in a pending lawsuit brought by the American Lung Association and several environmental watchdogs seeking disclosure of ingredients in its detergents. Is planting more than 4 million trees in new forests.

Redken Laboratories LLC
100% | 0%
Contributions: TOTAL: *$500*   DEM: *$500*   REP: *$0*
LOBBY SPENDING: *$0*
Subsidiary of L'Oréal SA. Has not signed the Compact for Safe Cosmetics.

Regis Corporation (RGS)
8% | 92%
Contributions: TOTAL: *$32,380*   DEM: *$2,750*   REP: *$29,630*
LOBBY SPENDING: *$0*
In 2007, the EEOC filed a lawsuit alleging civil rights violations. Has a written nondiscrimination policy covering sexual orientation but not gender identity.

Revlon, Inc.
Contributions: TOTAL: *$24,000*   DEM: *$15,900*   REP: *$8,100*
LOBBY SPENDING: *$0*

66% | 34%

Subsidiary of MacAndrews & Forbes Holdings, Inc. Has not signed the Compact for Safe Cosmetics. Supports the National Breast Cancer Coalition.

Rite Aid
Contributions: TOTAL: *$216,635*   DEM: *$140,635*   REP: *$76,000*
LOBBY SPENDING: *$1,040,000*

65% | 35%

Subsidiary of Leonard Green & Partners, LP. In 2009, a lawsuit was filed alleging that the company did not properly pay employees for overtime. In 2008, settled two lawsuits for a total of over $1.8 million in connection with allegedly selling baby formula and other products past their expiration dates and artificially inflating prices at its stores. In 2007, was sued over alleged union suppression. Is one of the top contributors to the Children's Miracle Network. Has a written nondiscrimination policy covering sexual orientation but not gender identity. Offers insurance coverage to employees' domestic partners. Insurance for transgender employees is offered, and treatment is covered.

Sally Beauty Holdings, Inc.
Contributions: TOTAL: *$6,550*   DEM: *$0*   REP: *$6,550*
LOBBY SPENDING: *$0*

0% | 100%

A pending lawsuit alleges it failed to properly compensate employees for overtime. In 2008, settled an EEOC lawsuit alleging racial discrimination.

Schering-Plough Corporation
Contributions: TOTAL: *$674,364*   DEM: *$299,869*   REP: *$374,495*
LOBBY SPENDING: *$4,320,000*

44% | 56%

A pending whistle-blower lawsuit was filed by four former employees for being terminated after disclosing illegal marketing and sales practices. Named as a codefendant in a pending lawsuit alleging violations of state consumer protection laws arising from the sale and marketing of Zetia and Vytorin. In 2009, paid $165 million to resolve a class action lawsuit alleging it failed to disclose manufacturing issues that delayed FDA approval for its allergy drug Clarinex. In 2008, agreed to pay $31 million for allegedly improperly pricing drugs purchased by the Medicaid program. In 2006, paid $435 million to the DOJ to settle allegations ranging from the improper marketing of drugs to defrauding the Medicare and Medicaid programs. One of its divisions also pleaded guilty to criminal wrongdoing. In 2009, began using a 1.7 megawatt solar energy system at one of its plants. In 2009, announced a license agreement to give developing countries access to technology for the manufacture of pandemic influenza vaccine. In 2007, provided 500,000 environmentally friendly inhalers. Its foundation provides $150,000 in science scholarships to New Jersey high schools. Has a written nondiscrimination policy covering sexual orientation and gender identity. Offers insurance coverage to employees' domestic partners. Insurance for transgender employees is offered, and some treatment is covered.

Sephora USA LLC

98% / 2%

Contributions: Total: *$13,175*   Dem: *$12,975*   Rep: *$200*
Lobby Spending: *$0*

Subsidiary of LVMH Moët Hennessy Louis Vuitton SA. In 2007, settled a class action lawsuit with the EEOC for $576,000 over allegations of racial discrimination.

Tom's of Maine, Inc.

86% / 14%

Contributions: Total: *$23,090*   Dem: *$19,790*   Rep: *$3,300*
Lobby Spending: *$0*

Subsidiary of Colgate-Palmolive Company. Does not conduct animal testing for its products. Most of its product packaging is made from 100% postconsumer recycled materials. Has pledged $1 million to the "Rivers Awareness Partnership" with American Rivers and River Network. Donates 10% of pretax profits to charitable organizations supporting the environment, human needs, the arts, and education. Employees are encouraged to use 5% of their paid time volunteering at nonprofit organizations.

Town Sports International Holdings, Inc.

59% / 41%

Contributions: Total: *$8,050*   Dem: *$4,750*   Rep: *$3,300*
Lobby Spending: *$0*

Private equity firm Bruckmann, Rosser, Sherrill & Co. owns more than 25% of the company. In 2006, settled a lawsuit resolving allegations that it acted in violation of the ADA.

Unilever N.V.

96% / 4%

Contributions: Total: *$178,700*   Dem: *$171,300*   Rep: *$7,400*
Lobby Spending: *$1,580,000*

Foreign owned. In 2008, scored 75 out of 100 in "The Climate Counts Company Scorecard Report." In 2008, announced that by 2015 all the palm oil used to make its products must be certified as deriving from sustainable sources. Has made a 35% reduction in carbon dioxide from energy per metric ton of production since 1995.

Unilever USA

100% / 0%

Contributions: Total: *$7,600*   Dem: *$7,600*   Rep: *$0*
Lobby Spending: *$1,580,000*

Subsidiary of Unilever N.V. In 2008, awarded grants to U.S. National Parks programs totaling $240,000. Is the longest-standing corporate partner of the National Park Foundation, to which it has provided more than $24 million in support. Has a written nondiscrimination policy covering sexual orientation and gender identity. Offers insurance coverage to employees' domestic partners. Insurance for transgender employees is offered, but treatment is not covered.

Walgreen Co.

64% / 36%

Contributions: Total: *$376,704*   Dem: *$239,553*   Rep: *$137,151*
Lobby Spending: *$2,480,000*

In 2008, paid $35 million to settle claims that it improperly switched patients to different versions of prescription drugs so it could increase the reimbursement amounts it received from Medicaid. In 2008, reached a $24 million settlement involving racial discrimination claims brought by the EEOC. In 2008, paid $9.9 million to resolve allegations of improperly billing Medicare for prescription drugs dispensed to people who were covered by both Medicare and private third-party insurance. Has 20 stores with solar panels. Partners with Friends of the Urban Forest. Offers free health screenings. Supports disaster relief efforts and food banks. Has a written nondiscrimination policy covering sexual orientation and gender identity. Offers insurance coverage to employees' domestic partners. Insurance for transgender employees is offered, but treatment is not covered.

Wyeth

52% ▬▬▬ 48%

Contributions: TOTAL: *$698,838*   DEM: *$365,628*   REP: *$333,210*
LOBBY SPENDING: *$5,782,568*

Has many pending lawsuits related to use of the menopause drugs Prempro and Premarin, for which a 2002 study turned up cancer links. Is named as a codefendant in a pending lawsuit for alleged off-label marketing of the drugs Aranesp and Enbrel. A 2009 Supreme Court decision upheld an award of $6.7 million to a musician who lost her arm after an injection of its prescription medication Phenergan. In 2007, a jury made a $134.5 million judgment against it in a lawsuit filed by three women who claimed its hormone replacement drugs caused their breast cancer. Listed by NAFE as one of the top 50 companies for female executives in 2009. *Working Mother* magazine listed it as one of the 100 Best Companies for Women in 2008. Has a written nondiscrimination policy covering sexual orientation but not gender identity.

Home and Garden

Chris Colin

One spring day in April 2009, Michelle Obama and students from a local elementary school took shovels to the South Lawn of the White House and planted a vegetable garden. Locally grown organic produce, kids learning about healthy food—only the pesticide industry could object, and indeed it did.

"As you go about planning and planting the White House garden, we respectfully encourage you to recognize the role conventional agriculture plays in the U.S.," wrote the Mid America CropLife Association, an association of several dozen companies from the agriculture chemical industry. The letter more or less urged the White House to consider the well-known advantages of spritzing one's arugula with a healthy dose of Roundup.

As PR efforts go, this one wilted on contact. The pesticide companies inadvertently branded themselves a desperate industry facing obsolescence at the hands of a forward-thinking administration. The truth is more complex. While the White House has indeed joined the growing sustainable-farming movement, the $20 billion lawn and garden industry remains powerful and well represented on K Street. (Obama's secretary of agriculture, Tom Vilsack, has what some consider uncomfortable ties to Monsanto, for example.)

Still, within the larger home and garden sector, there's a sense that things are changing. Pressure has been steadily mounting, for instance, to force appliance manufacturers to increase their products' energy efficiency. In California, which tends to lead the nation on such matters, the state's Energy Commission has trained its sights on televisions; along with their associated devices—DVD players, TiVos, and so on—televisions consume a full 10% of a home's electricity. If a recent proposal is passed, televisions sold in the state would have to cut their energy usage in half by 2013.

Taking a page from the pre-Obama auto industry, the Consumer Electronics Association has resisted the move toward efficiency standards. Industry observers have noted that, three decades ago, the same commission took on refrigerators, then a huge drain on the state's power grid. The efforts met with similar resistance, but today refrigerators consume just a quarter of the electricity they did then.

In general, the move toward reducing environmental impact is one of the bigger changes facing the home and garden sector. Among would-be reformers of the industry, efficiency is increasingly the holy grail. It's not a particularly sexy cause—it lacks the high-tech appeal of, say, tidal power—but its potential energy savings could dwarf those of many alternative energy proposals.

Ironically, it was President George W. Bush who brought national attention to the matter of "power vampires," or appliances that continue to suck power from outlets even when off. Bush was derided for the seemingly insignificant environmental gesture, but his science was solid. The advent of "standby mode" has meant a cost of 65 billion kilowatt hours of power each year in the United States and the release of over 80 billion pounds of carbon dioxide into the atmosphere. Indeed, the ubiquitous display clocks and memory chips on our assorted electronic devices are said to consume up to 8% of the country's total energy.

If Bush got a couple things right in the home sphere, he also built much of his presidency around one colossal miscalculation there. His "ownership society" was a central platform from the beginning, and American liberty was equated with holding the deed to one's own home. In truth, his push for us all to snap up real estate had more to do with pleasing the financial sector, but few felt compelled to split hairs. Home values were set to drift ever upward, common sense be damned, and all we had to worry about was finding a salesclerk at Home Depot.

The salesclerks are easier to spot now—the ones who haven't been laid off, anyway. As the imploding housing market continues to rock the industry, Home Depot and others wait to see what, exactly, the downturn will mean. Given diversification habits within these companies, the ramifications could be far-reaching: General Electric may call to mind your washing machine, for example, but it has also produced antipersonnel mine components. In addition to being a billion-dollar weapons manufacturer, General Electric owns a majority stake in NBC, which some critics have claimed was insufficiently critical of the administration's justifications for going to war in Iraq—and which, according to the *New York Times*, was enlisted in 2001 to help appeal an order that General Electric begin a costly cleanup of the Hudson River, into which it has dumped PCBs.

Even those companies that focus exclusively on this sector find themselves battling regulators and defending against ever-more-savvy consumers. Leading pesticide manufacturers, for instance, formed the benign-sounding Responsible Industry for a Sound Environment political action committee—clearly a misleading name. Spending millions each year on lobbyists, groups like this fight to limit regulation and in some cases to obscure data and lawsuits related to the damage their products can cause. Meanwhile, the lumber and paper industries have not only a powerful lobby, but also sympathetic politicians to frame their controversial practices as a jobs-versus-owls debate—even though these industries outsource more and more jobs to Mexico and elsewhere.

Nevertheless, activist groups have had some phenomenal successes. The world's largest supplier of home improvement products, Home Depot, Inc., faced a vast and ongoing protest against its sale of rainforest lumber. Fearing a broader backlash, the company eventually reversed many of its policies and has since taken up the cause of sustainable harvesting. Even General Electric has begun moving—glacially, some say—toward a greener business.

In many cases, the home and garden sector is no more confined to our homes and gardens than we are. Ushering the sector through the recession while correcting some of its more toxic habits will be a major project. Maybe there's no better place to start than a row of organic carrots in the South Lawn—gardens grow inch by inch, as the song tells us.

Top Ten Democratic Contributors

Home Depot, Inc.	$581,306
Deere & Company	$201,380
3M Company	$173,914
Container Store, The	$137,750
Bed Bath & Beyond	$136,600
GOJO Industries	$110,750
Shaklee Corporation	$70,549
Ecolab, Inc.	$51,600
Mattel, Inc.	$51,400
Russ Berrie and Company, Inc.	$49,300

Top Ten Republican Contributors

Home Depot, Inc.	$835,072
Deere & Company	$400,986
3M Company	$235,831
Kohler Company	$151,500
Bed Bath & Beyond	$107,050
True Manufacturing Co., Inc.	$103,700
Haworth, Inc.	$103,600
Williams-Sonoma, Inc.	$100,500
Ashley Furniture Industries, Inc.	$99,850
W. W. Grainger, Inc.	$99,342

Top Ten Lobbying Spenders

Deere & Company	$3,805,000
3M Company	$3,761,676
Home Depot, Inc.	$2,116,500
Mattel, Inc.	$1,270,000
Whirlpool Corporation	$950,000
Lowe's Companies, Inc.	$470,000
Tupperware Brands Corporation	$300,000
Toys "R" Us, Inc.	$195,000
Clorox Company, The	$170,000
S. C. Johnson & Son, Inc.	$132,981

42%   58%

3M Company
Contributions: TOTAL: *$409,745*   DEM: *$173,914*   REP: *$235,831*
LOBBY SPENDING: *$3,761,676*
A pending class action lawsuit alleges age discrimination. A second
pending age-discrimination class action lawsuit alleges violation of the
ADEA. Has received its fifth Energy Star Award for Sustained Excellence in Energy Management. Has cut its absolute greenhouse gas
emissions and solid waste. Foundation provided a $1 million grant to
The Nature Conservancy in 2008. Received a perfect score of 100 on
the Human Rights Campaign Corporate Equality Index. Has a written
nondiscrimination policy covering sexual orientation and gender iden-

tity. Offers insurance coverage to employees' domestic partners. Insurance for transgender employees is offered, and treatment is covered.

84 Lumber Co. LP
11% | 89%
Contributions: TOTAL: *$99,649*   DEM: *$11,100*   REP: *$88,549*
LOBBY SPENDING: *$0*
Privately held. Named as a codefendant in a 2009 class action lawsuit claiming it distributed and sold drywall that allegedly caused sulfur-related problems. Supports volunteer fire departments, the Red Cross, the United Way, and Habitat for Humanity. Has no written nondiscrimination policy covering sexual orientation or gender identity.

Aaron Brothers, Inc.
45% | 55%
Contributions: TOTAL: *$458*   DEM: *$208*   REP: *$250*
LOBBY SPENDING: *$0*
Subsidiary of Michaels Stores, Inc.; parent, Bain Capital LLC.

Ace Hardware Corporation
27% | 73%
Contributions: TOTAL: *$13,801*   DEM: *$3,750*   REP: *$10,051*
LOBBY SPENDING: *$0*
Privately held. Named as one of 55 codefendants in a lawsuit over alleged asbestos exposure. Partners with Little League. Foundation supports the Children's Miracle Network and the American Red Cross. Has a written nondiscrimination policy covering sexual orientation but not gender identity.

American Lawn Mower Company
0% | 100%
Contributions: TOTAL: *$12,600*   DEM: *$0*   REP: *$12,600*
LOBBY SPENDING: *$0*
Privately held.

Ariens Corporation
0% | 100%
Contributions: TOTAL: *$7,500*   DEM: *$0*   REP: *$7,500*
LOBBY SPENDING: *$0*
Privately held. In 2009, introduced the first all-electric riding lawn mower for the consumer market. Funded construction of a $1.5 million technology and engineering education center for students of Brillion High School.

Ashley Furniture Industries, Inc.
6% | 94%
Contributions: TOTAL: *$105,850*   DEM: *$6,000*   REP: *$99,850*
LOBBY SPENDING: *$0*
Privately held. Has reduced its air pollution emissions. Has no written nondiscrimination policy covering sexual orientation or gender identity.

BabyCenter, LLC
100% | 0%
Contributions: TOTAL: *$2,750*   DEM: *$2,750*   REP: *$0*
LOBBY SPENDING: *$0*
Subsidiary of Johnson & Johnson.

Bed Bath & Beyond

56% | 44%

Contributions: TOTAL: *$243,650*   DEM: *$136,600*   REP: *$107,050*
LOBBY SPENDING: *$0*

In 2009, settled a class action lawsuit that alleged it deceptively marketed its line of sheets by using exaggerated thread counts. Has a written nondiscrimination policy covering sexual orientation but not gender identity.

Black & Decker Corporation, The

35% | 65%

Contributions: TOTAL: *$15,951*   DEM: *$5,550*   REP: *$10,401*
LOBBY SPENDING: *$0*

Named as a codefendant in a pending case brought by California municipalities that alleges a plume of perchlorate has contaminated groundwater. Paid $50 million in 2008 to settle a lawsuit brought by the IRS. Requires its suppliers to ensure that their employees have the right to join lawful labor associations to represent them collectively. Outreach focuses on community revitalization and education. Offers its employees $5,000 toward the cost of adopting a child. Has a written nondiscrimination policy covering sexual orientation but not gender identity. Offers insurance coverage to employees' domestic partners.

Brady Industries

0% | 100%

Contributions: TOTAL: *$69,603*   DEM: *$250*   REP: *$69,353*
LOBBY SPENDING: *$0*

Privately held.

Briggs & Stratton Corporation

15% | 85%

Contributions: TOTAL: *$8,600*   DEM: *$1,250*   REP: *$7,350*
LOBBY SPENDING: *$0*

Named as a codefendant in a pending class action lawsuit alleging manufacturers of lawnmowers have purposely misstated horsepower valuations on their products in order to justify higher prices. Has reduced its toxic emissions by 90%. Established environmental audit committees to ensure suppliers practice environmentally sound business. Supports Big Brothers/Big Sisters, Goodwill Industries, Briggs & Al's Run & Walk for Children's Hospital, and Susan G. Komen Race for the Cure.

Bright Horizons Family Solutions, Inc.

100% | 0%

Contributions: TOTAL: *$25,050*   DEM: *$25,050*   REP: *$0*
LOBBY SPENDING: *$0*

Subsidiary of Bain Capital LLC. Ranked 80th on *Fortune* magazine's "100 Best Companies to Work For" in 2009. In 2009, DiversityInc recognized it as one of that year's 25 Most Noteworthy Companies. Foundation has created 200 play places for children in homeless shelters. Has a written nondiscrimination policy covering sexual orientation and gender identity. Offers insurance coverage to employees' domestic partners. Insurance for transgender employees is offered, but treatment is not covered.

Central Garden & Pet Company

67% | 33%

Contributions: TOTAL: *$757*   DEM: *$507*   REP: *$250*
LOBBY SPENDING: *$0*

Faces a pending lawsuit for selling pet products that are harmful to both pets and humans without proper warning labels.

Church & Dwight Co., Inc.

70% | 30%

Contributions: TOTAL: *$12,700*   DEM: *$8,850*   REP: *$3,850*
LOBBY SPENDING: *$120,000*

Named as a codefendant in a pending lawsuit brought by the American Lung Association and several environmental watchdog groups seeking disclosure of ingredients in its detergents. Uses 25% postconsumer recycled content in producing its laundry detergent bottles. Has a written nondiscrimination policy covering sexual orientation but not gender identity.

Clorox Company, The

79% | 21%

Contributions: TOTAL: *$29,324*   DEM: *$23,205*   REP: *$6,119*
LOBBY SPENDING: *$170,000*

In 2009, launched a recycling program for its Brita pitcher water filters. In 2008, scored 15 out of 100 in "The Climate Counts Company Scorecard Report." About 90% of its U.S. product cartons are made from 100% recycled content, and most of its retail displays are made from 100% postconsumer waste. Foundation supports education, youth development, and cultural and civic vitality. Has a written nondiscrimination policy covering sexual orientation and gender identity. Offers insurance coverage to employees' domestic partners. Insurance for transgender employees is offered, but treatment is not covered.

Container Store, The

100% | 0%

Contributions: TOTAL: *$137,750*   DEM: *$137,750*   REP: *$0*
LOBBY SPENDING: *$0*

Subsidiary of Leonard Green & Partners LP. Ranked 32nd on *Fortune* magazine's "100 Best Companies to Work For" in 2009. Has made *Fortune's* list of "100 Best Places to Work in America" every year since 1999, in part because it provides benefits for part-time employees and wages above the industry standard.

Cost Plus, Inc.

100% | 0%

Contributions: TOTAL: *$250*   DEM: *$250*   REP: *$0*
LOBBY SPENDING: *$0*

In 2009, settled a class action lawsuit that alleged it violated a provision of the Fair and Accurate Credit Transactions Act. The majority of its goods are constructed of farm-raised wood, recycled metal, recycled glass, and bamboo.

Deere & Company

33% | 67%

Contributions: TOTAL: *$602,366*   DEM: *$201,380*   REP: *$400,986*
LOBBY SPENDING: *$3,805,000*

In 2009, retirees filed a class action lawsuit alleging that changes to their benefits package dramatically altered the package. Named as a codefendant in a pending class action lawsuit alleging that manufacturers of lawnmowers have purposely misstated horsepower valuations on their products in order to justify higher prices. In 2006, began recruiting African American businessmen and women to become dealers after a lawsuit stated that there was not a single African American among the roughly 1,400 dealers nationwide. Its goal is to reduce its total global greenhouse gas emissions by 25% per dollar of revenue through 2014. Supports community betterment, higher education, and solutions for world hunger. Sponsors the national Future Farmers of America, the national 4-H Council, and MANRRS (Minorities in Agriculture, Natural Resources, and Related Sciences). Has a written nondiscrimination policy covering sexual orientation but not gender identity. Offers insurance coverage only to employees' opposite sex domestic partners.

Do It Best Corp.

0% — 100%

Contributions: TOTAL: *$25,450*   DEM: *$0*   REP: *$25,450*
LOBBY SPENDING: *$0*
Privately held.

Doane Pet Care Company

0% — 100%

Contributions: TOTAL: *$3,300*   DEM: *$0*   REP: *$3,300*
LOBBY SPENDING: *$0*
Subsidiary of Mars, Inc.. In 2008, settled, as a codefendant, a $24 million lawsuit over contaminated pet food linked to the deaths of perhaps thousands of dogs and cats.

Drs. Foster & Smith, Inc.

2% — 98%

Contributions: TOTAL: *$12,250*   DEM: *$250*   REP: *$12,000*
LOBBY SPENDING: *$0*
Privately held. Ships products using starch peanuts made on site that are 100% biodegradable and boxes that are made from 75% recycled/69% postconsumer recycled corrugated cardboard. Many of its products are made with recycled materials, biodegradable materials, or both.

Ecolab, Inc.

37% — 63%

Contributions: TOTAL: *$138,580*   DEM: *$51,600*   REP: *$86,980*
LOBBY SPENDING: *$100,000*
In 2009, paid $118,000 to settle a case brought under the amended Uniformed Services Employment and Reemployment Rights Act of 1994. Its goal is to reduce its U.S. greenhouse gas emissions by 20% per dollar sales from 2006 to 2012. Partners with Ronald McDonald House; also supports youth, education, the arts, and conservation. Has a written nondiscrimination policy covering sexual orientation but not gender identity. Offers insurance coverage to employees' domestic partners.

Ethan Allen Interiors, Inc.

55% — 45%

Contributions: TOTAL: *$18,250*   DEM: *$10,000*   REP: *$8,250*
LOBBY SPENDING: *$0*
A lawsuit brought by terminated employees for alleged age discrimination is pending. A pending class action lawsuit alleges failure to pay overtime, allow rest and meal breaks, and reimburse expense claims. Uses water-based materials for all packaging materials. Is launching a "green" line of products. Has a written nondiscrimination policy covering sexual orientation and gender identity. Offers insurance coverage to employees' domestic partners.

Euromarket Designs, Inc. (Crate and Barrel)
Contributions: TOTAL: *$17,835* DEM: *$17,835* REP: *$0*
LOBBY SPENDING: *$0*
100% / 0%
Foreign owned. Subsidiary of Otto GmbH & Co KG. Shopping bags are made from 30% postconsumer material and printed with water-based inks. Has a written nondiscrimination policy covering sexual orientation but not gender identity. Offers insurance coverage to employees' domestic partners.

Excellience Learning Corporation
Contributions: TOTAL: *$2,500* DEM: *$2,300* REP: *$200*
LOBBY SPENDING: *$0*
92% / 8%
Privately held. Subsidiary of Thoma Bravo LLC.

Fiskars Brands, Inc.
Contributions: TOTAL: *$500* DEM: *$500* REP: *$0*
LOBBY SPENDING: *$0*
100% / 0%
Foreign owned. Subsidiary of Fiskars Oyj Abp.

Gaiam, Inc.
Contributions: TOTAL: *$7,750* DEM: *$5,750* REP: *$2,000*
LOBBY SPENDING: *$0*
74% / 26%
Has purchased 1,500 trees to offset the carbon impact of its operations. Its catalog has earned the Forest Stewardship Council certification. Uses 100% recyclable and biodegradable packaging for all media. Partners with "Fair Trade."

Garden Ridge Corporation
Contributions: TOTAL: *$500* DEM: *$500* REP: *$0*
LOBBY SPENDING: *$0*
100% / 0%
Subsidiary of Three Cities Research, Inc.

Gerber Products Company
Contributions: TOTAL: *$200* DEM: *$0* REP: *$200*
LOBBY SPENDING: *$0*
0% / 100%
Subsidiary of Nestlé USA, Inc. Named as a codefendant in a class action lawsuit alleging negligence or wrongdoing after a study revealed that many of its products for children contain probable cancer-causing chemicals. A pending lawsuit alleges it deceptively marketed its "fruit juice" snacks. Is a codefendant in another pending class action lawsuit alleging misrepresentation of the health risks associated with exposure to BPA from its polycarbonate plastic baby bottles and training cups.

GOJO Industries
Contributions: TOTAL: *$110,750* DEM: *$110,750* REP: *$0*
LOBBY SPENDING: *$0*
100% / 0%
Privately held.

GUND, Inc.
Contributions: TOTAL: *$750* DEM: *$0* REP: *$750*
LOBBY SPENDING: *$0*
0% / 100%
Privately held. An official sponsor of the March of Dimes.

Hartmann, Inc.
6% | 94%
Contributions: TOTAL: *$38,700*   DEM: *$2,300*   REP: *$36,400*
LOBBY SPENDING: *$0*
Privately held. Subsidiary of Clarion Capital Partners.

Hartz Mountain Corporation, The
14% | 86%
Contributions: TOTAL: *$1,750*   DEM: *$250*   REP: *$1,500*
LOBBY SPENDING: *$0*
Foreign owned. Subsidiary of Sumitomo Corporation. Is a codefendant in a lawsuit filed by the NRDC for alleged illegal sale of pet products containing the known cancer-causing chemical propoxur without proper warning labels. In 2006, ceased producing its phenothrin-containing flea and tick products for cats; however, the EPA's product cancellation order did not apply to Hartz's flea and tick products for dogs, and Hartz continues to use phenothrin in a concentration of 85.7% in many of those products. Partners with several universities to research pet care.

Haworth, Inc.
4% | 96%
Contributions: TOTAL: *$108,200*   DEM: *$4,600*   REP: *$103,600*
LOBBY SPENDING: *$0*
Privately held. Has reduced its U.S. greenhouse gas emissions. Its LEED-certified facilities offset 100% of their energy requirements through renewable energy credits. Has achieved zero waste at one of its manufacturing plants. Partners with United Way, Susan G. Komen Race for the Cure, and Habitat for Humanity.

Henkel AG & Co. KGaA
70% | 30%
Contributions: TOTAL: *$45,650*   DEM: *$31,950*   REP: *$13,700*
LOBBY SPENDING: *$0*
Foreign owned. Has reduced water consumption by 48%, energy consumption by 40%, and waste generation by 37% since 1995.

Hill's Pet Nutrition, Inc.
69% | 31%
Contributions: TOTAL: *$16,600*   DEM: *$11,400*   REP: *$5,200*
LOBBY SPENDING: *$0*
Subsidiary of Colgate-Palmolive Co. Named as a codefendant in a pending class action lawsuit that alleges that pet food companies have fraudulently or negligently misrepresented and concealed the contents of their pet foods, engaged in deceptive and unfair trade practices, and failed to warn the public of the health risks to animals associated with a diet consisting of their commercial pet foods. In 2008, settled, as a codefendant, a $24 million lawsuit over contaminated pet food linked to the deaths of perhaps thousands of dogs and cats. Two new manufacturing plants are designed to obtain LEED certification. Has committed $1 million to the Morris Animal Foundation for feline research. Supports animal shelters by providing pet foods for free.

Home Depot, Inc.
41% | 59%
Contributions: TOTAL: *$1,416,378*   DEM: *$581,306*   REP: *$835,072*
LOBBY SPENDING: *$2,116,500*
Co-founder Bernie Marcus has described the Employee Free Choice Act as "the demise of civilization." A pending class action lawsuit alleges that it unfairly denied overtime pay and pension benefits.

Retired and current employees that invested in the 401(k) portfolio with Home Depot stock have alleged mismanagement of the funds in a pending class action ERISA lawsuit. In 2008, paid $14.5 million to settle a whistle-blower lawsuit alleging an employee was discharged in retaliation for refusal to make unwarranted chargebacks against vendors for merchandise that was undamaged. In 2008, settled a lawsuit based on allegations of employee abuse. Agreed to pay a $1.3 million penalty and implement a nationwide compliance program in 2008 to resolve alleged violations of the Clean Water Act. In 2007, paid nearly $10 million to settle allegations of failure to properly store and transport hazardous sludge. Its foundation is investing $400 million in grants for 100,000 affordable "green" homes and the planting and preservation of more than 3 million trees in urban areas. Has a written nondiscrimination policy covering sexual orientation but not gender identity. Offers insurance coverage to employees' domestic partners. Insurance for transgender employees is offered, but treatment is not covered.

Iams Company
0% / 100%
Contributions: Total: *$2,000*   Dem: *$0*   Rep: *$2,000*
Lobby Spending: *$0*
Subsidiary of Procter & Gamble. Named as a codefendant in a pending class action lawsuit that alleges that pet food companies have fraudulently or negligently misrepresented and concealed the content of their pet foods, engaged in deceptive and unfair trade practices, and failed to warn the public of the health risks to animals associated with a diet consisting of their commercial pet foods. In 2008, settled, as a codefendant, a $24 million lawsuit over contaminated pet food linked to the deaths of perhaps thousands of dogs and cats. Offers insurance coverage to employees' domestic partners.

IKEA International AS
100% / 0%
Contributions: Total: *$3,900*   Dem: *$3,900*   Rep: *$0*
Lobby Spending: *$0*
Foreign owned. Subsidiary of INGKA Holding B.V.

Jo-Ann Stores, Inc.
0% / 100%
Contributions: Total: *$500*   Dem: *$0*   Rep: *$500*
Lobby Spending: *$0*
In 2006, settled several ADA claims by making its stores more accommodating to individuals with disabilities.

KB Holdings, Inc. (KB Toys)
0% / 100%
Contributions: Total: *$1,500*   Dem: *$0*   Rep: *$1,500*
Lobby Spending: *$0*
Subsidiary of Bain Capital LLC. In 2008, filed chapter 11 bankruptcy for the second time in five years. Currently being liquidated.

Kohler Company
16% / 84%
Contributions: Total: *$180,972*   Dem: *$29,472*   Rep: *$151,500*
Lobby Spending: *$0*
Privately held. Its cast iron products are manufactured from 93% recycled and reclaimed material, and nearly all brass used to manufacture its faucets is recycled and reclaimed. Supplies kitchen and bath products for Habitat for Humanity homes.

La-Z-Boy, Inc.
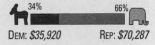
Contributions: TOTAL: *$7,050*   DEM: *$5,100*   REP: *$1,950*
LOBBY SPENDING: *$0*
Eight pending lawsuits allege retaliation against workers who filed workers' compensation claims after they were injured on the job. Partners with Ronald McDonald House Charities. Supports THE QUILT: Support for People Living with Cancer.

Learning Care Group, Inc.
Contributions: TOTAL: *$1,500*   DEM: *$0*   REP: *$1,500*
LOBBY SPENDING: *$0*
Subsidiary of Morgan Stanley.

Lenox Group, Inc.
Contributions: TOTAL: *$750*   DEM: *$750*   REP: *$0*
LOBBY SPENDING: *$0*
Subsidiary of Clarion Capital Partners LLC.

Linens-N-Things
Contributions: TOTAL: *$3,500*   DEM: *$1,200*   REP: *$2,300*
LOBBY SPENDING: *$0*
Subsidiary of LNT Acquisition LLC. Operations before February 15, 2009, remain with the bankruptcy estate of Linens-n-Things, Inc. Currently operates online only.

Lowe's Companies, Inc.
Contributions: TOTAL: *$106,207*   DEM: *$35,920*   REP: *$70,287*
LOBBY SPENDING: *$470,000*
In 2008, settled a gender discrimination lawsuit. In 2008, backed up its commitment to global forest conservation by supporting the Combat Illegal Logging Act of 2007. Underwrites Habitat for Humanity's Women Build program. In 2008, pledged $1 million to SkillsUSA. Has contributed $3 million to The Nature Conservancy and $3 million to the National Trust for Historic Preservation. Its foundation contributed more than $27.5 million to schools and community organizations. Partners with the National Urban League, the NAACP, the National Council of La Raza, the Organization of Chinese Americans, and the Japanese American Citizens League. Supports and partners with organizations for veterans and military families. Offers insurance coverage to employees' domestic partners.

Manhattan Group LLC
Contributions: TOTAL: *$10,295*   DEM: *$3,800*   REP: *$6,495*
LOBBY SPENDING: *$0*
Privately held.

Martha Stewart Living Omnimedia, Inc.
Contributions: TOTAL: *$5,200*   DEM: *$5,200*   REP: *$0*
LOBBY SPENDING: *$0*
Several pending lawsuits are related to alleged defective products. Partners with the Clinton Global Initiative on the "My Commitment" project. Offers employees three paid volunteer days per year.

Masco Corporation
24%   76%
Contributions: TOTAL: *$101,350*   DEM: *$24,000*   REP: *$77,350*
LOBBY SPENDING: *$0*
A pending lawsuit alleges it violated antitrust laws by conspiring with fiberglass insulation manufacturers to fix prices. Another pending class action lawsuit alleges that it violated federal and state wage and hour laws. In 2009, paid $8.5 million to settle a wages class action suit. Supports Habitat for Humanity, the Reach Initiative, and the Detroit Festival of Arts. Has a written nondiscrimination policy covering sexual orientation but not gender identity.

Mattel, Inc.
66%   34%
Contributions: TOTAL: *$77,450*   DEM: *$51,400*   REP: *$26,050*
LOBBY SPENDING: *$1,270,000*
In 2008, paid $12.5 million to settle a lawsuit brought by 39 states after some of its toys were found to contain dangerous levels of lead. Its foundation partners with the Special Olympics, the Make-A-Wish Foundation, Save the Children, and the Mattel Children's Hospital at UCLA. Has a written nondiscrimination policy covering sexual orientation and gender identity. Offers insurance coverage to employees' domestic partners. Insurance for transgender employees is offered, but treatment is not covered.

Maytag
33%   67%
Contributions: TOTAL: *$750*   DEM: *$250*   REP: *$500*
LOBBY SPENDING: *$0*
Subsidiary of Whirlpool Corporation.

Menard, Inc.
24%   76%
Contributions: TOTAL: *$22,151*   DEM: *$5,351*   REP: *$16,800*
LOBBY SPENDING: *$0*
Privately held. Was found in contempt for refusing to reinstate a former employee as part of a 2009 settlement, which also awarded $1.6 million in a lawsuit based on the Equal Pay Act, Title VII of the Civil Rights Act, and the Wisconsin Fair Employment Act.

Method
100%   0%
Contributions: TOTAL: *$1,250*   DEM: *$1,250*   REP: *$0*
LOBBY SPENDING: *$0*
Certified "cruelty free" by the Coalition for Consumer Information on Cosmetics. Products are biodegradable and contain no phosphates, phthalates, parabens, or bleach.

Michaels Stores, Inc.
49%   51%
Contributions: TOTAL: *$1,459*   DEM: *$708*   REP: *$751*
LOBBY SPENDING: *$0*
Subsidiary of Bain Capital LLC and The Blackstone Group LP. A pending lawsuit alleges that it unlawfully made deductions from employees' earnings and that it failed to pay overtime wages, provide meal periods, accurately record hours worked, and itemize employee wage statements. Has a written nondiscrimination policy covering sexual orientation but not gender identity.

Newell Rubbermaid, Inc.

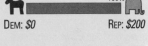

29%   71%

Contributions: TOTAL: *$53,318*   DEM: *$15,218*   REP: *$38,100*
LOBBY SPENDING: *$0*

Several pending lawsuits stem from deaths connected with infants becoming trapped in an allegedly defective crib. Recycles resin waste and corrugated cardboard. Is collaborating with organizations such as the Forest Stewardship Council to get green certifications for its product packaging. Philanthropic programs include K–12 programs, workforce reentry programs, and initiatives to support women's health. Has a written nondiscrimination policy covering sexual orientation and gender identity. Offers insurance coverage to employees' domestic partners. Insurance for transgender employees is offered, and treatment is covered.

Oil-Dri Corporation of America

0%   100%

Contributions: TOTAL: *$16,200*   DEM: *$0*   REP: *$16,200*
LOBBY SPENDING: *$0*

Traces the provenance of its products to the Bible. Increased use of GMOs adversely affects demand for its products.

Orchard Supply Hardware Stores Corporation

0%   100%

Contributions: TOTAL: *$200*   DEM: *$0*   REP: *$200*
LOBBY SPENDING: *$0*

Subsidiary of Sears Holdings Corporation. Partners with the Canary Foundation to address early cancer detection and donated $500,000 to the foundation in 2008. Offers insurance coverage to employees' domestic partners.

Pactiv Corporation

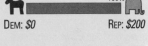

70%   30%

Contributions: TOTAL: *$1,650*   DEM: *$1,150*   REP: *$500*
LOBBY SPENDING: *$0*

Recycles 90% of scrap from its plastic manufacturing directly into products. Recycles aluminum, corrugated cardboard, scrap metals, and remaining plastic scrap through suppliers and recycling services.

Pet Valu, Inc.

0%   100%

Contributions: TOTAL: *$500*   DEM: *$0*   REP: *$500*
LOBBY SPENDING: *$0*

Privately held. In 2008, settled, as a codefendant, a $24 million lawsuit over contaminated pet food linked to the deaths of perhaps thousands of dogs and cats.

PETCO Animal Supplies Stores, Inc.

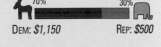

100%   0%

Contributions: TOTAL: *$940*   DEM: *$940*   REP: *$0*
LOBBY SPENDING: *$0*

Subsidiary of Leonard Green & Partners LP and TPG Capital LP. A pending lawsuit alleges that it sold pet products that are harmful to both pets and humans without proper warning labels. An EEOC lawsuit alleging an ADA violation is pending. In 2008, U.S. marshals, acting on behalf of the FDA, confiscated various animal food products stored under allegedly unsanitary conditions. Its shopping bags and pet carriers use recycled materials. Supports grassroots programs and organizations committed to improving animal welfare, educating responsible pet parents, and reducing the number of homeless animals that are put to death. Donated $3 million to local shelters in 2009. Has a written nondiscrimination policy covering sexual orientation but not gender identity.

Petmate
Contributions: TOTAL: *$2,300*   DEM: *$0*   REP: *$2,300*
LOBBY SPENDING: *$0*

Subsidiary of Westar Capital LLC. Formerly Doskocil Manufacturing Company, Inc. Uses 25% recycled materials in the manufacture of its products. Nearly all of its products are 100% recyclable.

PetSmart, Inc.
Contributions: TOTAL: *$11,550*   DEM: *$450*   REP: *$11,100*
LOBBY SPENDING: *$0*

A pending lawsuit stems from psittacosis-infected birds allegedly cross-infecting humans, leading to coma and death. Another pending lawsuit alleges that it sold pet products that are harmful to both pets and humans without proper warning labels. In 2008, paid $1.45 million to settle a class action lawsuit with more than 4,000 employees who allege they did not get lunch periods and rest breaks. Has funded more than $70 million in grants and programs benefiting animal welfare organizations. Its in-store pet adoption programs have saved the lives of more than 3 million pets. Has a written nondiscrimination policy covering sexual orientation but not gender identity. Offers insurance coverage to employees' domestic partners.

Pier 1 Imports, Inc.
Contributions: TOTAL: *$250*   DEM: *$0*   REP: *$250*
LOBBY SPENDING: *$0*

Seeking to avoid bankruptcy. Partners with UNICEF, generating more than $26 million for children around the world. Has a written nondiscrimination policy covering sexual orientation but not gender identity.

Pottery Barn
Contributions: TOTAL: *$480*   DEM: *$230*   REP: *$250*
LOBBY SPENDING: *$0*

Subsidiary of Williams-Sonoma, Inc. Its catalog is printed on FSC-certified paper. Many products are made of reclaimed or sustainable materials.

Pottery Barn Kids
Contributions: TOTAL: *$200*   DEM: *$0*   REP: *$200*
LOBBY SPENDING: *$0*

Subsidiary of Williams-Sonoma, Inc.

RC2 Corporation
Contributions: TOTAL: *$0*   DEM: *$0*   REP: *$0*
LOBBY SPENDING: *$82,500*

In 2008, paid $30 million and agreed to put in place new quality controls to settle a nationwide class action lawsuit for thousands of product claims for families who bought lead-tainted items such as Thomas the Tank Engine.

Restoration Hardware, Inc.

70%   30%

Contributions: TOTAL: *$9,900*   DEM: *$6,900*   REP: *$3,000*
LOBBY SPENDING: *$0*

Subsidiary of Catterton Partners and Tower Three Partners. Has a written nondiscrimination policy covering sexual orientation but not gender identity. Offers insurance coverage to employees' domestic partners.

Russ Berrie and Company, Inc.

100%   0%

Contributions: TOTAL: *$49,300*   DEM: *$49,300*   REP: *$0*
LOBBY SPENDING: *$0*

Sold its gift business to The Encore Group, Inc., which is now operating as The Russ Company, Inc. (Russ Gift). Its infant and juvenile business (composed of subsidiaries Kids Line, LLC; Sassy, Inc.; LaJobi, Inc.; and CoCaLo) will announce a new corporate name.

S. C. Johnson & Son, Inc.

36%   64%

Contributions: TOTAL: *$113,358*   DEM: *$40,758*   REP: *$72,600*
LOBBY SPENDING: *$132,981*

Privately held. A pending class action lawsuit alleges "deceptive environmental claims" in relation to its use of a seal of approval on its Windex product. In 2009, announced that it will begin disclosing chemical ingredients on its product labels and list them on its Web site. From 2000 to 2005, cut greenhouse gas emissions by 24%, representing an absolute reduction of 17%. Uses wind power at one of its plants. Donates 5% of pretax profits to philanthropic causes. Has a written nondiscrimination policy covering sexual orientation and gender identity. Offers insurance coverage to employees' domestic partners. Insurance for transgender employees is offered, but treatment is not covered.

Scotts Miracle-Gro Co.

2%   98%

Contributions: TOTAL: *$57,500*   DEM: *$1,300*   REP: *$56,200*
LOBBY SPENDING: *$0*

In 2009, the EPA issued "stop sale, use or removal" orders for 19 of the company's products that are unregistered and improperly labeled and that make false or misleading claims, contain statements that EPA did not approve as part of the products' registration, or make claims that were not supported by submissions of required scientific studies. In 2008, the EPA ordered it to stop the use of and remove four unregistered or improperly labeled pesticides. In 2007, paid $500,000 to settle charges brought by the Agriculture Department. The department alleged that the company failed to comply with U.S. rules while testing a genetically engineered grass. Has pledged to help fund a college education for 50 individuals who successfully participate in its mentoring program and graduate from high school. Has provided $1 million in financial support to and $500,000 in media products for Washington DC's National Garden, of which it is a founding sponsor.

Seventh Generation, Inc.

100%   0%

Contributions: TOTAL: *$8,300*   DEM: *$8,300*   REP: *$0*
LOBBY SPENDING: *$0*

Derives its name from the Great Law of the Iroquois that states, "In our every deliberation, we must consider the impact of our decisions on the next seven generations." Discloses a complete ingredient list for all products. Uses 100% recycled materials in its nonabsorbent paper products. Has decreased its normalized greenhouse gas emissions. Donates feminine care product packages to shelters. Annually donates 10% of pretax profits to nonprofit community, environmental, health, and responsible business organizations working for positive change.

Shaklee Corporation

84% | 16%

Contributions: TOTAL: *$83,974*   DEM: *$70,549*   REP: *$13,425*
LOBBY SPENDING: *$0*

Subsidiary of Activated Holdings LLC. Does not conduct animal testing for its products. Planted 1 million trees and took other actions to make its global operations 100% neutral for all six Kyoto-defined greenhouse gases. Its charitable foundation helps people directly affected by natural disasters and emergencies. Partners with the EPA, Ocean Alliance, Wild Dolphin Project, American Forests, and Healthy Child Healthy World.

Sherwin-Williams Company, The

9% | 91%

Contributions: TOTAL: *$79,950*   DEM: *$7,250*   REP: *$72,700*
LOBBY SPENDING: *$0*

Named as a codefendant in a pending lawsuit alleging manufacture of defective products that contained unsafe levels of benzene, failure to give proper warnings about the dangers of benzene, and improper storage of benzene-containing products. In 2007, paid $16 million in a lawsuit alleging price-fixing. Its VIP program supports building and maintenance projects at some of America's parks. Its Home Work initiative partners with public housing authorities to train residents to become professional painters. Offers employees adoption assistance of up to $3,000 and time off. Has a written nondiscrimination policy covering sexual orientation but not gender identity.

Stanley Works, The

3% | 97%

Contributions: TOTAL: *$15,762*   DEM: *$461*   REP: *$15,301*
LOBBY SPENDING: *$80,000*

Provides aid to Red Feather's American Indian Sustainable Housing Initiative. Partners with Habitat for Humanity and SkillsUSA. Has a written nondiscrimination policy covering sexual orientation but not gender identity.

Toro Company, The

4% | 96%

Contributions: TOTAL: *$5,550*   DEM: *$200*   REP: *$5,350*
LOBBY SPENDING: *$0*

Named as a codefendant in a pending class action lawsuit alleging that manufacturers of lawnmowers have purposely misstated horsepower valuations on their products in order to justify higher prices. Donates 2% of pretax domestic profits to the nonprofit sector.

Toys "R" Us, Inc.

90% | 10%

Contributions: TOTAL: *$9,800*   DEM: *$8,800*   REP: *$1,000*
LOBBY SPENDING: *$195,000*

Subsidiary of Bain Capital LLC, Kohlberg Kravis Roberts & Co., and Vornado Realty Trust. A pending lawsuit alleges racial discrimination against African American shoppers. Donated $1.9 million to Autism Speaks in 2009. Partners with Safe Kids Worldwide, Save the Children, and the Starlight Starbright Children's Foundation, with which it has built more than 70 playrooms benefiting pediatric patients. Has a written nondiscrimination policy covering sexual orientation and gender identity. Offers insurance coverage to employees' domestic partners. Insurance for transgender employees is offered, but treatment is not covered.

True Manufacturing Co., Inc.
Contributions: TOTAL: *$103,700* DEM: *$0* REP: *$103,700*
LOBBY SPENDING: *$0*
Privately held. Has committed to reducing its greenhouse gas emissions by 15% by 2013. Between 1998 and 2008, reduced its total water use by 58% and its natural gas consumption per square foot of manufacturing by 23%.

True Value Company
Contributions: TOTAL: *$4,950* DEM: *$500* REP: *$4,450*
LOBBY SPENDING: *$0*
Privately held cooperative of independently owned stores. Its foundation has donated $4 million to Cotter Boys and Girls Club of Chicago. Provides scholarships to children of employees and gives paint supplies to schools.

Tupperware Brands Corporation
Contributions: TOTAL: *$19,100* DEM: *$12,500* REP: *$6,600*
LOBBY SPENDING: *$300,000*
In 2009, avowed confidence in the safety of using polycarbonate in producing its products. Reuses plastic raw material. Is a national sponsor of the Boys and Girls Clubs of America's SMART Girls program. Has a written nondiscrimination policy covering sexual orientation but not gender identity.

Weber-Stephen Products Co.
Contributions: TOTAL: *$2,500* DEM: *$2,300* REP: *$200*
LOBBY SPENDING: *$0*
Privately held.

Whirlpool Corporation
Contributions: TOTAL: *$115,552* DEM: *$38,452* REP: *$77,100*
LOBBY SPENDING: *$950,000*
A pending lawsuit claims a hostile work environment arising from alleged racial discrimination. Retirees seek to retain specific health care benefits in a pending class action lawsuit. Other class action lawsuits allege defective products. In 2008, Whirlpool paid $14 million in a defective design lawsuit after a fatality occurred, allegedly as a result of a fire caused by a Whirlpool dryer. Settled a class action lawsuit for allegedly defective water heaters for over $2 million in 2008. Pig iron that goes into steel used in Whirlpool products can be traced to slave labor in Brazil. Has a greenhouse gas reduction goal of 6.6% by 2012. Has received the Energy Star Sustained Excellence award for four consecutive years. Donates a range and an Energy Star–certified refrigerator to every new Habitat for Humanity house built in North America. Has contributed more than $34 million in cash and donations to Habitat

for Humanity. Donates 2% of its pretax profits to charitable causes. Has a written nondiscrimination policy covering sexual orientation and gender identity. Offers insurance coverage to employees' domestic partners. Insurance for transgender employees is offered, but treatment is not covered.

Williams-Sonoma, Inc.

16%   84%

Contributions: TOTAL: *$119,948*   DEM: *$19,448*   REP: *$100,500*
LOBBY SPENDING: *$0*

In 2008, joined the Global Forest & Trade Network, the World Wildlife Fund's initiative to save the world's most valuable and threatened forests. Its catalog uses only paper that is certified by the FSC. Has a written nondiscrimination policy covering sexual orientation but not gender identity. Offers insurance coverage to employees' domestic partners.

WKI Holding Company, Inc.

84%   16%

Contributions: TOTAL: *$12,150*   DEM: *$10,150*   REP: *$2,000*
LOBBY SPENDING: *$0*
Privately held.

W. W. Grainger, Inc.

6%   94%

Contributions: TOTAL: *$105,692*   DEM: *$6,350*   REP: *$99,342*
LOBBY SPENDING: *$0*

In 2008, paid the federal government $6 million to settle a whistleblower lawsuit in which it was accused of overcharging the government and of relabeling materials made in trade-restricted countries before selling them to federal agencies. Focuses on disaster preparedness and partners with the Red Cross. Annually awards 100 community college scholarships for trade degrees. Has a written nondiscrimination policy covering sexual orientation but not gender identity.

Major Retailers

Chris Colin

Wal-Mart takes a lot of flak, but you've got to hand it to a major retailer that still finds time to infiltrate *Newsweek*. It's difficult to find another explanation for the magazine's February 2009 article "Our Corporate Saviors: 10 Companies That May Lead Us Out of Recession."

"Wal-Mart offers shoppers good merchandise at prices which become more and more attractive as the downturn continues," the article reads. Reasonable enough, but omitted from this bit of breathlessness was one minor detail: through low wages, poor health-care options, outsourcing, a ban on organizing, and a range of environmentally destructive practices, the largest private employer in the country also helped bring *on* the myriad conditions that led to the recession. The company's 1.4 million "associates" worldwide suddenly found those Wal-Mart prices more attractive than ever.

It's a great old trick: make your employees into customers, and your customers desperate enough to become employees. Indeed, from sprawl to outsourcing, monopolization, labor abuses, and cuts in health insurance and other employee benefits, the multibillion-dollar big-box store has found itself enmeshed in just about every issue relevant to the sector in general.

Of course, the country's major retailers have been crafty for some time now. The environmental impact—plus sheer ugliness—of these 150,000-square-foot stores is enormous, so they routinely promise all manner of benefits to the towns that let them in. There will be jobs, shopping convenience, and sales tax revenue for the local government. Here and there they meet resistance, but mostly they are welcomed. Over time, they have transformed the country's social and economic fabric. Where once communities clustered around a handful of modestly sized businesses, these operations are mammoth and far-flung. Chasing profits with impunity, these corporations frequently abandon one giant store for an even bigger facility if the numbers look better.

For years major retailers had momentum on their side, and an array of environmental and labor abuses simply came with that scale of business. The fight for market share forced major retailers to grow ever larger; as with many growth industries, this expansion tends to put the retailers at odds not just with local communities and environmentalists, but also with labor unions and smaller businesses that are unable to compete on the same level. It follows, then, that the sector has traditionally spent millions on lobbying and public relations. It has pushed at both federal and local levels for imminent domain rights, massive tax breaks, and the revision of local ordinances barring giant stores. Proponents of the big-box store and other major retailer operations argued that these institutions benefit both the consumer and the state, bringing in new jobs and taxes.

And now those arguments, as well as the stores themselves, are collapsing. Wal-Mart's recession-proof business model notwithstanding, the number of empty shells across the country has begun to multiply. Where some stores shrewdly exploit economic conditions, others merely succumb—with consequences no more pleasant for the worker or the planet. When Circuit City liquidated its 567 U.S. stores in early 2009, the nation's second largest appliance and electronics chain became merely the latest evidence that big-box stores can't keep the employment promises they make in every community they enter. As these stores shutter, the national landscape transforms yet again at the hands of major retail—this time, becoming a sprawl of vacated retail husks, each with its own story of blight, wasted building material, runoff from the construction phase, and so on.

As the recession has rocked the major retailers of the country, it has highlighted the awkward position they've arranged for themselves: as harmful as they've been to so many communities, they've so thoroughly restructured local economies that their disappearance is now harmful, too. With every store that folds, employees lose their paychecks—and, by extension, their means to keep the next store in business. Major retail has been ground zero for some of the economy's most destructive ripple effects.

But amid these negative trends, a new White House and revved-up unions have been fighting for change. The Employee Free Choice Act (EFCA), also known as "card check," would amend the National Labor Relations Act by making organizing considerably easier for employees, and union-busting tougher for employers. Major retailers, such as Wal-Mart (not to mention minor political parties such as the GOP), oppose the legislation. Starbucks, Costco, and Whole Foods have attempted to present a compromise—this fact alone represents a significant concession, given companies' historic resistance even to discussing the matter. President Obama, in what some hope augurs a broader shift, has indicated his support for the EFCA bill.

Even before Obama took office, there were hints that large, healthy paradigm shifts were in the works. In October 2008, Wal-Mart CEO H. Lee Scott announced plans to run the company entirely on renewable energy and produce zero waste. Here, the massive scale of the Wal-Mart operation could effect disproportionately large positive changes, just as its more insidious habits produced disproportionately large negative ones. When a company this size doubles the fuel efficiency of its truck fleet, or the amount of organic food it sells, the gestures go mainstream in a big way.

A dramatically new economic and political environment is clearly affecting this sector. (In a perhaps telling little footnote, industry sources reported that the top-selling 2009 wall calendar at major retailers across the country was one featuring Barack Obama.) With consumer spending constituting 70% of the national economy, the big-box stores, a new administration, and 300 million consumers will have to produce a new way of doing business in the years ahead.

Top Ten Democratic Contributors

United Parcel Service, Inc.	$1,287,247
FedEx Holding Corporation	$1,081,125
Wal-Mart Stores, Inc.	$914,228
Target Corporation	$233,838
Costco Wholesale Corporation	$218,490
Sears Holdings Corporation	$92,708
Winmark Corporation	$91,450
Replacements, Ltd.	$85,150
DHL Express (USA), Inc.	$15,334
Office Depot, Inc.	$10,291

Top Ten Republican Contributors

United Parcel Service, Inc.	$1,792,172
FedEx Holding Corporation	$1,455,034
Wal-Mart Stores, Inc.	$1,265,548
Target Corporation	$490,520
Sears Holdings Corporation	$84,874
Staples, Inc.	$76,850
Office Depot, Inc.	$21,376
DHL Express (USA), Inc.	$17,751
Costco Wholesale Corporation	$7,800
Sears, Roebuck and Co.	$5,850

Top Ten Lobbying Spenders

FedEx Holding Corporation	$15,295,000
Wal-Mart Stores, Inc.	$10,590,000
United Parcel Service, Inc.	$7,717,141
Target Corporation	$2,930,000
Sears Holdings Corporation	$561,285
Office Depot, Inc.	$260,000
OfficeMax, Inc.	$180,000
Staples, Inc.	$140,000
uBid.com	$40,000
DHL Express (USA), Inc.	$40,000

Big Lots, Inc.

46%   54%

Contributions: TOTAL: *$1,750*   DEM: *$800*   REP: *$950*

LOBBY SPENDING: *$0*

Agreed to pay $10 million to settle a class action lawsuit alleging failure to compensate hundreds of its California store managers for working overtime. A similar case is pending in Texas. Paid $300,000 to settle the sexual harassment claims of five women. Provided economic support for employees affected by Hurricane Katrina. Supports education and Toys for Tots. Has a written nondiscrimination policy covering sexual orientation but not gender identity.

Costco Wholesale Corporation

97%   3%

Contributions: TOTAL: *$226,290*   DEM: *$218,490*   REP: *$7,800*

LOBBY SPENDING: *$0*

Fought several battles to build controversial high-impact stores, including one in Mexico that would destroy a 3,000-year-old Olmec site. Pending lawsuit seeks damages for alleged common-law fraud, violations of the New Jersey Consumer Fraud Act, and negligent misrepresentation in its auto sales program. Pending class action lawsuit alleges it denies women employees promotions to high-paying management positions. Costco workers are among the highest paid in the retail industry. Is considered union friendly. In 2006, PETA purchased 65 shares of Costco in order to influence the company to purchase chicken only from suppliers that kill the animals humanely. Is installing solar arrays on the roofs of its stores in California and Hawaii. Has a written nondiscrimination policy covering sexual orientation and gender identity. Offers insurance coverage to employees' domestic partners. Insurance for transgender employees is offered, and some treatment is covered.

DHL Express (USA), Inc.
46% — 54%
Contributions: TOTAL: *$33,085*   DEM: *$15,334*   REP: *$17,751*
LOBBY SPENDING: <*$40,000*
Subsidiary of DHL Holdings (USA), Inc.; parent, Deutsche Post World Net in Germany. In 2009, Deutsche Post ceased all of its air and ground services within the United States. DHL Express (USA) still offers international shipping services to and from the United States. In 2008, settled a $25 million class action lawsuit due to glitches in its computer system. Facing a class action lawsuit alleging that it overbilled thousands of U.S. customers. In 2008, scored 67 out of 100 on "The Climate Counts Company Scorecard Report." Outreach includes disaster relief, education, environmental stewardship, and UNICEF. Has a written nondiscrimination policy covering sexual orientation but not gender identity. Offers insurance coverage to employees' domestic partners.

FedEx Holding Corporation
43% — 57%
Contributions: TOTAL: *$2,536,159*   DEM: *$1,081,125*   REP: *$1,455,034*
LOBBY SPENDING: *$15,295,000*
Ranked 90th on *Fortune* magazine's "100 Best Companies to Work For" in 2009. In 2008, scored 53 out of 100 on "The Climate Counts Company Scorecard Report." Has made significant investments in hybrid delivery trucks and solar power. Has developed a custom-facility lighting solution that reduces energy consumption by up to 93%. Recycles and purchases renewable-energy carbon offsets. Outreach includes disaster relief, education, safety, and health and human services. Is donating $5.5 million to a nonprofit organization dedicated to the prevention of blindness. Has a nondiscrimination policy covering sexual orientation but not gender identity. Some FedEx subsidiaries offer insurance coverage to employees' domestic partners. Insurance for transgender employees is offered, but treatment is not covered.

Kmart Corporation
14% — 86%
Contributions: TOTAL: *$5,000*   DEM: *$700*   REP: *$4,300*
LOBBY SPENDING: *$0*
Subsidiary of Sears Holdings Corporation. Accused of supporting sweatshop labor. Received a "D" on Green America's retailer scorecard, which alleges that it purchases clothing from known sweatshops and has sourced from countries with well-documented human and labor rights abuses. In 2006, agreed to pay $13 million to settle a class action lawsuit alleging it ignored federal regulations governing access for disabled customers. In 2006, a federal judge approved an $11.75 million settlement in a breach-of-fiduciary lawsuit brought by Kmart's 401(k) plan participants against Kmart's officers and directors. Supports the NAACP, the United Negro College Fund, the National Society of Hispanic MBAs, the U.S. Hispanic Chamber of Commerce, the Congressional Black Caucus, the Human Rights Campaign, and Catalyst, a nonprofit organization working to advance women in business.

Also partners with the National American Red Cross, March of Dimes, and Salvation Army. Has a written nondiscrimination policy covering sexual orientation and gender identity. Offers insurance coverage to employees' domestic partners. Insurance for transgender employees is offered, but treatment is not covered.

Mail Boxes Etc., Inc.

76% | 24%

Contributions: TOTAL: *$2,050*   DEM: *$1,550*   REP: *$500*
LOBBY SPENDING: *$0*
Subsidiary of United Parcel Service, Inc. Its foundation supports the Toys for Tots Literacy Program.

Office Depot, Inc.

32% | 68%

Contributions: TOTAL: *$31,667*   DEM: *$10,291*   REP: *$21,376*
LOBBY SPENDING: *$260,000*
Lawsuit regarding alleged violations of federal securities statutes could have implications for Office Depot workers participating in an employee stock plan, as well as shareholders and investors. Paid $4.75 million to settle charges of selling office products to the government that were manufactured in countries without reciprocal trade agreements with the United States. Settled a class action suit for $3.3 million for failure to pay overtime to assistant store managers. In 2007, paid $2.3 million to settle a claim that California customers were over-charged by faulty scanners. Listed as one of the top 50 companies for female executives by NAFE. Has reduced greenhouse gas emissions associated with its transport. Nearly 50% of its materials are recycled in North America. Supports the Forest & Biodiversity Conservation Alliance. Offers a Green Book™ Catalog containing environmentally preferable products and ideas for a "greener office." Its foundation supports programs that enhance quality of life for children, strengthen communities, encourage local and international economic growth, and empower schools. Has a written nondiscrimination policy covering sexual orientation but not gender identity. Offers insurance coverage to employees' domestic partners.

OfficeMax, Inc.

50% | 50%

Contributions: TOTAL: *$11,525*   DEM: *$5,800*   REP: *$5,725*
LOBBY SPENDING: *$180,000*
Faces a class action lawsuit for $1.5 billion for fraudulent stock sales and misrepresentation of earnings. Has reduced carbon emissions by enabling sleep mode on its computers and monitors. Is the first company to nationally distribute 100% postconsumer copier paper, which it developed, and the first to nationally distribute 100% postconsumer color copier paper manufactured by wind power. Offers 100% postconsumer recycled paper for self-serve copies. Does not purchase logs from endangered areas and gives preference to suppliers working well-managed forests. Supports education, civic improvement, and the arts. Has a written nondiscrimination policy covering sexual orientation and gender identity. Offers insurance coverage to employees' domestic partners. Insurance for transgender employees is offered, but treatment is not covered.

Replacements, Ltd.
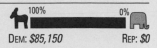
Contributions: TOTAL: *$85,150*   DEM: *$85,150*   REP: *$0*
LOBBY SPENDING: *$0*
Privately held. Awarded the American Psychological Association's "Psychologically Healthy Workplace" for 2009. Employs telecommuting, four 10-hour days, and organized carpools. Has a written nondiscrimination policy covering sexual orientation and gender identity. Offers insurance coverage to employees' domestic partners. Insurance for transgender employees is offered, and treatment is covered.

Sam's Club
Contributions: TOTAL: *$3,560*   DEM: *$700*   REP: *$2,860*
LOBBY SPENDING: *$0*
Subsidiary of Wal-Mart Stores, Inc.

Sears Holdings Corporation

Contributions: TOTAL: *$177,582*   DEM: *$92,708*   REP: *$84,874*
LOBBY SPENDING: *$561,285*
See individual subsidiaries for more information: Sears, Roebuck and Co., Kmart Corporation, Lands' End, Inc., and Orchard Supply Hardware Corporation. In 2007, a judge approved a $14.5 million settlement in a breach-of-fiduciary lawsuit brought by participants in Sears Holdings' 401(k) plans against Sears Holdings' officers and directors. Participates in the EPA's voluntary Responsible Appliance Disposal Program. Has an extensive recycling program. Is working to phase out PVC in its packaging and merchandise. Supports Rebuilding Together, the American Diabetes Association, St. Jude Children's Research Hospital, and the March of Dimes. Has a written nondiscrimination policy covering sexual orientation and gender identity. Offers insurance coverage to employees' domestic partners. Insurance for transgender employees is offered, but treatment is not covered.

Sears, Roebuck and Co.
Contributions: TOTAL: *$7,073*   DEM: *$1,223*   REP: *$5,850*
LOBBY SPENDING: *$0*
Subsidiary of Sears Holdings Corporation. One of 26 retailers that agreed to a $20 million settlement of a class action lawsuit by garment workers in Saipan alleging sweatshop practices. Received a "D-" on Green America's retailer scorecard, which alleges that the company purchases clothing from known sweatshops and has sourced from countries with well-documented human and labor rights abuses. A pending class action lawsuit alleges it sold defective washing machines. Another pending class action lawsuit alleges it improperly claimed that certain clothes dryers it sold contained stainless steel drums. In 2006, settled a class action suit over employees' overtime pay for $15 million. Received an "F" on the 2006 NAACP Economic Reciprocity Initiative report. Supports home renovation for low-income families and neighborhood revitalization. Has a written nondiscrimination policy covering sexual orientation and gender identity. Offers insurance coverage to employees' domestic partners. Insurance for transgender employees is offered, but treatment is not covered.

Staples, Inc.

10%   90%

Contributions: TOTAL: *$85,500*   DEM: *$8,650*   REP: *$76,850*
LOBBY SPENDING: *$140,000*

In 2009, $2.5 million was awarded to 343 employees who accused Staples of violating the FLSA for failing to pay overtime compensation. In 2007, paid $38 million to settle a class action lawsuit that alleged its overtime pay practices violated California laws. Partners with solar developer SunEdison, hosting 14 rooftop solar systems. Renewable energy sources now meet 20% of its total U.S. electricity requirements. Recycling program includes used ink and toner cartridges, personal electronics, rechargeable batteries, and office technology products. Offers more than 3,000 eco-preferable products. Provides financial support for disadvantaged youth and environmental causes. Has a written nondiscrimination policy covering sexual orientation and gender identity. Offers insurance coverage to employees' domestic partners. Insurance for transgender employees is offered, but treatment is not covered.

Target Corporation

32%   68%

Contributions: TOTAL: *$724,358*   DEM: *$233,838*   REP: *$490,520*
LOBBY SPENDING: *$2,930,000*

One of 26 retailers that agreed to a $20 million settlement with garment workers in Saipan for alleged sweatshop practices. Agreed to pay a $1.9 million settlement to immigrant janitors for failure to pay overtime and some taxes. Received a "D+" on Green America's retailer scorecard, which alleges that the company purchases clothing from known sweatshops and has sourced from countries with well-documented human and labor rights abuses. In 2008, paid $6 million to settle a lawsuit alleging that its Web site format discriminates against blind consumers. Received an "F" on the 2006 NAACP Economic Reciprocity Initiative report. In 2007, paid $775,000 to settle a lawsuit alleging a racially hostile work environment. Is a partner in the EPA's program to reduce municipal solid waste. Is a member of the U.S. Green Building Council. Some of its stores in California have solar panel systems. Uses LED lighting for outside signage in new stores. Contributes 5% of its income in support of education, the arts, social services, and volunteerism. Has a written nondiscrimination policy covering sexual orientation and gender identity. Offers insurance coverage to employees' domestic partners. Insurance for transgender employees is offered, but treatment is not covered.

uBid.com

Contributions: TOTAL: *$0*   DEM: *$0*   REP: *$0*
LOBBY SPENDING: *$40,000*

Subsidiary of Enable Holdings, Inc.; parent, Petters Group Worldwide, LLC. Has hosted auctions to raise funds to help end domestic violence.

United Parcel Service, Inc.
42%   58%

Contributions: TOTAL: *$3,079,419*   DEM: *$1,287,247*   REP: *$1,792,172*
LOBBY SPENDING: *$7,717,141*

Was forced to pay into union workers' retirement accounts for violation of federal law. A pending class action lawsuit asserts ADA violations.

Has faced several lawsuits for workplace injuries. In 2008, scored 40 out of 100 on "The Climate Counts Company Scorecard Report." Participated in the EPA's Climate Leaders program. Has implemented an e-waste recycling program. Operates the largest private fleet of alternative fuel vehicles in the transportation industry. Participates in the SmartWay Transport Partnership. Encourages employees to volunteer. Supports handicapped children, environmental stewardship, the United Way, and literacy. Assists nonprofit organizations to recruit and manage volunteer staff. Has a written nondiscrimination policy covering sexual orientation and gender identity. Offers insurance coverage to employees' domestic partners. Insurance for transgender employees is offered, but treatment is not covered.

Wal-Mart Stores, Inc.

42% | 58%

Contributions: TOTAL: *$2,179,776*   DEM: *$914,228*   REP: *$1,265,548*
LOBBY SPENDING: *$10,590,000*

Notorious for its refusal to allow workers to unionize, its dismal record on employee compensation, its poor benefits program, and its sourcing from known sweatshops. Paid an $11 million settlement to avoid federal criminal charges stemming from use of undocumented worker contractors. Has agreed to a settle 63 lawsuits that claim it violated U.S. labor laws by forcing employees to work off the clock. In 2009, agreed to pay $1 million and hire independent monitors to ensure price accuracy at its Arizona stores. In 2007, agreed to pay $1.4 million to settle a similar lawsuit. Listed by NAFE as one of the top 50 companies for female executives in 2009. Received an "F" on Green America's retailer scorecard, which alleges that the company purchases clothing from known sweatshops and has sourced from countries with well-documented human and labor rights abuses. Consumes vast tracts of natural habitat and promotes sprawl. Environmental goals include reducing greenhouse gases by 20%. Its foundations support programs that address hunger, homelessness, education, and job training. Has a written nondiscrimination policy covering sexual orientation but not gender identity. Refuses insurance coverage to employees' domestic partners. Insurance for transgender employees is offered, but treatment is not covered.

Winmark Corporation

94% | 6%

Contributions: TOTAL: *$97,050*   DEM: *$91,450*   REP: *$5,600*
LOBBY SPENDING: *$0*

Franchises retail chains that buy, sell, and consign used goods (and some new items) at more than 850 stores. The chains sell sports gear (Play It Again Sports), children's items (Once Upon A Child), and teen apparel (Plato's Closet).

Media and Entertainment

Norman Solomon

In their never-ending quest for ears and eyeballs, the nation's top media firms are engaged in a high-stakes dance with government regulators. Finding traction in some of Washington's powerful places can lead to huge benefits. A few words inserted into legislation on Capitol Hill, or a favorable vote by the Federal Communications Commission (FCC), can shift the balance sheets for multibillion-dollar conglomerates that provide the nation with much of its news and entertainment. Meanwhile, for the public, there's a lot more at stake than corporate profits.

Back in 1996, a landmark telecommunications "reform" act sailed through Congress; the skipper was President Bill Clinton, and his first mate was House speaker Newt Gingrich. Media consumers are still reeling from the effects. One of the results was a radio "land rush" that further deregulated the airwaves. So, for instance, Clear Channel Communications—a conservative radio chain—was able to grab ownership of more than 1,000 radio stations nationwide, including more than half a dozen in a single city. Another swift result of the new bipartisan law was Time Warner's merger with Turner Broadcasting; federal approval of the deal created the biggest media and entertainment corporation in the world.

During the first term of President George W. Bush, more deregulation boosted the dominance of just a few media giants, which tended to lavish their appreciative contributions most effusively on Republicans. But as the GOP's tide began to ebb midway through the decade, the media industry donations tilted toward the ascending Democratic Party. The shift has been dramatic for General Electric, which owns NBC and other major media outlets. But the trend even included Rupert Murdoch's News Corporation, the parent company of the famously right-wing Fox News.

While wolfing down previous competitors, huge media conglomerates have depended on the Justice Department and FCC to look the other way—making antitrust enforcement a thing of the past. It doesn't hurt to throw donations at both sides of the aisle as a perennial way of guarding against unpalatable legislation becoming law.

156

Many hundreds of national magazines and cable networks dot the nation's media terrain. But the vast majority are owned by just a few corporations. Their leverage in Washington doesn't just hinge on the checks that go to politicians. Large outlays for lobbying are part of the price of doing mass-media business.

The largesse devoted to campaign donations and lobbyists is part of a spiraling cycle: leverage in the corridors of governmental power helps the media conglomerates to grow still bigger, while the political sensibilities of corporate owners and managers routinely affect the tenor and limits of media coverage. That coverage, in turn, contributes to a media atmosphere conducive to the further domination of the media environment by burgeoning conglomerates. At the same time, perhaps the greatest amount of clout that the media industries exercise is bound up in the mix of news and punditry that assesses the performances of powerful government officials and the issues that confront them.

Over time, what we see and hear—or don't see and hear—is largely a consequence of such pay-to-play political games, which media conglomerates have been winning in Washington for a very long time. With the notable and crucial exception of the Internet, the substantive diversity of media has been steadily dwindling—even while the niche marketing of corporatized media products has diversified.

Cable and satellite TV options have exploded in number. Yet, the corporations that own the heavily promoted and capitalized channels are few in number. They hire the top managers, who hire the decision makers in executive suites and newsrooms. In the pursuit of profits, and often with unspoken ideological outlooks, the management of mass-media outlets routinely filters out diversifying possibilities from the nation's mass-distributed media diet.

Among the key television "gatekeepers" are the cable and satellite systems that determine which channels are to be featured or even made available to viewers. Thus, years into the founding of the worldwide satellite TV channel Al Jazeera English, the network was still unavailable to U.S. residents; they needed to visit the Internet to find programming that was readily available to TV viewers on several other continents.

No doubt the Web has opened up media diversity. Our choices are vastly greater than they were a decade ago. But the fast-moving media landscape is, overall, still dominated by a small number of media conglomerates. Not coincidentally, many of those with the widest reach can be found on the list of top contributors during the latest campaign cycle.

Although critics appropriately focus on news media as shapers of public attitudes and political apertures for the nation, the varied and far-reaching impacts of entertainment industries should not be discounted. They play an enormous role in shaping a mass culture that encourages and circumscribes a sense of shared preoccupations. What can be "green-lighted" is as much a product of self-censorship in Hollywood as what can be approved for the focus of investigative journalism in a newsroom. Creative artists who seek to push the political boundaries in ways that question corporate power are up against the walls that continue to be reinforced by conglomerates' pursuit of the bottom line.

The bipartisan contributions from media firms can be understood as part of a multilayered protection racket that serves the powerful in corporate suites as well as in Washington's corridors of power. Any individual, in either quarter, is apt to be expendable; shortfalls of revenue or votes can easily result in tumbling from some very high horses galloping along Wall Street or Pennsylvania Avenue. But the spiraling system of concentrated power in the realms of media and politics is ongoing. The results can be seen in the policy decisions of Washington, the media outlets that report the news, and the entertainment fare that fills the multiplex at the mall.

Top Ten Democratic Contributors

National Amusements, Inc.	$1,690,799
News Corporation, Ltd., The	$1,266,293
Walt Disney Company, The	$1,137,525
DISH Network Corp. (formerly EchoStar Communications)	$564,926
Vivendi S.A.	$508,230
DreamWorks Animation SKG, Inc.	$441,882
DreamWorks SKG	$405,361
Clear Channel Communications, Inc.	$397,342
Viacom International, Inc.	$381,200
Liberty Media Corporation	$300,790

Top Ten Republican Contributors

Clear Channel Communications, Inc.	$619,390
Liberty Media Corporation	$479,199
News Corporation, Ltd., The	$432,365
Walt Disney Company, The	$401,058
National Amusements, Inc.	$294,678
DISH Network Corp. (formerly EchoStar Communications)	$278,850
Hallmark Cards, Inc.	$232,203
Vivendi S.A.	$217,766
DirecTV Group, Inc.	$157,499
Viacom International, Inc.	$135,950

Top Ten Lobbying Spenders

National Amusements, Inc.	$13,473,000
Walt Disney Company, The	$10,430,000
News Corporation, Ltd., The	$9,690,000
Clear Channel Communications, Inc.	$7,080,000
Viacom International, Inc.	$4,410,000
Liberty Media Corporation	$3,726,000
DirecTV Group, Inc.	$3,210,000
Vivendi S.A.	$3,150,000
Amazon.com, Inc.	$2,962,000
Discovery Communications, Inc./ Discovery Channel Store	$1,750,000

Activision Blizzard, Inc.

39% | 61%

Contributions: TOTAL: *$158,535* DEM: *$62,334* REP: *$96,201*
LOBBY SPENDING: *$0*
Subsidiary of foreign-owned Vivendi S.A. In 2008, combined Activision with Vivendi Games to form Activision Blizzard. Has a written policy for protection of whistle-blowers from retaliation.

Amazon.com, Inc.

79%   21%

Contributions: Total: *$288,769*   Dem: *$228,435*   Rep: *$60,334*
Lobby Spending: *$2,962,000*

Agreed to pay $1.9 million to settle a class action lawsuit alleging fraud and violations of privacy. Received a score of 80 out of 100 on the 2008 Human Rights Campaign Corporate Equality Index. In 2008, scored 5 out of 100 on "The Climate Counts Company Scorecard Report." Its new corporate headquarters will meet LEED certification requirements. Developed a software program that determines the "right-sized" box for shipping any item, reducing packaging waste and transportation costs. Launched "AmazonGreen," a program that lists the best green products offered by Amazon.com. Has implemented energy-saving ideas. Outreach includes literacy programs and disaster relief. Has a written nondiscrimination policy covering sexual orientation but not gender identity. Offers insurance coverage to employees' domestic partners. Insurance for transgender employees is offered, but treatment is not covered.

AMC Entertainment Holdings, Inc.

51%   49%

Contributions: Total: *$12,749*   Dem: *$6,549*   Rep: *$6,200*
Lobby Spending: *$0*

AMC is controlled by JPMorgan Chase & Co. and Apollo Advisors. Owns one-quarter of MovieTickets.com. A pending lawsuit filed by the DOJ alleges ADA violations involving theater seating. Supports Variety - The Children's Charity, the Will Rogers Motion Picture Pioneers Foundation, and the Autism Society of America. It is a steward of several historic theaters in Kansas City, MO. Has a written nondiscrimination policy covering sexual orientation and gender identity. Offers insurance coverage to employees' domestic partners. Insurance for transgender employees is offered, but treatment is not covered.

Barnes & Noble, Inc.

96%   4%

Contributions: Total: *$205,862*   Dem: *$198,312*   Rep: *$7,550*
Lobby Spending: *$130,000*

A pending lawsuit filed in 2006 by a shareholder alleges violation of state and federal law in connection with the backdating of stock options. Raises awareness of autism and Down Syndrome, sponsors literacy programs, donates books to disadvantaged youth, and supports higher learning and the arts. Has a written nondiscrimination policy covering sexual orientation and gender identity. Offers health insurance coverage to employees' domestic partners. Insurance for transgender employees is offered, and treatment is covered.

Blockbuster, Inc.

75%   25%

Contributions: Total: *$16,892*   Dem: *$12,641*   Rep: *$4,251*
Lobby Spending: *$0*

A pending lawsuit alleges that it transferred customers' personal information to Facebook.com without permission. In 2009, agreed to pay $300,000 to resolve a lawsuit alleging it overcharged some customers for merchandise. Its "no more late fees" campaign earned a fine and restitution order when a judge ruled that the "restocking charge" constituted a late fee. Supports the NAACP, the League of United Latin American Citizens, the Children's Miracle Network, and the Boys & Girls Clubs of America. Has a written nondiscrimination policy covering sexual orientation but not gender identity. Offers insurance to employees' domestic partners.

Books-A-Million, Inc.

100% / 0%

Contributions: TOTAL: *$2,300* DEM: *$2,300* REP: *$0*
LOBBY SPENDING: *$0*

Operates three retail formats: Books-A-Million superstores, Bookland "traditional" stores, and Joe Muggs newsstands.

Borders Group, Inc.

82% / 18%

Contributions: TOTAL: *$18,419* DEM: *$15,019* REP: *$3,400*
LOBBY SPENDING: *$0*

Its foundation supports literacy programs, education, and the fine and performing arts. Has a written nondiscrimination policy covering sexual orientation and gender identity. Offers health insurance coverage to employees' domestic partners. Insurance for transgender employees is offered, and some treatment is covered.

Carmike Cinemas

0% / 100%

Contributions: TOTAL: *$500* DEM: *$0* REP: *$500*
LOBBY SPENDING: *$0*

Settled a lawsuit alleging its theater seating violates the ADA.

Cinemark Holdings, Inc.

0% / 100%

Contributions: TOTAL: *$76,250* DEM: *$250* REP: *$76,000*
LOBBY SPENDING: *$0*

Settled a lawsuit alleging its theater seating violates the ADA. In 2008, Cinemark's CEO gave $9,999 to the anti-gay Prop. 8 campaign that stripped marriage equality from the California constitution, prompting boycotts.

Clear Channel Communications, Inc.

39% / 61%

Contributions: TOTAL: *$1,016,732* DEM: *$397,342* REP: *$619,390*
LOBBY SPENDING: *$7,080,000*

Often held as a prime example of the dangers of media consolidation, Clear Channel has successfully lobbied to relax restrictions on concentrated media ownership. Facing 22 class action lawsuits alleging that it engaged in unlawful and anticompetitive activities in various regional ticket markets for live rock concerts. Supports children's hospitals and shelters, food banks, educational programs, health care, and cultural enhancement. Its foundation also supports the arts, education, and the environment, as well as cancer research. Has a written nondiscrimination policy covering sexual orientation and gender identity. Offers insurance coverage to employees' domestic partners. Insurance for transgender employees is offered, but treatment is not covered.

Clear Channel Outdoor Holdings, Inc.

24% / 76%

Contributions: TOTAL: *$46,950* DEM: *$11,450* REP: *$35,500*
LOBBY SPENDING: *$0*

Subsidiary of Clear Channel Communications, Inc. Several cities have protested its erection of billboards, especially the digital variety.

Named in a lawsuit alleging civil rights violations and illegal bid-rigging for contracts for signage.

Columbia House Company

Contributions: TOTAL: *$1,000*   DEM: *$0*   REP: *$1,000*
LOBBY SPENDING: *$0*

0% 100%

Subsidiary of Direct Brands; parent, investment firm Najafi Companies. Fined $1.6 million for more than 600 health and safety violations at its Indiana plant.

DirecTV Group, Inc.

Contributions: TOTAL: *$357,399*   DEM: *$199,900*   REP: *$157,499*
LOBBY SPENDING: *$3,210,000*

56% 44%

Subsidiary of Liberty Media Corporation, which plans to merge its Liberty Entertainment business with DirecTV. Two public pension funds are suing both companies over the plans to merge, alleging DirecTV shareholders are overpaying for assets it will get from the entertainment unit. A pending class action lawsuit alleges failure to tell customers they must pay a monthly lease fee and eventually return their receivers, even if they paid for them at retail. A pending class action lawsuit alleges it collected early termination fees without telling its customers. Has received almost 30,000 complaints through the Better Business Bureau since the beginning of 2006. Provides free programming to more than 5,000 schools. Sponsors *PTO Today* magazine's Parent Group of the Year for 2009. Has a written nondiscrimination policy covering sexual orientation but not gender identity.

Discovery Communications, Inc./ Discovery Channel Store

Contributions: TOTAL: *$185,208*   DEM: *$179,508*   REP: *$5,700*
LOBBY SPENDING: *$1,750,000*

97% 3%

Its global headquarters was awarded platinum-level LEED certification. Outreach includes the extension of science, environmental, and other educational programming in the United States and third-world countries. Social responsibility initiatives include the Discovery Channel Global Education Partnership and the Discovery Education 3M Young Scientist Challenge. Has a written nondiscrimination policy covering sexual orientation but not gender identity. Offers insurance coverage to employees' domestic partners.

DISH Network Corp. (formerly EchoStar Communications)

Contributions: TOTAL: *$843,776*   DEM: *$564,926*   REP: *$278,850*
LOBBY SPENDING: *$850,000*

67% 33%

In 2009, the DOJ and four states filed suit, alleging telemarketing that violates the Telephone Consumer Protection Act and state laws. In an EEOC-sponsored suit, paid $8 million to a blind applicant. Has no written nondiscrimination policy that covers sexual orientation or gender identity. Refuses insurance coverage to employees' domestic partners.

DreamWorks Animation SKG, Inc.

Contributions: TOTAL: *$519,432*   DEM: *$441,882*   REP: *$77,550*
LOBBY SPENDING: *$0*

85% 15%

Ranked 47th on *Fortune* magazine's "100 Best Companies to Work For" in 2009. Supports the Elizabeth Glaser Pediatric AIDS Foundation, the Salvation Army, and the Motion Picture and Television Fund.

DreamWorks SKG

100% / 0%

Contributions: TOTAL: *$405,361*   DEM: *$405,361*   REP: *$0*
LOBBY SPENDING: *$0*

Has a written nondiscrimination policy covering sexual orientation but not gender identity.

Hallmark Cards, Inc.

30% / 70%

Contributions: TOTAL: *$333,328*   DEM: *$101,125*   REP: *$232,203*
LOBBY SPENDING: *$640,000*

Privately held. In 2008, introduced a new line of cards for gay marriages that has been criticized by conservative Christian groups and the KKK. Seeks to obtain 100% of paper from sustainable sources by 2015. Striving to reduce energy use, water use, and waste by 25% by 2015. Partners with (PRODUCT)RED, UNICEF, and the Susan G. Komen Race for the Cure. Has a written nondiscrimination policy covering sexual orientation and gender identity. Offers insurance coverage to employees' domestic partners. Insurance for transgender employees is offered, but treatment is not covered.

Hasbro, Inc.

90% / 10%

Contributions: TOTAL: *$66,120*   DEM: *$59,720*   REP: *$6,400*
LOBBY SPENDING: *$400,000*

Adopted a labor code of conduct in response to a Chinese supplier found to have violated human and labor rights. However, in 2006, it was removed from the FTSE4Good Index series for failing to satisfy supply-chain labor standards. The FTSE4Good Index encourages investment in socially responsible companies that are included in the index only after meeting strict criteria. Partners in the EPA's Climate Leaders and WasteWise programs. Supports educational programs for children at risk and programs that give ill children respite. Has a paid employee volunteer program. Has a written nondiscrimination policy covering sexual orientation but not gender identity. Offers insurance coverage to employees' domestic partners.

Liberty Media Corporation

39% / 61%

Contributions: TOTAL: *$779,989*   DEM: *$300,790*   REP: *$479,199*
LOBBY SPENDING: *$3,726,000*

In 2009, two public pension funds filed a lawsuit over its plans to merge recently acquired DirecTV with its Liberty Entertainment business. The suit alleges DirecTV shareholders are overpaying for assets it will get from the entertainment unit. Its foundation has granted over $500,000 to Colorado charities. Has a written nondiscrimination policy covering sexual orientation but not gender identity.

Movie Gallery, Inc.

8% / 92%

Contributions: TOTAL: *$5,700*   DEM: *$450*   REP: *$5,250*
LOBBY SPENDING: *$0*

Adheres to the Video Software Dealers' Association "Pledge to Parents" that limits the rental of violent and sexualized video games to children. Philanthropy supports the Helen Keller Foundation.

National Amusements, Inc.

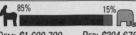

85%   15%

Contributions: TOTAL: *$1,985,477*   DEM: *$1,690,799*   REP: *$294,678*
LOBBY SPENDING: *$13,473,000*

Settled a lawsuit alleging its theater seating violates the ADA. Supports local food banks. Partnered with the SHADE Foundation by offering free movies in the summer to keep kids out of the sun.

Nederlander Organization

17%   83%

Contributions: TOTAL: *$87,400*   DEM: *$14,700*   REP: *$72,700*
LOBBY SPENDING: *$0*

Also does business as The Nederlander Producing Company of America. Operates theater companies and dinner theaters and produces concerts and live theater. Offers insurance coverage to employees' domestic partners.

Netflix, Inc.

99%   1%

Contributions: TOTAL: *$128,185*   DEM: *$127,385*   REP: *$800*
LOBBY SPENDING: <*$40,000*

Accused in a lawsuit filed in 2009 of conspiring with Wal-Mart to monopolize the market for the sale and rental of online DVDs. Environmental contribution: if Netflix members drove to and from a rental store, they would consume 800,000 gallons of gasoline and release more than 2.2 million tons of carbon dioxide emissions annually. Has no written nondiscrimination policy covering sexual orientation or gender identity.

News Corporation, Ltd., The

75%   25%

Contributions: TOTAL: *$1,698,658*   DEM: *$1,266,293*   REP: *$432,365*
LOBBY SPENDING: *$9,690,000*

Accused of championing conservative causes. Has successfully lobbied to relax restrictions on concentrated media ownership. Criticized for complying with Chinese free-speech restrictions in order to expand its lucrative operations. In 2008, scored 63 out of 100 in "The Climate Counts Company Scorecard Report." Seeks to decrease its 2006 carbon footprint by 10% by 2012. Has a written nondiscrimination policy covering sexual orientation but not gender identity. Offers insurance coverage to employees' domestic partners.

Powell's Books, Inc.

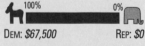

100%   0%

Contributions: TOTAL: *$67,500*   DEM: *$67,500*   REP: *$0*
LOBBY SPENDING: *$0*

The largest independent bookstore in the United States. Criticized for its contentious negotiations with union members. Its online arm is held up as the green alternative to Amazon.com, Inc., and Barnes & Noble, Inc. Its NW Portland warehouse will have one of the largest solar arrays in Oregon. Has an agreement with Portland General Electric to purchase Clean Wind[SM] Power, offsetting 165,000 pounds of carbon each year. Its delivery trucks use biodiesel fuel. Partners with Green Press Initiative. Offers its employees a discount on bus passes. Those who bike to work may receive an annual bicycle maintenance subsidy. Outreach includes literacy programs, free speech and civil rights advocacy, and support of public schools and libraries.

Regal Entertainment Group
74% 26%
Contributions: TOTAL: *$16,708* DEM: *$12,408* REP: *$4,300*
LOBBY SPENDING: *$0*

Settled a lawsuit alleging its theater seating violates the ADA. Provides free movies to children in the summer and gives the deaf and hearing impaired access to open-captioned films. National charitable partners include the American Red Cross, Boys & Girls Clubs of America, Variety - The Children's Charity, Make-A-Wish Foundation, and Will Rogers Motion Pictures Pioneers Foundation. Has a written nondiscrimination policy covering sexual orientation but not gender identity.

Sony Music Entertainment
81% 19%
Contributions: TOTAL: *$134,275* DEM: *$108,825* REP: *$25,450*
LOBBY SPENDING: *$1,008,000*

Subsidiary of Sony Corporation of America; parent, Sony Corp. BMG Music Service is no longer accepting new members. In 2008, sued for violations of the Children's Online Privacy Protection Act of 1998. Had to pay $1 million to settle claims that it improperly collected personal information from at least 30,000 children and disclosed some of the information to other registered users. Paid a $10 million settlement in a lawsuit alleging payola and other fraud. One of six music industry companies named in a class action complaint alleging conspiracy to block the growth of online music downloads in an effort to protect compact disc sales.

Ticketmaster Entertainment, Inc.
69% 31%
Contributions: TOTAL: *$40,677* DEM: *$28,102* REP: *$12,575*
LOBBY SPENDING: *$320,000*

A pending nationwide class action lawsuit filed in 2009 alleges that Ticketmaster Entertainment, Inc. and its wholly owned subsidiary Ticketsnow.com, Inc. conspired to monopolize the event ticket market. Has faced at least a dozen antitrust lawsuits and a congressional investigation. Has many enemies: bands, venues, and small-ticket concessions. Has a written nondiscrimination policy covering sexual orientation but not gender identity.

TiVo, Inc.
96% 4%
Contributions: TOTAL: *$6,050* DEM: *$5,800* REP: *$250*
LOBBY SPENDING: *$310,000*

Offers employees a free shuttle to local transit locations. Offers insurance coverage to employees' domestic partners.

Trans World Entertainment Corporation
0% 100%
Contributions: TOTAL: *$500* DEM: *$0* REP: *$500*
LOBBY SPENDING: *$0*

One of 16 music industry companies agreeing to a $143 million settlement in a price-fixing scheme.

Viacom International, Inc.
74% 26%
Contributions: TOTAL: *$517,150* DEM: *$381,200* REP: *$135,950*
LOBBY SPENDING: *$4,410,000*

Chairman Sumner Redstone controls a majority of Viacom through his National Amusements movie theater chain. Has paid multiple indecency settlements to the FCC. Agreed to pay $1.5 million to the FCC for violations of limits on advertising in children's television programs on Nickelodeon. Has a business conduct statement and supplier compliance policy. In 2008, scored 4 out of 100 in "The Climate Counts Company Scorecard Report." Its foundation supports and participates in nearly 20 global social, political, and environmental initiatives. Has a written nondiscrimination policy covering sexual orientation and gender identity. Offers insurance coverage to employees' domestic partners. Insurance for transgender employees is offered, and some treatment is covered.

Vivendi S.A.

70%   30%

Contributions: TOTAL: *$725,996*   DEM: *$508,230*   REP: *$217,766*
LOBBY SPENDING: *$3,150,000*

Foreign owned. Uses renewable energy at some of its facilities. Released the music industry's first completely recyclable CD package. In 2008, joined the United Nations Global Compact. Supports United Nations food and agriculture programs. Has a written nondiscrimination policy covering sexual orientation but not gender identity. Offers insurance coverage to employees' domestic partners.

Walt Disney Company, The

74%   26%

Contributions: TOTAL: *$1,538,583*   DEM: *$1,137,525*   REP: *$401,058*
LOBBY SPENDING: *$10,430,000*

Charged with contracting with sweatshop laborers. In 2007, Students and Scholars Against Corporate Misbehavior detailed labor violations in Disney factories in China. Ranked 29th on DiversityInc's list of the "Top 50 Companies for Diversity" in 2009. In 2008, scored 25 out of 100 in "The Climate Counts Company Scorecard Report." Environmental goals include zero waste, zero net direct greenhouse gas emissions from fuels, reduced indirect greenhouse gas emissions from electricity consumption, minimized water use, and minimized product footprint. Supports the arts, children's hospitals, Boys & Girls Clubs of America, Make-A-Wish Foundation, and Starlight Children's Foundation. Has a written nondiscrimination policy covering sexual orientation and gender identity. Offers insurance coverage to employees' domestic partners. Insurance for transgender employees is offered, and treatment is covered.

Warner Music Group Corporation

89%   11%

Contributions: TOTAL: *$299,348*   DEM: *$267,548*   REP: *$31,800*
LOBBY SPENDING: *$953,853*

One of six music industry companies named in a class action complaint alleging conspiracy to block the growth of online music downloads in an effort to protect compact disc sales. Environmental initiatives include reducing its greenhouse gas emissions and offsetting its carbon footprint, converting CD/DVD products to environmentally friendly packaging, practicing ecologically superior paper procurement, reducing waste, enhancing recycling, and "greening" its large-scale corporate events. Has a written nondiscrimination policy covering sexual orientation but not gender identity.

Restaurants

Jane Black

With more than 13 million workers, the restaurant industry is the nation's second largest private employer. And it's one of the few industries that continues to grow despite the brutal economic downturn. Sales in 2009 are expected to rise 2.5% to $566 billion, about 4% of the gross domestic product, with a total economic impact of $1.5 trillion. No wonder, then, that Congress pays close attention to the wishes of the restaurant lobby.

Led by the National Restaurant Association, the industry overwhelmingly supports Republicans. In 2008, the association donated nearly $1 million, 81% of which went to Republicans. Overall, the industry was more balanced: $7.1 million, or 62% of contributions, went to Republicans. But that state of affairs was largely due to the extraordinary political times. (Barack Obama, Hillary Clinton, and John McCain were the top three recipients in 2008.) Over the last 15 years, industry contributions have averaged 72.5% to Republicans, who tend to oppose taxes and regulations.

The restaurant industry lobbies on a broad range of issues, including food safety, public health, tax and labor laws, health care, and immigration. The industry has even weighed in on tort reform as it tries to limit its exposure to litigation on unhealthful foods. Americans spend 48% of their food dollars at restaurants and, with obesity rates at an all-time high, it's difficult for the industry to deny any responsibility.

For years, the industry opposed any regulation of ingredients (such as trans fats) or labeling requirements, supporting voluntary standards instead. Restaurant food isn't making people fat, the National Restaurant Association argued; irresponsible consumption and a lack of exercise are the culprits.

But the widespread acceptance of obesity as a public health threat has compelled the industry to change its strategy. Take menu labeling. Public health advocates contend that posting calories and nutrition information on menu boards at chain restaurants would help consumers make more-informed decisions. After all, studies show that making healthful choices isn't as easy as it seems. A 2007 California poll showed that, on average, only 10% of respondents could pick the most healthful item from a short list of common fast foods.

The industry initially opposed federal rules, but in light of city and state regulations, it backed its own bill, the Labeling Education and Nutrition (LEAN) Act of 2009. The LEAN Act called for nutrition information to be posted somewhere in chain establishments, but it did not require the information to be on the menu boards where consumers would certainly see it. The bill also preempted stricter local regulations, which the industry says are too varied for national corporations to follow. Now the industry has cut a deal with public health advocates. In exchange for preemption, it agreed that chains with 20 or more outlets should post calories on menus and menu boards; additional information will be available on request.

The industry is also involved in the wider debate about health care, a top priority for the Obama administration. The lobby had supported association health plans, which are designed to let small businesses join together across state lines to obtain economies of scale and to give tax credits to companies that chip in 60% of employees' premiums. (Remember, though, that the biggest donors are large corporations such as McDonalds and Wendy's; 91% of National Restaurant Association members are small businesses with fewer than 50 employees.)

Obama's vision for health care is more far-reaching, however. The industry admits that proposals for association health plans are no longer in play. At press time, the industry had not backed a specific plan, but it will be sure to weigh in on the structure of any national health-care plan and, more importantly, on who pays for it.

Labor issues also are taking center stage in Washington. The sudden momentum behind the Employee Free Choice Act (EFCA), which makes it easier for workers to unionize, took the industry by surprise. The industry opposes a so-called card-check system, wherein employees sign a card in favor of representation instead of voting by private ballot, saying it increases the risk of coercion. Many Democrats went on the record supporting the bill in 2007, when, under President George W. Bush, it had little chance of passage. Now with Democrat majorities in both houses of Congress, the bill has new life, and the industry has mobilized against it.

The industry continues to focus on other labor issues—keeping down the minimum wage, for example. With food costs rising worldwide, capping labor costs is essential to restaurants, which on average have slim profits of 4% to 6%.

Immigration reform is part of that fight. The industry continues to back an increase for what it calls an "arbitrary" cap on H-2B visas, which allow seasonal resorts to hire help from outside the United States. On the larger question of immigration reform, the lobby is fighting to ensure that the responsibility to police illegal immigrants does not fall to employers. For example, the industry vigorously opposed so-called no-match rules, whereby employers would be responsible for checking Social Security numbers against a national database. The industry argued that data irregularities and potential false positives made the system unworkable, especially for small businesses. Instead, the industry supports a more "comprehensive" approach that includes a path to citizenship for immigrants without criminal records.

Top Ten Democratic Contributors

Wendy's/Arby's Group, Inc.	$289,118
McDonald's Corporation	$273,154
Riese Organization	$132,150
Sonny's Real Pit Bar-B-Q	$111,050
Darden Restaurants, Inc.	$96,808
OSI Restaurant Partners LLC	$94,450
Ilitch Holdings, Inc.	$92,250
Yum! Brands, Inc.	$71,166
Brinker International, Inc.	$54,600
Sonic Corp.	$46,500

Top Ten Republican Contributors

OSI Restaurant Partners LLC	$670,009
McDonald's Corporation	$331,615
MJKL Enterprises, Inc.	$296,600
Wendy's/Arby's Group, Inc.	$261,250
Big Boy Restaurants LLC	$157,950
Darden Restaurants, Inc.	$151,368
Waffle House, Inc.	$116,450
Brinker International, Inc.	$88,859
ARAMARK Corporation	$79,175
CKE Restaurants, Inc.	$76,400

Top Ten Lobbying Spenders

Darden Restaurants, Inc.	$1,617,526
Yum! Brands, Inc.	$1,461,795
ARAMARK Corporation	$870,000
McDonald's Corporation	$617,432
Burger King Corporation	$279,648
Brinker International, Inc.	$160,000
OSI Restaurant Partners LLC	$159,362
Wendy's International, Inc.	$80,000
Outback Steakhouse, Inc.	$40,000
CKE Restaurants, Inc.	$30,000

15%   85%

AFC Enterprises, Inc. (Popeyes)
Contributions: TOTAL: *$5,000*   DEM: *$750*   REP: *$4,250*
LOBBY SPENDING: *$0*
Agreed to pay $15 million to settle a class action lawsuit alleging securities violations. Foundation supports various charities. Has a written nondiscrimination policy covering sexual orientation but not gender identity.

88%   12%

Applebee's International, Inc.
Contributions: TOTAL: *$6,035*   DEM: *$5,285*   REP: *$750*
LOBBY SPENDING: *$0*
Subsidiary of DineEquity Corp. Facing a class action lawsuit after an E.W. Scripps media investigation found that it and other popular chain restaurants touted "healthy" dishes that contained more calories and fat than the eateries claimed. Has a written nondiscrimination policy covering discrimination on the basis of race and sexual orientation but not gender identity. Offers health insurance coverage to employees' domestic partners.

34%   66%

ARAMARK Corporation
Contributions: TOTAL: *$119,945*   DEM: *$40,770*   REP: *$79,175*
LOBBY SPENDING: *$870,000*
A pending lawsuit in Massachusetts alleges violation of the state's tipping law. Ranked number one in its industry in *Fortune* magazine's 2009 list of "World's Most Admired Companies." Strives to offer foods that are produced locally and in a sustainable manner. Practices waste reduction, reuse, and recycling. Supports disaster relief and helps provide access to food, clothing, and healthy environments. Contributes to organizations making a meaningful impact.

0%   100%

Arby's Restaurant Group, Inc.
Contributions: TOTAL: *$5,850*   DEM: *$0*   REP: *$5,850*
LOBBY SPENDING: *$0*
Subsidiary of Wendy's/Arby's Group, Inc. Agreed to retrofit 100 stores each year to comply with the ADA after it was sued for ADA violations. Foundation supports leadership, education, and youth-mentoring initiatives. Has given over $25 million to Big Sisters of America. Has a written nondiscrimination policy covering sexual orientation but not gender identity.

Auntie Anne's, Inc.

0%   100%

Contributions: TOTAL: *$14,828*   DEM: *$0*   REP: *$14,828*
LOBBY SPENDING: *$0*

Anne Beiler started the company in 1988 to help fund a faith-based family assistance foundation. Supports children's and Christian causes, donating more than $3 million to hospitals. Provides scholarship and home down-payment gift programs for its employees.

Big Boy Restaurants LLC

0%   100%

Contributions: TOTAL: *$157,950*   DEM: *$0*   REP: *$157,950*
LOBBY SPENDING: *$0*

Gives back to the communities it serves.

Bob Evans Farms, Inc.

100%   0%

Contributions: TOTAL: *$601*   DEM: *$601*   REP: *$0*
LOBBY SPENDING: *$0*

A pending lawsuit alleges ADA violations. Outreach focuses on breast cancer awareness and on families and children in the communities where it operates. Has a written nondiscrimination policy covering sexual orientation but not gender identity.

Boston Market Corporation

72%   28%

Contributions: TOTAL: *$975*   DEM: *$700*   REP: *$275*
LOBBY SPENDING: *$0*

Subsidiary of Sun Capital Partners, Inc. The UAW called for a consumer boycott because of unfair labor and supplier practices. Paying up to $14 million to settle two class action lawsuits for alleged violations of California wage and hour laws. Agreed to pay $150,000 to settle federal charges alleging sexual harassment and disability discrimination. Outreach includes a partnership with Give Kids the World.

Brinker International, Inc.

38%   62%

Contributions: TOTAL: *$143,459*   DEM: *$54,600*   REP: *$88,859*
LOBBY SPENDING: *$160,000*

Received a score of 100 out of 100 from the Human Rights Campaign. Supports children, health, arts and culture, and social services; does not support religious organizations. Has a written nondiscrimination policy covering sexual orientation and gender identity. Offers insurance coverage to employees' domestic partners. Insurance for transgender employees is offered, and treatment is covered.

Bruegger's Enterprises, Inc.

100%   0%

Contributions: TOTAL: *$500*   DEM: *$500*   REP: *$0*
LOBBY SPENDING: *$0*

Subsidiary of Sun Capital Partners, Inc. Supports nonprofit groups involved in disease prevention or the support of underprivileged children.

Burger King Corporation

41%   59%

Contributions: TOTAL: *$90,050*   DEM: *$37,350*   REP: *$52,700*
LOBBY SPENDING: *$279,648*

Subsidiary of Burger King Holdings, Inc. Without cause, fired at least 27 employees in its affiliated restaurants in Honduras after they were rumored to be organizing to demand better working conditions. Pending lawsuit for alleged discrimination against African American employees. Named in several sexual harassment lawsuits. In 2008, scored 0 out of 100 in "The Climate Counts Company Scorecard Report." Installation of new broilers has reduced gas consumption 52% and cut electricity consumption almost 90%. Foundation supports organizations that alleviate hunger, prevent disease, and support youth programs.

California Pizza Kitchen, Inc.

3% | 97%

Contributions: TOTAL: *$7,250*   DEM: *$250*   REP: *$7,000*
LOBBY SPENDING: *$0*

Partnered with Kraft Foods, Inc. on its frozen pizza line. A pending class action lawsuit alleges overtime and labor violations. Has stated it will not use ingredients from cloned animals. Supports Starlight Children's Foundation and communities in which the company has a presence. Has a written nondiscrimination policy covering sexual orientation but not gender identity.

Carlson Restaurants Worldwide, Inc.

31% | 69%

Contributions: TOTAL: *$23,300*   DEM: *$7,250*   REP: *$16,050*
LOBBY SPENDING: *$0*

Subsidiary of the Carlson Companies, Inc. In 2006, the Physicians Committee for Responsible Medicine brought a lawsuit against Carlson and seven other restaurant chains/groups seeking to prevent them from continuing to sell grilled chicken products to consumers without warnings about the products' carcinogenic effects.

Carl's Jr.

0% | 100%

Contributions: TOTAL: *$3,500*   DEM: *$0*   REP: *$3,500*
LOBBY SPENDING: *$0*

Subsidiary of CKE Restaurants, Inc. Has granted more than $400,000 in scholarship monies. Has no written nondiscrimination policy covering sexual orientation or gender identity.

CEC Entertainment, Inc.

0% | 100%

Contributions: TOTAL: *$2,000*   DEM: *$0*   REP: *$2,000*
LOBBY SPENDING: *$0*

Operates the Chuck E. Cheese's chain of pizza parlors. A pending lawsuit filed by a customer alleges racial discrimination. Paid $300,000 in damages for firing a mentally disabled man for no cause. The company has since increased sensitivity training for employees.

Cheesecake Factory, Inc., The

54% | 46%

Contributions: TOTAL: *$4,751*   DEM: *$2,550*   REP: *$2,201*
LOBBY SPENDING: *$0*

The EEOC filed a class action lawsuit in 2008 accusing it of failing to take action following numerous complaints of sexual harassment. Foundation supports cancer research and hunger and disaster relief. Has a written nondiscrimination policy that excludes sexual orientation and gender identity. Refuses insurance coverage to employees' domestic partners.

Chevys, Inc.

100% DEM: *$500*   0% REP: *$0*

Contributions: TOTAL: *$500*   DEM: *$500*   REP: *$0*
LOBBY SPENDING: *$0*

Subsidiary of Real Mex Restaurants. Supports community-building organizations. Will host a fund-raiser at its restaurant and give up to 25% of the proceeds to the customer's nonprofit organization of choice. Offers insurance coverage to employees' domestic partners.

Chick-Fil-A, Inc.

10% DEM   90% REP

Contributions: TOTAL: *$35,785*   DEM: *$3,464*   REP: *$32,321*
LOBBY SPENDING: *$0*

Settled (for an undisclosed sum) a religious discrimination lawsuit with a Muslim franchisee whose relationship was terminated because he refused to take part in a Christian group prayer. The company's corporate purpose includes the mandate to "glorify God." It bases its management values on various biblical precepts. Foundation supports a foster care program, a summer camp, and marriage enrichment retreats. Also supports Christian causes, children's issues, and education. Written nondiscrimination policy excludes sexual orientation and gender identity. Refuses insurance coverage to employees' domestic partners.

Chili's Grill and Bar

100% DEM   0% REP

Contributions: TOTAL: *$750*   DEM: *$750*   REP: *$0*
LOBBY SPENDING: *$0*

Subsidiary of Brinker International, Inc.

Chipotle Mexican Grill, Inc.

100% DEM   0% REP

Contributions: TOTAL: *$500*   DEM: *$500*   REP: *$0*
LOBBY SPENDING: *$0*

Food is unprocessed, seasonal, family-farmed, sustainable, naturally raised, hormone free, and organic. Two of its restaurants are seeking LEED certification. Supports education, youth sports, and community improvement projects. Has a written nondiscrimination policy covering sexual orientation but not gender identity.

Church's Chicken, Inc.

47% DEM   53% REP

Contributions: TOTAL: *$4,350*   DEM: *$2,050*   REP: *$2,300*
LOBBY SPENDING: *$0*

Subsidiary of Arcapita, Inc.; parent, Arcapita Bank BSC in Bahrain. A pending lawsuit against the Islamic investment bank that owns the Church's Chicken fast-food chain alleges that a franchise failed because the bank's strict adherence to the religious code of Shari'a prohibited the owners from selling pork. Supports Special Olympics Georgia.

CKE Restaurants, Inc.

1% DEM   99% REP

Contributions: TOTAL: *$77,400*   DEM: *$1,000*   REP: *$76,400*
LOBBY SPENDING: *$30,000*

Has been boycotted by gay rights activists and feminists due to the president and CEO's donations to conservative groups and participation in the antiabortion movement. The company hired Playboy founder

Hugh Hefner as a spokesperson with the motto "Because some guys don't want the same thing day after day." Supports education, hunger cessation, and community leadership. Has no written nondiscrimination policy covering sexual orientation or gender identity. Refuses insurance coverage to employees' domestic partners.

Cold Stone Creamery, Inc.
15% | 85%
Contributions: TOTAL: *$6,600*   DEM: *$1,000*   REP: *$5,600*
LOBBY SPENDING: *$0*

Subsidiary of Kahala Corp. Supports the Make-A-Wish Foundation and local schools and charitable organizations. Has no written nondiscrimination policy covering sexual orientation or gender identity.

Cracker Barrel Old Country Store, Inc.
21% | 79%
Contributions: TOTAL: *$70,000*   DEM: *$15,000*   REP: *$55,000*
LOBBY SPENDING: *$0*

In 2006, paid $2 million to settle a lawsuit for sexual and racial harassment brought by the EEOC. The NAACP has alleged racial discrimination against African American customers. Its foundation supports preservation and establishment of historic monuments, natural sites, and parks. Also supports education, human services, and cultural issues. Has a written nondiscrimination policy covering sexual orientation but not gender identity. Refuses insurance coverage to employees' domestic partners.

Darden Restaurants, Inc.
39% | 61%
Contributions: TOTAL: *$248,176*   DEM: *$96,808*   REP: *$151,368*
LOBBY SPENDING: *$1,617,526*

Paid $9.5 million to settle two class action lawsuits brought by California employees of its Red Lobster and Olive Garden chains. Settled multiple racial discrimination lawsuits brought by customers. Its headquarters is surrounded by special "biosoil" that promotes reabsorption and prevents runoff. In 2008, scored 0 out of 100 in "The Climate Counts Company Scorecard Report." Focuses philanthropy on arts and culture, social services, nutrition, education, and preservation of natural resources. Has a minority supplier program. Has a written nondiscrimination policy covering sexual orientation but not gender identity. Offers insurance coverage to employees' domestic partners.

Denny's Corporation
100% | 0%
Contributions: TOTAL: *$7,050*   DEM: *$7,050*   REP: *$0*
LOBBY SPENDING: *$0*

A pending $28 million lawsuit brought by Arab American customers alleges racial discrimination. Settled several racial discrimination lawsuits for $54 million. Sponsors scholarship programs and supports at-risk children and human rights initiatives. Has no written nondiscrimination policy covering sexual orientation or gender identity.

Domino's Pizza, Inc.
10% | 90%
Contributions: TOTAL: *$50,799*   DEM: *$4,837*   REP: *$45,962*
LOBBY SPENDING: *$0*

Private equity firm Bain Capital owns nearly 30% of the company. Faulted for its child labor record. Has allocated $7 million to employees who have been victims of fire, accidents, illness, or natural disasters. Supports minority interest groups, community welfare, hunger relief, education, arts and culture, and children's charities. Has a written nondiscrimination policy covering sexual orientation but not gender identity. Refuses insurance coverage to employees' domestic partners. Insurance for transgender employees is offered, and some treatment is covered.

Einstein Noah Restaurant Group (formerly New World Restaurant Group)

Contributions: TOTAL: *$200*   DEM: *$200*   REP: *$0*
LOBBY SPENDING: *$0*

100%   0%

In 2008, agreed to pay up to $2.5 million to settle two lawsuits filed by former employees for unpaid overtime and breaks.

Hard Rock Cafe International, Inc.

Contributions: TOTAL: *$3,750*   DEM: *$3,750*   REP: *$0*
LOBBY SPENDING: *$0*

100%   0%

Subsidiary of Seminole Hard Rock Entertainment, Inc.; parent, Seminole Tribe of Florida, Inc. Uses only environmentally safe cleaning materials and recycled paper products. Supports treatment programs for substance abuse, several children's charities, disaster relief, Habitat for Humanity, Amnesty International, cancer research, environmental conservation, and the arts. Has a written nondiscrimination policy covering sexual orientation but not gender identity. Offers insurance coverage to employees' domestic partners.

Hardee's Food Systems, Inc.

Contributions: TOTAL: *$200*   DEM: *$0*   REP: *$200*
LOBBY SPENDING: *$0*

0%   100%

Subsidiary of CKE Restaurants, Inc. Paid an $87,000 settlement in a child labor lawsuit. Supports breast cancer awareness and early detection. Has no written nondiscrimination policy covering sexual orientation or gender identity.

Hooters of America, Inc.

Contributions: TOTAL: *$300*   DEM: *$0*   REP: *$300*
LOBBY SPENDING: *$0*

0%   100%

Paid $2 million to settle a class action suit filed by men denied the opportunity to serve as "Hooters girls." Ordered to create gender-neutral positions. Multiple instances of high-figure punitive damage awards to former female employees who complained of sexual harassment. Supports the Make-A-Wish Foundation and the Juvenile Diabetes Foundation.

Ilitch Holdings, Inc.

Contributions: TOTAL: *$168,650*   DEM: *$92,250*   REP: *$76,400*
LOBBY SPENDING: *$0*

55%   45%

Holding company for the Little Caesars pizza chain. Fought with preservationists in Detroit to purchase and subsequently demolish a historic hotel to build a parking lot. Supports community development, human services, education, and recreation. Ilitch Charities supports children's homes, youth sports, and various charities.

International Dairy Queen, Inc.
Contributions: TOTAL: *$500*   DEM: *$500*   REP: *$0*
LOBBY SPENDING: *$0*

100% — DEM: $500 | 0% — REP: $0

Subsidiary of Berkshire Hathaway. Supports education and the Children's Miracle Network.

Jack in the Box, Inc.
Contributions: TOTAL: *$2,900*   DEM: *$1,000*   REP: *$1,900*
LOBBY SPENDING: *$0*

34% — DEM: $1,000 | 66% — REP: $1,900

Its foundation supports youth mentoring and a variety of charitable organizations. Its primary charitable partner is Big Sisters. Has a written nondiscrimination policy covering sexual orientation but not gender identity.

Kahala Corp.
Contributions: TOTAL: *$6,600*   DEM: *$1,000*   REP: *$5,600*
LOBBY SPENDING: *$0*

15% — DEM: $1,000 | 85% — REP: $5,600

Supports the Make-A-Wish Foundation.

KFC Corporation
Contributions: TOTAL: *$500*   DEM: *$0*   REP: *$500*
LOBBY SPENDING: *$0*

0% — DEM: $0 | 100% — REP: $500

Subsidiary of Yum! Brands, Inc. Is accused of wildly fluctuating employee work hours to avoid providing benefits and protections, including maternity leave and severance pay. Was boycotted by PETA. Supports scholarship programs, hunger cessation, and road repairs.

Krispy Kreme Doughnuts, Inc.
Contributions: TOTAL: *$2,000*   DEM: *$0*   REP: *$2,000*
LOBBY SPENDING: *$0*

0% — DEM: $0 | 100% — REP: $2,000

Paid $75 million to settle a class action lawsuit by shareholders alleging insider trading and false and misleading statements. Provides summer camp experiences to ill children. Has no written nondiscrimination policy covering sexual orientation or gender identity.

Landry's Restaurants, Inc.
Contributions: TOTAL: *$38,500*   DEM: *$24,700*   REP: *$13,800*
LOBBY SPENDING: *$0*

64% — DEM: $24,700 | 36% — REP: $13,800

CEO Tilman Fertitta is accused in a pending lawsuit of stealing control of the company by systematically reducing the offering price, then buying stock on the open market. He now owns 54% of the shares. A pending class action lawsuit alleges violations of federal labor laws for requiring servers to give up a portion of tips to offset charges levied by credit card companies.

Little Caesar Enterprises, Inc.
Contributions: TOTAL: *$1,250*   DEM: *$250*   REP: *$1,000*
LOBBY SPENDING: *$0*

20% — DEM: $250 | 80% — REP: $1,000

Subsidiary of Ilitch Holdings, Inc. Its foundation feeds the homeless and provides disaster relief.

Marie Callender Pie Shops, Inc.
33% — 67%
Contributions: TOTAL: *$750*   DEM: *$250*   REP: *$500*
LOBBY SPENDING: *$0*
Subsidiary of Castle Harlan, Inc. The frozen food line, with the exception of pies, is licensed to ConAgra Foods, Inc.

**McCormick & Schmick's
Seafood Restaurants, Inc.**
0% — 100%
Contributions: TOTAL: *$1,750*   DEM: *$0*   REP: *$1,750*
LOBBY SPENDING: *$0*
In 2008, paid $1.1 million to settle a class action lawsuit concerning race discrimination claims by African American hourly employees. Each restaurant donates goods, services, banquet and meeting space, and dining certificates or meals to charitable organizations.

McDonald's Corporation
45% — 55%
Contributions: TOTAL: *$604,769*   DEM: *$273,154*   REP: *$331,615*
LOBBY SPENDING: *$617,432*
The UFCW calls the company "very antiunion." Accused of several labor violations overseas. In 2008, scored 27 out of 100 in "The Climate Counts Company Scorecard Report." Approximately 82% of its consumer packaging in its nine largest markets is made from renewable materials. Operates "green restaurants" in Sweden and the United States and is constructing others in Brazil, Canada, and France. Supports cancer research, youth programs, HIV/AIDS research, and disaster relief. Has a written nondiscrimination policy covering sexual orientation but not gender identity. Offers insurance coverage to employees' domestic partners. Insurance for transgender employees is offered, and some treatment is covered.

MJKL Enterprises, Inc.
0% — 100%
Contributions: TOTAL: *$297,100*   DEM: *$500*   REP: *$296,600*
LOBBY SPENDING: *$0*
Operates 59 Carl's Jr. restaurants, 60 Hardee's restaurants, 12 Pizza Patron restaurants, and 3 Bill's Ghost and Spirit convenience stores. Is converting corporate fleet vehicles to operate on fuel derived from waste vegetable oil collected at its Arizona franchise locations.

Morton's Restaurant Group, Inc.
27% — 73%
Contributions: TOTAL: *$3,750*   DEM: *$1,000*   REP: *$2,750*
LOBBY SPENDING: *$0*
Investment firm Castle Harlan owns almost 30% of the company. Supports the Make-A-Wish Foundation.

Nathan's Famous, Inc.
0% — 100%
Contributions: TOTAL: *$1,500*   DEM: *$0*   REP: *$1,500*
LOBBY SPENDING: *$0*
Specialty Foods Group makes Nathan's hot dogs for retail sale. Supports Feeding America.

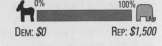

Olive Garden Italian Restaurant
Contributions: TOTAL: *$350*   DEM: *$0*   REP: *$350*
LOBBY SPENDING: *$0*

0%   100%

Subsidiary of Darden Restaurants, Inc. Sponsors local charity and school events and the Leukemia & Lymphoma Society. Has a written nondiscrimination policy covering sexual orientation but not gender identity. Offers insurance coverage to employees' domestic partners.

On The Border Mexican Grill & Cantina
Contributions: TOTAL: *$409*   DEM: *$0*   REP: *$409*
LOBBY SPENDING: *$0*

0%   100%

Subsidiary of Brinker International, Inc.

OSI Restaurant Partners LLC
Contributions: TOTAL: *$764,459*   DEM: *$94,450*   REP: *$670,009*
LOBBY SPENDING: *$159,362*

12%   88%

Subsidiary of Bain Capital LLC. Four class action lawsuits allege that OSI violated the federal Fair and Accurate Credit Transactions Act. Supports disaster relief. Has no written nondiscrimination policy covering sexual orientation or gender identity.

Outback Steakhouse, Inc.
Contributions: TOTAL: *$25,620*   DEM: *$8,900*   REP: *$16,720*
LOBBY SPENDING: *<$40,000*

35%   65%

Subsidiary of OSI Restaurant Partners LLC. In 2006, the EEOC filed a lawsuit alleging gender discrimination because it did not promote women to top management positions. Supports U.S. troops fighting in Afghanistan and Iraq by bringing them mobile catering units. Has no written nondiscrimination policy covering sexual orientation or gender identity.

Palm Management Corp.
Contributions: TOTAL: *$5,600*   DEM: *$0*   REP: *$5,600*
LOBBY SPENDING: *$0*

0%   100%

Participant in the Women's Foodservice Forum, which promotes career advancement for executive women. Member of the MultiCultural Foodservice & Hospitality Alliance. Provides support for the fight against domestic violence. Has a written nondiscrimination policy covering sexual orientation but not gender identity. Offers insurance coverage to employees' domestic partners.

Panda Restaurant Group, Inc.
Contributions: TOTAL: *$5,800*   DEM: *$3,800*   REP: *$2,000*
LOBBY SPENDING: *$0*

66%   34%

Pending class action lawsuit alleging employees were purposely misclassified so they would not be eligible for paid overtime. Supports children's causes in communities where the company has a presence. Has given millions of dollars of in-kind donations to numerous nonprofit organizations, schools, and hospitals.

Papa John's International, Inc.
Contributions: TOTAL: *$2,000*   DEM: *$2,000*   REP: *$0*

100%   0%

LOBBY SPENDING: *$0*

Supports education, cerebral palsy research, children's causes, the arts, Special Olympics, and the American Diabetes Association. Has no written nondiscrimination policy covering sexual orientation or gender identity. Refuses insurance coverage to employees' domestic partners.

Pizza Hut, Inc.   32%   68%
Contributions: TOTAL: *$52,101*   DEM: *$16,650*   REP: *$35,451*
LOBBY SPENDING: *$0*

Subsidiary of Yum! Brands, Inc. In 2006, settled a class action overtime lawsuit for $15 million.

Pizza Inn, Inc.   0%   100%
Contributions: TOTAL: *$500*   DEM: *$0*   REP: *$500*
LOBBY SPENDING: *$0*

Supports community-based programs that focus on the needs of schools, churches, seniors, and other local care-giving organizations.

Quiznos Master LLC   50%   50%
Contributions: TOTAL: *$2,400*   DEM: *$1,200*   REP: *$1,200*
LOBBY SPENDING: *$0*

Lawsuits pending in four states allege it does not give prospective franchise owners all pertinent facts about restaurant locations and business operations. Lawsuits filed by a few dozen franchisees in Pennsylvania allege that it engages in a "pattern of racketeering" and generates "grossly inflated profits" at the expense of franchises, which usually fail. Supports disaster relief, health initiatives, diversity, and education within the communities in which it operates. Has no written nondiscrimination policy covering sexual orientation or gender identity.

Red Lobster   33%   67%
Contributions: TOTAL: *$3,018*   DEM: *$1,000*   REP: *$2,018*
LOBBY SPENDING: *$0*

Subsidiary of Darden Restaurants, Inc. Has a written nondiscrimination policy covering sexual orientation but not gender identity. Offers insurance coverage to employees' domestic partners.

Riese Organization   100%   0%
Contributions: TOTAL: *$132,410*   DEM: *$132,150*   REP: *$260*
LOBBY SPENDING: *$0*

Runs restaurants under National Restaurants Management. Owns and operates 113 chain restaurants in the New York City area and develops its own proprietary restaurant concepts. Lawsuit filed in 2008 for $600 million by four female workers who claim that widespread sexual harassment at its Hawaiian Tropic Zone escalated into rape.

Ruby Tuesday, Inc.   5%   95%
Contributions: TOTAL: *$19,800*   DEM: *$1,000*   REP: *$18,800*
LOBBY SPENDING: *$0*

Pending lawsuit brought by the EEOC alleges sexual harassment. The menu is printed on paper made with wind-generated electricity. Is reducing its landfill waste by 320 tons per year by challenging its salad dressing vendors to use sleeker pouches.

Ruth's Hospitality Group, Inc. (formerly Ruth's Chris Steak House, Inc.)

0% ——————————— 100%

Contributions: TOTAL: *$26,600* DEM: *$0* REP: *$26,600*
LOBBY SPENDING: *$0*

Facing a 2008 RICO class action lawsuit alleging that it systematically hires undocumented workers and lets them use the Social Security numbers of previous workers. It also claims the restaurant hires undocumented workers on a "large scale," pays them in cash, knowingly accepts I-9 immigration forms containing false information, and otherwise knowingly violates immigration and employment laws.

Smith & Wollensky Restaurant Group, Inc.

100% ——————————— 0%

Contributions: TOTAL: *$2,500* DEM: *$2,500* REP: *$0*
LOBBY SPENDING: *$0*

Subsidiary of Patina Restaurant Group LLC. Has faced racial discrimination lawsuits brought by employees working at various locations. Offers insurance coverage to employees' domestic partners.

Sonic Corp.

100% ——————————— 0%

Contributions: TOTAL: *$46,500* DEM: *$46,500* REP: *$0*
LOBBY SPENDING: *$0*

Is the subject of three pending suits brought by the EEOC. Supports educational causes within the State of Oklahoma.

Sonny's Real Pit Bar-B-Q

92% ——————————— 8%

Contributions: TOTAL: *$121,250* DEM: *$111,050* REP: *$10,200*
LOBBY SPENDING: *$0*

Supports various community initiatives throughout the Southeast, including education, arts and humanities, charitable efforts, youth development, and human services.

Taco Bell Corp.

62% ——————————— 38%

Contributions: TOTAL: *$9,050* DEM: *$5,600* REP: *$3,450*
LOBBY SPENDING: *$0*

Subsidiary of Yum! Brands, Inc. A pending class action lawsuit in California alleges that barriers make access at corporate-owned Taco Bell restaurants in that state difficult for those with disabilities. Its foundation supports programs that inspire teens to graduate from high school.

TruFoods LLC

0% ——————————— 100%

Contributions: TOTAL: *$1,000* DEM: *$0* REP: *$1,000*
LOBBY SPENDING: *$0*

T.G.I. Friday's

62% ——————————— 38%

Contributions: TOTAL: *$1,175* DEM: *$725* REP: *$450*
LOBBY SPENDING: *$0*

Subsidiary of Carlson Restaurants Worldwide, Inc. Settled a $5 million lawsuit for unpaid wages and other damages resulting from its refusal to permit its employees to take legally required breaks. Has a written non-discrimination policy covering sexual orientation and gender identity. Offers insurance coverage to employees' domestic partners. Insurance for transgender employees is offered, and some treatment is covered.

Uno Restaurant Holdings Corp.

Contributions: Total: *$2,527*   Dem: *$0*   Rep: *$2,527*

0%   100%

Lobby Spending: *$0*

Subsidiary of Centre Partners Management LLC. Violated the "whistle-blowers' protection act" in a pattern of termination after employees reported food safety violations. Offers schools the opportunity to partner with its restaurants to raise money.

Waffle House, Inc.

Contributions: Total: *$117,200*   Dem: *$750*   Rep: *$116,450*

1%   99%

Lobby Spending: *$0*

Has faced numerous racial discrimination, sexual harassment, and violation of civil rights lawsuits. Supports the American Red Cross, the American Cancer Society, and the Walk for Autism.

Wendy's/Arby's Group, Inc.

Contributions: Total: *$550,368*   Dem: *$289,118*   Rep: *$261,250*

53%   47%

Lobby Spending: *$0*

Supports U.S. adoption programs, as well as leadership, education, and mentoring initiatives in the communities it serves.

Wendy's International, Inc.

Contributions: Total: *$31,700*   Dem: *$16,100*   Rep: *$15,600*

51%   49%

Lobby Spending: *$80,000*

Subsidiary of Wendy's/Arby's Group, Inc. Criticized for rejecting a fair wage campaign launched by the Coalition of Immokalee Workers, a group of South Florida farm workers. In 2008, scored 0 out of 100 in "The Climate Counts Company Scorecard Report." Supports adoption advocacy and education. Has a written nondiscrimination policy covering sexual orientation and gender identity. Refuses insurance coverage to employees' domestic partners.

White Castle System, Inc.

Contributions: Total: *$53,450*   Dem: *$1,000*   Rep: *$52,450*

2%   98%

Lobby Spending: *$0*

Supports Detroit's "Angels' Night."

Yum! Brands, Inc.

Contributions: Total: *$127,516*   Dem: *$71,166*   Rep: *$56,350*

56%   44%

Lobby Spending: *$1,461,795*

Has been cited for sourcing toys from sweatshops and abusing labor standards in its stores. Beijing KFC employees filed at least four lawsuits against the company for unfair employment practices. In 2008, scored 1 out of 100 in "The Climate Counts Company Scorecard Report." Has refused to discuss its role in Amazon rainforest destruction. Supports college scholarships, community hunger-relief initiatives, and programs that focus on reading incentives and mentoring of at-risk teens. Has a written nondiscrimination policy covering sexual orientation but not gender identity. Offers insurance coverage to employees' domestic partners. Limited insurance for transgender employees is offered, but treatment is not covered.

Sporting Goods

Dave Zirin

No one claims that the sporting goods business has been synonymous with social responsibility. A trillion-dollar global industry, it has scoured the earth for cheap labor and state-sponsored subsidies. In the race to the ethical bottom, the athletic-industrial complex has routinely laced 'em up—all in an effort to maximize profit.

But there have been some bright spots. During the 1990s, for example, United Students against Sweatshops helped raise awareness about the sketchy supply chain for sporting goods. It held rallies and protests and even challenged sports demigods like Michael Jordan and Jerry Rice to be accountable for the products they endorsed. In the global South, there is a consensus among many political leaders, and even some activists, that the situation has vastly improved over the last decade. Most U.S. companies now put out a corporate social responsibility (CSR) report that documents the myriad ways they are attempting to create a humane workplace. Make no mistake: in this business, image matters.

So does lifestyle. In fact, many sporting goods companies say that's what they're really selling. In today's "red state–blue state" environment, some of those lifestyles carry a political charge. Snowboarding and hunting aren't just hobbies; they're social identities that consumers signal with their purchases. Not surprisingly, these identities reflect the political polarization we encounter elsewhere.

We see the same split in the industry's top political contributors. The busiest 21 firms gave Democrats $338,708, while Republicans received $325,725, a near-even split. But most companies didn't split their political envelopes evenly. Instead, they gave to the party that helped them extend their brand. In the age of Obama, companies catering to upscale extreme sports focused on the youth market and gave to the Democrats. Burton Snowboards, for example, gave $129,853, all to the donkeys. As the party of Karl Rove, the Republicans focused on God, guns, and gays. Smith & Wesson, the famous gun manufacturer, rewarded them accordingly.

The strategy might suggest that sporting goods companies have gone legit. No longer would they be a pariah industry, operating in the dark in fear of the investigative light. But despite their efforts, questions remain about whether they have improved or just become more effective in hiding the abuse.

Awards are now given to the companies that produce the best corporate social responsibility reports. But these reports reflect the *aspirations* of a company rather than the reality. They aren't written by workers, but by management. They certainly don't include the fact that improvements often came about because workers fought for workplace reforms actively resisted by the company.

China is where the question of appearance versus reality holds the most relevance. It has become the great exporter to the United States, shipping everything from sporting goods to American flags produced under the watchful eye of those strange bedfellows: U.S. capital and the Chinese Communist Party. Of course, China also hosted that ultimate marketing machine for sporting goods, the 2008 Olympic Games. The event was even blessed by President George W. Bush, who became the first sitting U.S. president to attend opening ceremonies on foreign soil.

Jim Keady, a former professional soccer player and coach at St. John's University in Queens, New York, is now the codirector of the antisweatshop organization Educating for Justice. "One of the key ways to define a sweatshop is whether workers have the right to develop an independent, democratic voice in the workplace, either by creating a worker-owned cooperative or an independent trade union," he said to me. "In China both cooperatives and independent trade unions are illegal." Even *Business Week*, that interoffice memo of the corporate suites, has written, "American importers have long answered criticism of conditions at their Chinese suppliers with labor rules and inspections. But many factories have just gotten better at concealing abuses." Any improvements in China can't be traced to pressure from U.S. companies. Instead, they're more likely due to a volatile labor situation. As many as 9,000 strikes occurred in China last year—all of them illegal, and many of them violent.

If the sporting goods business is truly about lifestyle choices, we can start with the choices U.S.

companies make about their business practices. But if the business is really about the bottom line, then all of us, producers and consumers, might have the inside track in the race to the bottom.

Top Ten Democratic Contributors

NIKE, Inc.	$183,515
Burton Snowboards	$153,400
Recreational Equipment, Inc. (REI)	$23,701
Radio Flyer, Inc.	$20,000
Cascade Designs, Inc.	$19,955
Outdoor Research, Inc.	$17,000
Smith & Wesson	$15,000
Trek Bicycle Corporation	$14,440
Adidas AG	$10,670
L. L. Bean, Inc.	$10,608

Top Ten Republican Contributors

New Balance Athletic Shoe, Inc.	$148,200
NIKE, Inc.	$95,961
Jas. D. Easton, Inc.	$34,700
Columbia Sportswear Company	$28,800
Smith & Wesson	$27,775
Hodgdon Powder Company, Inc.	$23,300
Sierra Trading Post, Inc.	$19,600
L. L. Bean, Inc.	$17,800
Scheels All Sports, Inc.	$16,100
Cabela's, Inc.	$15,100

Top Ten Lobbying Spenders

NIKE, Inc.	$930,000
Smith & Wesson	$680,000
Cascade Designs, Inc.	$550,000
New Balance Athletic Shoe, Inc.	$288,000
Patagonia, Inc.	$90,000
Victorinox Swiss Army, Inc.	$80,000
Recreational Equipment, Inc. (REI)	$70,000
Outdoor Research, Inc.	$40,000
Acushnet Company	$40,000
Columbia Sportswear Company	$40,000

Acushnet Company
Contributions: TOTAL: *$500*   DEM: *$500*   REP: *$0*
LOBBY SPENDING: <*$40,000*
Subsidiary of Fortune Brands, Inc. Its supplier citizenship policy states that it is dedicated to operating ethically, protecting the environment, and supporting the communities in which it does business.

Adidas AG
54%   46%
Contributions: TOTAL: *$19,770*   DEM: *$10,670*   REP: *$9,100*
LOBBY SPENDING: *$30,000*
Foreign owned. Has sourced from countries with wide-spread, well-documented human and labor rights abuses and encourages sweat-shop labor with its supplier practices. Among the founding companies of the Fair Labor Association. Is eliminating PVCs and reducing toxic solvents. Supports initiatives to aid children and young adults and funds causes around the world.

Amer Sports Corporation
9%   91%
Contributions: TOTAL: *$12,576*   DEM: *$1,176*   REP: *$11,400*
LOBBY SPENDING: *$0*
Foreign owned. Subsidiary of Amer Group PLC in Finland. Has sourced from countries with wide-spread, well-documented human and labor rights abuses. Manufactures the world's first regenerative ski boot made from biopolymers, cotton, and bamboo fiber. Subsidiary Precor has increased incentives for employees who use alternative trans-portation or drive vehicles that get 40+ miles to the gallon. Supports sports and education in Tanzania, as well as breast cancer research and awareness.

Big 5 Sporting Goods Corporation
100%   0%
Contributions: TOTAL: *$250*   DEM: *$250*   REP: *$0*
LOBBY SPENDING: *$0*
A pending lawsuit brought by a physically disabled consumer alleges ADA violations.

Burton Snowboards
100%   0%
Contributions: TOTAL: *$153,400*   DEM: *$153,400*   REP: *$0*
LOBBY SPENDING: *$0*
Committed to going fur-free. Founder of Chill, an international nonprofit intervention program benefiting inner-city and at-risk youth. Offers insurance coverage to employees' domestic partners.

Cabela's, Inc.
0%   100%
Contributions: TOTAL: *$15,100*   DEM: *$0*   REP: *$15,100*
LOBBY SPENDING: *$0*
Accepted public funds for a new Texas store but sued to keep its use of that money secret from taxpayers. Filed a lawsuit asking a judge to evict a reclusive elderly woman who is living on property near a Cabela's project. Outreach includes partnerships with the Congressio-nal Sportsmen's Caucus, the NRA, and several other fish, game, and environmental organizations.

Callaway Golf Company
75%   25%
Contributions: TOTAL: *$2,000*   DEM: *$1,500*   REP: *$500*
LOBBY SPENDING: *$0*
Outreach in communities with a company presence, targeting at-risk youth and those underserved by health care. Foundation supports cancer research, hunger cessation, veterans and their families, and the Humane Society. Has a written nondiscrimination policy covering

sexual orientation but not gender identity. Offers insurance coverage to employees' domestic partners.

Cannondale Bicycle Corporation

100% ← | 0% →

Contributions: TOTAL: *$500*   DEM: *$500*   REP: *$0*
LOBBY SPENDING: *$0*

Subsidiary of Dorel Industries, Inc., in Canada. Supports the International Mountain Biking Association, as well as Bikes Belong and its mission to get more people riding bicycles more often.

Cascade Designs, Inc.

98% ← | 2% →

Contributions: TOTAL: *$20,455*   DEM: *$19,955*   REP: *$500*
LOBBY SPENDING: *$550,000*

Supports conservation projects for public lands, wilderness areas, and waterways.

Coleman Company, Inc., The

61% ← | 39% →

Contributions: TOTAL: *$5,800*   DEM: *$3,550*   REP: *$2,250*
LOBBY SPENDING: *$0*

Subsidiary of Jarden Corporation. Supporter of outdoor conservation efforts.

Columbia Sportswear Company

12% ← | 88% →

Contributions: TOTAL: *$32,790*   DEM: *$3,990*   REP: *$28,800*
LOBBY SPENDING: *<$40,000*

Supports organizations that specialize in human assistance, conservation, the environment, youth, and arts and education programs. Has a written nondiscrimination policy covering sexual orientation but not gender identity.

Converse, Inc.

100% ← | 0% →

Contributions: TOTAL: *$7,428*   DEM: *$7,428*   REP: *$0*
LOBBY SPENDING: *$0*

Subsidiary of NIKE, Inc. Partner in (PRODUCT) RED campaign. Has a written nondiscrimination policy covering sexual orientation and gender identity. Offers insurance coverage to employees' domestic partners. Insurance for transgender employees is offered, and treatment is covered.

Eddie Bauer Holdings, Inc.

100% ← | 0% →

Contributions: TOTAL: *$500*   DEM: *$500*   REP: *$0*
LOBBY SPENDING: *$0*

Sources from countries with widespread, well-documented human and labor rights abuses and encourages sweatshop labor with its supplier practices. Among the founding companies of the Fair Labor Association. Has used prison labor. Raised $5 million for reforestation efforts in several U.S. states and Canadian provinces. Has a written nondiscrimination policy covering sexual orientation but not gender identity.

Hibbett Sports, Inc.

0% ← | 100% →

Contributions: TOTAL: *$13,800*   DEM: *$0*   REP: *$13,800*
LOBBY SPENDING: *$0*

Settled a lawsuit for $755,000 in 2008 filed by three former employees alleging they were owed back wages for overtime. Supports the United Way.

Hodgdon Powder Company, Inc.
Contributions: TOTAL: *$23,300*   DEM: *$0*   REP: *$23,300*
LOBBY SPENDING: *$0*

Its mission statement reads, in part, "we will deal with integrity and honesty, reflecting that people are more important than dollars and that our purpose is to bring credit to our Lord Jesus Christ."

Huffy Corporation
Contributions: TOTAL: *$5,050*   DEM: *$750*   REP: *$4,300*
LOBBY SPENDING: *$0*

One of 16 companies that agreed to pay $14.9 million to the federal government and the State of California in cleanup costs for the San Gabriel Valley Superfund Site. Paid $50,000 to the State of Wisconsin to settle allegations of air pollution violations. Has a long history of union strikes. Huffy made its last bike in the United States in 1999.

Jarden Corporation
Contributions: TOTAL: *$21,900*   DEM: *$9,450*   REP: *$12,450*
LOBBY SPENDING: *$0*

Paid $8 million in a class action lawsuit alleging that it issued false and misleading statements to the market, artificially inflating its stock. Has no written nondiscrimination policy covering sexual orientation or gender identity.

Jas. D. Easton, Inc.
Contributions: TOTAL: *$34,700*   DEM: *$0*   REP: *$34,700*
LOBBY SPENDING: *$0*

Operates as Easton Sports, Inc., subsidiary of Easton-Bell Sports, Inc. Its environmental policy states that it will "continuously improve practices to minimize environmental impacts and prevent pollution." Supports archery programs for youth in the San Diego, CA, area.

L. L. Bean, Inc.
Contributions: TOTAL: *$28,408*   DEM: *$10,608*   REP: *$17,800*
LOBBY SPENDING: *$0*

Member of the Fair Labor Association. Scored 73 out of 100 in the 2008 Human Rights Campaign Corporate Equality Index. Catalogs contain 20% recycled fiber. Uses solar power to heat water for its corporate offices. Nine of its retail stores are built to LEED standards. Member of the EPA's Climate Leaders program. Outreach focuses on conservation and recreation, education, and culture and the arts. Has a written nondiscrimination policy covering sexual orientation and gender identity. Offers insurance coverage to employees' domestic partners. Insurance for transgender employees is offered, but treatment is not covered.

Modell's Sporting Goods
Contributions: TOTAL: *$15,200*   DEM: *$7,300*   REP: *$7,900*
LOBBY SPENDING: *$0*

Subsidiary of Henry Modell & Company, Inc. In 2007, ordered to pay $500,000 in a racial discrimination lawsuit, which it might appeal. Supports families, youth, education, and physical activity. Its stores distribute gift cards to local nonprofit organizations, schools, recreation centers, sports teams, and leagues.

New Balance Athletic Shoe, Inc. 2% 98%
Contributions: TOTAL: *$151,000* DEM: *$2,800* REP: *$148,200*
LOBBY SPENDING: *$288,000*
Despite its "Made in the USA" labels, 75% of its shoes are made overseas. Has a long history of labor violations in its footwear manufacturing plant in China. Sponsors the Rock N' Roll marathon series and partners with the Susan G. Komen Race for the Cure.

NIKE, Inc. 66% 34%
Contributions: TOTAL: *$279,476* DEM: *$183,515* REP: *$95,961*
LOBBY SPENDING: *$930,000*
Has sourced from countries with widespread, well-documented human and labor rights abuses. Cofounder of the Fair Labor Association. According to Global Labor Strategies, Nike is among the major corporations lobbying against China's Draft Labor Contract Law that aims to secure minimal labor standards for workers. In 2008, scored 82 out of 100 in "The Climate Counts Company Scorecard Report." Purchases a majority of its energy needs from green sources. Established "Nike Considered Design" to create products that minimize environmental impact and use environmentally preferred materials. Foundation supports programs that promote health and gender equality. Has a written nondiscrimination policy covering sexual orientation and gender identity. Offers insurance coverage to employees' domestic partners. Insurance for transgender employees is offered, and treatment is covered.

North Face, Inc., The  100% 0%
Contributions: TOTAL: *$250* DEM: *$250* REP: *$0*
LOBBY SPENDING: *$0*
Subsidiary of the VF Corporation. Offsets energy use of its North American operations with 100% wind energy through renewable energy credits. Partners with the EPA Climate Leaders program. Supports community development overseas, as well as the protection and conservation of threatened wild places. Has a written nondiscrimination policy covering sexual orientation but not gender identity.

Outdoor Research, Inc. 100% 0%
Contributions: TOTAL: *$17,000* DEM: *$17,000* REP: *$0*
LOBBY SPENDING: *<$40,000*
Partners with Summit for Someone, a mountaineering fundraiser that benefits Big City Mountaineers, a nonprofit recreational mentoring program for at-risk teens.

Patagonia, Inc. 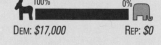 100% 0%
Contributions: TOTAL: *$7,260* DEM: *$7,260* REP: *$0*
LOBBY SPENDING: *$90,000*
Subsidiary of Lost Arrow Corporation. Uses organic cotton in its clothing production. Member of the Fair Trade Association. Has awarded over $31 million in cash and in-kind donations to environmental groups. Built its own power plant at its headquarters. Has a clothing recycling program. Outreach includes protection of wildland ecosystems and

biodiversity in the Patagonia region of Chile and Argentina. Has a written nondiscrimination policy covering sexual orientation but not gender identity. Offers insurance coverage to employees' domestic partners.

Play It Again Sports
Contributions: TOTAL: *$2,000*   DEM: *$1,500*   REP: *$500*
LOBBY SPENDING: *$0*
75% / 25%
Subsidiary of Winmark Corporation.

Quiksilver, Inc.
Contributions: TOTAL: *$6,500*   DEM: *$6,500*   REP: *$0*
LOBBY SPENDING: *$0*
100% / 0%
Its Roxy handbags were found to have a high level of lead, according to the Center for Environmental Health. Leader in customer privacy. Foundation supports environmental, educational, health, and youth-related projects.

Radio Flyer, Inc.
Contributions: TOTAL: *$20,000*   DEM: *$20,000*   REP: *$0*
LOBBY SPENDING: *$0*
100% / 0%
Virtually all production takes place in China. Offers insurance coverage to employees' domestic partners.

Rawlings Sporting Goods Company, Inc.
Contributions: TOTAL: *$1,000*   DEM: *$0*   REP: *$1,000*
LOBBY SPENDING: *$0*
0% / 100%
Subsidiary of K2, Inc. Communicates its environmental expectations to its supplier base.

Recreational Equipment, Inc. (REI)
Contributions: TOTAL: *$23,701*   DEM: *$23,701*   REP: *$0*
LOBBY SPENDING: *$70,000*
100% / 0%
Ranked 12th on *Fortune* magazine's "100 Best Companies to Work For" in 2009. Plans to become climate neutral by 2020. Is installing solar electric technology in 11 of its stores. Aspires to become a zero waste-to-landfill business by 2020. Outreach includes environmental stewardship and grants to environmental projects. Has a written nondiscrimination policy covering sexual orientation and gender identity. Offers insurance coverage to employees' domestic partners. Insurance for transgender employees is offered, and treatment is covered.

Reebok International Ltd.
Contributions: TOTAL: *$16,600*   DEM: *$7,500*   REP: *$9,100*
LOBBY SPENDING: *$30,000*
45% / 55%
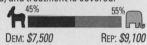
Subsidiary of Adidas AG. According to the National Labor Committee, women at its factory in Honduras are paid 19 cents per jersey--less than three-tenths of 1% of the jersey's $75 retail price. Is one of the founders of the Fair Labor Association. Has a record of supporting trade unionists. Has a written nondiscrimination policy covering sexual orientation but not gender identity. Offers insurance coverage to employees' domestic partners.

Scheels All Sports, Inc.

0% ▬▬▬▬▬▬▬▬▬▬ 100%

Contributions: TOTAL: *$16,100*   DEM: *$0*   REP: *$16,100*
LOBBY SPENDING: *$0*

The Reno-Sparks Scheels became the world's largest all-sports store in 2008. Many of its stores offer company recycling. Uses eco-friendly landscaping. Supports ride-your-bike-to-work month and local tree planting. Supports local athletic programs, education, conservation, social services and health, and the United Way.

Sierra Trading Post, Inc.

0% ▬▬▬▬▬▬▬▬▬▬ 100%

Contributions: TOTAL: *$19,600*   DEM: *$0*   REP: *$19,600*
LOBBY SPENDING: *$0*

Company Web site states that "business ethics must be consistent with the faith of the owners in Jesus Christ and his teachings." Its catalogs are 100% recyclable and are printed on paper that comes from North American forests certified to be managed by the Sustainable Forest Initiative. Uses solar domes, automatic lighting shutoffs, and other energy-saving devices in its buildings.

Smith & Wesson

35% ▬▬▬▬▬▬▬▬▬▬ 65%

Contributions: TOTAL: *$42,775*   DEM: *$15,000*   REP: *$27,775*
LOBBY SPENDING: *$680,000*

Sponsors a variety of firearm sporting events across the country.

Sports Authority, Inc., The

55% ▬▬▬▬▬▬▬▬▬▬ 45%

Contributions: TOTAL: *$1,822*   DEM: *$1,000*   REP: *$822*
LOBBY SPENDING: *$0*

Subsidiary of Leonard Green & Partners L.P. The company's e-tailing Web site is operated by GSI Commerce, Inc. Outreach includes partnerships with the National Sports Center for the Disabled and communities where it does business. Has no written nondiscrimination policy covering sexual orientation or gender identity.

Trek Bicycle Corporation

100% ▬▬▬▬▬▬▬▬▬▬ 0%

Contributions: TOTAL: *$14,440*   DEM: *$14,440*   REP: *$0*
LOBBY SPENDING: *$0*

Has funded trail development with the International Mountain Bicycling Association and provided support to the League of American Bicyclists' Bicycle Friendly Community Program. Supports Cancer Council South Australia and the World Bicycle Relief's Project Zambia.

Victorinox Swiss Army, Inc.

100% ▬▬▬▬▬▬▬▬▬▬ 0%

Contributions: TOTAL: *$535*   DEM: *$535*   REP: *$0*
LOBBY SPENDING: *$80,000*

Foreign owned. Subsidiary of Victorinox AG. Its manufacturing plant is heated primarily through energy recovered from its own manufacturing operations. One hundred adjacent apartments share this heat source. Other environmental conservation measures include recycling of industrial waste.

Telecommunications and Internet

Michael Calabrese

Unknown to most consumers, a battle is raging over the future of the Internet—one that has perhaps reached a progressive turning point with the election of Barack Obama. The stakes are enormous: as the world goes digital, online, and wireless, will the networks be open or closed? Will users have complete freedom of expression and choice online, or will they be restricted to toll-gated "channels" of content? Will there be affordable and universal service to high-speed broadband, or will the gap between the digital haves and have-nots further exacerbate inequalities in opportunity and outcomes?

On one side are the incumbent phone and cable giants, which, together with the broadcasting industry and a few captive equipment suppliers, are trying to leverage their investments in politicians to suppress competition and consumer choice. On the other side are the emerging Internet giants—such as Google, Amazon, and eBay—which are fighting a rearguard action to keep the Internet as open, affordable, and innovative as possible. A burgeoning movement of consumer advocates and media reform activists has generally allied with the disruptive Internet and start-up companies, which, although clearly self-interested, at least have business models that profit from Internet freedom.

The hottest flash point in this struggle over control of the Internet is the debate over "network neutrality." Network neutrality is the principle of Internet freedom: the principle that users should have the right to access any online content, run any application, or access any Web service without interference from their Internet service provider (ISP). This end-to-end networking freedom is how the old copper-wire phone networks have operated for over a century under traditional common carrier regulation. Telephone companies are required to give everyone nondiscriminatory access to the network on reasonable terms—and they cannot block, degrade, or charge different rates to different customers on the basis of the customers' affiliation or the content of the customers' speech.

The 1996 Telecommunications Act was ostensibly intended to promote competition and consumer choice, but in 2002, the Bush Federal Communications Commission (FCC) managed to repeal the principle of common carriage, claiming in Orwellian fashion that the Internet should not be regulated because it is not a "communications service." Under the ideological banner of deregulation (and the ground cover of millions of dollars in campaign contributions), the Baby Bells and Big Cable were allowed to close their monopoly last-mile networks to interconnection by potential broadband competitors (hence the death of upstart ISPs like Earthlink)—and, in theory, to control the content and services flowing as digital bits through their pipes.

Each of the telecom and cable giants has tried to chip away at Internet freedom. The most brazen bad actors have been the cable giants. In 2007, Comcast was caught red-handed using a "spoofing" technology to block peer-to-peer file transfers by its customers. When consumer groups filed a complaint claiming Comcast was targeting BitTorrent—the most popular video file-sharing application—because it feared competition with its own video-on-demand offerings, the company at first denied, then later conceded, that it was attempting to "shape" the traffic on its network. After the FCC outlawed this practice, Time Warner Cable announced that it would retaliate by moving its Internet service from flat-rate pricing to a metering regime that imposes steep penalties—and even service termination—on customers who use far more than the average amount of network capacity in a given month.

The rapidly consolidating wireless industry has been even more aggressive in asserting a right to block consumer choice among competing devices, applications, and content over its networks. For example, Verizon Wireless refused to give a text messaging code to NARAL, a pro-choice group, so that it could communicate with activists during a political action campaign. Text messaging is an important and rapidly growing platform for free speech and political organizing. Although Verizon reversed its decision after a public outcry, it continues to fight a petition filed by public interest groups asking the FCC to rule that text messaging deserves the same common carrier protections as voice calling. AT&T censored the

Webcast of a Pearl Jam concert because the group sang lyrics critical of President Bush. AT&T quickly backpedaled and claimed that its "content monitors" had made a mistake, but civil libertarians noted that any degree of censorship by an ISP should be deemed an illegal breach of Internet freedom.

Wall Street Journal consumer technology columnist Walt Mossberg frequently refers to the big four wireless carriers (Verizon, AT&T, Sprint, and T-Mobile) as the "Soviet Ministries," because they deny consumers the choice to use any device or application or to access any Web content or service over their networks. The Apple iPhone, available exclusively on AT&T's network, is the exception that proves the rule. Although Apple had the market power to negotiate control over the design and applications allowed to operate on the iPhone, the devices are locked to AT&T's network (unless illegally hacked), and certain applications (such as Voice over Internet calling, or VoIP) are not permitted to transmit over AT&T's network at all because they compete with the carrier's own services or affiliates. Skype, a subsidiary of the Internet auction giant eBay, has been blocked by each of the wireless carriers from offering free or low-cost VoIP services over their allegedly "unlimited" broadband data networks.

By contrast, Clearwire, an upstart wireless ISP using super-fast WiMAX technology, has a business model premised on a promise to simply sell broadband connections and not diminish Internet freedom. Although the new Clearwire is partly owned by Sprint, it relies for capital on investments by Intel and Google, which insisted the company adopt an open-access policy.

Google continues to be the big company most aligned with progressive technology activists in Washington, but there are also those who criticize its targeted advertising model as a threat to personal privacy. They say it's spooky that users of Gmail, for example, find that the ads appearing alongside their e-mail and searches on Google will correspond to key words (such as "cancer" or "Caribbean cruise") used in their personal e-mails. Google claims that it doesn't associate individual online behavior with personal identity (only with the MAC address that uniquely identifies each computing device, and it deletes even that anonymous information after a year or so). Nonetheless, privacy activists argue that companies like Google should use "behavioral advertising" only if users affirmatively "opt in" (rather than forcing consumers to "opt out," as is the current practice).

One new issue that promises to be at the top of Washington's telecom agenda well into 2010 is the debate over a national broadband deployment policy. The Internet may have been invented and taken root first in America, but during the Bush years, the United States dropped from 3rd to 16th internationally in terms of broadband adoption. A smaller share of homes in America have broadband—and at far slower speeds and far higher prices—than in most of the world's advanced economies. The economic stimulus enacted in February 2009 provided $7.2 billion for broadband projects and directed the FCC to come up with a plan for universal service.

Meanwhile, the telecom incumbents are lobbying furiously for tax breaks and more public airwaves licenses for incumbent providers, while consumer and digital inclusion activists are making the case for more public spending on open-access fiber infrastructure and municipally owned and operated networks. On this issue, even high-tech goliaths like Microsoft and Intel are mostly on the side of public investment in digital inclusion and competition. Citizens should tune in to activist campaigns by progressive tech groups like MoveOn and Free Press. After all, the future of the Internet hangs in the balance.

Top Ten Democratic Contributors

AT&T, Inc.	$2,531,482
Time Warner, Inc.	$2,505,667
Comcast Corporation	$2,226,666
Google, Inc.	$1,503,549
Verizon Communications, Inc.	$1,385,085
Qualcomm, Inc.	$619,662
Qwest Communications International, Inc.	$547,231
Level 3 Communications, Inc.	$491,385
Cablevision Systems Corporation	$477,334
Yahoo!, Inc.	$437,661

Top Ten Republican Contributors

AT&T, Inc.	$2,875,123
Verizon Communications, Inc.	$1,500,459
Comcast Corporation	$1,275,936
Time Warner, Inc.	$595,001
Qwest Communications International, Inc.	$586,678
Google, Inc.	$326,323
Deutsche Telekom AG	$325,265
T-Mobile USA, Inc.	$325,265
Corning, Inc.	$271,766
eBay, Inc.	$261,180

Top Ten Lobbying Spenders

Verizon Communications, Inc.	$32,387,000
AT&T, Inc.	$32,214,784
Comcast Corporation	$21,419,323
Time Warner, Inc.	$13,391,192
Qualcomm, Inc.	$13,030,000
Deutsche Telekom AG	$8,592,025
T-Mobile USA, Inc.	$8,502,025
Cox Enterprises, Inc.	$6,990,000
Sprint Nextel Corporation	$6,157,500
Qwest Communications International, Inc.	$6,001,345

ALLTEL Corporation
39% | 61%

Contributions: TOTAL: *$320,110* DEM: *$125,385* REP: *$194,725*
LOBBY SPENDING: *$700,000*

Subsidiary of Verizon Communications. Several lawsuits allege its cell phone customers are charged for mobile content without authorization. A pending class action lawsuit claims it is breaking the law by not allowing customers to opt out of text service and by charging them for unsolicited texts. Offers wireless handset recycling. Supports disaster relief, college scholarships, and the Susan G. Komen Breast Cancer Foundation. Has a written nondiscrimination policy covering sexual orientation but not gender identity. Refuses insurance coverage to employees' domestic partners. Insurance for transgender employees is offered, but treatment is not covered.

America Online (AOL) LLC
71% | 29%

Contributions: TOTAL: *$180,212* DEM: *$128,752* REP: *$51,460*
LOBBY SPENDING: *$0*

Subsidiary of Time Warner, Inc., previously referred to as AOL Time Warner. A pending lawsuit alleges violation of the federal electronic privacy law after AOL of Virginia made available the Internet search records of more than 650,000 of its members. Uses energy-saving devices in its office buildings, some of which are LEED certified. Supports children's health and safety and online public service advertising. Has a written nondiscrimination policy covering sexual orientation and gender identity. Offers insurance coverage to employees' domestic partners. Insurance for transgender employees is offered, but treatment is not covered.

AT&T, Inc.   47%   53%
Contributions: TOTAL: *$5,406,605*   DEM: *$2,531,482*   REP: *$2,875,123*
LOBBY SPENDING: *$32,214,784*

A major player in the telecommunications lobby, through which it campaigns for industry deregulation. In 2006, the Electronic Frontier Foundation filed a class action lawsuit alleging it violated the law and customer privacy by collaborating with the NSA in its illegal program to wiretap and data-mine Americans' communications. Ranked 2nd on DiversityInc's list of the "Top 50 Companies for Diversity" in 2009. Known for accommodating employees with disabilities. In 2008, in conjunction with Cell Phones for Soldiers, recycled more than 2.5 million wireless devices. Donates technology equipment to schools. Funds high school success programs and provides support for military personnel, hunger cessation, and reading programs. Has a written nondiscrimination policy covering sexual orientation and gender identity. Offers health insurance to employees' domestic partners. Insurance for transgender employees is offered, and treatment is covered.

Cablevision Systems Corporation   76%   24%
Contributions: TOTAL: *$627,341*   DEM: *$477,334*   REP: *$150,007*
LOBBY SPENDING: *$860,000*

Provides free broadband Internet access to schools and participates in Cable in the Classroom. Owns Madison Square Garden, whose "Cheering for Children" effort provides after-school programs. Supports the fight against pancreatic cancer. Has a written nondiscrimination policy covering sexual orientation but not gender identity. Offers insurance coverage to employees' domestic partners.

Charter Communications, Inc.   62%   38%
Contributions: TOTAL: *$120,847*   DEM: *$75,147*   REP: *$45,700*
LOBBY SPENDING: *$1,330,000*

Filed for Chapter 11 bankruptcy reorganization in 2009. Has been criticized for poor customer support and frequent billing consistency issues, causing the BBB to post a warning to consumers about the company. In 2007, *PCWorld* ranked Charter's cable Internet service the worst among 14 major ISPs. Participates in Cable in the Classroom. Has a written nondiscrimination policy covering sexual orientation but not gender identity.

Comcast Corporation   64%   36%
Contributions: TOTAL: *$3,502,602*   DEM: *$2,226,666*   REP: *$1,275,936*
LOBBY SPENDING: *$21,419,323*

Has vigorously resisted union campaigns. Settled a lawsuit for allegedly misleading customers with its advertising and marketing practices, agreeing to pay $1 million, improve its customer service, and change its advertising. Participates in Cable in the Classroom; helps libraries raise funds to purchase computers. Supports the National Urban League and the National Council of La Raza. Has a written nondiscrimination policy covering sexual orientation but not gender identity. Offers insurance coverage to employees' domestic partners. Insurance for transgender employees is offered, but treatment is not covered.

Corning, Inc.   51%   49%
Contributions: TOTAL: *$549,432*   DEM: *$277,666*   REP: *$271,766*
LOBBY SPENDING: *$1,370,547*

Has a recycling program for used electronic equipment. Foundation supports education, health care, and environmental preservation. Has a written nondiscrimination policy covering sexual orientation and gender identity. Offers insurance coverage to employees' domestic partners. Insurance for transgender employees is offered, but treatment is not covered.

Cox Communications, Inc.   48%   52%
Contributions: TOTAL: *$170,263*   DEM: *$81,050*   REP: *$89,213*
LOBBY SPENDING: *$20,000*

Subsidiary of Cox Enterprises, Inc. Ranked 17th on DiversityInc's list of the "Top 50 Companies for Diversity" in 2009. One of its headquarters uses solar panels for energy; another sends 75% of its cafeteria waste to a composting facility and donates its fry oil for conversion to biodiesel. Is transitioning its vehicle fleet to flex-fuel and hybrid cars. Participates in Cable in the Classroom. Supports Boys & Girls Clubs of America. Has a written nondiscrimination policy covering sexual orientation and gender identity. Offers insurance coverage to employees' domestic partners. Insurance for transgender employees is offered, and some treatment is covered.

Cox Enterprises, Inc.   61%   39%
Contributions: TOTAL: *$311,983*   DEM: *$191,735*   REP: *$120,248*
LOBBY SPENDING: *$6,990,000*

Privately held. Environmental goals include reducing its annual carbon footprint 20% by 2017. Created an eco-friendly headquarters. Uses soy-based colored ink and recycled paper for newspapers. Supports its communities and the environment through sponsorships, donations, and employee volunteerism. Has a written nondiscrimination policy covering sexual orientation and gender identity. Offers insurance coverage to employees' domestic partners. Insurance for transgender employees is offered, and some treatment is covered.

Deutsche Telekom AG   55%   45%
Contributions: TOTAL: *$726,281*   DEM: *$401,016*   REP: *$325,265*
LOBBY SPENDING: *$8,592,025*

Foreign owned. Facing a lawsuit brought by more than 800 law firms representing more than 16,000 Telekom shareholders who say the company inflated the value of its real estate holdings and misled them. Supports the Kyoto Protocol. Its recycling rate in Germany is nearly 100%. Uses fuel cells to supply part of the energy needed for its buildings. Offers a free recycling program for cell phones and components. Provides free Internet access to German schoolchildren, a help line for young people in need, and a parent help line. Also supports corporate volunteerism, environmental protection, and philanthropy to help socially and physically challenged people.

EarthLink, Inc.

66% | 34%

Contributions: TOTAL: *$94,131*   DEM: *$62,032*   REP: *$32,099*
LOBBY SPENDING: *$2,760,000*

Investment firms Coghill Capital, Steel Partners, and Sterling Capital each own about 10% of the company. Has a written nondiscrimination policy covering sexual orientation and gender identity. Offers insurance coverage to employees' domestic partners. Insurance for transgender employees is offered, but treatment is not covered.

eBay, Inc.

56% | 44%

Contributions: TOTAL: *$595,763*   DEM: *$334,583*   REP: *$261,180*
LOBBY SPENDING: *$4,130,000*

Ranked 83rd on *Fortune* magazine's "100 Best Companies to Work For" in 2009. Offers an online marketplace for ethically sourced and eco-friendly products. In 2008, scored 5 out of 100 in "The Climate Counts Company Scorecard Report." In 2009, launched the "eBay Green Team," which champions smart ways to shop green and encourages comparatively sustainable buying choices. In 2008, opened a building constructed to the LEED gold standard. Foundation supports childhood literacy, animal welfare, and Oxfam America. Also supports employee-matching donations of money or time to organizations. Has a written nondiscrimination policy covering sexual orientation and gender identity. Offers insurance coverage to employees' domestic partners. Insurance for transgender employees is offered, but treatment is not covered.

Embarq Corporation

47% | 53%

Contributions: TOTAL: *$468,732*   DEM: *$218,507*   REP: *$250,225*
LOBBY SPENDING: *$1,180,000*

Named in a pending class action lawsuit in which online subscribers accuse their ISPs and a California technology company of unlawfully tracking their Internet-use habits. Supports arts and culture, education, and human services. Awards grants to nonprofit organizations at which its employees volunteer. Has a written nondiscrimination policy covering sexual orientation and gender identity.

Facebook, Inc.

99% | 1%

Contributions: TOTAL: *$65,050*   DEM: *$64,300*   REP: *$750*
LOBBY SPENDING: *$0*

Microsoft is its exclusive partner for serving banner advertising, and as such Facebook serves only advertisements that exist in Microsoft's advertisement inventory. Supports entrepreneurs building businesses on Facebook Platform with seed-funding grants.

Google, Inc.

82% | 18%

Contributions: TOTAL: *$1,829,872*   DEM: *$1,503,549*   REP: *$326,323*
LOBBY SPENDING: *$4,360,000*

A pending lawsuit alleges it violated the unfair competition law when it was contracted to place targeted advertisements through its Adword program but instead placed them on low-quality sites. Ranked 4th on *Fortune* magazine's "100 Best Companies to Work For" in 2009. In 2008, scored 55 out of 100 in "The Climate Counts Company Scorecard

Report." Is retrofitting offices with "green" technology and adopting plug-in vehicles. A solar power system generates energy for one of its locations. Offers employees a car-sharing program. Has a written non-discrimination policy covering sexual orientation and gender identity. Offers insurance coverage to employees' domestic partners. Insurance for transgender employees is offered, and treatment is covered.

IAC/InterActiveCorp
83% | 17%

Contributions: TOTAL: *$168,869* DEM: *$140,469* REP: *$28,400*
LOBBY SPENDING: *$2,351,496*

A click fraud suit against subsidiary Citysearch.com is pending. Supports autism awareness. Has a written nondiscrimination policy covering sexual orientation but not gender identity. Offers insurance coverage to employees' domestic partners.

IDT Corporation
33% | 67%

Contributions: TOTAL: *$258,068* DEM: *$84,225* REP: *$173,843*
LOBBY SPENDING: *$1,700,000*

A pending 2004 class action suit filed by call center workers alleges discriminatory treatment of non-Jewish employees. IDT founder is known for his work with modern orthodox Jewish causes. Company supports a program that works with student athletes in underserved communities and several educational institutions. Its employees support a van that delivers food in Newark, NJ. Has a written nondiscrimination policy covering sexual orientation but not gender identity.

Knowledge Learning Corporation
62% | 38%

Contributions: TOTAL: *$14,100* DEM: *$8,800* REP: *$5,300*
LOBBY SPENDING: *$190,000*

Subsidiary of Knowledge Universe, Inc. Foundation donates to the Juvenile Diabetes Research Foundation, Ronald McDonald House, and Project CURE.

Knowledge Universe, Inc.
12% | 88%

Contributions: TOTAL: *$57,100* DEM: *$6,900* REP: *$50,200*
LOBBY SPENDING: *$20,000*

After serving time for securities fraud in the early 1990s, chairman Michael Milken founded the Prostate Cancer Foundation and the non profit, nonpartisan Milken Institute, which researches economic issues and policy making. Every year, he awards $25,000 each to more than 100 teachers.

Level 3 Communications, Inc.
89% | 11%

Contributions: TOTAL: *$553,610* DEM: *$491,385* REP: *$62,225*
LOBBY SPENDING: *$1,020,816*

A pending lawsuit alleges that its SEC filings and other communications were materially false and misleading in their failure to disclose problems with absorption of acquisitions. Has a written nondiscrimination policy covering sexual orientation but not gender identity. Offers insurance coverage to employees' domestic partners.

MCI, Inc.
26% | 74%

Contributions: TOTAL: *$8,175*   DEM: *$2,125*   REP: *$6,050*
LOBBY SPENDING: *$0*

Subsidiary of Verizon Communications, Inc. Changed name from World-Com back to MCI, Inc., following an Enron-style accounting scandal that plagued the companies after their merger. Supports programs to improve educational opportunities for disadvantaged youth and small and minority-owned businesses. Has a written nondiscrimination policy covering sexual orientation but not gender identity. Offers insurance coverage to employees' domestic partners. Insurance for transgender employees is offered, and some treatment is covered.

MySpace.com
96% | 4%

Contributions: TOTAL: *$8,473*   DEM: *$8,122*   REP: *$351*
LOBBY SPENDING: *$0*

Subsidiary of Fox Interactive Media; parent, News Corporation, Ltd. Four families whose underage daughters were sexually abused after meeting people they encountered on MySpace sued News Corp., alleging it was negligent in failing to create safety measures. In response, the company added new security features.

Qualcomm, Inc.
75% | 25%

Contributions: TOTAL: *$827,232*   DEM: *$619,662*   REP: *$207,570*
LOBBY SPENDING: *$13,030,000*

Ranked 16th on *Fortune* magazine's "100 Best Companies to Work For" in 2009. Its buildings are designed to promote environmental stewardship. In 2008, named "Recycler of the Year" by the City of San Diego, CA. Supports science, technology, engineering, and math education. Promotes healthy communities and the arts. Has a written nondiscrimination policy covering sexual orientation and gender identity. Offers insurance coverage to employees' domestic partners. Insurance for transgender employees is offered, but treatment is not covered.

Qwest Communications International, Inc.
48% | 52%

Contributions: TOTAL: *$1,133,909*   DEM: *$547,231*   REP: *$586,678*
LOBBY SPENDING: *$6,001,345*

Its former cochair and CEO is serving a six-year prison term for insider trading. Paid over $17 million in fines to the FCC for violation of federal law. Employs members of the CWA union. Offers a cell phone recycling program that also raises money for public school districts and educational initiatives. Its foundation has partnered with Boys and Girls Clubs, Big Sisters, and Goodwill Industries. Provides matching funds to nonprofit organizations to which its employees donate. Has a written nondiscrimination policy covering sexual orientation but not gender identity. Offers insurance coverage to employees' domestic partners.

Skype Technologies SA
100% | 0%

Contributions: TOTAL: *$10,200*   DEM: *$10,200*   REP: *$0*
LOBBY SPENDING: *$0*
Subsidiary of eBay, Inc.

Sprint Nextel Corporation

61% | 39%

Contributions: TOTAL: *$518,340* DEM: *$318,702* REP: *$199,638*
LOBBY SPENDING: *$6,157,500*

Faces several class action lawsuits over its early termination fees. Is an EPA Climate Leaders Partner. Is increasing its use of renewable energy. Restored wetlands and natural landscape at its headquarters. One of its campus buildings has LEED certification. Has a cell phone recycling program. Corporate giving is focused on K-12 public education and diversity. Local and regional investments also support arts and culture and youth development. Has a written nondiscrimination policy covering sexual orientation and gender identity. Offers insurance coverage to employees' domestic partners. Insurance for transgender employees is offered, but treatment is not covered.

Symantec Corporation

85% | 15%

Contributions: TOTAL: *$437,844* DEM: *$373,349* REP: *$64,495*
LOBBY SPENDING: *$1,279,615*

Has adopted the "Calvert Women's Principles," the first global code of corporate conduct focused exclusively on advancing women in the workplace. Aims to reduce its carbon emissions by 15% by 2012. Achieved LEED gold certification for one of its campuses. Supports science, technology, engineering, and math education; environmental protection; and online safety. Has a written nondiscrimination policy covering sexual orientation and gender identity. Offers insurance coverage to employees' domestic partners. Insurance for transgender employees is offered, but treatment is not covered.

TDS Telecommunications

57% | 43%

Contributions: TOTAL: *$58,300* DEM: *$33,000* REP: *$25,300*
LOBBY SPENDING: *$280,000*

Subsidiary of Telephone and Data Systems, Inc. Supports local youth, school, library, and hunger cessation programs. Has a written nondiscrimination policy covering sexual orientation but not gender identity.

Telephone and Data Systems, Inc.

62% | 38%

Contributions: TOTAL: *$138,129* DEM: *$85,754* REP: *$52,375*
LOBBY SPENDING: *$2,167,880*

Supports various local charities. Has a written nondiscrimination policy covering sexual orientation but not gender identity.

Time Warner Cable, Inc.

55% | 45%

Contributions: TOTAL: *$573,988* DEM: *$315,605* REP: *$258,383*
LOBBY SPENDING: *$490,000*

Subsidiary of Time Warner, Inc. In 2008, settled a class action lawsuit alleging that it sold its subscribers' personal information to other companies for marketing purposes. A pending lawsuit alleges unlawful business acts and practices and deceptive advertising. Ranked 38th on DiversityInc's list of the "Top 50 Companies for Diversity" in 2009. Its environmental efforts include paperless operations, reduced power use, and recycling. Uses the LEED sustainability rating system as a standard protocol for all facility construction. Outreach includes public service announcements and free cable and high-speed broadband connections to schools. Has a written nondiscrimination policy covering sexual orientation and gender identity. Offers insurance coverage to employees' domestic partners. Insurance for transgender employees is offered, but treatment is not covered.

Time Warner, Inc.

81%   19%

Contributions: TOTAL: *$3,100,668*   DEM: *$2,505,667*   REP: *$595,001*
LOBBY SPENDING: *$13,391,192*

Concerns have been raised about its role in media consolidation and its impact on public access to information from diverse sources. In 2008, scored 19 out of 100 in "The Climate Counts Company Scorecard Report." Is increasing the amount of certified fiber in its magazines to 80%. Supports education and the arts, as well as several employee volunteer programs. Has a written nondiscrimination policy covering sexual orientation and gender identity. Offers insurance coverage to employees' domestic partners. Insurance for transgender employees is offered, but treatment is not covered.

T-Mobile USA, Inc.

55%   45%

Contributions: TOTAL: *$726,281*   DEM: *$401,016*   REP: *$325,265*
LOBBY SPENDING: *$8,502,025*

Subsidiary of Deutsche Telekom AG. A pending class action lawsuit claims that it is breaking the law by not allowing customers to opt out of text service and for charging them for unsolicited texts. Another lawsuit alleges that it charges cell phone customers for mobile content without authorization. Cited by the CWA as "antiworker." Ranked 96th on *Fortune* magazine's "100 Best Companies to Work For" in 2009. Offers a handset recycling program, the net proceeds of which benefit a program supporting at-risk kids. Offers subscribers free access to wireless text-messaged Amber alerts. Has a written nondiscrimination policy covering sexual orientation but not gender identity. Offers insurance coverage to employees' domestic partners.

United Online, Inc.

90%   10%

Contributions: TOTAL: *$35,408*   DEM: *$31,858*   REP: *$3,550*
LOBBY SPENDING: *$30,000*

Supports Ronald McDonald House Charities, in part by donating computers and Internet access.

United States Cellular Corporation (U.S. Cellular)

53%   47%

Contributions: TOTAL: *$55,650*   DEM: *$29,575*   REP: *$26,075*
LOBBY SPENDING: *$1,595,000*

Subsidiary of Telephone and Data Systems, Inc. A pending class action lawsuit claims it is breaking the law by not allowing customers to opt out of text service and by charging for unsolicited texts. Another lawsuit alleges it charges cell phone customers for mobile content without authorization. Has supported programs serving disadvantaged youth, families, and seniors. Offers subscribers free access to wireless text-messaged Amber alerts.

Verizon Communications, Inc.
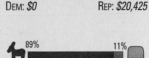
Contributions: TOTAL: *$2,885,544*   DEM: *$1,385,085*   REP: *$1,500,459*
LOBBY SPENDING: *$32,387,000*

Has provided customers' telephone records to federal authorities in emergency cases without court orders hundreds of times since 2005. In 2006, paid almost $49 million to settle a landmark class action lawsuit alleging pregnancy discrimination. Listed by NAFE in the top 50 companies for female executives in 2009. Ranked 12th on DiversityInc's list of the "Top 50 Companies for Diversity" in 2009. Is reducing its carbon emissions. Contributes money to American Forests, which plants a tree on behalf of shareholders who receive communications electronically. Supports education, health, domestic violence prevention, and the National Council of La Raza. Has a written nondiscrimination policy covering sexual orientation but not gender identity. Offers health insurance coverage to employees' domestic partners. Insurance for transgender employees is offered, and some treatment is covered.

Vonage Holdings Corp.
Contributions: TOTAL: *$37,562*   DEM: *$23,212*   REP: *$14,350*
LOBBY SPENDING: *$1,874,190*

Supports medical research, hunger cessation, disaster relief, and education.

Western Wireless Corporation
Contributions: TOTAL: *$20,425*   DEM: *$0*   REP: *$20,425*
LOBBY SPENDING: *$0*

Subsidiary of ALLTEL Corporation.

Yahoo!, Inc.
Contributions: TOTAL: *$492,222*   DEM: *$437,661*   REP: *$54,561*
LOBBY SPENDING: *$3,975,700*

In 2007, settled a lawsuit brought by families of two Chinese cyber-dissidents who were jailed for their writings after Yahoo! revealed their identities to the Chinese government. In 2006, Reporters Without Borders performed censorship tests on Chinese versions of Internet search engines and found Yahoo! to be the worst offender. Closed chat rooms to help fight child exploitation. Has been named one of the "Best Employers for Minorities" by *Black Collegian* magazine and as one of the best places for GLBT equality, according to the Human Rights Campaign Foundation. In 2008, scored 37 out of 100 in "The Climate Counts Company Scorecard Report." Supports alternative commuting and purchases carbon-offset credits. Hosts a Web site dedicated to "green" living. Has a written nondiscrimination policy covering sexual orientation and gender Identity. Offers insurance coverage to employees' domestic partners. Insurance for transgender employees is offered, but treatment is not covered.

YouTube LLC
Contributions: TOTAL: *$12,950*   DEM: *$12,950*   REP: *$0*
LOBBY SPENDING: *$0*

Subsidiary of Google, Inc. Has a written nondiscrimination policy covering sexual orientation and gender identity. Offers insurance coverage to employees' domestic partners. Insurance for transgender employees is offered, and treatment is covered.

Travel and Leisure

Malia Everette

The global travel and leisure industry is huge, multi-faceted, and dynamic. In 2007, international tourism generated $856 billion, or 30% of the world's service exports. The following year, global arrivals grew 2% to reach 924 million. According to the World Tourism Organization, that figure will climb to 1.6 billion by 2020.

Like other growth sectors, the travel and leisure industry can change society for good or ill. In particular, it can aid sustainable development or enable the exploitation of cultures and ecosystems. On the positive side of the ledger is what international travel can do to inspire a heightened sense of citizen diplomacy. This sense is especially critical after eight years of the Bush administration. What better way for Americans to heal torn relationships than to travel to and learn about other nations, including those estranged by U.S. foreign policy?

Although President Obama's election in 2008 created fresh possibilities for such citizen diplomacy, the concept is not new. President John F. Kennedy expressed it succinctly almost 50 years ago:

> Travel has become one of the great forces for peace and understanding in our time. As people move throughout the world and learn to know each other's customs and to appreciate the qualities of individuals of each nation, we are building a level of international understanding, which can sharply improve the atmosphere for world peace.

This approach to travel will likely gather momentum, especially in the current economy, wherein a growing number of Americans want not only value but also meaning for their vacation dollar.

Although global travel is expected to increase, all is not well with the industry. The global recession has sent major luxury and adventure travel operators into bankruptcy, and others are hoping to ride out a year or two of losses. At the same time, there are bright spots in the areas of sustainable tourism, ecotourism, service learning or "voluntourism," and philanthropy tourism. Travel service providers, domestic and international tour operators, hoteliers, and airlines can expect challenges inspired not only by increasing costs of energy but also by rising environmental and social concerns among travelers.

Here in the United States, the travel and leisure industry employs 7.7 million workers and creates more that $740 billion in spending annually, but conventional inbound operators and service providers have been severely affected by the decrease in tourism. In March 2009, industry leaders met with President Obama to discuss the role travel can play in strengthening the American economy. They focused on two areas: the need to welcome more international visitors and the nationwide downturn in meetings and events.

The list of this industry's top political contributors, dominated by casinos and gaming tribal nations, is telling. Last year, gaming revenue nationwide was down 4.7%, and jobs fell slightly; this despite the fact that one-quarter of the adult U.S. population visited a casino in 2008, and racetrack casinos increased their revenues 17.2% to nearly $6.2 billion. There are now 44 "racinos" in 12 states, with more on the way. In that sense, the gaming sector is betting on further support and expansion.

In the meantime, airlines and hotel resort chains have experienced significant declines. Surveys show that 75% of Americans are planning a vacation this year, but 42% of them are staying closer to home. As businesses and organizations scale back on conferences, events, and travel costs, the industry has increased its efforts to garner government support.

Amid this change, a superb opportunity has emerged for conscious consumers. With their tourist dollars, they can make greener and more socially responsible choices, thereby catalyzing the leisure industry and supporting sustainable travel options. So go ahead, make a booking. As Fitzhugh Mullan once advised, "Stop worrying about the potholes in the road and celebrate the journey."

Top Ten Democratic Contributors

MGM Mirage, Inc.	$634,559
Harrah's Entertainment, Inc.	$456,470
San Manuel Band of (Serrano) Mission Indians	$435,472
Pechanga Band of (Luiseño) Mission Indians	$383,305
AMR Corporation (American Airlines)	$370,691
Morongo Band of Mission Indians	$352,073
Mississippi Band of Choctaw Indians	$331,850
National Thoroughbred Racing Association, Inc. (NRTA)	$325,500
National Basketball Association (NBA)	$320,730
Chickasaw Nation	$313,901

Top Ten Republican Contributors

Marriott International, Inc.	$759,316
Enterprise Rent-A-Car Company	$752,766
MGM Mirage, Inc.	$657,172
Las Vegas Sands Corp.	$429,774
Station Casinos, Inc.	$409,950
AMR Corporation (American Airlines)	$388,764
Wynn Resorts, Limited	$381,225
Chickasaw Nation	$259,446
National Thoroughbred Racing Association, Inc. (NRTA)	$258,000
Morongo Band of Mission Indians	$248,239

Top Ten Lobbying Spenders

AMR Corporation (American Airlines)	$11,460,000
Delta Air Lines, Inc.	$7,950,000
Northwest Airlines Corporation	$6,103,213
UAL Corporation (United Airlines)	$4,697,327
Continental Airlines, Inc.	$4,208,968
US Airways Group, Inc.	$2,948,858
Marriott International, Inc.	$2,270,000
Royal Caribbean Cruises Ltd.	$2,210,000
National Football League (NFL)	$2,158,000
Southwest Airlines Co.	$1,970,000

Accor North America

Contributions: TOTAL: *$2,750*   DEM: *$0*   REP: *$2,750*
LOBBY SPENDING: *$0*

Foreign owned by Accor S.A. Hosts an annual women's leadership summit. The purchase of wind energy for all nine U.S. Sofitel locations qualified it as an EPA Green Power Partner. Plants trees, uses water-saving devices and "green" cleaning products, and prints its directories with soy ink on recycled paper. Supports the Bureau of Services for the Visually Impaired, the Susan G. Komen Race for the Cure, Goodwill,

AIDS Walk, the Holocaust Memorial, and hunger cessation programs. Has no written nondiscrimination policy covering sexual orientation or gender identity.

AirTran Holdings, Inc.
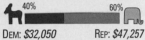

Contributions: TOTAL: *$79,307*   DEM: *$32,050*   REP: *$47,257*
LOBBY SPENDING: *$550,000*

In 2008, scored 4 out of 100 in "The Climate Counts Company Scorecard Report." Supports Susan G. Komen Race for the Cure, Habitat for Humanity, the March of Dimes, domestic violence prevention, and families of soldiers in Iraq. Has a written nondiscrimination policy covering sexual orientation but not gender identity. Refuses insurance coverage to employees' same-sex domestic partners.

Alaska Air Group, Inc.

Contributions: TOTAL: *$105,335*   DEM: *$65,815*   REP: *$39,520*
LOBBY SPENDING: *$960,000*

In 2007, introduced bilingual airport kiosks. In 2008, scored 15 out of 100 in "The Climate Counts Company Scorecard Report." Has eliminated paper ticket jackets, saving roughly 850 pulp trees per year. Has recycling programs. Is a corporate partner of The Nature Conservancy. Supports health and human services, arts and cultural programs, and civic organizations. Has a written nondiscrimination policy covering sexual orientation and gender identity. Offers insurance coverage to employees' domestic partners. Insurance for transgender employees is offered, but treatment is not covered.

AMR Corporation (American Airlines)

Contributions: TOTAL: *$759,455*   DEM: *$370,691*   REP: *$388,764*
LOBBY SPENDING: *$11,460,000*

Opposes enhanced crew-rest and other safety requirements recently enacted by the FAA. The DOJ settled a class action lawsuit that claimed the carrier illegally denied benefits to pilots while they were serving in National Guard and reserve units. In 2008, was fined $7.1 million for allegedly violating employee drug- and alcohol-testing procedures and for knowingly flying airplanes that broke maintenance regulations. In 2008, scored 35 out of 100 in "The Climate Counts Company Scorecard Report." Aims to reduce carbon emissions by 30% by 2025. Annually recycles about 10 million cans and donates the proceeds to the Wings Foundation, which assists flight attendants who have critical needs. Supports hundreds of nonprofit organizations in the countries it serves. Has a written nondiscrimination policy covering sexual orientation and gender identity. Offers insurance coverage to employees' domestic partners. Insurance for transgender employees is offered, but treatment is not covered.

Avis Budget Group, Inc.

Contributions: TOTAL: *$72,550*   DEM: *$40,550*   REP: *$32,000*
LOBBY SPENDING: *$260,000*

Formerly Cendant Corporation. Cendant's former chairman is imprisoned for his part in an accounting fraud scandal. A class action lawsuit filed by a consumer advocacy group in 2007 alleged that a spike in rental fees in California in 2006 was the result of illegal price-fixing. Car washes at Avis and Budget facilities reuse at least 80% of their waste-water. Participates in the EPA's SmartWay program. The Avis Budget fleet includes gas/electric hybrid vehicles. Allied with Carbonfund.org; renters can make their rental 100% carbon neutral. Has a written non-discrimination policy covering sexual orientation but not gender identity. Offers insurance coverage to employees' domestic partners. Insurance for transgender employees is offered, and some treatment is covered.

Avis Rent A Car System LLC

0% — 100%

Contributions: TOTAL: *$4,900*   DEM: *$0*   REP: *$4,900*
LOBBY SPENDING: *$0*

Subsidiary of Avis Budget Group, Inc. Supports the Make-A-Wish Foundation and the American Red Cross. Supports national organiza-tions involved in health care research and minority education/eco-nomic development. Has a written nondiscrimination policy covering sexual orientation but not gender identity. Offers insurance coverage to employees' domestic partners. Insurance for transgender employees is offered, and some treatment is covered.

Best Western International, Inc.

12% — 88%

Contributions: TOTAL: *$6,100*   DEM: *$750*   REP: *$5,350*
LOBBY SPENDING: *$0*

Is organized as a not-for-profit membership association. A dissident group of owners has been fighting for more transparency in Best West-ern's unorthodox corporate governance. Partnered with World Vision to develop a child sponsorship program for children living in poverty. Does not have standardized benefits throughout membership.

Carey International, Inc.

0% — 100%

Contributions: TOTAL: *$250*   DEM: *$0*   REP: *$250*
LOBBY SPENDING: *$0*

Subsidiary of Avis Budget Group, Inc. Operates as Carey Limousine.

Carlson Companies, Inc.

32% — 68%

Contributions: TOTAL: *$77,895*   DEM: *$24,575*   REP: *$53,320*
LOBBY SPENDING: *$0*

Privately held. Often named one of the 100 Best Companies for Working Mothers by *Working Mother* magazine. For three consecutive years, 2006–2008, was named one of the "Best Places to Work for GLBT Equality." In 2008, scored 11 out of 100 in "The Climate Counts Com-pany Scorecard Report." Its foundation supports education and the United Way. Cofounded the World Childhood Foundation, which serves vulnerable children in 14 countries. Has a written nondiscrimination policy covering sexual orientation and gender identity. Offers insurance coverage to employees' domestic partners. Insurance for transgender employees is offered, but treatment is not covered.

Carlson Hotels Worldwide

100% — 0%

Contributions: TOTAL: *$750*   DEM: *$750*   REP: *$0*
LOBBY SPENDING: *$0*

Subsidiary of Carlson Companies, Inc. Supports the Code of Conduct to Protect Children against Sexual Exploitation in Travel and Tourism. Its environmental programs focus on improving indoor air quality; reduc-

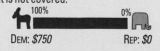

ing, reusing, and recycling solid waste; and conserving energy and water. Partners with The CarbonNeutral Company to invest in environmental protection. Offers insurance coverage to employees' domestic partners. Insurance for transgender employees is offered, but treatment is not covered.

Carnival Corporation

64%   36%
Contributions: TOTAL: *$328,405*   DEM: *$209,650*   REP: *$118,755*
LOBBY SPENDING: *$400,000*

A class action suit filed in 2008 accuses it and other cruise lines of violating federal antitrust laws by assessing fuel surcharges after ticket purchases. Subsidiary Holland America has been accused of accepting kickbacks from shore-excursion providers. Its Princess Cruise and Holland America ships can plug into hydroelectric power while in port, reducing air pollution from idling. Holland America has begun using ships with hybrid-powered systems.

Celebrity Cruises, Inc.
100%   0%
Contributions: TOTAL: *$250*   DEM: *$250*   REP: *$0*
LOBBY SPENDING: *$0*

Subsidiary of Royal Caribbean Cruises Ltd. Treats all sewage and discharges it far from shore. Has introduced shipboard gas turbine engines, which greatly reduce smokestack emissions. Supports marine conservation and education. Has a written nondiscrimination policy covering sexual orientation but not gender identity. Offers insurance coverage to employees' domestic partners. Insurance for transgender employees is offered, but treatment is not covered.

Chickasaw Nation
55%   45%
Contributions: TOTAL: *$573,347*   DEM: *$313,901*   REP: *$259,446*
LOBBY SPENDING: *$935,000*

Operates 13 casinos, 7 travel plazas and trading posts, 6 tobacco stores, 2 radio stations, a theater, and a bank. Subsidiary Chickasaw Nation Industries is a holding company with over a dozen limited liability companies that operate as subsidiaries. These companies are engaged in diverse lines of business, including information technology, medical support, construction, and aviation and aerospace technologies.

Choice Hotels International, Inc.
90%   10%
Contributions: TOTAL: *$257,722*   DEM: *$230,822*   REP: *$26,900*
LOBBY SPENDING: *$0*

Committed to employee development, diversity initiatives, and minority ownership incentives. Foundation supports food aid, tourism, and education. Supports employee volunteerism and has a charitable matching program. Offers scholarships to children of employees. Has a written nondiscrimination policy covering sexual orientation but not gender identity.

Clarion
100%   0%
Contributions: TOTAL: *$250*   DEM: *$250*   REP: *$0*
LOBBY SPENDING: *$0*

Subsidiary of Choice Hotels International, Inc. Settled a federal disability discrimination suit brought on behalf of five mentally challenged housekeepers.

Classic Residence by Hyatt
100% 0%

Contributions: Total: *$4,220*   Dem: *$4,220*   Rep: *$0*
Lobby Spending: *$0*
Subsidiary of Global Hyatt Corporation. In 2009, made a significant donation of furniture and other items to Scottsdale, AZ, charities. Offers tuition reimbursement to employees.

Comfort Inn
88% 12%

Contributions: Total: *$8,251*   Dem: *$7,301*   Rep: *$950*
Lobby Spending: *$0*
Subsidiary of Choice Hotels International, Inc. A pending federal lawsuit was filed in 2009 by a Filipino woman who says she and other workers from the Philippines were tormented by South Dakota hotel operators.

Comfort Suites
67% 33%

Contributions: Total: *$750*   Dem: *$500*   Rep: *$250*
Lobby Spending: *$0*
Subsidiary of Choice Hotels International, Inc.

Continental Airlines, Inc.
50% 50%

Contributions: Total: *$476,900*   Dem: *$236,701*   Rep: *$240,199*
Lobby Spending: *$4,208,968*
In 2008, scored 20 out of 100 in "The Climate Counts Company Scorecard Report." Conducted the first biofuel-powered demonstration flight of a U.S. commercial airliner. Has increased its fuel efficiency per passenger mile by 35% since 1997. Offers customers an opportunity to purchase carbon offsets for their trip. Is committed to constructing its facilities according to Energy Star and LEED standards when feasible. Supports community organizations in the arts, culture, sports, education, and health. Has a written nondiscrimination policy covering sexual orientation and gender identity. Offers insurance coverage to employees' domestic partners. Insurance for transgender employees is offered, but treatment is not covered.

Country Inns & Suites by Carlson
0% 100%

Contributions: Total: *$200*   Dem: *$0*   Rep: *$200*
Lobby Spending: *$0*
Subsidiary of Carlson Hotels Worldwide. Sponsors the Emmy Award-winning Reading Rainbow program featured on PBS television.

Courtyard
50% 50%

Contributions: Total: *$500*   Dem: *$250*   Rep: *$250*
Lobby Spending: *$0*
Subsidiary of Marriott International, Inc.

Crowne Plaza Hotels & Resorts
83% 17%

Contributions: Total: *$1,500*   Dem: *$1,250*   Rep: *$250*
Lobby Spending: *$0*
Subsidiary of InterContinental Hotels Group PLC. A pending lawsuit alleges racial discrimination at one of its locations. Has no written nondiscrimination policy covering sexual orientation or gender identity.

Days Inn Worldwide, Inc.
56% 44%

Contributions: Total: *$3,556*   Dem: *$2,005*   Rep: *$1,551*

Lobby Spending: *$0*

Subsidiary of AmeriHost Franchise Systems, Inc.; parent, Wyndham Worldwide Corporation. Settled a price-gouging lawsuit in which the State of Florida alleged that consumers were overcharged for basic necessities during a hurricane state of emergency.

Delta Air Lines, Inc.

44% — 56%

Contributions: Total: *$341,454*   Dem: *$151,101*   Rep: *$190,353*
Lobby Spending: *$7,950,000*

Its pilots and flight dispatchers are represented by unions; the rest of its workforce, unlike other legacy air carriers, is nonunion. Targeted in a $1 billion class action suit for its practice of penalizing travelers who deplane without completing a multistop ticket. In 2008, scored 5 out of 100 in "The Climate Counts Company Scorecard Report." Supports the Breast Cancer Research Foundation, The Conservation Fund, and Habitat for Humanity. Provided a $1 million scholarship endowment at Morehouse College. Has a written nondiscrimination policy covering sexual orientation but not gender identity. Offers insurance coverage to employees' domestic partners. Insurance for transgender employees is offered, and some treatment is covered.

Dollar Thrifty Automotive Group, Inc.

48% — 52%

Contributions: Total: *$43,850*   Dem: *$21,100*   Rep: *$22,750*
Lobby Spending: *$30,000*

A pending class action lawsuit alleges that a spike in rental fees in California in 2006 was the result of illegal price-fixing by it and other rental-car companies. Supports health and human services organizations. Has a written nondiscrimination policy covering sexual orientation and gender identity. Offers insurance coverage to employees' domestic partners. Insurance for transgender employees is offered, but treatment is not covered.

Econo Lodge

0% — 100%

Contributions: Total: *$1,500*   Dem: *$0*   Rep: *$1,500*
Lobby Spending: *$0*

Subsidiary of Choice Hotels International, Inc.

Embassy Suites Hotels

100% — 0%

Contributions: Total: *$250*   Dem: *$250*   Rep: *$0*
Lobby Spending: *$0*

Subsidiary of Hilton Hotels Corporation. Supports the Lance Armstrong Foundation.

Enterprise Rent-A-Car Company

24% — 76%

Contributions: Total: *$985,516*   Dem: *$232,750*   Rep: *$752,766*
Lobby Spending: *$760,000*

A pending class action lawsuit alleges that a spike in rental fees in California in 2006 was the result of illegal price-fixing by it and other rental-car companies. Settled a major class action suit alleging ADA violations. Offers customers carbon-offset purchases. Its charitable foundation will match customer contributions dollar-for-dollar up to a total of $1 million. Is adding 5,000 hybrids to its fleet. Offers flex-fuel

vehicles for rental. Enterprise's foundation is underwriting the planting of 50 million trees. Supports the Everglades Foundation and the Missouri Botanical Garden. Has a written nondiscrimination policy covering sexual orientation but not gender identity. Offers insurance coverage to employees' domestic partners. Insurance for transgender employees is offered, but treatment is not covered.

Expedia, Inc.

99%   1%

Contributions: TOTAL: *$27,999*   DEM: *$27,799*   REP: *$200*
LOBBY SPENDING: *$779,500*

Several cities have sued Web-based travel clearinghouses such as Expedia for alleged failure to pay millions of dollars in hotel taxes. Co-founded the World Heritage Alliance, a joint initiative with the United Nations Foundation to promote sustainable tourism. Has a written nondiscrimination policy covering sexual orientation but not gender identity. Offers insurance coverage to employees' domestic partners. Insurance for transgender employees is offered, but treatment is not covered.

Fairfield Resorts, Inc.

0%   100%

Contributions: TOTAL: *$7,150*   DEM: *$0*   REP: *$7,150*
LOBBY SPENDING: *$0*

Subsidiary of Wyndham Worldwide Corporation. Employees alleging gender harassment and bias filed a $50 million federal lawsuit in 2008 and are seeking class action status against the properties. More than 40 workers from Mongolia, Slovakia, Russia, and Ukraine are suing Fairfield and five companies that staff the resorts, saying they are owed three years in overtime pay.

Fairmont Hotels & Resorts, Inc.

100%   0%

Contributions: TOTAL: *$1,000*   DEM: *$1,000*   REP: *$0*
LOBBY SPENDING: *$0*

Foreign owned. Sustainability efforts include recycling and organic waste diversion in the hotel's kitchens, distributing household goods and food to those in need, and purchasing green power. Offers community and conservation opportunities for guests. Supports cultural and historical preservation.

Four Points by Sheraton

100%   0%

Contributions: TOTAL: *$250*   DEM: *$250*   REP: *$0*
LOBBY SPENDING: *$0*

Subsidiary of Starwood Hotels & Resorts Worldwide, Inc.

Four Seasons Hotels, Inc.

86%   14%

Contributions: TOTAL: *$5,250*   DEM: *$4,500*   REP: *$750*
LOBBY SPENDING: *$0*

Subsidiary of Cascade Investment LLC. Ranked 92nd on *Fortune* magazine's "100 Best Companies to Work For" in 2009. Engages in practices that conserve natural resources and reduce environmental impact. Donates organic food waste to farmers in Costa Rica. Supports youth mentoring programs and cancer research. Has a written nondiscrimination policy covering sexual orientation but not gender identity. Offers insurance coverage to employees' domestic partners.

Frontier Airlines Holdings, Inc.
Contributions: Total: *$11,000*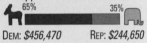
Lobby Spending: *$120,000*

54% Dem 46% Rep *$5,100*

Its corporate giving program has been suspended due to restructuring under Chapter 11 bankruptcy protection that was filed in 2008. Has no written nondiscrimination policy covering sexual orientation or gender identity.

Global Hyatt Corporation
Contributions: Total: *$75,275* Dem: *$49,525* Rep: *$25,750*
Lobby Spending: *$0*

66% 34%

Privately held. Recognized for diversity policies in recruiting and employing minorities. In 2008, scored 7 out of 100 in "The Climate Counts Company Scorecard Report." Is installing one of the nation's largest solar hot water systems in a Scottsdale, AZ, hotel. Supports the Make-A-Wish Foundation, Multiple Sclerosis Society, and Y-ME Breast Cancer organization. Offers paid leave for employees to volunteer. Has a written nondiscrimination policy covering sexual orientation and gender identity. Offers insurance coverage to employees' domestic partners. Insurance for transgender employees is offered, but treatment is not covered.

Hampton Inn
Contributions: Total: *$2,300* Dem: *$1,150* Rep: *$1,150*
Lobby Spending: *$0*

50% 50%

Subsidiary of Hilton Hotels Corporation. Supports Save-A-Landmark.

Harrah's Entertainment, Inc.
Contributions: Total: *$701,120* Dem: *$456,470* Rep: *$244,650*
Lobby Spending: *$720,000*

65% 35%

Subsidiary of Apollo Advisors and TPG Capital L.P. Ordered to pay $1 million in damages to a former employee who claimed she was fired for letting the Missouri Gaming Commission in on illegal activity. Participates in the EPA's Climate Leaders program. Recycles cooking oil waste and cardboard. Donates 1% of profits to charitable causes. Supports employee volunteerism and has a matching grant program supporting educational institutions. Has a written nondiscrimination policy covering sexual orientation and gender identity. Offers insurance coverage to employees' domestic partners. Insurance for transgender employees is offered, but treatment is not covered.

Hertz Corporation, The
Contributions: Total: *$25,000* Dem: *$12,100* Rep: *$12,900*
Lobby Spending: *$0*

48% 52%

Investment firms Clayton Dubilier & Rice, The Carlyle Group, and Merrill Lynch Global Private Equity own about 55% of Hertz. A pending class action lawsuit alleges that a spike in rental fees in California in 2006 was the result of illegal price-fixing by it and other rental-car companies. Seeks to do business with qualified minority/woman-owned/disadvantaged business enterprises. Has no written nondiscrimination policy covering sexual orientation or gender identity.

Hilton Garden Inn
79%   21%
Contributions: Total: *$3,215*   Dem: *$2,550*   Rep: *$665*
Lobby Spending: *$0*
Subsidiary of Hilton Hotels Corporation. Packages for its fresh "to-go" food items are 100% compostable. Its exterior signs are virtually 100% LED, and its beds are completely recyclable. Partners with the National Gardening Association.

Hilton Hotels Corporation
53%   47%
Contributions: Total: *$135,894*   Dem: *$71,594*   Rep: *$64,300*
Lobby Spending: *$540,000*
Subsidiary of The Blackstone Group LP. In 2008, scored 23 out of 100 in "The Climate Counts Company Scorecard Report." By 2014, it seeks to reduce its energy consumption by 20% and water consumption by 10%. Supports cancer prevention and treatment, environmental programs, and U.S. Paralympics. Undertook a five-year, $11.2 million initiative in 2006 to improve housing, health, and development of at-risk children in Los Angeles and Minneapolis/St. Paul. A grant of $1 million to CARE supports children affected by HIV/AIDS in Zambia. Guests can convert "HHonors" points to charitable donations. Has a written nondiscrimination policy covering sexual orientation and gender identity. Offers insurance coverage to employees' domestic partners. Insurance for transgender employees is offered, but treatment is not covered.

Holiday Inn Hotels & Resorts
27%   73%
Contributions: Total: *$137,130*   Dem: *$36,880*   Rep: *$100,250*
Lobby Spending: *$0*
Subsidiary of InterContinental Hotels Group PLC. Has no written non-discrimination policy covering sexual orientation or gender identity.

Homewood Suites by Hilton
35%   65%
Contributions: Total: *$1,150*   Dem: *$400*   Rep: *$750*
Lobby Spending: *$0*
Subsidiary of Hilton Hotels Corporation. Supports the National Coalition for the Homeless and Kids Help Phone, Canada's free counseling service.

Howard Johnson International, Inc.
69%   31%
Contributions: Total: *$3,185*   Dem: *$2,185*   Rep: *$1,000*
Lobby Spending: *$0*
Subsidiary of AmeriHost Franchise Systems, Inc.; parent, Wyndham Worldwide Corporation.

Hyatt Hotels Corporation
60%   40%
Contributions: Total: *$2,500*   Dem: *$1,500*   Rep: *$1,000*
Lobby Spending: *$0*
Subsidiary of Global Hyatt Corporation.

InterContinental Hotels & Resorts
37%   63%
Contributions: Total: *$171,855*   Dem: *$63,230*   Rep: *$108,625*
Lobby Spending: *$730,000*
Subsidiary of InterContinental Hotels Group PLC.

JetBlue Airways Corporation
Contributions: TOTAL: *$67,926* DEM: *$26,800* REP: *$41,126*
LOBBY SPENDING: *$10,000*

39% 61%

In 2009, joined a lawsuit opposing new FAA safety rules aimed at pilot fatigue. In 2008, scored 11 out of 100 in "The Climate Counts Company Scorecard Report." Contributes to Carbonfund.org to offset carbon emissions associated with crew member travel. Outreach focuses on cancer prevention and awareness, children, education, and the environment. Has a written nondiscrimination policy covering sexual orientation but not gender identity. Offers insurance to employees' domestic partners. Insurance for transgender employees is offered, but treatment is not covered.

Knights Franchise Systems, Inc.
(Knights Inn)
Contributions: TOTAL: *$1,700* DEM: *$1,700* REP: *$0*
LOBBY SPENDING: *$0*

100% 0%

Subsidiary of AmeriHost Franchise Systems, Inc.; parent, Wyndham Worldwide Corporation.

Las Vegas Sands Corp.
Contributions: TOTAL: *$430,624* DEM: *$850* REP: *$429,774*
LOBBY SPENDING: *$710,000*

0% 100%

Operates several casinos in the United States and Macao, and the Sands Expo Center trade show and convention center in Las Vegas. Offers extensive benefits for employees. Foundation supports youth education programs, minority empowerment, and improvement projects in inner cities. Has no written nondiscrimination policy covering sexual orientation or gender identity.

Loews Hotels Holding
Corporation
Contributions: TOTAL: *$179,381* DEM: *$176,431* REP: *$2,950*
LOBBY SPENDING: *$0*

98% 2%

Subsidiary of Loews Corporation. Its Minority Business Enterprise Program gives small minority- or women-owned businesses the opportunity to become vendors. Uses environmentally friendly cleaning products. Supports hunger cessation and literacy programs and donates used goods such as linens and furniture to local organizations and shelters.

LQ Management LLC
(La Quinta Inns)
Contributions: TOTAL: *$5,201* DEM: *$500* REP: *$4,701*
LOBBY SPENDING: *$0*

10% 90%

Subsidiary of The Blackstone Group LP. Is committed to attracting age 50+ job seekers. Has no written nondiscrimination policy covering sexual orientation or gender identity.

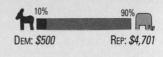

Major League Baseball Commissioners Ofc.

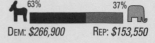

Contributions: TOTAL: *$420,450* DEM: *$266,900* REP: *$153,550*
LOBBY SPENDING: *$1,960,000*

With the NRDC, created the Team Greening Program. Supports programs for disadvantaged children, baseball families in need, cancer research and patient advocacy, and veterans.

Marriott International, Inc.

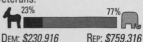

Contributions: TOTAL: *$990,232* DEM: *$230,916* REP: *$759,316*
LOBBY SPENDING: *$2,270,000*

Member of a task force on developing human rights principles for the hotel industry. Ranked 78th on *Fortune* magazine's "100 Best Companies to Work For" in 2009. Listed by NAFE in the top 50 companies for female executives in 2009. Ranked 4th on DiversityInc's list of the "Top 50 Companies for Diversity" in 2009. In 2008, scored 40 out of 100 in "The Climate Counts Company Scorecard Report." The EPA has placed the ENERGY STAR label on more than 275 of its hotels. Supports disaster relief, Habitat for Humanity, and Feeding America. Has a written nondiscrimination policy covering sexual orientation and gender identity. Offers insurance coverage to employees' domestic partners. Insurance for transgender employees is offered, but treatment is not covered.

Mashantucket Pequot Tribal Nation

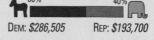

Contributions: TOTAL: *$480,205* DEM: *$286,505* REP: *$193,700*
LOBBY SPENDING: *$610,000*

Owns and operates what may be the world's most profitable casino, Foxwoods Resort Casino in Connecticut. Its development company projects include commercial gaming, tribal gaming, hotels, condos, resort facilities, and golf courses. Supports organizations and programs that aid Native American tribes, human services, community development, education, and the environment.

MGM Grand Hotel, LLC

Contributions: TOTAL: *$48,800* DEM: *$30,800* REP: *$18,000*
LOBBY SPENDING: *$0*

Subsidiary of MGM Mirage, Inc.; parent, Tracinda Corporation. Federal and state judges have issued conflicting decisions in nine lawsuits involving more than 300 condo purchasers against the developers of Signature at MGM Grand. At issue is whether the developers insinuated that ownership of the units would bring big profits. Selling condos as investments, unless units are registered as securities, is illegal.

MGM Mirage, Inc.

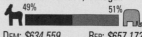

Contributions: TOTAL: *$1,291,731* DEM: *$634,559* REP: *$657,172*
LOBBY SPENDING: *$690,000*

Subsidiary of Tracinda Corporation. Ranked 19th on DiversityInc's list of the "Top 50 Companies for Diversity" in 2009. Outreach focuses on diversity, education, childhood development, hunger cessation, disaster relief, and community development. Offers $5,000 to employees for adoption assistance. Has a written nondiscrimination policy covering sexual orientation but not gender identity. Offers insurance to employees' domestic partners. Insurance for transgender employees is offered, but treatment is not covered.

Mississippi Band of Choctaw Indians

76%   24%

Contributions: TOTAL: *$437,950*   DEM: *$331,850*   REP: *$106,100*
LOBBY SPENDING: *$580,000*

Owns and operates several resorts and casinos, as well as manufacturing, service, retail, and tourism enterprises. Is one of the 10 largest employers in Mississippi.

Morongo Band of Mission Indians

59%   41%

Contributions: TOTAL: *$600,312*   DEM: *$352,073*   REP: *$248,239*
LOBBY SPENDING: *$535,000*

Operates the Morongo Casino Resort and Spa, one of the largest casinos in California. The tribe has become the largest private sector employer in the Banning-Beaumont region. In 2008, California voters gave approval for it and three other tribes to operate an additional 17,000 slot machines in an effort to help balance California's budget through gambling dollars. The Morongos' annual turkey donation program benefits 65 groups in Riverside and Los Angeles counties.

National Basketball Association (NBA)

99%   1%

Contributions: TOTAL: *$325,230*   DEM: *$320,730*   REP: *$4,500*
LOBBY SPENDING: *$597,000*

Its "Basketball without Borders" program sponsors camps worldwide where promising basketball players receive training in leadership, life skills, healthy and safe living, and HIV/AIDS prevention. NBA Cares has raised more than $105 million for charity and built more than 415 places where kids and families can live, learn, or play.

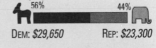

56%   44%

National Football League (NFL)

Contributions: TOTAL: *$52,950*   DEM: *$29,650*   REP: *$23,300*
LOBBY SPENDING: *$2,158,000*

NFL Charities supports programs and initiatives that deliver education and youth services. It also designates funds to assist the foundations of current and former players and awards sports-related medical research grants. Through a partnership with Scholastic, Inc., the NFL and NFL Players Association funded development of an educational program that walks youngsters through issues such as diversity, cultural awareness, and community. Has a written nondiscrimination policy covering sexual orientation but not gender identity.

18%   82%

National Hockey League (NHL)

Contributions: TOTAL: *$2,800*   DEM: *$500*   REP: *$2,300*
LOBBY SPENDING: *$110,000*

Supports the Salvation Army. Its Hockey is for Everyone program provides support to nonprofit youth hockey organizations across North America. Hockey Fights Cancer, a joint initiative of the NHL and the National Hockey League Players' Association, has raised over $10 million.

National Thoroughbred Racing Association, Inc. (NRTA)

56% | 44%

Contributions: TOTAL: *$583,500*   DEM: *$325,500*   REP: *$258,000*
LOBBY SPENDING: *$730,000*

NTRA Charities' mission is to promote and support charities in or related to the thoroughbred industry. Its Barbaro Memorial Fund supports research to ensure the safety of racing's equine athletes.

Northwest Airlines Corporation

43% | 57%

Contributions: TOTAL: *$433,064*   DEM: *$187,867*   REP: *$245,197*
LOBBY SPENDING: *$6,103,213*

Subsidiary of Delta Air Lines, Inc. A pending lawsuit alleges failure to comply with the ADA, the Air Carrier Act, and the Rehabilitation Act. In 2008, scored 39 out of 100 in "The Climate Counts Company Scorecard Report." Partners with The Nature Conservancy.

Omni Hotels Corporation

4% | 96%

Contributions: TOTAL: *$18,300*   DEM: *$700*   REP: *$17,600*
LOBBY SPENDING: *$0*

Subsidiary of TRT Holdings, Inc. Chosen as one of the "Best Companies to Work for in Texas" in 2009. Has a written nondiscrimination policy covering sexual orientation but not gender identity.

Orbitz Worldwide, Inc.

95% | 5%

Contributions: TOTAL: *$10,700*   DEM: *$10,200*   REP: *$500*
LOBBY SPENDING: *$414,683*

Subsidiary of Travelport Limited; parent, The Blackstone Group LP. Several cities have sued Orbitz and other Web-based travel clearinghouses, claiming failure to pay millions of dollars in hotel taxes. Partners with CarbonFund.org to allow customers to offset their travel-related carbon footprint. Has a written nondiscrimination policy covering sexual orientation and gender identity. Offers insurance coverage to employees' domestic partners. Insurance for transgender employees is offered, but treatment is not covered.

Park Plaza Hotels & Resorts

100% | 0%

Contributions: TOTAL: *$500*   DEM: *$500*   REP: *$0*
LOBBY SPENDING: *$0*

Subsidiary of Carlson Hotels Worldwide.

Pechanga Band of (Luiseño) Mission Indians

64% | 36%

Contributions: TOTAL: *$597,454*   DEM: *$383,305*   REP: *$214,149*
LOBBY SPENDING: *$0*

Owns and operates the Pechanga Resort & Casino, touted as the largest casino in the western United States. Is Temecula Valley's number one employer and the second largest private employer in Riverside County, CA. Offers childcare for employees.

PGA TOUR, Inc.

63% | 37%

Contributions: TOTAL: *$20,537*   DEM: *$12,850*   REP: *$7,687*
LOBBY SPENDING: *$870,000*

Supports education, health and human services, youth development, and community services.

Priceline.com, Inc.
19% | 81%
Contributions: TOTAL: *$16,000*   DEM: *$3,100*   REP: *$12,900*
LOBBY SPENDING: *$0*

Several cities have sued Priceline, along with other Web-based travel clearinghouses, claiming failure to pay millions of dollars in hotel taxes.

Quality Inn
72% | 28%
Contributions: TOTAL: *$2,650*   DEM: *$1,900*   REP: *$750*
LOBBY SPENDING: *$0*

Subsidiary of Choice Hotels International, Inc.

Radisson Hotels & Resorts
100% | 0%
Contributions: TOTAL: *$2,500*   DEM: *$2,500*   REP: *$0*
LOBBY SPENDING: *$0*

Subsidiary of Carlson Hotels Worldwide; parent, Carlson Companies, Inc. A lawsuit brought under the ADA is pending.

Ramada Worldwide, Inc.
77% | 23%
Contributions: TOTAL: *$2,151*   DEM: *$1,651*   REP: *$500*
LOBBY SPENDING: *$0*

Subsidiary of AmeriHost Franchise Systems, Inc.; parent, Wyndham Worldwide Corporation. In 2008, paid $35,000 to settle an EEOC complaint alleging sexual harassment.

Red Roof Inns, Inc.
0% | 100%
Contributions: TOTAL: *$597*   DEM: *$0*   REP: *$597*
LOBBY SPENDING: *$0*

Subsidiary of Citigroup's Global Special Situations Group and Westbridge Hospitality Fund.

Renaissance Hotels & Resorts
100% | 0%
Contributions: TOTAL: *$750*   DEM: *$750*   REP: *$0*
LOBBY SPENDING: *$0*

Subsidiary of Marriott International, Inc.

Residence Inn
0% | 100%
Contributions: TOTAL: *$300*   DEM: *$0*   REP: *$300*
LOBBY SPENDING: *$0*

Subsidiary of Marriott International, Inc.

Ritz-Carlton Hotel Company, L.L.C., The
65% | 35%
Contributions: TOTAL: *$21,650*   DEM: *$14,150*   REP: *$7,500*
LOBBY SPENDING: *$0*

Subsidiary of Marriott International, Inc. In 2007, two class action lawsuits claiming violations of wage and hour laws were filed. In 2008, donated over $8.55 million in products and services to charitable organizations. Has a written nondiscrimination policy covering sexual orientation but not gender identity. Offers insurance coverage to employees' domestic partners.

Royal Caribbean Cruises Ltd.

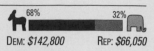

68%   32%

Contributions: Total: *$208,850*   Dem: *$142,800*   Rep: *$66,050*
Lobby Spending: *$2,210,000*

In 2008, it and subsidiary Celebrity Cruises, Inc., were ordered to refund $21 million worth of fuel surcharges levied after travelers booked their vacations. Has invested in advanced wastewater purification systems and has installed water-reduction technology and appliances and high-efficiency electrical appliances. Has invested $10 million in efforts to restore and maintain a healthy marine environment and to promote awareness of ocean and coastal issues. Has a written nondiscrimination policy covering sexual orientation but not gender identity. Offers insurance coverage to employees' domestic partners. Insurance for transgender employees is offered, but treatment is not covered.

Sabre Holdings Corporation

74%   26%

Contributions: Total: *$11,258*   Dem: *$8,357*   Rep: *$2,901*
Lobby Spending: *$0*

Subsidiary of Silver Lake Partners and TPG Capital. Corporate headquarters is LEED-certified campus. Community outreach programs include Math Can Take You Places and Travel for Good. Has a written nondiscrimination policy covering sexual orientation and gender identity. Offers insurance coverage to employees' domestic partners. Insurance for transgender employees is offered, but treatment is not covered.

San Manuel Band of (Serrano) Mission Indians

76%   24%

Contributions: Total: *$570,272*   Dem: *$435,472*   Rep: *$134,800*
Lobby Spending: *$620,000*

Owns and operates the San Manuel Indian Bingo and Casino, one of the largest employers in Riverside and San Bernardino counties. Has joint ventures with other organizations and tribal nations, including two hotels/resorts, a mixed-use development project, and a restaurant.

Sheraton Hotels & Resorts Worldwide, Inc.

93%   7%

Contributions: Total: *$7,350*   Dem: *$6,850*   Rep: *$500*
Lobby Spending: *$0*

Subsidiary of Starwood Hotels & Resorts Worldwide, Inc.

Sleep Inn

45%   55%

Contributions: Total: *$1,100*   Dem: *$500*   Rep: *$600*
Lobby Spending: *$0*

Subsidiary of Choice Hotels International, Inc.

Southwest Airlines Co.

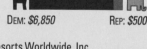

35%   65%

Contributions: Total: *$299,591*   Dem: *$105,222*   Rep: *$194,369*
Lobby Spending: *$1,970,000*

A class action lawsuit was filed in 2009 after the airline disclosed that dozens of its planes missed safety inspections. In 2008, scored 37 out of 100 in "The Climate Counts Company Scorecard Report." Received Silver LEED status for its Oakland Airport terminal. Participates in the Air

Transport Association of America's initiative to reduce greenhouse gas emissions by 30% by 2025. Has a medical transportation grant program. Has a written nondiscrimination policy covering sexual orientation and gender identity. Offers insurance coverage to employees' domestic partners. Insurance for transgender employees is offered, but treatment is not covered.

Starwood Hotels & Resorts Worldwide, Inc.
82% | 18%
Contributions: Total: *$80,201*   Dem: *$65,801*   Rep: *$14,400*
Lobby Spending: *$760,000*
A pending class action lawsuit alleges breach of lodging contracts through imposition of mandatory charges above the room rate agreed on at the time of reservation. In 2008, scored 24 out of 100 in "The Climate Counts Company Scorecard Report." Partners with Habitat for Humanity and the Juvenile Diabetes Research Foundation. Has a written nondiscrimination policy covering sexual orientation and gender identity. Offers insurance coverage to employees' domestic partners.

Station Casinos, Inc.
26% | 74%
Contributions: Total: *$552,950*   Dem: *$143,000*   Rep: *$409,950*
Lobby Spending: *$850,000*
Subsidiary of Colony Capital LLC. Owns and operates 10 hotel casinos in Las Vegas under the Station and Fiesta brand names and eight smaller casinos in the Vegas area. Also manages the Thunder Valley Casino in Sacramento, CA, for the United Auburn Indian Community. Is known for its high employee-satisfaction ratings. Supports programs helping to solve some of its community's challenges. Has no written nondiscrimination policy covering sexual orientation or gender identity.

St. Regis Hotels & Resorts
100% | 0%
Contributions: Total: *$200*   Dem: *$200*   Rep: *$0*
Lobby Spending: *$0*
Subsidiary of Starwood Hotels & Resorts Worldwide, Inc.

Super 8 Worldwide, Inc.
15% | 85%
Contributions: Total: *$6,850*   Dem: *$1,000*   Rep: *$5,850*
Lobby Spending: *$0*
Subsidiary of AmeriHost Franchise Systems, Inc., parent, Wyndham Worldwide Corporation.

Travelocity.com LP
72% | 28%
Contributions: Total: *$10,025*   Dem: *$7,225*   Rep: *$2,800*
Lobby Spending: *$0*
Subsidiary of Sabre Holdings Corporation; both are privately held by Silver Lake Partners and TPG Capital. Several cities have sued Travelocity, along with other Web-based travel clearinghouses, claiming failure to pay millions of dollars in hotel taxes. Partners with the Conservation Fund to allow customers to offset their travel-related carbon footprint. Has a written nondiscrimination policy covering sexual orientation and gender identity. Offers insurance coverage to employees' domestic partners. Insurance for transgender employees is offered, but treatment is not covered.

Travelodge Hotels, Inc.
Contributions: TOTAL: *$250*   DEM: *$250*   REP: *$0*
LOBBY SPENDING: *$0*
100% / 0%
Subsidiary of AmeriHost Franchise Systems, Inc.; parent, Wyndham Worldwide Corporation.

Trump Entertainment Resorts, Inc.
Contributions: TOTAL: *$5,000*   DEM: *$2,700*   REP: *$2,300*
LOBBY SPENDING: *$0*
54% / 46%
In 2009, filed for Chapter 11 bankruptcy. A pending lawsuit alleges labor violations.

Trump Organization, The
Contributions: TOTAL: *$140,650*   DEM: *$67,200*   REP: *$73,450*
LOBBY SPENDING: *$0*
48% / 52%
Privately held. Owns several pieces of high-end real estate in New York, as well as hotels, resorts, residential towers, and golf courses in major U.S. markets and abroad. Owns 28% of Trump Entertainment Resorts. Foundation supports St. Jude Children's Research Hospital.

UAL Corporation (United Airlines)
Contributions: TOTAL: *$438,904*   DEM: *$304,472*   REP: *$134,432*
LOBBY SPENDING: *$4,697,327*
69% / 31%
Shed its pension/retirement obligations to its employees in bankruptcy court. A pending lawsuit involves labor violations and alleged racial discrimination. In 2009, paid $3 million to a former employee for alleged retaliation over complaints of gender discrimination. In 2009, paid $850,000 and was ordered to change its overtime policy to settle a lawsuit alleging ADA violations. Has invested in alternative fuel vehicles. Foundation supports education, health, diversity, arts, and culture initiatives. Has an employee volunteer and charitable gift program. Has a written nondiscrimination policy covering sexual orientation and gender identity. Offers insurance coverage to employees' domestic partners. Insurance for transgender employees is offered, but treatment is not covered.

US Airways Group, Inc.
Contributions: TOTAL: *$256,119*   DEM: *$68,804*   REP: *$187,315*
LOBBY SPENDING: *$2,948,858*
27% / 73%
Disabled passengers have brought two pending discrimination lawsuits. Appealed a suit brought by a disabled employee who claimed ADA violations. Scrapped employee pension plans following an extensive court battle. In 2008, scored 0 out of 100 in "The Climate Counts Company Scorecard Report." Supports social responsibility and diversity projects through employee volunteerism and contributions of air transportation. Has a written nondiscrimination policy covering sexual orientation and gender identity. Offers insurance coverage to employees' domestic partners. Insurance for transgender employees is offered, but treatment is not covered.

Vanguard Car Rental USA, Inc.
Contributions: TOTAL: *$13,800*   DEM: *$12,300*   REP: *$1,500*
LOBBY SPENDING: *$0*

89% / 11%

Subsidiary of Enterprise Rent-A-Car Company. Has introduced bio-diesel-fueled cars into some of its fleets.

Virgin Group Ltd.
25% | 75%
Contributions: TOTAL: *$3,050*   DEM: *$750*   REP: *$2,300*
LOBBY SPENDING: *$750,000*
Foreign owned. Has committed to invest $3 billion in renewable energy. Partners with the National Network for Youth and the National Alliance to End Homelessness. Offers scholarships to its School of Entrepreneurship in South Africa.

W Hotels Worldwide
100% | 0%
Contributions: TOTAL: *$250*   DEM: *$250*   REP: *$0*
LOBBY SPENDING: *$0*
Subsidiary of Starwood Hotels & Resorts Worldwide, Inc.

Westin Hotels & Resorts
0% | 100%
Contributions: TOTAL: *$250*   DEM: *$0*   REP: *$250*
LOBBY SPENDING: *$0*
Subsidiary of Starwood Hotels & Resorts Worldwide, Inc.

Women's National Basketball Association (WNBA)
100% | 0%
Contributions: TOTAL: *$1,000*   DEM: *$1,000*   REP: *$0*
LOBBY SPENDING: *$0*
Supports the American Heart Association, youth basketball programs, breast health awareness, literacy programs, and the U.N. Foundation. encourages women to learn about the importance of physical fitness.

Wyndham Worldwide Corporation
64% | 36%
Contributions: TOTAL: *$54,415*   DEM: *$34,949*   REP: *$19,466*
LOBBY SPENDING: *$550,000*
A pending class action lawsuit alleges a discriminatory and gender-biased work environment at Wyndham's Las Vegas property, as well as federal civil rights and FMLA violations. In 2008, scored 10 out of 100 in "The Climate Counts Company Scorecard Report." Is installing solar panels. Supports Hole in Wall Camps, Christel House International, and Starlight Children's Foundation. Has a written nondiscrimination policy covering sexual orientation and gender identity. Offers insurance coverage to employees' domestic partners. Insurance for transgender employees is offered, but treatment is not covered.

Wynn Resorts, Limited
18% | 82%
Contributions: TOTAL: *$466,275*   DEM: *$85,050*   REP: *$381,225*
LOBBY SPENDING: *$80,000*
CEO Steve Wynn is a codefendant in a pending lawsuit alleging failure to pay for health care services for employees and beneficiaries under Wynn Resorts' self-insured health care plan. In 2007, the NLRB filed five lawsuits alleging discrimination, suspension, and termination in retaliation for pro-union activities. In 2007, the casino's dealers voted for a union, but they still lack a negotiated contract. In 2007, a lawsuit alleging ADA violations was filed. Has a written nondiscrimination policy covering sexual orientation but not gender identity.

Vehicles, Parts, and Gas

Chris Colin

The American auto industry understands image better than anyone—these are the people who gave us the tail fin, and who burned "cherry red" forever into the national lexicon. Tough, then, to explain how the chief executives of the Big Three automakers could fail to see the profound uncoolness of flying private jets to their panhandling sessions at the U.S. Capitol.

In truth, the PR blunder that day in November 2008 was just one of many remarkable miscalculations over the years. For decades, American carmakers have been perfecting the art of the poor decision, from putting all their eggs in the SUV basket to lobbying against higher fuel-efficiency standards. But while the industry had been sputtering for miles, the recession represented a brick wall—suddenly those poor decisions added up to a question of survival. The industry that was once the 800-pound gorilla on Capitol Hill was suddenly facing extinction. And the political party that had so often wrestled with this behemoth now found itself performing a rescue.

Why? Why throw billions of tax dollars at some of the most obstinate, poorly run, and unprogressive companies around?

After all, for years—and contrary to public desire—the U.S. auto lobby worked tirelessly to keep Congress from increasing fuel-efficiency standards. It also worked to dilute safety standards and pushed for import quotas from Japan. It learned to get around fuel-efficiency standards by arguing that SUVs were light trucks, not passenger vehicles, which are required to meet more rigorous standards. It even joined the tort reform movement popularized under the current business-friendly administration, working to limit liability in class action suits.

Both automakers and auto dealers—an even larger lobby—have given predominantly to Republicans over the years. Ties between carmakers and the Bush administration were especially close, as *U.S. News & World Report* has detailed. Chief of Staff Andrew Card was formerly General Motors Corporation's top lobbyist and head of a trade group of major domestic automakers. Jacqueline Glassman, chief counsel for the National Highway and Traffic Safety Administration

224

(NHTSA), was once a top lawyer for DaimlerChrysler AG. In a few cases—cases in which lives have actually been lost—the money trail from lobby to government has been too glaring for the public to ignore. In 2000, when Firestone sat through accident after accident before recalling its faulty tires, it was eventually noted that the very officials guiding NHTSA policy were the ones benefiting most from the auto lobby.

The response to this and other potential setbacks was a sophisticated PR campaign. Despite overwhelming data to the contrary, the Alliance of Auto Manufacturers claimed that the higher percentage of deaths in SUV accidents (compared with car accidents) came from lower seatbelt use; similar distortions were made about rollover tendency. At the same time, an even more insidious greenwashing trend has spread throughout the sector. Even as Ford Motor Company—with the worst fuel efficiency of any U.S. automaker—worked feverishly to gut California's clean air regulations, it publicly trumpeted its commitment to "clean-running" vehicles.

Given this track record, why did the Obama administration feel obliged to give the industry the biggest jump start of its existence? In a sense, there are 3.1 million answers. That's the number of people employed by all auto-related businesses in the country, the number that would otherwise find their livelihoods threatened. And they're good livelihoods. When workers lose auto industry jobs, studies show, they seldom find anything else that pays as well or that delivers the kind of benefits that the United Auto Workers managed to secure. Ford, GM, and Chrysler may be profoundly mismanaged, but their grip is on the economy's dead man's switch.

But there's another answer, too, one that's not just about saving good jobs. When a progressive administration oversees the semi-nationalization of an industry, that administration takes the wheel to some degree. So it was that in May 2009, President Obama shocked the nation with news that he was imposing the first emissions standard and mileage requirement for the entire nation. The administration said the move would reduce greenhouse gases by 900 million metric tons in a six-and-a-half-year period—roughly equivalent to removing 177 million cars from the road.

The announcement capped a protracted and bitter saga dating back, naturally, to the Bush years. In 2005, California had requested a waiver from the Environmental Protection Agency (EPA) to toughen emissions standards beyond those of the rest of the country. The EPA ignored the request as long as possible, then eventually denied it—touching off accusations that the White House had illegally pressured the EPA to do so. Senator Barbara Boxer, chair of the Environment and Public Works Committee, argued that the head of the agency, Stephen L. Johnson, had been coerced by the administration.

"You know, a funny thing happened on the way to the White House," Boxer told the press at the time. "Mr. Johnson goes into the White House with a briefing that tells him to fight for the waiver, and then the waiver's not granted."

President Obama's announcement made the EPA brouhaha history, along with a good many other chapters from past years. Still, it's worth remembering exactly how much reach the auto industry had: from the White House, to the legislative branch, to the very agency meant to regulate it. It remains to be seen what kind of reach Detroit will have in the future. Officials didn't say whether that bailout money had come with strings attached, or if automakers had simply realized, at last, which way the political and environmental winds were blowing.

The years ahead will reveal just how much of a U-turn the Big Three—or perhaps Big Two—can manage. The auto lobby had decades to get its claws in the NHTSA, the Republican Party, and energy policy makers. But that's the thing about flying your private jet to Washington and holding out your cup: we all own a piece now.

Top Ten Democratic Contributors

Ford Motor Company	$549,618
General Motors Corporation	$486,027
Chrysler LLC	$423,894
Koch Industries, Inc.	$357,505
ExxonMobil Corporation	$333,799
Sunoco, Inc.	$272,750
Chevron Corporation	$269,816
BP PLC	$215,915
Valero Energy Corporation	$201,750
ConocoPhillips	$175,200

Top Ten Republican Contributors

Koch Industries, Inc.	$2,180,108
ExxonMobil Corporation	$1,085,223
Valero Energy Corporation	$890,622
Chevron Corporation	$802,201
ConocoPhillips	$521,146
Pilot Corporation	$491,575
Anadarko Petroleum Corporation	$491,450
General Motors Corporation	$483,259
Chrysler LLC	$472,143
Marathon Oil Corporation	$450,529

Top Ten Lobbying Spenders

ExxonMobil Corporation	$45,940,000
General Motors Corporation	$28,061,000
Koch Industries, Inc.	$25,091,750
Chevron Corporation	$22,024,000
BP PLC	$15,090,000
Ford Motor Company	$14,819,000
Marathon Oil Corporation	$12,580,000
ConocoPhillips	$12,548,621
Toyota Motor Corporation	$11,169,150
Nissan Motor Co., Ltd.	$7,650,000

Advance Auto Parts, Inc.

25% / 75%

Contributions: TOTAL: *$10,175*   DEM: *$2,550*   REP: *$7,625*
LOBBY SPENDING: *$0*
Supports youth alcohol education, diabetes research, the Make-A-Wish Foundation, the United Way, and the Children's Miracle Network. Has a written nondiscrimination policy covering sexual orientation and gender identity.

AM General LLC

51% / 49%

Contributions: TOTAL: *$302,600*   DEM: *$153,600*   REP: *$149,000*
LOBBY SPENDING: *$860,000*
MacAndrews & Forbes Holdings, Inc., owns about 70% of the company. Has no written nondiscrimination policy covering sexual orientation or gender identity.

AMERCO

54% / 46%

Contributions: TOTAL: *$13,550*   DEM: *$7,350*   REP: *$6,200*
LOBBY SPENDING: *$0*
Holding company for U-Haul International, Inc. Reuses reclaimed rainwater and has permeable ground cover in its parking lots. Returns spent lead-acid batteries to the supplier to be recycled. Offers a biodegradable packing peanut. Supports hunger relief, clothing donations, and housing. Has no written nondiscrimination policy covering sexual orientation or gender identity.

Anadarko Petroleum Corporation

9%   91%

Contributions: TOTAL: *$542,450*   DEM: *$51,000*   REP: *$491,450*
LOBBY SPENDING: *$2,130,000*

In 2009, ordered to pay $1 million for Clean Water Act violations and another $8 million for environmental cleanup and oil-spill prevention projects. Has no written nondiscrimination policy covering sexual orientation or gender identity.

Ashland, Inc.

13%   87%

Contributions: TOTAL: *$239,558*   DEM: *$31,208*   REP: *$208,350*
LOBBY SPENDING: *$1,560,000*

Two pending lawsuits brought by former employees allege that exposure to benzene caused them to develop leukemia. In 2006, Ashland resolved EPA allegations that it failed to comply with national emissions standards for hazardous air pollutants. Assisted in the development of a major nature preserve. Helps sponsor Ohio River Sweep. Supports community organizations focusing on education, arts, disaster relief, and health and human services. Has a written nondiscrimination policy covering sexual orientation but not gender identity.

AUDI AG

0%   100%

Contributions: TOTAL: *$1,000*   DEM: *$0*   REP: *$1,000*
LOBBY SPENDING: *$0*

Subsidiary of Volkswagen AG. A combined heat, power, and refrigeration plant generates steam and electricity at its site in Ingolstadt, Germany, reducing natural gas consumption and carbon dioxide emissions. Recycles all its metal. Has a written nondiscrimination policy covering sexual orientation and gender identity. Offers insurance coverage to employees' domestic partners. Insurance for transgender employees is offered, but treatment is not covered.

AutoNation, Inc.

20%   80%

Contributions: TOTAL: *$106,690*   DEM: *$21,200*   REP: *$85,490*
LOBBY SPENDING: *$0*

Pending lawsuit brought by consumers alleges deceptive trade practices. Supports local health and welfare efforts. Has a written nondiscrimination policy covering sexual orientation but not gender identity.

AutoZone, Inc.

18%   82%

Contributions: TOTAL: *$83,150*   DEM: *$14,800*   REP: *$68,350*
LOBBY SPENDING: *$0*

In 2007, paid $1.5 million in a civil environmental and consumer protection enforcement lawsuit. Supports education, human services, and civic endeavors. Has a written nondiscrimination policy covering sexual orientation but not gender identity. Refuses insurance coverage to employees' domestic partners.

Bayerische Motoren Werke AG

69%   31%

Contributions: TOTAL: *$2,553*   DEM: *$1,750*   REP: *$803*
LOBBY SPENDING: *<$40,000*

Foreign owned. Has been financially involved in Burma, potentially strengthening that country's illegal military junta. Operates maquilas.

Participates in the United Nations Global Compact. Environmental goals include using 30% fewer resources in 2012 than it did in 2006 and reducing water, energy, waste, and VOC emissions for each vehicle produced by 5% each year. Uses natural fibers as a base for its interior components. Developed the first production-ready vehicle to be powered by hydrogen. Integrates environmental and recycling requirements into its product creation process. No less than 15% of all the plastic components used in BMW vehicles are made of recyclates. Supports intercultural learning, educational projects, HIV/AIDS research, alternative-fuel development, and environmental research.

BP PLC

40% | 60%

Contributions: TOTAL: *$535,324*   DEM: *$215,915*   REP: *$319,409*
LOBBY SPENDING: *$15,090,000*

Foreign owned. Pending lawsuits allege that it knowingly aided South Africa's apartheid regime. A pending lawsuit brought by the State of Alaska seeks compensation for pipeline leaks. In 2009, BP Products North America, Inc., a unit of BP PLC, agreed to spend nearly $180 million to resolve clean air law violations. One of 12 oil refinery companies that paid a portion of a $422 million settlement in 2008 for using MTBE despite known environmental risks and potential health risks. In 2008, was rated the 29th worst polluter on PERI's Toxic 100 index. Created an alternative energy unit and has made investments in four low-carbon technologies. Supports entrepreneurship, economic growth, health education, and education in rural areas. Has a written nondiscrimination policy covering sexual orientation and gender identity. Offers insurance coverage to employees' domestic partners. Insurance for transgender employees is offered, but treatment is not covered.

Bridgestone Americas Holding, Inc.

49% | 51%

Contributions: TOTAL: *$192,405*   DEM: *$95,050*   REP: *$97,355*
LOBBY SPENDING: *$2,240,000*

Subsidiary of Bridgestone Corporation in Japan. Multiple labor violations have been documented at its rubber plants. Has a recycling program for used oil, batteries, and tires. Has established six wildlife habitat areas on its land. Supports Habitat for Humanity and Keep America Beautiful. Has a written nondiscrimination policy covering sexual orientation and gender identity. Does not offer insurance coverage to employees' domestic partners. Limited insurance for transgender employees is offered, but treatment is not covered.

Chesapeake Energy Corporation

21% | 79%

Contributions: TOTAL: *$480,771*   DEM: *$100,800*   REP: *$379,971*
LOBBY SPENDING: *$835,000*

In a lawsuit brought in 2009, its board members were accused of breach of fiduciary duty for granting a $75 million bonus to CEO Aubrey K. McClendon. The lawsuit also levels "unlawful insider trading" allegations against former Oklahoma U.S. Sen. Don Nickles and two other Chesapeake board members. In 2007, a jury awarded a $404 million verdict in favor of plaintiff landowners and against subsidiary Chesapeake Appalachia LLC and others for unpaid royalties. Ranked 73rd on *Fortune* magazine's "100 Best Companies to Work For" in 2009. Supports community and public service improvements, education, health care, youth programs, and environmental protection.

Chevron Corporation
Contributions: TOTAL: *$1,072,017* DEM: *$269,816* REP: *$802,201*
LOBBY SPENDING: *$22,024,000*

The *Multinational Monitor* named Chevron one of the "10 Worst Corporations" of 2008. One of 12 oil refinery companies that paid a portion of a $422 million settlement in 2008 for using MTBE despite known environmental risks and potential health risks. Implicated in violent events and human rights violations in Nigeria. Has engaged in toxic dumping in several U.S. states and in the Amazon rainforest. According to the Center for Public Integrity, Chevron is a potentially responsible party for 95 Superfund sites. Supports sustainable livelihoods, access to basic human services, and education in the areas in which it operates. Pledged $18 million for a program to support public school education in school districts affected by hurricanes Katrina and Rita. Has a written nondiscrimination policy covering sexual orientation and gender identity. Offers insurance coverage to employees' domestic partners. Limited insurance for transgender employees is offered, but treatment is not covered.

Chrysler LLC
Contributions: TOTAL: *$896,037* DEM: *$423,894* REP: *$472,143*
LOBBY SPENDING: *$5,847,782*

In June 2009, Fiat S.p.A. acquired Chrysler, enabling its exit from Chapter 11 bankruptcy. Received a $14 billion bailout from the government—taxpayer money it may be using to continue its campaign against higher fuel-efficiency standards. Operates maquilas. According to the Center for Public Integrity, Chrysler is a potentially responsible party at 50 Superfund sites. Has reduced annual energy use by more than 18% from 2002 levels in its North American facilities. Eleven of its vehicle models have SmartWay certification. Received a perfect score on the 2008 Human Rights Campaign Corporate Equality Index. Supports arts and culture, education, diversity, disaster relief, and youth development. Has a written nondiscrimination policy covering sexual orientation and gender identity. Offers insurance coverage to employees' domestic partners. Insurance for transgender employees is offered, and treatment is covered.

CITGO Petroleum Corporation
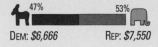
Contributions: TOTAL: *$14,216* DEM: *$6,666* REP: *$7,550*
LOBBY SPENDING: *$845,000*

Subsidiary of PDVSA USA, Inc.; parent is PDVSA in Venezuela. One of 12 oil refinery companies that paid a portion of a $422 million settlement in 2008 for using MTBE despite known environmental risks and potential health risks. According to a pending class action lawsuit filed in 2006, hundreds of people were physically injured and put out of work after waste oil from CITGO's storage tanks was released into Louisiana's Calcasieu Ship Channel. Supports the Muscular Dystrophy Association, the United Way, and Habitat for Humanity.

ConocoPhillips
Contributions: Total: *$696,346*   Dem: *$175,200*   Rep: *$521,146*
Lobby Spending: *$12,548,621*

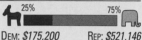

A pending lawsuit brought by 80 poisoning victims, cancer patients, and relatives of former workers alleges that it acted irresponsibly by not ensuring protection against certain chemicals. One of 12 oil refinery companies that paid a portion of a $422 million settlement in 2008 for using MTBE despite known environmental risks and potential health risks. In 2008, paid a $1.2 million civil penalty for more than 2,000 violations of the Clean Water Act. Settled a $100 million class action lawsuit brought by Pensacola, FL, residents, some of whom owned property bought and condemned by the EPA. In 2008, was rated as the 13th worst polluter on PERI's Toxic 100 index. Has worked with communities in Canada to protect endangered caribou. Supports education, arts, and environmental programs. Has a written nondiscrimination policy covering sexual orientation but not gender identity. Offers insurance coverage to employees' domestic partners. Insurance for transgender employees is offered, but treatment is not covered.

CSK Auto Corporation
Contributions: Total: *$3,000*   Dem: *$0*   Rep: *$3,000*
Lobby Spending: *$0*

Subsidiary of O'Reilly Automotive. Shareholders have filed a lawsuit against it, and the SEC may bring an enforcement action against it for violating federal securities laws. Two former executives were indicted on charges that they schemed to manipulate the company's earnings. Has no written nondiscrimination policy covering sexual orientation or gender identity.

Daimler AG
Contributions: Total: *$15,257*   Dem: *$9,814*   Rep: *$5,443*
Lobby Spending: *$1,456,997*

Foreign owned. In 2007, Daimler sold 80% of Chrysler to Cerberus Capital Management. Pending lawsuits allege that former Daimler Chrysler and other multinational corporations knowingly aided South Africa's apartheid regime. Is the second largest European arms manufacturer. Manufactures the Smart Car. Has increased the range and boosted the performance of fuel cells. Mercedes Benz South Africa is recognized for its support of HIV-positive workers. Daimler supports social welfare, science, culture, and sports programs.

Devon Energy Corporation
Contributions: Total: *$472,490*   Dem: *$44,200*   Rep: *$428,290*
Lobby Spending: *$1,325,000*

In 2007, paid $5 million to settle a class action suit alleging that it illegally deducted hidden fees from the amounts that it paid royalty owners for natural gas production. Ranked 13th on *Fortune* magazine's "100 Best Companies to Work For" in 2009. Recognized for water recycling and conservation. Is a partner in the EPA's Natural Gas STAR Program, a voluntary effort to reduce methane emissions. Recognized for reclaiming other operators' oil and gas fields in New Mexico. Supports youth and education, health and human services, and environmental protection. Has no written nondiscrimination policy covering sexual orientation or gender identity.

Driven Brands, Inc.
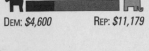
Contributions: TOTAL: *$15,779*   DEM: *$4,600*   REP: *$11,179*
LOBBY SPENDING: *$0*
Formerly Meineke Holding Company.

ExxonMobil Corporation
Contributions: TOTAL: *$1,419,022*   DEM: *$333,799*   REP: *$1,085,223*
LOBBY SPENDING: *$45,940,000*
Has benefited from over $5 billion in taxpayer subsidies over the last decade. Pending lawsuits allege that it knowingly aided South Africa's apartheid regime. Continues to appeal an Alaskan court-ordered fine in the wake of the 1989 *Valdez* spill. Is spearheading efforts to open the Arctic National Wildlife Refuge to drilling. In 2008, was rated as the 9th worst polluter on PERI's Toxic 100 index. Boasts a commitment to preserving biodiversity but simultaneously fights policies to cut greenhouse gas emissions. A May 2007 report by Greenpeace says that ExxonMobil continues to fund groups that deny or downplay global warming. Has several carbon capture and storage projects. Is providing $100 million to Stanford University's Global Climate and Energy Project. Supports health and safety programs, education, and community development. Refuses to adopt an antidiscrimination policy. Has no written nondiscrimination policy covering sexual orientation or gender identity. Refuses insurance coverage to employees' domestic partners.

Flying J, Inc.
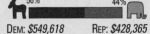
Contributions: TOTAL: *$9,400*   DEM: *$0*   REP: *$9,400*
LOBBY SPENDING: *$0*
Filed for Chapter 11 bankruptcy protection in December 2008. A pending lawsuit alleges that it disabled leak detection systems and failed to fix problems at underground tank systems at six of its seven truck and car travel plazas in California. Ordered to pay over $100,000 for water pollution violations at two of its truck stops in Iowa. Several locations have been assessed fines for diesel fuel spills, sewage ordinance violations, and dumping of petroleum-contaminated water. Supports fund-raisers for local schools.

Ford Motor Company
Contributions: TOTAL: *$977,983*   DEM: *$549,618*   REP: *$428,365*
LOBBY SPENDING: *$14,819,000*
Pending lawsuits allege that it and other multinational corporations knowingly aided South Africa's apartheid regime. Ranked 28th on DiversityInc's list of the "Top 50 Companies for Diversity" in 2009. Listed by NAFE as one of the top 50 companies for female executives in 2009. Member of the United Nations Global Compact. Has lobbied against tighter efficiency and emissions regulations. In 2008, was rated the 17th worst polluter on PERI's Toxic 100 index. Since 2000, has reduced its energy use by 30% and carbon dioxide emissions by 39%. Promotes employee volunteerism and works closely with Habitat for Humanity. Supports innovation and education, community develop-

ment, and auto-related safety education. Has a written nondiscrimination policy covering sexual orientation and gender identity. Offers insurance coverage to employees' domestic partners. Insurance for transgender employees is offered, and treatment is covered.

General Motors Corporation

50% / 50%

Contributions: TOTAL: *$969,286*   DEM: *$486,027*   REP: *$483,259*
LOBBY SPENDING: *$28,061,000*

Filed for bankruptcy protection in 2009. Pending lawsuits allege that it knowingly aided South Africa's apartheid regime. Named in a lawsuit alleging managers at one plant ignored defective seat belts and braking systems. Former African American managers filed a pending $7.4 billion racial discrimination suit. In 2008, was rated the 18th worst polluter on PERI's Toxic 100 index. GM's Central Foundry Division plant in New York is on the Superfund National Priority List. Opposes climate change regulations and higher emissions standards. Invested $1 billion in research on hydrogen fuel cell vehicles. Received a perfect score on the 2008 Human Rights Campaign Corporate Equality Index. Aids in disaster relief and donates to cultural, educational, and societal causes. Has a written nondiscrimination policy covering sexual orientation and gender identity. Offers insurance coverage to employees' domestic partners. Insurance for transgender employees is offered, and treatment is covered.

Goodyear Tire & Rubber Company, The

36% / 64%

Contributions: TOTAL: *$266,930*   DEM: *$94,950*   REP: *$171,980*
LOBBY SPENDING: *$4,980,000*

Agreed, with five other rubber manufacturers, to spend a total of $19 million on cleanup at an Ohio Superfund landfill. Also agreed, along with seven other companies, to pay $120 million for cleanup of a contaminated dump site in Texas. In 2008, was rated the 19th worst polluter on PERI's Toxic 100 index. Its manufacturing facilities reuse and recycle everything from their manufacturing efforts. Has set a near-zero water discharge target for its new plant in China. Its plant in Peru sponsors recyclable-material collection programs. Glass collected for donations to a nonprofit group aids disabled and orphaned children. Supports employee volunteerism and makes in-kind donations. Has a written nondiscrimination policy covering sexual orientation but not gender identity.

Harley-Davidson, Inc.

37% / 63%

Contributions: TOTAL: *$62,851*   DEM: *$23,050*   REP: *$39,801*
LOBBY SPENDING: *$575,000*

Has a strong history of positive union relations. Supports education, community revitalization, and arts and culture. Its foundation supports the Muscular Dystrophy Association and veterans initiatives. Has a written nondiscrimination policy covering sexual orientation but not gender identity.

Hess Corporation

Contributions: TOTAL: *$474,857*   DEM: *$112,832*   REP: *$362,025*
LOBBY SPENDING: *$2,120,000*

One of 12 oil refinery companies that paid a portion of a $422 million settlement in 2008 for using MTBE despite known environmental risks and potential health risks. In 2008, ordered to pay a penalty of $1.1 million for storage violations. Aims to lessen its environmental impact through energy efficiency and recovery efforts and carbon capture and trading. Supports disaster relief, humanitarian aid, and infrastructure development. In 2006, contributed $20 million for an educational initiative in Equatorial Guinea. Has a written nondiscrimination policy covering sexual orientation but not gender identity.

Honda Motor Co., Ltd.

Contributions: TOTAL: *$9,365*   DEM: *$4,257*   REP: *$5,108*
LOBBY SPENDING: *$4,129,194*

Settled a class action lawsuit alleging that the odometers in some models racked up more miles than they should have. Offers a hydrogen fuel cell-powered vehicle for retail sale and opened the world's first fuel cell-vehicle dealership network. Recycles up to 86% of automobile components and has introduced water-based paints. Its experimental Home Energy Station generates hydrogen from natural gas for use in fuel cell vehicles while supplying electricity and hot water to the home. Community activities include reforestation and forest conservation, environmental cleanup, and ecology education. Has a written nondiscrimination policy covering sexual orientation but not gender identity.

Hyundai Motor Company

Contributions: TOTAL: *$5,375*   DEM: *$2,025*   REP: *$3,350*
LOBBY SPENDING: *$790,000*

Foreign owned. A pending class action lawsuit alleges that the factory-installed flywheel and clutch in the 2003 Hyundai Tiburon prematurely fails and that the company refuses to replace it under warranty. All of its vehicles are certified low-emission vehicles, and six of its models are certified ultra-low-emission vehicles. For every 2009 Genesis purchased, Hyundai will offset the car's carbon emissions for one year by conserving and reforesting 3,000 acres of tropical forest in the Brazilian Cerrado.

Jiffy Lube International, Inc.

Contributions: TOTAL: *$18,200*   DEM: *$0*   REP: *$18,200*
LOBBY SPENDING: *$0*

Subsidiary of Shell Oil Company; parent Royal Dutch/Shell Group. Agreed to step up environmental protection and to pay $500,000 in civil fines and legal fees after it was charged in 2008 for not properly storing antifreeze and motor oil. As a system, Jiffy Lube collects more used oil than any company in North America. This oil is re-refined and used for industrial applications. Raises funds for the American Heart Association, St. Jude Children's Research Hospital, and the Make-A-Wish Foundation. Has a written nondiscrimination policy covering sexual orientation and gender identity. Offers insurance coverage to employees' domestic partners. Insurance for transgender employees is offered, and some treatment is covered.

Kawasaki Heavy Industries, Ltd.

100% | **0%**

Contributions: TOTAL: *$200*   DEM: *$200*   REP: *$0*
LOBBY SPENDING: *$0*

Foreign owned. Developed a green gas engine with the highest power generation efficiency (48.5%) in the world. Achieved a recycling rate of 87.2% in 2008. Offers a family-friendly workplace and extensive support for childcare. Supports a forest restoration project, global warming prevention, coastal conservation, and disaster relief.

Kia Motors Corporation

38% | **62%**

Contributions: TOTAL: *$5,375*   DEM: *$2,025*   REP: *$3,350*
LOBBY SPENDING: *$790,000*

Foreign owned. Subsidiary of Hyundai Motor Co. Produces vehicles to meet the U.S. standard for an ultra-low-emission vehicle. Supports traffic safety and mobility for people with disabilities.

Koch Industries, Inc.

14% | **86%**

Contributions: TOTAL: *$2,537,613*   DEM: *$357,505*   REP: *$2,180,108*
LOBBY SPENDING: *$25,091,750*

Is known for its ability to get criminal charges dropped and huge penalties knocked down. In 2009, subsidiary Invista agreed to pay a $1.7 million civil penalty and make as much as $500 million in improvements to settle environmental violations. Subsidiary Georgia-Pacific is accused of stripping lands bare and paying only a small fee to the federal government for what it took from the public. Participates in reclamation and recycling programs and programs that promote sustainable forest management. Foundation supports Habitat for Humanity, human services, education, and the arts. Has no written nondiscrimination policy covering sexual orientation or gender identity.

Les Schwab Tire Centers

0% | **100%**

Contributions: TOTAL: *$500*   DEM: *$0*   REP: *$500*
LOBBY SPENDING: *$0*

In a lawsuit filed in 2006, two female employees allege that they were denied promotional opportunities and that the company has an institutional process of discrimination against women; the company had never employed a female manager.

Marathon Oil Corporation

28% | **72%**

Contributions: TOTAL: *$623,200*   DEM: *$172,671*   REP: *$450,529*
LOBBY SPENDING: *$12,580,000*

The New Mexico Environment Department is suing it over thousands of alleged air emissions violations. One of 12 oil refinery companies that paid a portion of a $422 million settlement in 2008 for using MTBE despite known environmental risks and potential health risks. Charged with profiteering following hurricanes Katrina and Rita. Subject to a SEC probe for its payments to the government of Equatorial Guinea. Participates in the American Petroleum Institute's Climate Challenge, committing to improve refinery energy efficiency 10% by 2012. Has transformed more than 1,400 acres of its property into habitat certified by the Wildlife Habitat Council. Supports the Colorado River Initiative, the Susan G. Komen Race for the Cure, and a malaria control project in Equatorial Guinea. Has a written nondiscrimination policy covering sexual orientation but not gender identity. Refuses insurance coverage to employees' domestic partners.

Mazda Motor Corporation
25% | 75%
Contributions: TOTAL: *$1,000* DEM: *$250* REP: *$750*
LOBBY SPENDING: *$250,000*
Ford Motor Company holds a 13% stake in the company. By 2011, expects to develop a diesel engine that is cheaper and about as fuel-efficient as some hybrid cars. Aims to raise the fuel economy of its fleet 30% by 2015. Is developing hydrogen rotary engine vehicles. Supports charitable organizations that promote literacy, cross-cultural understanding, environmental conservation, and social welfare.

Meineke Car Care Centers, Inc.
35% | 65%
Contributions: TOTAL: *$13,179* DEM: *$4,600* REP: *$8,579*
LOBBY SPENDING: *$0*
Subsidiary of Driven Brands, Inc.; parent, Carousel Capital Partners.

Mercedes-Benz USA, Inc.
88% | 13%
Contributions: TOTAL: *$2,000* DEM: *$1,750* REP: *$250*
LOBBY SPENDING: *$1,336,997*
Subsidiary of Daimler AG. A pending class action lawsuit alleges that it sold cars equipped with an emergency response system known to soon become obsolete. Is launching two hybrid vehicles and, starting in 2012, zero-emission fuel-cell vehicles. In the current C-Class, 85% of the material is recyclable and 95% is reusable. The current S-Class contains 27 components made from renewable resources. Its dealership in Peoria, AZ, is a LEED-certified building.

Michelin North America, Inc.
37% | 63%
Contributions: TOTAL: *$52,350* DEM: *$19,500* REP: *$32,850*
LOBBY SPENDING: *$930,554*
Foreign owned. Subsidiary of Compagnie Generale des Etablissements Michelin. Settled a class action lawsuit alleging that it and Honda deceived customers about the replacement costs and repairs of "run-flat" tires. Nine plants are members of the EPA National Performance Track program for environmental improvements beyond requirements. Several of its plants use a system of cogeneration, whereby electricity can be produced and steam recovered from heat. Supports K-12 math and science, Clemson University, and environmental activities with the South Carolina Wildlife Federation. Has a written nondiscrimination policy covering sexual orientation but not gender identity.

Midas, Inc.
100% | 0%
Contributions: TOTAL: *$3,600* DEM: *$3,600* REP: *$0*
LOBBY SPENDING: *$0*
The internationally franchised company is now branding itself as a total auto maintenance destination.

Nissan Motor Co., Ltd.
100% | 0%
Contributions: TOTAL: *$1,500* DEM: *$1,500* REP: *$0*
LOBBY SPENDING: *$7,650,000*

Renault owns almost 45% of Nissan. A class action lawsuit accuses it of purposely designing its vehicles' odometers to inflate the mileage driven. Was party to an industry lawsuit aimed at blocking stricter emissions legislation in California. Has one of the most fuel-efficient vehicle fleets. Supports Habitat for Humanity and literacy and science programs. Has a written nondiscrimination policy covering sexual orientation but not gender identity. Offers insurance coverage to employees' domestic partners. Insurance for transgender employees is offered, but treatment is not covered.

Occidental Petroleum

26% | 74%

Contributions: TOTAL: *$582,751*   DEM: *$153,600*   REP: *$429,151*
LOBBY SPENDING: *$5,425,257*

A pending lawsuit brought by Peru's Achuar indigenous peoples demands cleanup of and reparations for environmental damage allegedly caused by Occidental over a 30-year period. Has spilled more than 2.9 million barrels of crude oil and has polluted more than 1,625 miles of river. In 2008, was rated the 49th worst polluter on PERI's Toxic 100 index. Supports economic development, hunger cessation, and disaster relief. Has a written nondiscrimination policy covering sexual orientation but not gender identity.

O'Reilly Automotive, Inc.

32% | 68%

Contributions: TOTAL: *$17,351*   DEM: *$5,600*   REP: *$11,751*
LOBBY SPENDING: *$0*

The EEOC brought a pending lawsuit on behalf of African American employees at one distribution center.

Penske Corporation

0% | 100%

Contributions: TOTAL: *$71,000*   DEM: *$250*   REP: *$70,750*
LOBBY SPENDING: *$225,324*

Owns about 40% of publicly traded auto dealer Penske Automotive Group (formerly United Auto Group). Its truck leasing division participates in the EPA's SmartWay Transport Partnership, and it received the EPA's highest score for environmental performance. Supports Habitat for Humanity, the United Way, and disaster relief. Has a written nondiscrimination policy covering sexual orientation but not gender identity.

Pep Boys — Manny, Moe & Jack

100% | 0%

Contributions: TOTAL: *$250*   DEM: *$250*   REP: *$0*
LOBBY SPENDING: *$0*

A pending class action lawsuit alleges violations of federal and state wage and hour laws. Founded the Motorist Assurance Program to promote fairness in the auto service industry by curbing superfluous repair and overcharging. Has no written nondiscrimination policy covering sexual orientation or gender identity.

Pilot Corporation

0% | 100%

Contributions: TOTAL: *$493,075*   DEM: *$1,500*   REP: *$491,575*
LOBBY SPENDING: *$0*

CVC Capital partners holds a 47.5% interest. In 2008, Florida's attorney general issued it subpoenas for investigation of price gouging in the days following Hurricane Ike. Supports youth foundations, hunger cessation, nature conservation, and health and wellness programs.

Porsche Automobile Holding SE

Contributions: TOTAL: *$500*   DEM: *$0*   REP: *$500*
LOBBY SPENDING: *$240,000*

Foreign owned. Has more than 50% controlling interest in Volkswagen AG. All current models can be driven on up to 10% biofuel (ethanol); the Cayenne model can be driven on up to 25% biofuel.

Precision Auto Care, Inc.

Contributions: TOTAL: *$6,268*   DEM: *$6,268*   REP: *$0*
LOBBY SPENDING: *$0*

Partners with Vehicles for Change, a nonprofit organization committed to changing lives with donated cars.

Royal Dutch/Shell Group

Contributions: TOTAL: *$340,575*   DEM: *$163,425*   REP: *$177,150*
LOBBY SPENDING: *$6,404,283*

Foreign owned. Named in a lawsuit brought by the residents of an Alaskan village who allege that oil and utility companies' greenhouse gas emissions are destroying the village by melting Arctic sea ice. Pending lawsuits allege that it knowingly aided South Africa's apartheid regime. Its operations in Nigeria have led to complaints by human rights groups. In 2008, was rated the 42nd worst polluter on PERI's Toxic 100 index. Investing in environmental projects, like second-generation biofuels, and is encouraging governments to take urgent action to build an international policy framework for managing greenhouse gases. Foundation supports small enterprises and entrepreneurship in Africa and addresses poverty and environmental challenges linked to globalization and energy use. Has a written nondiscrimination policy covering sexual orientation and gender identity. Offers insurance coverage to employees' domestic partners. Insurance for transgender employees is offered, and some treatment is covered.

Ryder System, Inc.

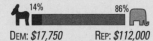

Contributions: TOTAL: *$129,750*   DEM: *$17,750*   REP: *$112,000*
LOBBY SPENDING: *$480,000*

Invests in new engine technologies and transportation best practices that can reduce overall energy demands. Recycles used oil. One of its buildings is ENERGY STAR rated. Participates in the EPA's SmartWay Transportation program. Has a written nondiscrimination policy covering sexual orientation and gender identity. Offers insurance coverage to employees' domestic partners. Insurance for transgender employees is offered, but treatment is not covered.

Saab Automobile AB

Contributions: TOTAL: *$0*   DEM: *$0*   REP: *$0*
LOBBY SPENDING: *$160,000*

Subsidiary of General Motors Corporation. Filed for bankruptcy protection in early 2009. Has developed hybrid and bioethanol concept cars. Has a written nondiscrimination policy covering sexual orientation and gender identity. Offers insurance coverage to employees' domestic partners. Insurance for transgender employees is offered, and treatment is covered.

Sinclair Oil Corporation
7% | 93%

Contributions: Total: *$130,400*   Dem: *$8,900*   Rep: *$121,500*
Lobby Spending: *$330,000*

In 2007, paid a $5 million criminal penalty and was ordered to make a community service payment of $500,000 to the River Parks Authority for Clean Water Act violations. Has accumulated more fines from the Oklahoma Department of Environmental Quality (ODEQ) than any other Oklahoma entity. Has refused to dismantle its Arkansas River refinery despite state revitalization plans and ODEQ violations.

Sunoco, Inc.
48% | 52%

Contributions: Total: *$571,100*   Dem: *$272,750*   Rep: *$298,350*
Lobby Spending: *$2,504,283*

One of 12 oil refinery companies that paid a portion of a $422 million settlement in 2008 for using MTBE despite known environmental risks and potential health risks. Paid $3.6 million to settle a federal lawsuit for a crude oil spill in a wildlife refuge and agreed to over $300 million in environmental improvements. Settled a price-gouging lawsuit, without admitting wrongdoing, in the aftermath of Hurricane Katrina. Endorses the CERES Principles and has taken some environmental protection steps, including installing pollution control devices. Donates home heating oil to some Delaware Valley residents. Supports education, youth programs, and community programs and organizations. Has a written nondiscrimination policy covering sexual orientation but not gender identity.

Toyota Motor Corporation
52% | 48%

Contributions: Total: *$56,280*   Dem: *$29,330*   Rep: *$26,950*
Lobby Spending: *$11,169,150*

Foreign owned. Owns a 51% stake in Daihatsu Motor Co., Ltd. Criticized for producing vehicles used by the military of the Burmese dictatorship, as well as for firing over 200 workers in the Philippines in 2006 during a dispute over union recognition. Toyota Motor North America ranked 40th on DiversityInc's list of the "Top 50 Companies for Diversity" in 2009. Lobbied against fuel efficiency legislation in California. Has been embroiled in Clean Air Act-violation lawsuits. One of its complexes received LEED gold certification. Has announced plans to test a plug-in hybrid car. Is creating a wind-powered logistic services facility. In 2008, donated $5 million in support of national parks. Supports education, arts, and culture in local communities. Has a written nondiscrimination policy covering sexual orientation and gender identity. Offers insurance coverage to employees' domestic partners. Insurance for transgender employees is offered, but treatment is not covered.

Valero Energy Corporation
18% | 82%

Contributions: Total: *$1,092,372*   Dem: *$201,750*   Rep: *$890,622*
Lobby Spending: *$1,403,000*

One of 12 oil refinery companies that paid a portion of a $422 million settlement in 2008 for using MTBE despite known environmental risks and potential health risks. Ordered to pay a $4.25 million civil penalty

and spend $232 million for new and upgraded pollution controls at its refineries in three states, and had to fund environmental projects to help communities affected by refinery emissions in 2007. Ranked 93rd on *Fortune* magazine's "100 Best Companies to Work For" in 2009. In 2008, was rated the 16th worst polluter on PERI's Toxic 100 index. Has invested more than $5 billion in environmental projects. Has entered ethanol production and built wind-powered turbines. Supports the United Way, the Muscular Dystrophy Association, and children's charities. Has a written nondiscrimination policy covering sexual orientation but not gender identity. Offers insurance coverage to employees' domestic partners.

Volkswagen AG

29%   71%

Contributions: TOTAL: *$3,500*   DEM: *$1,000*   REP: *$2,500*
LOBBY SPENDING: *$2,604,457*

Foreign owned. Supports the United Nations Global Compact. Established a humanitarian fund on behalf of people compelled to work at the company during World War II. Operates maquilas. Up to 95% of its vehicles are recyclable. Uses rainwater to aid in water conservation at its plants. Support and development of women employees is a company focus. Has set up programs to aid those with HIV/AIDS in South Africa. Supports historic preservation, arts and culture, and education.

Volkswagen of America, Inc.

40%   60%

Contributions: TOTAL: *$2,500*   DEM: *$1,000*   REP: *$1,500*
LOBBY SPENDING: *$311,230*

Subsidiary of Volkswagen AG. Environmental goals include developing synthetic biofuels and alternative drive concepts, such as natural gas and hybrids. Aims to offer carbon-neutral mobility. Developing biofuels that can be distributed with existing infrastructure and that can be used in vehicles currently on the market. Supports the American Cancer Society and the United Way. Matches employee donations and offers paid time off to volunteer. Has a written nondiscrimination policy covering sexual orientation and gender identity. Offers insurance coverage to employees' domestic partners. Insurance for transgender employees is offered, but treatment is not covered.

Volvo Car Corporation

100%   0%

Contributions: TOTAL: *$400*   DEM: *$400*   REP: *$0*
LOBBY SPENDING: *$0*

Subsidiary of Ford Motor Company. In 2008, the United Auto Workers went on strike at a Volvo truck plant in Virginia to defend health and safety protections. Supports the United Nations Global Compact. Allows state-sanctioned worker unions in its Chinese manufacturing operations. Offers a true multifuel car, thanks to an aftermarket conversion. All fabrics, threads, carpets, and safety belts are produced in a way that prevents or limits emissions of harmful substances. Is developing hybrid alternatives. Supports diversity and health and safety programs. Has a written nondiscrimination policy covering sexual orientation and gender identity. Offers insurance coverage to employees' domestic partners.

Yamaha Motor Co., Ltd.
Contributions: TOTAL: *$0*   DEM: *$0*   REP: *$0*
LOBBY SPENDING: *$420,000*

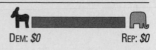

Foreign owned. Subsidiary of Yamaha Corporation. In 2009, Yamaha Motor Corp. USA recalled the Rhino and suspended sales after U.S. regulators found the vehicles had been responsible for at least 46 deaths. Is offering a free repair program to address safety issues. In 2006, the California Attorney General Office filed a $19.6 million civil suit against Yamaha Motor Corp. USA and two of its dealers for allegedly circumventing air pollution control laws and importing motorcycles not certified for sale in California. Its 2010 goal is to reduce its carbon dioxide per unit of sales by 30% of its 1990 level. Has a voluntary recycling program for its motorcycles and boats. Is converting factories from petroleum-based fuel to natural gas. Uses solar energy in six locations. Supports biodiversity conservation, forest regeneration, safety education, and leadership development.

Index